Where I Have Never Been

In the series *Asian American History and Culture*, edited by Cathy Schlund-Vials, Shelley Sang-Hee Lee, and Rick Bonus. Founding editor, Sucheng Chan; editors emeriti, David Palumbo-Liu, Michael Omi, K. Scott Wong, and Linda Trinh Võ.

ALSO IN THIS SERIES:

Cynthia Wu, *Sticky Rice: A Politics of Intraracial Desire*
Marguerite Nguyen, *America's Vietnam: The Longue Durée of U.S. Literature and Empire*
Vanita Reddy, *Fashioning Diaspora: Beauty, Femininity, and South Asian American Culture*
Audrey Wu Clark, *The Asian American Avant-Garde: Universalist Aspirations in Modernist Literature and Art*
Eric Tang, *Unsettled: Cambodian Refugees in the New York City Hyperghetto*
Jeffrey Santa Ana, *Racial Feelings: Asian America in a Capitalist Culture of Emotion*
Jiemin Bao, *Creating a Buddhist Community: A Thai Temple in Silicon Valley*
Elda E. Tsou, *Unquiet Tropes: Form, Race, and Asian American Literature*
Tarry Hum, *Making a Global Immigrant Neighborhood: Brooklyn's Sunset Park*
Ruth Mayer, *Serial Fu Manchu: The Chinese Supervillain and the Spread of Yellow Peril Ideology*
Karen Kuo, *East Is West and West Is East: Gender, Culture, and Interwar Encounters between Asia and America*
Kieu-Linh Caroline Valverde, *Transnationalizing Viet Nam: Community, Culture, and Politics in the Diaspora*
Lan P. Duong, *Treacherous Subjects: Gender, Culture, and Trans-Vietnamese Feminism*
Kristi Brian, *Reframing Transracial Adoption: Adopted Koreans, White Parents, and the Politics of Kinship*
Belinda Kong, *Tiananmen Fictions outside the Square: The Chinese Literary Diaspora and the Politics of Global Culture*
Bindi V. Shah, *Laotian Daughters: Working toward Community, Belonging, and Environmental Justice*
Cherstin M. Lyon, *Prisons and Patriots: Japanese American Wartime Citizenship, Civil Disobedience, and Historical Memory*
Shelley Sang-Hee Lee, *Claiming the Oriental Gateway: Prewar Seattle and Japanese America*
Isabelle Thuy Pelaud, *This Is All I Choose to Tell: History and Hybridity in Vietnamese American Literature*
Christian Collet and Pei-te Lien, eds., *The Transnational Politics of Asian Americans*
Min Zhou, *Contemporary Chinese America: Immigration, Ethnicity, and Community Transformation*
Kathleen S. Yep, *Outside the Paint: When Basketball Ruled at the Chinese Playground*
Benito M. Vergara Jr., *Pinoy Capital: The Filipino Nation in Daly City*

A list of additional titles in this series appears at the back of this book.

Where I Have Never Been

Migration, Melancholia, and Memory in Asian American Narratives of Return

Patricia P. Chu

TEMPLE UNIVERSITY PRESS
Philadelphia • Rome • Tokyo

TEMPLE UNIVERSITY PRESS
Philadelphia, Pennsylvania 19122
tupress.temple.edu

Copyright © 2019 by Temple University—Of The Commonwealth System
 of Higher Education
All rights reserved
Published 2019

Author's note on the cover photo: "Sophie in Longsheng," © Lee B. Ewing, is a memento of my family's first trip to China in 2007. Inspired by my research for this book, I found and met many aunts, uncles, and cousins with whom my parents had lost touch after migrating to the United States. During this trip we also visited the Longji Terraces in Guizhou Province, known for the seven-hundred-year-old practice of growing rice on terraced fields in the mountains. The cover image, in which my daughter surveys the scene with her camera, is provided by Lee B. Ewing.

Title page photograph: © Lee B. Ewing

Library of Congress Cataloging-in-Publication Data

Names: Chu, Patricia P., author.
Title: Where I have never been : migration, melancholia, and memory in Asian
 American narratives of return / Patricia P. Chu.
Other titles: Migration, melancholia, and memory in Asian American narratives
 of return | Asian American narratives of return
Description: Philadelphia : Temple University Press, 2019. | Series: Asian American history
 & culture | Includes bibliographical references and index. |
Identifiers: LCCN 2018021245 (print) | LCCN 2018034177 (ebook) |
 ISBN 9781439902271 (E-book) | ISBN 9781439902257 (hardback : alk. paper) |
 ISBN 9781439902264 (paper : alk. paper)
Subjects: LCSH: American literature—Asian American authors—History and criticism. |
 Asian Americans in literature. | American literature—20th century—History and
 criticism. | American literature—21st century—History and criticism. | Emigration and
 immigration in literature. | Homeland in literature. | Return in literature. | Melancholy
 in literature. | Memory in literature. | Asian Americans—Ethnic identity. | BISAC:
 LITERARY CRITICISM / American / Asian American. | SOCIAL SCIENCE /
 Ethnic Studies / Asian American Studies.
Classification: LCC PS153.A84 (ebook) | LCC PS153.A84 C487 2019 (print) |
 DDC 810.9/895073—dc23
LC record available at https://lccn.loc.gov/2018021245

9 8 7 6 5 4 3 2 1

For Lee, Eleanor, and Sophie Ewing

Contents

	Acknowledgments	*ix*
	A Note on Names and Spelling	*xiii*
1	Narratives of Return: A Transpacific Tradition	*1*
2	"Ears Attuned to Two Cultures": Reconciling Accounts in Josephine Khu's *Cultural Curiosity*	*45*
3	Transpacific Echoes in the Family Memoir: Sojourns and Returns in Lisa See's *On Gold Mountain*	*63*
4	"The One Who Mediates": Mimicry, Melancholia, and Countermemory in Denise Chong's *The Concubine's Children*	*105*
5	Working through Diasporic Melancholia: Winberg and May-lee Chai's *The Girl from Purple Mountain*	*123*
6	"A Being . . . from a Different World": Yung Wing and the Making of a Global Subjectivity	*145*
7	"To Bring the Dead to Life": Countermemories in Lydia Minatoya's *The Strangeness of Beauty* and Ruth Ozeki's *A Tale for the Time Being*	*177*
	Coda	*209*
	Notes	*219*
	Works Cited and Additional Sources	*231*
	Index	*247*

Acknowledgments

TO SURVIVE MY APPRENTICESHIP as a self-trained scholar of Asian American literature, I relied on the support of three crucial communities where I have felt at home: the George Washington University English Department, my colleagues in Asian American studies, and my family. This book marks the second phase of my thinking in my effort to transcend the field's original focus on the continental United States and to understand the diasporic histories that have shaped Asian American communities and their literature. Naturally, in pursuing such a dream over the course of fifteen years, I have enjoyed the hospitality, witty and incisive conversations, and material support of many people, more than I can name.

This book was produced with the aid and support of my department chairs at the English Department of George Washington University, including Marshall Alcorn, Jeffrey Cohen, Robert McRuer, Faye Moskowitz, Christopher Sten, and Gayle Wald. Among my other beloved colleagues, I particularly wish to thank Judith Plotz for decades of inspiration and friendship; the late Jim Miller (whose advice led me to Taiwan, where I conceived the idea for this book); and Kavita Daiya, Jennifer Green-Lewis, Jennifer James, Alexa Joubin, Tony López, Evelyn Schreiber, and Jane Shore for collegial conversation. For practical support and funny stories, I thank Connie Kibler and Linda Terry. For the privilege of exchanging ideas over the years, I thank my students, especially my teaching assistants, Sreyoshi Sarkar and Elizabeth Moser, and Amy Nelson Bangerter, whose research led me to study Yung Wing's autobiography.

I am grateful to my colleagues at the Academica Sinica in Taipei, Fudan University in Shanghai, National University of Singapore, the University of Pamplona, the University of Waterloo and Wilfrid Laurier University in Ontario, and Xiamen University for hosting memorable and inspiring conferences that have encouraged me to widen the lenses of my scholarship and teaching beyond the continental United States.

To the American Studies Association (ASA), the Japanese Association for American Studies (JAAS), and the Japan–United States Friendship Commission—as well as my kind hosts in Japan, including Mark and Kuniko Davidson—I offer my thanks for the 2005 opportunity to represent the ASA at the JAAS conference, to meet fellow scholars of American studies in Japan, and to explore that beautiful country. My chapter on Japanese American engagements with Japanese history, a daunting topic for this Chinese American scholar, is offered here as a journeyman's effort to understand the legacies of Japan through the lens of Asian American writing.

This research has also been informed by two related projects I undertook during the same period. First was a study of the career of Chu Ching-nung, my paternal grandfather, funded by a University Facilitating Fund grant from George Washington University. A return trip to China was funded in 2009 by a Robert H. Smith Research Fellowship awarded by the National Gallery of Art to my husband, the professional photographer Lee B. Ewing; he and I collaborated to provide an illustrated lecture on the history of my mother's family members in China.

For the opportunity to teach at the University of Macau in the spring of 2017, which provided an appropriately international and Chinese setting for completing my book, I thank my dean, Ben Vinson, and the University of Macau Faculty of Humanities dean, Hong Gang Jin. For practical support, scintillating conversation, and splendid meals during that term, I thank Augusta Alves, Keith Appler, Man Yin Chiu, John Corbett, Lee Erwin, Kit Kelen, Eric Kong, Martin Montgomery, Damian Shaw, See Kam Tan, and Katrine K. Wong—as well as David McAleavey and Kathy Perry, my fellow travelers from Washington. For their administrative assistance, I thank Tina Chao, Taoran Sun, and Zoe Wong. I am grateful to Wenyi Chu for guiding my efforts at literary expression in Mandarin and to my students for the rare privilege of teaching Asian American literature to Chinese students in Macao. For their outstanding teaching and hospitality in Xizhou, Shanghai, and Washington, I thank John Flower and Pamela Leonard.

In the field of Asian American studies, I salute the following senior scholars for their inspiring work in the field and their generous personal advice and assistance over the years: King-kok Cheung, Elaine H. Kim, Robert G. Lee, Shirley Geok-lin Lim, the late Amy Ling, Lisa Lowe, Gail Nomura, Gary

Okihiro, Steve Sumida, and Sau-ling Cynthia Wong. For sharing invaluable selections of their work over the years, I thank Floyd Cheung, Mark Chiang, Sharon Delmendo, Lavina Dhingra, David L. Eng, Madeline Hsu, Martin Manalansan, Viet Thanh Nguyen, and Andy Chih-ming Wang. For additional fellowship and conversation, I thank Norman Bock, Leslie Bow, John Cheng, Lawrence-Minh Bùi Davis, Rocío Davis, Donald Goellnicht, Victor Jew, Rachel C. Lee, Jeanne Pfaelzer, Christine So, Min Hyoung Song, Rajini Srikanth, and K. Scott Wong.

For the special boon of close reading and keen editorial advice, I thank Carolyn Betensky, Floyd Cheung, Monica Chiu, Kavita Daiya, Cathy Schlund-Vials, my eagle-eyed editors Rose Elfman and Joan Polsky Vidal, and Eleanor Ty, my most generous and exacting interlocutor. Each of them has helped me improve this manuscript greatly.

To Janet Francedese, I offer many thanks for her early and continued support and for nurturing my generation of scholars in Asian American studies. I am grateful to Cathy Schlund-Vials and Sara Jo Cohen for affirming their confidence and excitement in this project when I was at the end of my rope and for graciously granting me the time needed to bring this project to fruition. At Temple University Press, I appreciate the warmth and professional expertise of Ann-Marie Anderson, Gary Kramer, Nikki Miller, and Kate Nichols.

Marianne Noble Manson, Marybeth McMahon, Betty Shave, Martha Weiss, and their families have shared savory meals and sparkling insights about sympathy, Shakespeare, stories, cicadas, and children. Thanks go to Anne Meyer, John Ockenga, and Elizabeth Zinner for grace and wisdom. My relatives in China and America, including Fu Rao, Xu Youwen, and Zhu Fangwen, have inspired me with their courage, warmth, and generosity, and I am particularly grateful for the affection and attention of Lily Chu, Otto Chu, Bruce Ewing, Tom Ewing, Vicky Lee, Joan Scott, and Gerry Weaver over the years.

Most of all, I am grateful for the company and care of my family, Lee, Eleanor, and Sophie Ewing, and for their gifts of music, beauty, wit, and love.

—Patricia P. Chu
June 17, 2018
Washington, DC

A Note on Names and Spelling

MY SOURCES use several different systems for spelling Chinese names, including pinyin, the modern system; the Wade-Giles system typically used by U.S. scholars prior to 1979; and spellings improvised by U.S. immigration officials and others. Chinese names from older texts by Yung Wing and Karl Gützlaff may reflect Cantonese pronunciation or have been spelled using other systems.

In their home contexts, Chinese, Japanese, and Korean names are typically listed surname first, without a comma. Most Chinese surnames have just one syllable, and the majority of Chinese given names have two syllables. In discussing most Asian scholars, including Chinese immigrant scholars, I follow Western usage, with the surname following the given name. For the following writers and historical figures, however, I adopt the surname-first usage, either because it is most familiar or because it corresponds with my sources:

Ba Jin (Pa Chin, Li Fei-kan)
Chang Chih-chung
Chang Yu-i (Zhang Youyi)
Chan Sam
Chao Ts'ai Piao
Chen Mengjia
Chiang Kai-shek
Chiang Monlin

Chiang Yee
Chow Guen
Chu Ching-nung
Fong Dun Shung
Fong Guai King
Fong Lai
Fong Quong
Fong Yun
Hong Huoxiu (Hung Siu Chune)
Hung Jin
Hu Shi (Hu Shih)
Lao She (pseudonym for Shu Ch'ing-ch'un)
Leong May-ying
Liang Afa (Leang Afah)
Liang Cheng
Lin Yutang
Lin Zexu (Lin Tse-hsü), Viceroy
Liu Xiaobo
Lu Hsun (Lu Xun)
Mao Zedong (Mao Tse-tung)
Ngon Hung
Nieh Hualing
Si Ping
Sui Sin Far (pseudonym for Edith Maude Eaton)
Sun Yatsen (Sun Yat-sen)
Tsao Mei-en (Ruth Chai)
Tuan Yi-Fu
Tu Wei-ming
Wen Yiduo (Wen I-to)
Wong Sam
Wu Ningkun
Ye Mingchen (Yeh Ming Hsin)
Yung Wing (Cantonese; the Mandarin pronunciation is spelled Rong Hong)
Zhao Luorui (Lucy Chao)
Zhou Enlai (Chou En-lai)

In Chapter 6, Yung Wing and Karl Gützlaff refer to many places whose names are now rendered differently. Here are the contemporary versions, with the older terms in parentheses:

Fuzhou (Fuchow)
Guangdong Province (Kwangtung Province)
Guangzhou (Canton): capital city of Guangdong Province
Hangzhou (Hangchau)
Korea (Corea)
Macao (Macau)
Ryūkyū Islands (Loo-choo Islands)
Suzhou (Suchau)
Thailand (Siam)
Wangxia (Wang-hsia)
Xiamen (Amoy)
Yangzhou (Yang Chow)

Where I Have Never Been

1

Narratives of Return

A Transpacific Tradition

> I am to return to China, where I have never been.
> —Maxine Hong Kingston, *The Woman Warrior*, 76

Prologue

SOME YEARS AGO, I returned to Asia for the first time in my adult life to present a paper on "narratives of return"—a newly minted category I soon learned was deceptively simple—at a conference in Taipei. In researching accounts of diasporic Chinese offspring who returned to their parents' ancestral country, I had learned that I was not alone in the experience of growing up in America with a felt affinity to the imagined community and turbulent history of China while living far from it. My parents had passed away, and when I landed in Taipei, heard Mandarin—familiar yet opaque—and saw Chinese faces, I felt a strange joy, as if returning to my family. At dawn, as I looked out the window of my guest house on the campus of the Academia Sinica, I saw men and women in loose clothes performing their *tai qi* exercises on the handkerchief of grass surrounded by the hotel driveway. Inevitably, their wide, slow steps and circling arms reminded me of my late father, the only person I had ever seen practicing *tai qi* in my hometown. Now that I had arrived in an unknown country where morning *tai qi* was more common than jogging, the feeling was bittersweet.

Many years earlier, I had explained to a close friend that the garrulous mother in Maxine Hong Kingston's memoir, *The Woman Warrior*, was not the least bit typical of my family or of the other Chinese families I knew. Among the families of immigrant professors, doctors, and engineers with whom I grew up in Pittsburgh, not one of the fathers or mothers told Chinese ghost stories, chanted about Fa Mu Lan, or told stories about life in China. On the contrary, the mothers gave the impression that they lived to tell their children to eat more, put on a warm jacket, and press steadily forward to a secure future in America, preferably as a scientist, engineer, or doctor. Despite the fact that my father, a scholar of Chinese history, taught Chinese language and literature at the University of Pittsburgh, we children (or at least, we younger children) were not instructed in Chinese history, Chinese language and literature, or family history at home. If anything, my mother wanted to be sure that we learned algebra early and took an interest in computer programming.

Perhaps it was unusual, even among Chinese Americans, that I had never visited China while my parents were still alive, but I thought I could trace this omission—not only to the cold war politics that cut off so many ties between mainland Chinese and their families in the West but also to the specific culture of my family. Both my father and my mother were the eldest children of large families; their fathers belonged to two generations that had felt responsible for leading China into the modern age. My paternal grandfather, Chu Ching-nung (Zhu Jingnong), was a prominent educator who served as vice minister of education under the Republic of China and also a lifelong friend of the scholar and diplomat Hu Shi (Hu Shih). My maternal grandfather, Chao Ts'ai Piao, whom I knew only as a kindly old man, had been a lieutenant general in the Nationalist army under Chiang Kai-shek. With these credentials, both my grandfathers became political exiles when the Chinese Communist Party drove the Nationalists out of mainland China in 1949; neither ever returned to live on the mainland, and both lived out their last years in America. My father and uncle had already come to the United States to study by 1949, but my grandfathers left their wives and all their other children behind; of eleven remaining children, only my mother and one more uncle would ever be able to leave the mainland. My father, who had been a Nationalist officer in the war against the Japanese and had celebrated their departure in 1945 by arranging for graduate study in the United States, did not consider it prudent to return after 1949. From Seattle, where he was studying, he wrote to my mother, whom he had met when she was a teenager, inviting her to come to his new city to complete her college education—interrupted in 1949—and to become his wife. To protect us American-born children from the intrigues of the past and entanglements in the future, they never went back, they encouraged us to perfect our English, and they told us almost nothing about the family they had left behind. Profoundly mistrustful of all things Communist, both my father and my mother died without saying anything about contacting their Chinese relatives. Among their personal papers, I found a few letters from family members and many, in Chinese, from friends I had never heard of. Though deterred for so many decades from visiting China, I followed in the footsteps of my father and grandfathers—literally, by attending and teaching at universities where they had been students and teachers, and figuratively, by becoming a scholar of Asian American literature. This choice enabled me to transfer my literary imagination from England (the country I had entered in my teens by reading Austen, Orwell, Shakespeare, and Shaw) to China. I was therefore deeply touched when I found *Cultural Curiosity*, historian Josephine Khu's collection of personal essays by the children of diasporic Chinese about their first-time visits to China, and I resolved to write this book.

Return, Melancholia, and Remembrance of Scholars Past

The experience of returning to China—or, more broadly, of latter-generation Asian Americans visiting their parents' or ancestors' homelands—is a germinal motif in Asian American literature that has not yet been fully examined. At the outset of the field, the scholars and writers inventing Asian American literary studies were hard pressed to claim recognition as *American* writers with a place in the *American* tradition. Early anthologists such as Kai-yu Hsu, Helen Palubinskas, Jeffery Paul Chan, Frank Chin, Lawson Fusao Inada, and Shawn Wong created a nascent Asian American literary tradition by focusing on texts written and published in English and centered on Asian Americans within the United States. Although texts with Asian settings and protagonists who crossed the Pacific have been available since at least 1909, the early scholars of Asian American literature did not fully address their transpacific nature. Elaine H. Kim's early, influential study *Asian American Literature: An Introduction to the Writings and Their Social Context*, for instance, discussed some texts set wholly or partially in Asia or the Pacific but also focused largely on literature about the struggles of new arrivals and their children (whom I call the first and second generations, respectively) to claim a place in America; claiming America remains a central theme of the literature and the scholarship. Since then, the postnational turn in Asian American studies, the increased focus on postcolonialism and globalization in American studies, and the participation of multilingual scholars with expertise in other literatures have provided new tools and paradigms for reimagining Asian American literature as something both more inclusive and less cohesive, more like a literature of global diasporas. This critical broadening (which I discuss below) has coincided with an explosion of Asian American publications and of memoir and travel writing in general, as well as with the rise of creative nonfiction and various forms of roots journeys by Asian Americans and others.[1] The theme of return is now so widely recognized that it has been taken up by numerous scholars as well as creative writers; it appears in popular media from cookbooks and travel articles to feature films and documentaries.² At the same time, a growing body of scholarship has theorized the autobiographical impulse, the memory and memorials, and the forms of mourning and melancholia particular to U.S. minority subjects and communities.

I argue that there is within Asian American literature a body of texts that includes narratives of returns to Asia: both literal return visits by Asian emigrants and symbolic returns, first visits by diasporic offspring that symbolize returns to their roots. This motif has grown stronger, particularly among Chinese American authors, since the 1980s, due both to publishing trends in the United States and to globalizing trends favoring increased travel and rapid communications, including China's policies of openness since the 1980s. I argue that this literature addresses and seeks to remedy widely held anxieties about cultural loss and the erasure of personal and family histories from public memory. Moreover, the writers of return narratives register and respond to the melancholic ghosts of personal and family losses through acts of remembrance—or, more specifically, through the use of *countermemory*, defined by George Lipsitz as memory rooted in "the local, the immediate, and the personal," starting with "the particular and the specific" and building "outward toward a total story." According to Lipsitz, "counter-memory looks to the past for the hidden histories excluded from dominant narratives" and "forces revision of existing histories by supplying new perspectives about the past" (212–213, qtd. in Davis, *Relative Histories* 15–16). Speaking specifically of the stakes in an Asian American context, Viet Thanh Nguyen has described Asian American countermemory as an "oppositional" practice that contests "dominant memory" and is "engaged in recovering what has been forgotten about and forgotten by Asian Americans":

> Since Asian immigrants began arriving in large numbers in the 19th century, other Americans had not seen them as part of an American imagined community. Americans excluded Asian immigrants from American memory, rendered symbolically, for example, in photographs of the completion of the Transcontinental Railroad that did not include any of the thousands of Chinese workers who were crucial in building it. Against this exclusion and erasure from dominant memory, Asian Americans engaged in practices of countermemory.... Countermemory is oppositional memory, the memory of the subordinated and the marginalized, memory from below versus memory from above. Much of Asian American memory is an exercise of countermemory, one engaged with recovering what has been forgotten about and forgotten by Asian Americans. ("Memory" 154)

Within my study, narratives of return address retrievals of not only Asian or Asian American stories occluded from mainstream American history and memory but also stories that Asian Americans themselves are liable to silence or forget. In *Relative Histories: Mediating History in Asian American Family Memoirs*, Rocío G. Davis links countermemory to Marianne Hirsch's definition of *postmemory*, which characterizes the kind of memory work involved in family memoirs and is "distinguished from memory by generational distance and from history by deep personal connection" (Hirsch, *Family* 22, qtd. in Davis, *Relative Histories* 16–17). For Hirsch, postmemory is connected to its source "not through recollection but through an imaginative investment and creation" (*Family* 22, qtd. in Davis, *Relative Histories* 16–17). Davis's study beautifully illustrates the ways that, within Asian American family memoirs, countermemory draws on the local and the personal to question official histories; postmemory, which transcends individual memory by crossing generations, is consciously shaped by the author's deep personal connections to her material and by her creative and imaginative agency (16–17). My study is indebted to her for these and other insights. Because loss, memory, historical erasure, and countermemory are not limited to Asian Americans, I hope my work resonates with studies of other literary traditions, though they are outside my scope here.

In addition to exploring the tropes of return and melancholia, which I discuss below, this book engages with scholarship on questions of form, genre, and reading practices. Narratives of return, it turns out, can appear within numerous genres, including drama, film, short stories, novels, travel narratives, ethnography, oral history, and various forms of life writing including autobiography, memoir, and family memoir. Given the range of genres and the tendency for many contemporary writers to write texts that complicate, combine, or confound genre expectations, it is beyond the scope of this work to survey the criticism of every genre deployed by writers of return narratives; nor does this study hold narratives of return to strict definitions of genres, themes, and plot devices. It does, however, describe the defining concerns of each kind of narrative introduced. As a literary critic of minority literature and of women's writing, I seek to resist the "window" paradigm of reading, in which the author's narrative choices are perceived as transparent and the literary text is read and judged as an objective document about the lives it describes. Such a paradigm implicitly assumes that the (minority or woman) author is a glorified clerk, lacking narrative versatility and mastery. Rather, I join with autobiography theorists and other scholars of Asian American literature to defend the poststructuralist premise that all the narratives are texts artfully and deliberately formed by their authors (or auteurs, for film), and that the formal elements of these texts are as significant as the stories they tell. In my view, the object of study may be (in the case of a nonfiction writer, for instance) not only the external events of the author's life but also the author's process of thinking about and rendering her or his life as a story. In reading a novel, I am concerned with not only the novelist's factual research or perceived accuracy but also the rhetorical effects of departures from verisimilitude: the contrived coincidence or happy end, the red herrings and unresolved questions, and those vital moments when characters misbehave. Drawing on autobiography theory, my reading practice highlights the tension between the published text and the author's source materials in order to emphasize the author's artifice (not as bad faith or inaccuracy but as creative agency) and the rhetorical effects of writers' literary choices. In arguing that Asian American narratives of return seek to address what I term "racial melancholia" through narrative acts of countermemory and postmemory, I also assert that the writers' interventions include acts of dissent from more established master narratives: both national narratives and, particularly in the cases of women writers, family narratives about success, failure, and the relative valuation of individuals within clans, families within communities, or communities within nations. In the tradition of Lisa Lowe's *Immigrant Acts*, I argue that in texts that might seem wayward or rambling, Asian American authors break expectations about genre, authority, and factuality in order to tell a new story, and they usually tell readers that this is what they are doing. Like Barbara Christian and Donald C. Goellnicht, I also read creative writers as producers of theory in their own forms, usually through storytelling (Christian 226, Goellnicht 341–342).

Finally, this book is inspired by the personal journeys of my two grandfathers, who earned advanced degrees in America and returned to help defend and modernize China in the early twentieth century, and of my parents, who entered the United States as students in the 1940s and stayed to become U.S. citizens. As an English professor focused on Asian American literary studies, I have sought to understand their stories in the contexts of Chinese history, Asian American history, postcolonial theory, and Asian American literature. I felt that the perspectives of the educated Chinese who studied abroad and returned to serve China in the Republican period (1911–1949) had largely been forgotten. Modern references to wartime Chinese history, it seemed, focused more on Chiang Kai-shek's failures of military and civilian leadership than on the idealism of modernizing reformers such as my father, my grandfather, and my grandfather's close friend Hu Shi. Most attention, of course, is focused on more recent events. Asian American studies, focused on immigration and social justice within the United States, has historically marginalized the stories of educated Chinese who studied here and returned to China, or who arrived in the United States before 1965. And the postcolonial theorists I read in graduate school focused on British and European imperialism, everywhere but in East Asia. Discussions of U.S. neoimperialism, in the Pacific Rim and elsewhere, came later. To my knowledge, Asian American studies has included little theorization of Japanese imperialism or of the evolution of China's self-image, from the imperial center of the Qing era to the collapsing dynasty, which sought to ward off Western imperialism with a new model for Chinese modernity, to the rising power of the late twentieth and early twenty-first century. And many of the working-class models for Asian American self-images, developed by West Coast or Hawaiian scholars, seemed not to describe my parents, a professor and his college-educated wife who settled (in Gary Okihiro's useful phrase) "east of California" (qtd. in E. Lee, "Asian American Studies" 250nn10–11). Part of my book is driven by a personal interest in the task of historicizing the unwritten narrative of my ancestors' arrivals in the United States and the desire to see the fields of Asian American and American studies encompass and more seriously consider the roles of educated Asian immigrants of the early twentieth century. In revisiting stories about my Grandfather Chu, and researching chapters on Yung Wing, the Chai family, and other educated Chinese, I have been delighted to discover extensive work on the topic of Sino-American educational exchange from Yung Wing to the present era (e.g., Bieler; M. Hsu, "Befriending" [*Journal*], "Befriending" [*Trans-Pacific*]; LaFargue; H. Li; Qian; Rhoads; and Ye), which informs my chapters on Yung Wing and the Chais. My other chapters seek to expand the scope of Asian American cultural inquiry similarly. In Chapter 7, I draw from among the many narratives in which Japanese American writers tell stories that seek to understand Japan in the 1920s, 1930s, and 1940s in order to describe the methods used by novelists Lydia Minatoya and Ruth Ozeki to pose questions about the responsibilities of Japanese people to engage with questions of history and memory.

Why Now? History, Memory, and Decolonizing Asian Histories

Why read Asian American narratives of return, and why read them now? In one form or another, travel narratives have always been part of Western culture and identity, and as Americans grow more and more economically dependent on and culturally connected with other peoples through travel and new media, U.S. interest in other cultures has never been greater. Within the academic and publishing worlds, the movement for some decades has been to demand space for new voices and new subjectivities that have heretofore been silent or invisible.

In his overview study *Travel Writing*, Carl Thompson notes:

> From the fifteenth to the twentieth centuries, the genre played an integral role in European imperial expansion, and the travel writing of this period is accordingly highly revealing of the activities of European travellers abroad, and of the attitudes and ideologies that drove European expansionism. Similarly, modern travel writing can yield significant insights in the ideologies and practices that sustain the current world order. (3)

In the same decade in which Asian American studies found a foothold in academia, the Palestinian scholar Edward W. Said published *Orientalism* (1978), a founding text of postcolonial studies, arguing that European travelers' perceptions of other peoples and cultures were shaped by the writings of previous travelers and that these writings, which depicted non-Western peoples as exotic, emotional, and childlike in their inability to think rationally and to govern themselves, constituted discourses that justified Western colonialism. Said's insights, coupled with the turn to cultural studies in English and American studies, opened the way for academics to attend to what had been deemed the "minor, somewhat middle-brow form" of travel writing, elevating it to a legitimate object of study (Thompson 2). Following Said's cue, postcolonial studies developed as a field that illuminated the colonial and imperial subtexts of cultural texts from canonical works of literature to "middlebrow" travel narratives, while also bringing new prominence to the publications of writers from regions and nations formerly colonized by the European powers. In this context, contemporary travel writing has emerged as a genre that, through its narratives of individual contact with "other" cultures and peoples, helps to negotiate cultural anxieties about the changing relationships in this era of globalization, particularly between Western powers and their citizens, on one hand, and formerly colonized cultures and peoples, on the other.

Some critics remain suspicious of the genre. Dinah Roma Sianturi asks whether travel writing ultimately can "divest itself of its imperial origins . . . [and] move forward and achieve discursive maturity" (qtd. in Youngs 3n16). In the introduction to their 1998 survey *Tourists with Typewriters: Critical Reflections on Contemporary Travel Writing*, Patrick Holland and Graham Huggan argue that contemporary travel writing "frequently provides an effective alibi for the perpetuation or reinstallment of ethnocentrically superior attitudes to 'other' cultures, peoples, and places," as well as flattering the "nostalgically retrograde" middle-class reader with distinctions between the tasteful "traveler" and the common "tourist" (viii). And in *The Picador Book of Journeys* (2002), Robyn Davidson asserts that popular interest in travel narratives "is marked by nostalgia for an era when home and abroad, occident and orient, centre and periphery were unproblematically defined" and for "the illusion that there is still an uncontaminated Elsewhere to discover" (6, qtd. in Thompson 5). Others, however, defend the genre as fostering "an internationalist vision, and implicitly, a cosmopolitan attitude that encourages tolerance, understanding, and a sense of global community" (White 251, qtd. in Thompson 6) and, at its best, as seeking "to overcome cultural distance through a protracted act of understanding" (Porter 3, qtd. in Thompson 7).

When Asian American authors create their own travel narratives, they consciously enter and often critique this tradition by complicating the traditional image of the cosmopolitan traveler—predominantly white and male—as a global and imperial subject visiting prospective, current, or future colonies or trading partners. By focusing specifically on the subset of Asian American narratives of return, I argue that when Asian Americans write of visiting their personal or ancestral homelands, their texts depict ambivalent interactions with family members and new acquaintances who may register as unfamiliar but who also share a common language, past, or culture that the traveler must negotiate. For instance, the Sri Lankan Canadian author Michael Ondaatje's return narratives explicitly discuss the double vision of the returning diasporic traveler. In his memoir *Running in the Family*, he interlaces family anecdotes and scenes of family interviews in Sri Lanka with the writings of British colonial visitors and native writers, implicitly challenging readers to consider to which group he belongs. In his novel *Anil's Ghost* (2000), Ondaatje describes the human rights investigation done in his homeland by an expatriate Sri Lankan, Anil, and her Sri Lankan colleague, Gamini, in a period of civil war and government corruption. Anil recalls Gamini's critique of American movies and English books that end with the visitor departing from the war zone and gazing down from his airplane window: "He's going home. So the war, to all purposes, is over. That's enough reality for the West" (285–286). At the novel's climax, Anil is forced to present their investigation results alone, in a hostile public forum, after their evidence has been stolen, while Gamini observes from the audience. When she says, "I think you murdered hundreds of *us*," openly accusing the government of murdering its citizens—and she includes herself as a Sri Lankan with the pronoun "us"—Gamini recognizes her courage, after fifteen years abroad, in giving "a citizen's evidence" (272, emphasis added). For Asian American women writers, as I discuss later, the critique of the cosmopolitan travel narrative can also proceed by calling up female traditions of oral history and women's life writing.

Indeed, as literary critic Rajini Srikanth has pointed out, American readers need to retrain themselves to conceptualize their culture as genuinely inclusive of subjects formerly viewed as outsiders, and to see the nation as global, transnational, and deeply interconnected with other sites around the world. Srikanth argues that readers should reconsider the supposed polarity between nationalism and cosmopolitanism as a productive dialectic. For instance, she posits that "a meaningful relationship between people begins with a willingness to acknowledge each other's painful histories; such acknowledgement is particularly difficult when the parties involved have themselves been responsible for the tragedies" (23), and that it is also true that "only when nations appreciate each other['s]" traumas and match their actions (foreign policies) accordingly will there be a likelihood of global cooperation" (27).

Srikanth's argument anticipates those of critical refugee studies and scholars of Southeast Asian culture and memory such as Viet Thanh Nguyen and Cathy J. Schlund-Vials. In *Nothing Ever Dies: Vietnam and the Memory of War*, Nguyen argues that American readers should resist the hegemony of nationalistic public memory by striving for a "complex ethics of memory, a just memory that strives both to remember one's own and others," while Schlund-Vials argues in *War, Genocide, and Justice: Cambodian American Memory Work* that Cambodian American cultural production works to counter "historical amnesias" in migrants' sites of origin and their countries of settlement, and to imagine or "engender . . . alternative modes for and practices of justice," beginning with remembrance (4).[3] For me, as for these authors, the ongoing task of transforming our knowledge involves retraining readers, in part by including literature by Asian Americans and other minority writers alongside other narratives of Westerners visiting the East. Specifically, this project includes not only the reading of travel narratives but also the reading and writing of return narratives: narratives in which immigrants return to their homelands or second-generation North Americans return to their ancestors' homelands to reclaim that aspect of their heritage, identity, and culture.

One explanation for the public's continued and renewed interest in the theme of return is that contemporary narratives of return—by writers of all ethnicities—negotiate cultural anxieties about modernity, history, and memory. In his overview of "memory discourses" of the past half century, Andreas Huyssen describes how they emerged in the West in the 1960s, in the wake of decolonization and new social movements in search of alternative and revisionist histories: "The search for other traditions and the tradition of 'others' was accompanied by multiple statements about endings: the end of history, the death of the subject, the end of the work of art, the end of metanarratives" (12). In other words, the search for formerly invisible stories and traditions has been accompanied by various forms of skepticism about the authority and objectivity of historical writing. At the same time, historical and other cultural references have become both more prolific and less clearly grounded in their original histories and cultures. As distinct cultures give way to a homogenizing global culture, and as memories of the past become decontextualized and appropriated by the present, there is a sense of greater anxiety about the loss of traditional cultures and ways of life as well as the loss of invisible or less-known histories; similar concerns arise about those histories that are appropriated and removed from their contexts by mainstream culture. According to Huyssen, the historical past formerly gave "coherence and legitimacy to family, community, nation, and state . . . but those links have weakened as national traditions and historical pasts have been deprived of geographic and political groundings as they are reorganized in the processes of cultural globalization" (4).

Huyssen asks whether such groundings are being forgotten and erased, as feared, or actually renegotiated. He suggests that a wave of memorial sites and events in Europe, the United States, and East Asia, accompanied by a brisk business in forms of history, memory, and nostalgia (including museums, retro consumer goods, historical documentaries, autobiography, historical novels, and public celebrations of national anniversaries), is a manifestation of a widespread fear that, in the wake of discourses critiquing the authority and objectivity of history, and the loss of the "coherence and legitimacy" that history is supposed to lend to everyday life and the public life of nations, we will forget the past and, eventually, our present (14). Indeed, he finds, since the 1980s issues of memory and forgetting have become dominant all over the world, but as "the culture of memory" spreads, the fault line between mythic and real pasts grows harder to draw (15–16). Despite the seeming globalization of memory discourses, much of the work they do—such as the commemoration of past wrongs by new regimes seeking legitimacy—must be done nationally and locally. Huyssen asks whether memory cultures in general can be read as reaction formations to economic globalization, since they involve reconstructing a local or national account of the past that informs the present (16). On one level, this seems like a persuasive conclusion. Srikanth, for instance, suggests precisely that nations must understand the particular traumas of individuals and of other nations in order to develop responsible and effective foreign policies.

However, while Huyssen acknowledges minority memory cultures, his work seems primarily focused on local or national projects of public memory—official memories—with emphasis on European examples. Whereas Huyssen emphasizes local or national memory projects as a response to the perceived threats of globalization, I suggest that for Asian Americans, the rise of a memory-driven trope, the narrative of return, is also a way to expand Asian American subjectivities and histories beyond the borders of the United States. It is a move to reclaim or remember the Asian histories that an earlier wave of Asian American scholarship neglected and to engage with the collective work of Asian American countermemory described by Viet Thanh Nguyen ("Memory" 154). Moreover, Asian American return narratives function to combat the perceived demand that Asians join a public American culture in which Asian histories are far from prominent, and Asian American histories are arguably even less visible. If, as Asian American scholars claim, the erasure and forgetting of individual particularities is demanded as a condition of claiming U.S. subjectivity, then Asian Americans are admittedly not unique among ethnic and racial minorities in negotiating this demand. However, Asian Americans may feel called to honor multiple pasts among which there is, institutionally, less discursive space for the stories of Asian ancestors. Like other Americans, Asian American schoolchildren are taught to commemorate U.S. history as a narrative driven by European settlers and immigrants, Native Americans, and African Americans, and to mourn (or in some cases to celebrate) the loss of a way of life in which their particular ancestors may not have actually taken part and from which Asians have been actually and symbolically excluded (S. Chan, *Asian Americans*; E. H. Kim, *Asian American* 3–13; L. Lowe, *Immigrant Acts* 1–36; Srikanth 51–55). Therefore, a primary impulse of Asian American scholarship and literature has been simply to locate, record, describe, and imagine the stories of Asian immigrants and their offspring in America. Hence, oral history, autoethnography, autobiography, memoir, and the bildungsroman are central genres of Asian American literature.

At the same time, Asian Americans face the task of finding out about traditional pasts—historical pasts, ways of life—in our ancestral homelands even as those homelands have undergone rapid change in the eras of modernization and globalization. Also, as the Taiwan-based cultural critic Kuan-Hsing Chen has noted, modern Asian states must come to terms with their twentieth-century histories in order to avoid replicating the mistakes of imperialism in the twenty-first century, a three-part process he calls "decolonization," "de-imperialization," and "*de–cold war*" (3–4). Chen argues that globalization, as an opening of all markets to global trade and competition, has the potential to promote greater exploitation of less developed nations by more developed ones. In many regions, smaller countries seek to tame the forces of globalization by organizing their own regional systems of trade and cooperation such as the "African Union, the Latin American Integration Association, the European Union, and the Association of Southeast Asian Nations" (K. Chen 5). In East Asia, however, this process has been impeded by the failure to confront Asia's particular legacies of intra-Asian imperialism and colonization. This failure, he writes, is due to the imposition of cold war antagonisms and boundaries shortly after the end of World War II and the resulting focus on economic development. He seems to say that Japan, South Korea, and Taiwan substituted allegiance to the United States for the internal scrutiny needed for three processes: *decolonization*, "the attempt of the previously colonized to reflectively work out a historical relation with the former colonizer, culturally, politically, and economically"; *deimperialization*, "in which the colonizing or imperializing population examines "the conduct, motives, desires, and consequences of the imperialist history that has formed its own subjectivity"; and *de–cold war*, the imperative to "confront and explore the legacies and ongoing tensions of the cold war" (3–4). For instance, Chen asserts that Japan has never fully examined its history and responsibility as the colonizer of Taiwan, Korea, and Manchuria and an occupier of mainland China because immediately after Japan's surrender in 1945, it was occupied by the United States and reconstructed as a U.S. ally. (In this process, as Sebastian Conrad has argued, Japan internalized accounts of the war that focused on the United States while largely forgetting its own actions in Asia until the 1980s, when the voices of other Asian nations made themselves heard [92–94].) Therefore, Chen asserts, other East Asian nations do not trust Japan to take part as an equal partner in regional integration, both because it is so dependent on the United States and because they fear that without clearer introspection, Japan is prone to repeat its history. South Korea and Taiwan, former Japanese colonies, have not fully acknowledged prewar colonial legacies in which for some subjects, Japan connoted not only an oppressive occupation but also (in the case of Taiwan at least) a force for modernization (toward which these countries may also feel ambivalent). Failing to reckon with the ambivalence generated by the experiences of colonization, right-wing regimes in Korea and Taiwan have adopted pro-American, anti-Communist mindsets that suppress dissent by equating it with pro-Communism. In Chen's view, these countries will not be fully prepared to form strong regional alliances until they have loosened their practical dependence (in terms of trade, aid, and defense) on the United States, their profound cultural identifications with the United States, and their deep-seated mistrust of Japan and Communist China (K. Chen 5–13).

Finally, mainland China was formerly the center of Asia, as the "Chinese empire" (which, Chen notes, is itself a Western term) dominated Asia until the incursion of Western imperialism in the mid-nineteenth century (K. Chen 269n1). This history has left other nations with residual suspicion and the Chinese culture with imperial ambition, which must be examined if China is to deimperialize. For the various nations, Chen warns against a simple decolonization process in which, rather than fully examining investments left over from the colonial period, a former colony defines itself primarily through resentment of the former colonial power and reactionary nationalism, a process that still leaves intact both the centrality of the colonizer and the primacy of imperialism as a model for national success. In China, the Communist-versus-Nationalist conflict and eventual civil war were manifestations of competing models for modernization (the Soviet socialist model versus the Western model of liberal democracy and capitalism). After 1949, the Nationalists tilted Taiwan toward the U.S. model and the Communists turned China toward the Soviet model. Chen, however, argues that China must seek the openness of that moment in the 1950s when the country sought to connect with other nonaligned ("third world") nations: "Chinese solidarity with the colonized third world, which began in the context of the 1955 Bandung conference in Indonesia, was a crucial step in the opening up and reformulation of the self-centered worldview found throughout the history of the Chinese empire," as exemplified in the 1950s, 1960s, and 1970s when the translation of world literature into Chinese manifested China's openness to a "third world decolonization era" (K. Chen 11–12). Readers questioning whether China could or would cultivate openness to other nations without an imperialist agenda may consult Chen's full argument and observe how China's "One Belt, One Road" plan (for global trade, inspired by the ancient Silk Road shipping routes) unfolds. According to one expert, "China's Belt and Road initiative is starting to deliver useful infrastructure, bringing new trade routes and better connectivity to Asia and Europe. . . . But [President] Xi [Jinpeng] will struggle to persuade skeptical countries that the initiative is not a smokescreen for strategic control."[4] Here, we need note only that Chen hopes Chinese intellectuals will search for a model in which Chinese development does not depend on reinstating China as an imperial or neoimperial center within Asia.

While most Asian American creative writers do not presume to lead in such intra-Asian debates, this book suggests that the memory work that is typical of Asian American return narratives—both biographical and fictional—may be understood as participating in multiple vital conversations. It is not only an aspect of the "memory discourses" that Huyssen and memory scholars have identified as a response to the questioning of history but also a crucial part of a larger, transpacific dialogue that may contribute to the work of decolonization, deimperialism, and de–cold war, although Asian American perspectives inevitably differ from those of Asians in Asia. Although Chen's articulation of his model postdates or coincides with much of the writing I examine here, most of the writers I have studied are aware that their international journeys and their published travel narratives are engaging not only with the writers' interpersonal relationships but also with larger dialogues about the history that shapes contemporary relations among China, Japan, and other East Asian nations. Among millennial Chinese American writers looking back at their ancestors, for instance, the postcolonial task of reimagining China's national narratives of modernization and its vexed relations with the West is undertaken, implicitly or explicitly, as the writers strive to weave that master narrative into the fabric of their family return narratives. And a number of stories of return to Japan, which in the eighties tended to address American fears of Japanese competition, have more recently engaged with its imperialist history.[5] In many of these return narratives, Asian American writers portray their ancestors as defying or reinventing old-country expectations and traditions and themselves as negotiating with modern natives' expectations about them, the diasporic visitors. Moreover, these writers may also question U.S. imperialism or cold war ideology, acting as cultural theorists and critics in their own right. Yet most of their analyses focus on the personal. To engage with the larger issues of shifting regional dynamics would in some cases occlude the authors' fundamental aim of imagining, or bearing witness to, personal stories of exploration and discovery of their ancestral pasts—stories that demand to be told before the people in them are forgotten. One task these writers set for readers, then, may be to attend to their personal stories while also observing how their work engages with the ideological project proposed by Chen.

Globalizing Asian American Culture and Identity: Additional Dialogues

This work participates in the ongoing rethinking of Asian American culture and identity in a global context, in which Asian American identities are understood to be hybrid, diasporic, or transnational. In their introduction to *Transnational Asian American Literature: Sites and Transits*, Shirley Geok-lin Lim, John Blair Gamber, Stephen Hong Sohn, and Gina Valentino identify three periods of scholarship that helpfully contextualize the discipline's reframing. In the first, prior to 1982, academics primarily produced anthologies of creative writing with scholarly introductions. The literature was at first defined as consisting of Chinese American, Japanese American, and Filipino American authors (though Korean American writers were soon added), and the focus was often, if not exclusively, on those who had been born in the United States and spoke English (5). Although a few immigrant writers, such as Sui Sin Far and Carlos Bulosan, did become central to early Asian American studies, the critical focus was on the formation of a literature that would raise consciousness about the struggles of Asian Americans to claim belonging in the United States, both culturally and legally. This nation-centered focus was articulated most provocatively by Jeffery Paul Chan, Frank Chin, Lawson Fusao Inada, and Shawn Wong (Chin et al., *Aiiieeeee!*; Chan et al., *The Big Aiiieeeee!*). As recalled by S. G. Lim, her coauthors, and S. C. Wong, this focus was discussed and refined in the next period of scholarship (1982–1995) by scholars such as King-kok Cheung, Sau-ling

Cynthia Wong, and Elaine H. Kim (K. Cheung, S. C. Wong [*Reading*], and E. H. Kim [*Asian American Literature*], discussed in S. G. Lim et al. 6–7 and S. C. Wong, "Denationalization"). This group also introduced new paradigms that pushed the field beyond its initial national focus. For instance, Stephen H. Sumida extended the symbolic borders of Asian American literature to include works from and about Hawaii; Oscar Campomanes described Filipino literature as one of exile, arguing for the inclusion of expatriate Filipino authors as definitive representatives of their group's literature; and Amy Ling anticipated the introduction of transnational models of subjectivity with her model of women writers who moved between [the] worlds of China, the United States, and other places (Sumida; Campomanes; Ling, *Between Worlds*). The third period of Asian American scholarship, defined by Lim, Gamber, Sohn, and Valentino as 1995 to the present, has been described as a flowering of "metacritical" scholarship in which researchers debate the shape of the field while building on early work; scholars in this period have also extended the geographic boundaries of "Asian Americans" to include authors rooted in the Pacific Rim, Southeast Asia, and South Asia and are considering the appropriateness of including "West Asia" within Asian American studies (Srikanth 1; Ty, *Unfastened* xx). (However, as Eleanor Ty notes, it is still not a common practice to include West Asia under the Asian North American umbrella, as "some scholars of the Middle Eastern diaspora prefer to be in the category 'Arab and Arab American studies'" [*Unfastened* xx].) Lim, Gamber, Sohn, and Valentino describe this latest period as one when Asian American literary and cultural studies are "traversed by theories associated with postmodernism, poststructuralism, psychoanalysis, and discourses on globalization, diaspora, transnationalism and postcolonialism" (S. G. Lim et al. 8–14; Srikanth 1). Ty suggests that these periods are less distinct in the areas of literary and cultural production but that one major change there did occur around the 1990s, when "creative works shifted from those that were mainly autoethnographic to those that are no longer tied to ethnic and national identities" (*Unfastened* xviii).

Transnational Asian American Literature is just one of many recent books inviting scholars and readers to rethink the U.S. boundaries that dominated the field in its early years, a reconsideration Sau-ling Cynthia Wong has called the "denationalization" of Asian American literature studies (S. C. Wong, "Denationalization"). I would like to engage here, briefly, with four of these publications: *The World Next Door*, by Rajini Srikanth; *Recovered Legacies: Authority and Identity in Early Asian American Literature*, edited by Keith Lawrence and Floyd Cheung; Lim, Gamber, Sohn, and Valentino's *Transnational Asian American Literature*; and *Unfastened: Globality and Asian Northern American Narratives*, by Eleanor Ty.

The World Next Door responds to the questions "What is South Asian American writing and what insights can it offer us about living in the world at this particular moment of tense geopolitics and interlinked economies?" (Srikanth 1). Srikanth argues that this body of work demands new reading practices, for it challenges the very idea of America that underwrites many readings of American literature. She argues for discarding binary thinking (16–19), learning to appreciate the unknowable (20–23), cultivating a "cosmopolitan consciousness" empathetic to others and their histories (23–27), and understanding the world as "a network of interconnected peoples" (27–33). Such an understanding requires Americanist scholars to look beyond the "exceptionalism" that sees the nation as uniquely created to further "freedom, democracy, and the liberty to pursue one's life objectives" and to ask how U.S. hegemony may have contributed to events such as 9/11 (33–37). She invites readers not only to attend to writers of South Asian origin or texts pertaining to South Asia–related themes but also to create a reading practice that is empathetic, inclusive, respectful of differences, globally aware, and politically responsible.

Like Srikanth's, my project considers the links Asian Americans have with other nations, beyond the borders of the United States. As her methodological questions emerge from confronting a particular group of texts in a specific moment, mine also arise inductively, from my encounters with the theme of return and the questions of interpretation that arise from this scholarly period (1995 to the present). But whereas Srikanth is primarily concerned with the responsibility of scholars and readers in the United States to question American exceptionalism, my questions remain focused on the individual perceptions and life stories of the writers I study. To be sure, questions of empathy and of locating and processing others' and our own national histories are critical to the texts I discuss. But if Srikanth's central question is *How should we read?*, mine is *What is an Asian American narrative of return, and what is at stake in such a journey?* Her primary focus is on South Asian American texts while mine is on Chinese American and Japanese American texts; I examine their representations of personal, family, and national histories; the themes of mourning and remembering; and how these processes affect individuals. Fundamentally, my reading practice is intended to focus on the agency of the authors in shaping readers' perceptions of themselves and their protagonists, in dialogue with existing discourses including the genres in which the authors write.

Along with Keith Lawrence, Floyd Cheung, and the contributors to their collection *Recovered Legacies*, I also seek to transcend presentist readings, particularly strongly ideological readings defined by late twentieth-century ideas of cultural naturalism, fixed ideas of authenticity, or the tendency to judge writers according to whether they resist or accommodate white supremacy in cultural nationalist terms (Lawrence and Cheung 2–5). In contrast to their book, mine is devoted largely to recent publications. But like them, I turn to early twentieth-century Chinese authors such as Yung Wing and seek to understand their writings as literary performances in the context of contemporaneous Sino-American relations. Like Floyd Cheung ("Early Chinese"), Georgina Dodge, and Sylvia Yanagisako, I question the practice of devaluing so-called elite writers by claiming they are not positioned to experience and write about being Asian American.[6] I also question the view exemplified by Elaine H. Kim's assessment that early immigrant writers who were "elites" were likely not to address race because they were generally removed from the troubles of their working-class countrymen (*Asian American* 24–25, qtd. and discussed in Dodge 73–74) as well as the underlying assumption, as Yanagisako writes in her critique of Asian American history courses, that "the past that constitutes Asian American subjectivity—the collective conscience and sense of being and acting in the world—is . . . a working-class one" (283).[7] Cheung recuperates early writers Yan Phou Lee and Yung Wing from accusations of elitist superficiality by arguing that Lee sought to contest exclusion legislation by using the authority of "autoethnography" to respond to whites with a reverse ethnographic gaze and that, in order to increase the political capital of Chinese in the United States, Yung sought to establish that Chinese and China were "manly" and deserving of respect ("Early Chinese" 25–31). Yung's autobiography performed masculine heroism coupled with political reliability in order to increase the prestige of Chinese in the United States, even as Yung privately supported revolutionary elements in China (F. Cheung, "Early Chinese" 33–34, "Political Resistance" 88–93). In short, Cheung argues that these elites did care very much about the fates of common Chinese and sought to improve their lot through word and action.

Dodge makes a different argument, drawing on the example of Etsu Sugimoto, the self-described *Daughter of the Samurai*. While she concedes that Sugimoto's biography did emerge from the part of her life when she lived in a white middle-class enclave and socialized with upper-class European American women, she argues that Sugimoto's life experience and interests went beyond writing only to please such readers; that her book captures her deeply intersubjective sense of Japanese literature, identity, and culture in a way that anticipates Dorinne Kondo's work on Japanese identity; that, as a self-supporting, widowed head of household sympathetic to American feminism, Sugimoto was not always sheltered from economic struggle; and that she was self-conscious and informative about her privileged position. That is, Dodge argues that privilege alone should not invalidate or marginalize the writings of authors who are truly curious, perceptive, and socially aware, even if they do not write primarily about the working classes. More important, she argues that *Daughter* is an innovative "hybrid" narrative, drawing on the Japanese "I-novel" and the American immigrant autobiography: "Like Sugimoto herself, [the book] crosses borders and, rather than assimilating with the adopted culture, molds it to her indigenous expectations and values" (61). Taking to heart these critics' efforts to expand the tools for reading and assessing such authors, I pose additional questions about the class assumptions some scholars have brought to the study of early twentieth-century immigrant and diasporic writing.

In my exploration of the return narratives of Chinese who studied in America and returned to China, I find that Yung Wing was only the first of many—tens of thousands of Chinese students over the course of 150 years—who drew on American and Western ideas with the object of bettering China as well as the lives of diasporic Chinese, including working-class Chinese in North America. (Indeed, the Chinese Self-Strengthening Movement, which rose to prominence as early as the 1860s, had as its motto, "Chinese learning for the foundation, Western learning for practical use" [qtd. in Leung 392, qtd. in F. Cheung, "Early Chinese" 33].) My argument—which expands on Floyd Cheung's view of Yung—is that many of these elites, most of whom were specifically sent by the Chinese governments of their times to gain expertise to help China, were very interested in the conditions of ordinary Chinese, both in China and in America. What they published, even in autobiographical modes of writing, must be read as designed not only to amuse the American public or sell books but also to help this larger national cause. Moving beyond the narrower scope of the United States to include diasporic or transpacific concerns, the publications of intellectuals who returned to China provide a telling context for the struggles of Chinese in America prior to 1965.

Finally, I am responding to Lawrence and Cheung's invitation to consider further what it means to extend the category "Asian American" to authors and texts whose sensibilities were formed well before the Asian American movement of the 1960s as well as to Chinese with a diasporic or transpacific consciousness. Consider the following historical examples. In 1905, angered by the treatment of Chinese in America, Chinese both at home and abroad organized a boycott of U.S. goods in protest (S. Chan, *Asian Americans* 96–97). In 1938, both Chinese Americans and Japanese Americans organized boycotts of Japanese goods and lobbied for an embargo on sending war materials, especially scrap metal, to Japan (Price). Would we consider these transpacific efforts "Asian American"? The examples continue. A Chinese man who has studied in America recalls the first arrival in his village of matches, clocks, and kerosene and observes that these Western goods were followed by missionaries, commerce, and the breakdown of an ancient economic structure (M. Chiang 34–38). A Cantonese revolutionary educated in Honolulu, Hong Kong, and London is inspired by the American political economist Henry George to organize a new government around "Three Principles of the People." A Chinese student at Cornell writes to his good friend, a student in Washington, D.C., proposing that the Chinese renounce traditional methods of poetry composition, switch from classical language to the vernacular, and model their poetry after Western modernist poetry; when he returns home to China, he popularizes Henrik Ibsen's play *A Doll's House* and arranges lecture tours for John Dewey and Margaret Sanger. A fourth, having studied in America, is assassinated in his home country after crossing his government too often in defense of academic freedom for his university and colleagues. A fifth, divorced by her husband after he studied in England while she remained at home, founds the first women's bank of China and tells her story to her Chinese American great-niece. A sixth is thrown into a labor camp for many years: after studying in the United States and returning to help rebuild his country after the civil war, he has been too open about his incredulity that the government would really persecute people for such minor offenses as missing political rallies.[8] In what sense might these be "Asian American" stories? Given that the term "Asian American" did not exist as a racial or literary category prior to 1968 (Dirlik, "Asians" 518), how do we determine which authors are "Asian American" prior to that? If we choose to exclude U.S.-educated Chinese intellectuals from our concept of Asian American authors—either because of their elite status or because of their Chinese or transpacific focus, what important writers and stories might we be missing?

In *Transnational Asian American Literature*, Lim, Gamber, Sohn, and Valentino share an interest in broadening the idea of Asian American literature to foreground the "diasporic, mobile, transmigratory nature of Asian American experience," in which subjects connect with the United States but are not limited to this country (1). This comprehensive introductory survey of major Asian American literary criticism captures how models of immigration and assimilation within U.S. borders have dominated the formation of Asian American studies and Asian American literature while coexisting with an interest in framing Asian American studies globally. As suggested above, I am working within the framework these authors describe. At the same time, I am intrigued by the approach taken by Rocío Davis, whose essay on the Asian American *childhood* defines it as a subset of autobiography, distinguishes the Asian American version from the European American one, and asserts that the Asian American *childhood* is marked by the unraveling of resolutions—pertaining to the subject's incorporation into society—that one might otherwise expect to find in these narratives (Davis, *Begin* 7–31). Like Davis, I seek first to describe and then to question a central theme, the narrative of return.

In *Unfastened*, Ty also reconsiders Asian American literature in a global context and then surveys and redefines tropes of mobility. Choosing the term "globality" to emphasize social, political, and cultural elements rather than the economic and corporate connotations of "globalization," she considers negative and positive accounts of globalization (the original term) and then charts a middle course between the two extremes, portraying globality as a mixed phenomenon that varies from case to case (Miyoshi; Dirlik, *Postcolonial Aura*; Imbert; R. Cohen, qtd. in Ty, *Unfastened* xii–xv, xxiv–xv). Ty recalls Sau-ling Cynthia Wong's influential distinction between a mainstream American literary tradition, in which mobility is figured as a liberatory "extravagance" (implicitly, a white male prerogative), and Asian American literature, in which mobility is more typically associated with "necessity," as in the cases of Asian emigrants seeking a better livelihood in America, Filipino migrant workers forced to follow the crops, or Japanese Americans being sent to internment camps away from their homes on the West Coast (S. C. Wong, *Reading* 13–14, 118–127, qtd. in Ty, *Unfastened* xv–xxiv). Ty also cites the "exilic" and "between worlds" models of Oscar Campomanes and Amy Ling as models of Asian American mobility that portray Asian Americans as constrained and lacking in agency (*Unfastened* xxvi). She acknowledges Aihwa Ong's definition of "flexible citizenship" as a strategy used by Chinese businessmen for whom multiple citizenship is used "to accumulate capital and power," contrasting their agency with the more constrained conditions of Filipinos who "move across the globe as migrant workers, domestics, and health care and hospitality workers" and the "millions of women from poor countries" who migrate to serve as "nannies, maids, and sometimes sex workers" in rich countries (Ong 6; Ehrenreich and Hochschild 2, qtd. in Ty, *Unfastened* xxvi). Yet she advocates rethinking the negative connotations of terms like "dislocation" and "displacement" in favor of James Clifford's positive view of travel and contact as "crucial sites for an unfinished modernity" (Clifford, *Routes* 2, qtd. in Ty, *Unfastened* xxvi). Noting that "displacement as perpetual exile and unbelonging goes against the strategy of 'claiming America' by and for Asian Americans, while displacement as movement, that is, taking the place of something else, suggests agency and subjectivity," she reframes Asian American migration in terms of modern, voluntary travel (*Unfastened* xxvi–xxvii). She seeks to read Asian Americans as creating new meanings through their journeys and as "travelers, explorers, and subject[s] of quest narratives"—that is, as authors and interpreters rather than supernumeraries (xxviii). Contesting other presumptions that have framed the field of Asian American literary studies, she notes three patterns: Asian Americans often do not see culture and identity as static categories to be claimed but rather thematize "the fluidity of contemporary transcultural identities and the layering of subject positions"; they focus not only on Asian-white relations and intrafamilial relations but also on relations among Asian Canadians, Asian Americans, and other ethnic groups; and they often depart from realism by using postmodernist techniques such as parody, exaggeration, irony, and decentered narration (xxix–xxx).

Because this book looks back to Yung Wing's nineteenth-century migrations to and from the United States, and to other stories of early Chinese immigration and return in the late nineteenth and early twentieth century, it serves as a reminder that contemporary globalization is rooted in transpacific migrations and colonial relations that were already under way in the 1800s. Though limited by space, I place Yung and his successors—the Chinese American scholars, merchants, and laborers of the late nineteenth and early twentieth centuries—into dialogue with larger histories of Sino-American scholarly exchange, trade, and labor migration. I also consider the efforts of late twentieth-century Japanese American writers to interrogate Japan's role in World War II in order to understand that history and how it shapes our modern context. Citing Sau-ling Cynthia Wong's thesis about Asian American mobility, Ty rightly raises the question of whether Asian American mobility is necessarily devoid of "extravagance" (S. C. Wong, *Reading* 118–127); she seeks to reinterpret Asian Americans as voluntary "travellers, explorers, and subjects of quest narratives" who use their travels and encounters as means to achieve, express, and shape an "unfinished modernity" (Ty, *Unfastened* xxvii; Clifford, *Routes* 2, qtd. in Ty, *Unfastened* xxvi). Expanding on existing criticism, I discuss involuntary migrations by figures as varied as common laborers, concubines, and refugee scholars. However, because I rely on accounts composed by Asian Americans themselves, I also emphasize the writers' labors to define themselves and those they portray as modern travelers and explorers, seekers and shapers of meaning and modernity. Like Ty, I emphasize the fluid, situational nature of Asian American cultures and subject positions. Whereas Ty seeks to go beyond themes she frames as traditional and well understood, such as Asian-white relations and intergenerational tensions, my emphasis on return narratives focuses on those themes but seeks to transform them by bringing attention to factors that may have escaped discussion until now. These include Yung's framing of identity in the semicolonial context of the late Qing Dynasty and his perennial outsider status, the ambiguous status of Lisa See's ancestors as a pioneering Chinatown family of mixed race, interracial tensions within other mixed-race families, and nuances in contemporary authors' portrayal of their identities (as fluid, situational, and plural subject positions constructed through intersubjective exchanges) and their cultures (as syncretic, dynamic, and complexly layered). Finally, although this study favors novels and various forms of life writing, I seek to push readers beyond a reflexive perception of Asian American works as realist texts that function as transparent windows into the authors' actual experiences. Instead, I emphasize the complexity and variation of the authors' literary techniques, which include using fictionalized monologues to dramatize the interiority of historical figures, problematizing historical documents, and creating unreliable and decentered narrators. Because of my wish to highlight these minority authors' varied and sometimes vexed relations to the task of augmenting, correcting, or recentering official history, my study is grounded by questions about the writing and reception of history as a larger, shared public narrative. While my book focuses on writers of Chinese and Japanese descent in order to situate the stories examined within those particular cultures, it is intended to stimulate discussion about similar narratives by authors of other groups. Whereas Ty focuses on the everyday as a site of the creation of meaning, my work engages with studies of race and affect, including theories of racial melancholia, mourning, countermemory, and postcolonial melancholia.

An Overview: Racial Melancholia, Postcolonial Melancholia, and Deimperialization

Readers new to Asian American literature may be struck by the high percentage of texts in which depression, isolation, mourning, and melancholy figure prominently.[9] Asian American narratives of return, in which authors explicitly seek to confront, comprehend, and carry forward the ghosts of the past, are particularly strong sites of rhetorical memory work that may be likened to the psychic work of mourning. For this reason, I refer in numerous chapters to the theory of racial melancholia, developed by cultural critics Anne Anlin Cheng and David L. Eng and psychoanalyst Shinhee Han in relation to Asian Americans and other "minoritarian" subjects, which became well known during the composition of this book (Eng, "Melancholia" 1278). Drawing on theories by Sigmund Freud and Frantz Fanon, as well as more recent work (by Judith Butler, Douglas Crimp, José Esteban Muñoz, and Kaja Silverman), Cheng, Eng, and Han have brought Freud's theories of mourning and melancholia to bear on questions of Asian American psychology. In brief—at the risk of providing a summary that is overly schematic and linear—Freud posits that mourning normally involves a long psychic process of renouncing a lost and beloved object (a person, country, or ideal) by revisiting, and breaking, all the psychic ties that connected the mourner to the object. This process culminates in the mourner's recognition of the permanence of that loss, the ability to attach to a new "libidinal object," and the termination of his or her debilitating dejection (Freud 242, 244–245). However, when mourners are unable to complete this process of mourning, "get over" their loss, and attach to a new libidinal object, instead remaining in a state of deep, disabling dejection, they are considered to be experiencing "melancholia" (245–246). With either mourning or melancholia, the bereaved person initially seeks to retain ties to the lost object, but in cases of melancholia the process is more complicated. The beloved person could be alive, but lost as an object of love (as in the case of a romantic breakup), in which case the loss is "of a more ideal kind" (245). In other cases of melancholia, a loss has occurred, but neither the therapist nor the patient sees clearly what is lost. Freud writes that the patient might know "*whom* he has lost but not *what* he has lost in him," signaling "an object-loss which is withdrawn from consciousness," unlike the loss in mourning, "in which there is nothing about the loss that is unconscious" (245). For Freud, the state is difficult to treat because, in contrast to mourning patients, melancholic patients cannot consciously perceive or articulate the nature of their losses, and also because these patients unconsciously seek to preserve their ties to the lost objects as if to keep them alive and present in their psyches. As Anne Anlin Cheng puts it, "Loss is denied as loss and incorporated as part of the ego. . . . [C]onsequently, as Freud reminds us, by incorporating and identifying with the ghost of the lost one, the melancholic takes on the emptiness of that ghostly presence and in this way participates in his/her own self-denigration" ("Melancholy" 50). In other words, when mourners are too attached to the absent one or lost object to renounce it, they may identify with the object, unconsciously incorporating it into their own egos. (Emphasizing the obscurity of this process, Freud describes how melancholic patients, who cannot express their rage at the lost one's abandonment directly, instead describe *themselves* as worthless and unforgivable, to a degree that is understandable only if one posits that passionate anger and judgment are feelings they cherish yet cannot acknowledge for the lost one, who is overtly idealized in the patients' accounts while they denigrate themselves [244].) While Freud's discussion seems to describe patients mourning *people*, Asian American scholars have developed a theory to describe minority subjects mourning a plethora of losses associated with immigration, including some that are abstract. These losses combine with the melancholic affect of becoming minority subjects whose cultural and material exclusion is used to preserve an image of normal U.S. citizenship and subjectivity as implicitly white. Cheng, however, describes "the melancholy of race" as a condition that troubles *both* whites and oppressed minorities: whites are haunted by the memory of minorities whose presence and histories of oppression they overtly deny but covertly remember, while oppressed minorities internalize the demand to identify with the majority yet are actually unable to win full inclusion and recognition. Cheng concludes: "While the formation of American culture may be said to be a history of legalized exclusions (Native Americans, African-Americans, Jews, Chinese-Americans, Japanese-Americans . . .), it is, however, also a history of misremembering those denials" ("Melancholy" 50). Thus, both the majority and the minorities "cleave" from and to each other through this system of "ghostly identification," with the result of perpetuating existing inequities (60).

In his 2000 essay "Melancholia in the Late Twentieth Century," the cultural critic David L. Eng suggests that melancholia is widespread: it has, for instance, been theorized as intrinsic to traditional gender formation. However, heterosexual males are not rendered melancholic by the process of relinquishing and internalizing *their* original love object (the mother) because they are compensated with the ability to identify with the father. By contrast, he argues, "women, homosexuals, people of color, and postcolonials are all coerced to relinquish and yet to identify with socially disparaged objects on their psychic paths to subjectivity. This ambivalent attachment to devalued objects . . . comes to define—indeed, to produce—minoritarian subjectivities" (1278). (For more detail on theories of melancholia and gender formation, see Chow 571–574.) In "A Dialogue on Racial Melancholia," Eng and Han suggest that for Asian immigrants to America, the theory of racial melancholia may provide a suggestive framework for examining ambivalence or depression resulting from inability to complete the classical trajectory of assimilation, in which the immigrant might "get over" the losses of leaving the old country by transferring his or her attachment to an ideal of inclusion in the new one. Since structural assimilation is perennially incomplete for Asians, who faced legalized exclusions for decades and still encounter cultural and political marginalization, racial melancholia results (345). Following José Esteban Muñoz's appropriation of Raymond Williams's term, Eng and Han propose that this form of melancholia be considered as a depathologized "'structure of feeling,' a structure of everyday life" (Muñoz 74, qtd. in Eng and Han, "Dialogue" 363) or an emergent form of consciousness that is shared and felt but not yet formally recognized or codified in fixed forms or practices in the cultural production of a particular community at a particular time.[10] My arguments below are deeply indebted to Eng and Han's articulation of the patterns of consciousness they observed in numerous young Asian Americans, patterns they attribute to the ambivalent positioning of Asian Americans as citizens who must aspire to a membership contingent on (honorary) whiteness, a condition which, as a group, Asian Americans can never fully attain (Eng and Han, "Dialogue" 363). Finally, Eng and Han follow

Muñoz, Judith Butler, and Douglas Crimp in suggesting that the process of internalizing the ghostly memory of those one cannot mourn in public can provide an empowering source of agency for minoritarian subjects and communities; in this context, refusal to relinquish the memory of the dead may be an essential seed for community cohesion and resistance (363–367).

The theory of racial melancholia provides a useful and resonant framework with which to consider rhetorical responses to various levels of loss and exclusion without resorting to psychoanalyzing individual authors or characters. That is, it provides an additional theory through which to examine how the material, cultural, and political conditions of exclusion are connected to the psychological affects of these texts, without psychoanalyzing their protagonists and narrators. (In practice, this distinction is difficult to maintain, but it is my aim.) The growing number of scholars writing about racial melancholia have used the theory to claim that, in various texts, Asian American subjects (appearing as either characters or narrators) are portrayed as struggling with conditions that are not only depressing to individuals but also based on permanent structural problems that generate melancholia. To summarize: in an Asian American subject, racial melancholia may include the internalization of an ambivalent attachment to whiteness; the confrontation with an impossible demand to separate oneself from others who represent racial otherness even as they embody one's own ethnicity, race, and origin; the involuntary transmission of the resulting melancholia, unspoken, to others, particularly one's children; a lack of conscious awareness of, or an inability to articulate, the roots of one's pain; a disdain for oneself or one's fellow minority subjects and an idealization of the racial other; an unexplained sense of lack of wholeness due to the unconscious and obscure nature of racial melancholia; or any combination of the above. Yet racial melancholia may also be a mechanism by which minoritarian subjects may "(re)construct identity and take [their] dead with [them] to the various battles [they] must wage" (Muñoz 74, qtd. in Eng and Han, "Dialogue" 363).

Many of the studies published since Eng's and Han's landmark essays in 2003 and 2006 have focused on how particular Asian American texts illustrate, complicate, or expand these basic theoretical ideas (Eng, "Transnational Adoption"; Eng and Han, "Desegregating"; Eng and Han, "Dialogue"). Rather than claim that racial melancholia is unique to Asian Americans, I want to emphasize the broad roots of racial melancholia theory from its inception. Asian American theorizations of racial melancholia are founded on claims that the ego is inherently melancholic. In "Melancholia in the Late Twentieth Century," for instance, Eng recalls that Freud himself concluded in 1923 that some melancholic identifications and disidentifications were fundamental to gender formation or, implicitly, universal; Eng suggests, however, that "minoritarian" subjects (women, gender minorities, racial minorities, and postcolonial subjects) experience melancholia in unique ways, each of which should be examined in context (1278). For instance, although I do not undertake the analysis here, I think it would be fruitful to consider experiences of melancholia in texts by and about nonminority adoptees; migrants from other cultures very different from American culture; "white" minority subjects, such as Jewish, Irish, or Italian immigrants; or diasporic Middle Eastern subjects, and to question what constitutes *racial* melancholia. In comparing Asians with white immigrants, prominent scholars have challenged the assumption that Asians resemble European immigrants and will follow European trajectories of assimilation (the ethnic hypothesis). On the contrary, they argue, anti-Asian discrimination is rooted in intransigent perceptions of Asians as fundamentally different from whites, and, as a result of these perceptions, Asians have historically faced and still face race-based barriers to citizenship and assimilation (the racial hypothesis [Okihiro; Omi and Winant; L. Lowe, *Immigrant Acts*; Gotanda]). However, I hope that my work is useful to those who recognize that, in Leslie Bow's nuanced and productive terms, Asian Americans and many others occupy a telling "interstitial" position in the black-white racial structure of U.S. culture. Asian Americans' underexamined position, and their methods of negotiating various situations, may productively be compared with the interstitial status and strategies of other minorities (Bow 4–5, 11–12).

My immediate task, however, is to consider how the Asian American subjects of these narratives register, directly or indirectly, forms of racial melancholia particular to their circumstances and how they use acts of memory and narration to contain or counteract such melancholia. In reading these texts, I argue that for Asian American subjects, a major source of racial melancholia is the unacknowledged nature of their losses and the absence of a public or private discourse to describe and hence to justify their pain. Just as Douglas Crimp wrote about the pain of being unable to mourn the deaths of abject young gay men during the AIDS crisis, Asian Americans are among those minorities whose claims to melancholia are viewed skeptically, precisely because they experience pains and injustices that are not publicly acknowledged or remembered (Crimp qtd. in Eng, "Melancholia" 1279). In reading family memoirs by Denise Chong and Winberg and May-lee Chai, I ask how narrative acts and objects of memory are used rhetorically to counter family histories rife with loss and unacknowledged anguish. In the chapter on Japanese North American literature, I suggest that racial melancholia informs the texts' treatments of prewar and wartime Japan. In short, I argue that these texts register melancholic responses to the protagonists' historic conditions of undescribed loss and suffering, yet they also consciously address melancholic conditions through acts of countermemory and postmemory, in which the authors seek out and shape their families' unwritten stories and use them to counter official narratives (Davis, *Relative Histories* 15–16).

In Chapter 7 and in my Coda, I also consider how *postcolonial melancholia* may be at work in Asian American texts concerned with China's and Japan's transitions into modernity. In *Postcolonial Melancholia*, Paul Gilroy adapts the work of German psychoanalytic writers Alexander and Margarete Mitscherlich, who, he writes, observed that Germans had failed to "face and work through the larger evil of which their love for [Adolf Hitler] had been part" (99). In the Mitscherlichs' view, the Germans had projected their national guilt onto Hitler and his immediate accomplices, denied the "destructiveness and wickedness of Germany's war aims," lost "the ability to recall whole segments of the national past," and remained haunted by the "loss of a fantasy of omnipotence" (Gilroy 98–99). Gilroy argued that Britain must also question why some modern Britons prefer to focus on their nation's part in the war against Nazis while forgetting its many colonial and postcolonial wars: modern British people must acknowledge the "brutalities of colonial rule enacted in their name and to their benefit," "work through the grim details of imperial and colonial history," and build a truly inclusive, multicultural sense of nationality, which he calls "conviviality" (99–101). Failure to perform these tasks results in postcolonial melancholia, summed up by Neil Roberts this way: "Britain's postimperial, postcolonial melancholia designates a condition whereby the current polity's repeated failure to let go of their imperial past reproduces in the present an imperial impulse," typically targeted against postcolonial immigrants and their British-born offspring (164). (Of course, Gilroy actually says Britain needs to examine more fully the costs and failures of its imperial past before letting go of its idealized version of it.)

Placing Gilroy's ideas into dialogue with Kuan-Hsing Chen's work, we may recall that Chen calls for East Asia analysts to work on the simultaneous processes of *deimperialization* (self-examination to be done by the former imperial power or colonizers), *decolonization* (self-examination to be done by the formerly colonized), and *de–cold war* (scrutiny by Asian countries of the cultural and political investments they made in the United States or other powers under the pressures of the cold war). In Chen's terms, Gilroy's book asks the British to undertake tasks of deimperialization on order to overcome their postcolonial melancholia. In using the term "postcolonial melancholia" to consider East Asia, I rely on Chen's summary, which problematizes the terms "imperialism" and "colonialism" in the context of East Asian history. He points out that postcolonial theory does not exactly match Chinese history, since China was neither a colony of the Western powers nor ruled by Japan. As Chen notes, China began the nineteenth century as a major empire; it had foreign powers claim concessions, not colonies, on the mainland; and the first "real colony in Northeast Asia was arguably Hong Kong," ceded to England in 1842 (K. Chen 5). Japan established the puppet state of Manchukuo in northeastern China in 1932 and officially invaded China in 1937. When Japan colonized Taiwan and Korea, Taiwan was not part of China. Thus, most of China experienced imperialism but not outright colonialism, which Chen defines as "a deepening of imperialism" (6). He observes, "The difficulty with Northeast Asian regional integration is partially caused by the discomfort the region's population felt under first the long-term dominance of the Chinese empire, and then the strain of prewar Japanese imperialism and colonialism" (6).

Thus, one might ask whether China, as a former empire that experienced Western and Japanese imperialism, suffered or suffers from a Chinese version of postcolonial melancholia and if so, what forms such melancholia would take. At the risk of simplification, I suggest that both the Republic of China and the People's Republic of China (PRC) were founded on critiques of the flaws of Chinese feudalism, which would seem to preclude melancholic attachment to the Qing empire, at least. On the other hand, both regimes suffered from figures who sought to emulate imperial power, and the complex legacies of Mao Zedong and the suffering he instigated still linger in public memory, not fully available for public critique. In the contemporary moment, as the PRC consolidates its power and seeks to expand its global influence, it does so partly by censoring portions of modern Chinese history whose grim details undermine its moral legitimacy—much as Britons discount the costs of colonialism, or Germans once failed to recognize their own complicity with the Nazi regime. For instance, the PRC internally censors mention of the Anti-Rightist movement in the 1950s, the Cultural Revolution, and the Tiananmen demonstrations of 1989. A January 2017 op-ed posted on the *Shanghai Daily News* website describes the late Nobel laureate and former Tiananmen demonstrator Liu Xiaobo as "a Chinese criminal convicted of inciting subversion of state power," the award as an "infamous decision," and the Dalai Lama as a "political exile who attempts to split Tibet from China" (Wang and Wang).[11] Thus "whole segments of the national past" are officially obscured in the PRC, while the history of Japanese imperialism and the anti-Japanese war are readily recalled there, just as Britain's struggle against the Nazis is in England, in order to enhance nationalism. Though the description of postcolonial melancholia does not precisely fit here, these details and Chen's analysis suggest that in the case of the PRC, further deimperialization is needed to counter a melancholic attachment to an idealized version of modern Chinese nationalism that endangers intra-Asian cooperation. How, then, do Chinese American authors and their narratives of return relate to this work?

Because of my investment in Chinese American narratives of return addressing the early twentieth century and augmenting the current understanding of Chinese American representations of this period, I do not address the modern equivalent of postcolonial melancholia in China here. However, it tacitly informs my reading of the first full-length Chinese American narrative of return, Yung Wing's 1909 autobiography, as I analyze how he registers the dark underbelly of late Qing history. Though *My Life in China and America* defends Chinese sovereignty and Chinese people, I argue, Yung was far from attached to the Qing Dynasty itself; on the contrary, he repeatedly criticizes it. Also, though Yung seems to love America and to claim belonging there, he also participates in his own form of decolonization as a naturalized Chinese American: he questions Western imperialism and the complicity of missionaries and travel writers with it. Moreover, by discussing the vulnerability of the Chinese people under the Qing, both within China and abroad, he exposes his own engagement with that vulnerability. Following the lead of Lisa Lowe's study of slave narratives in *The Intimacies of Four Continents*, I argue that Yung performs this rhetorical work by drawing on the genres of the missionary travel narrative and the slave narrative.

While I am discussing the theoretical question of transposing postcolonial melancholia into the East Asian context, I also turn to Japan, which similarly shifts between the positions of the colonized and the colonizer. As noted by Chen, Japan experienced Western imperialism in the nineteenth century, but it annexed Okinawa in 1872, occupied Taiwan in 1895, annexed Korea in 1910, set up Manchukuo in 1932, and formally invaded China in 1937, aspiring to lead and rule a "Greater East Asia Co-prosperity Sphere" that would rival the Western powers. Instead, Japan lost the war in 1945, was occupied by the allies, and became a protectorate of the United States. During this process, it never experienced colonization, but the Japanese process of properly understanding the nation's wartime actions and responsibilities was short-circuited by U.S. occupation, reconstruction, and Japan's reconstitution as a U.S. ally in the cold war. According to Chen, Japan must deimperialize, "resolv[ing] its guilt for the damage it caused its neighbors by the imperialist Greater East Asia Co-prosperity Sphere project," but it must also decolonize, "work[ing] out its contradictory attitudes of resentment and gratitude toward the United States" (6–10), although, like China, Japan has never been a colony. Chapter 7 sketches the debates about Japanese historical memory and considers how two Japanese American narratives of return, both novels, participate in deimperialization by describing the educations of migrants returning to Japan as they question Japanese imperialism. Drawing on a transnational feminist tradition of Japanese writing, including the I-novel, the memoirs of Japanese feminists, and the deimperializing scholarship of Emiko Ohnuki-Tierney about the kamikaze pilots of World War II, the novelists Lydia Minatoya and Ruth Ozeki exemplify the skillful balance struck by many Japanese American narratives of return. Their works demonstrate sympathy for the suffering and constraints of Japanese in the imperial, wartime, and postwar eras as well as awareness of the need to probe and question this period.

Narratives of Return: A Literary Overview

Like Eleanor Ty, I have "unfastened" the geopolitical borders of Asian America. I confess that my definition of "narratives of return" is fluid as well, including texts that exemplify, merge, and reform several genres. Because the trope of return is so germinal to Asian American literature, I do not provide an exhaustive survey of examples. (My Works Cited and Additional Sources list includes a hundred texts depicting actual and symbolic returns, as well as several closely related texts.) However, I have selected for close study five texts focusing on Chinese American narratives of return that span events from 1828 through 2002, with publication dates ranging from 1909 through 2002. Among these, I chose to include the autobiography of the early educational pioneer Yung Wing in order to emphasize the importance of Chinese Americans in the nineteenth century and of educated Chinese throughout the more than 150 years of Chinese-American contact and immigration. The thirteen personal narratives collected by Josephine Khu highlight the experiences of overseas Chinese symbolically returning to China for the first time in the 1980s and 1990s, a period when U.S. interest in China was accentuated by the opening of China to the West and a new era of multiculturalism, which contributed to the flourishing of Asian American literature in the United States and Canada. I have chosen the family history memoirs of Lisa See, Denise Chong, and Winberg and May-lee Chai both because of their literary merits and because I feel it is important to balance the more familiar stories of working-class Chinese (treated as unskilled laborers for immigration purposes, usually with peasant backgrounds and usually originating in southern China) with the stories of a merchant family and a family of highly educated scholars to give a richer and more complete picture of Chinese Americans and the literature they have produced. See depicts a uniquely full portrait of an extended family founded by a mixed-race merchant couple; Chong documents the lives of a peasant-laborer family in the specific context of Cantonese-Canadian immigration; and the Chais, a father-daughter author team, provide an unusual double narration marked by their difference in gender and generation.

Japanese Americans, as one of the longer-settled Asian American groups, have produced a substantial body of texts deemed central to Asian American literature. However, until recently, there were few English-language texts by Japanese Americans addressing the issues of Japanese imperialism, despite the fact that Japanese invasion and occupation were vividly recalled by Chinese American, Korean American, and Filipino American writers. As Theodore Goossen has argued, there is in Japanese North American literature a sense that the creative writers had more to say about this topic than they cared to publish for the larger American public, or that it was too difficult for them to write candidly about Japanese imperialism in the public sphere until larger historical discussions had taken place. Hence, my Japanese North American chapter uses the trope of return to address the silence in early Asian American literature about Japanese imperialism of the early twentieth century. Early classic texts of the 1950s and 1970s avoided discussing Japanese imperialism directly, focusing instead on injustices such as the internment of Japanese North Americans and the bombing of Hiroshima and Nagasaki (see Kogawa [who is Japanese Canadian]; Okada; Murayama; and Sone). In the 1980s and 1990s, several academic writers (including a white scholar) published favorable travel and return narratives seeking to counter images of Japan as a fearsome economic rival by presenting it as a site of gracious, hospitable academic exchange and elegant traditions, with an economy driven primarily by artisans and small family businesses (see C. Davidson; Kondo; Minatoya, *Talking*; Mura); more recently, Japan has been portrayed as a modern nation characterized by prosperity, homogeneity, academic competition, familial alienation, overwork, sexism, and hostility to outsiders, both in fiction and life writing (see, e.g., Backer; D. Lee; Mori; Ozeki) and in fictional and scholarly representations of third-generation Japanese Brazilian guest workers (Yamashita; Tsuda, *Diasporic Homecomings* and *Strangers*). Among the many Japanese American return narratives, I have chosen to focus on texts that examine Japan in the 1920s and 1930s from several distinct perspectives: those of a returning emigrant woman and her Japanese American niece (sent to study in Japan) in the 1920s and 1930s, who witness the rise of Japanese militarism (Minatoya, *Strangeness*); and that of a twenty-first-century Japanese schoolgirl who returns to Japan after living in California, who looks back on Japan's imperial era through the story of her great-uncle, who served and died in World War II as a kamikaze pilot (Ozeki).

As my discussion should suggest, I do not wish to imply that Chinese and Japanese American narratives of return represent Asian American narratives of return exhaustively. Indeed, my original plan was to write a book that included texts about by and about many additional ethnic groups. However, in the course of writing, I have been drawn to formal and historical questions that require a narrower approach. The topic of Japanese American portrayals of Japan, for instance, merits more discussion than I could provide here.

I particularly regret giving up, for now, the personally moving and politically resonant topic of Korean adoptees and their narratives of returning and searching for their birth families in Korea, which first led me to Eng's work on racial melancholia.[12] I hope that readers share my view that narratives by and about returnees of other groups deserve additional space and separate study. Nor have I made an effort to redress the gender imbalance that has emerged in my final choice of texts, despite my earlier plans to include many additional texts by men. I can say only that I believe, on the basis of my broader reading, that racial melancholia and the will to address it through writing and countermemory are certainly not limited to women; by placing these particular texts into dialogue, however, I hope to foster future discussions of the theme of return that will acknowledge women's texts as central to this literature.

Narratives of Return: Types and Tropes of Return

At this point, before turning to the texts I have selected, it may be useful to delineate the various categories of return narratives that I have encountered. To begin, I must distinguish between *actual* returns, by Asian emigrants to homelands they know personally, and *symbolic* returns, in which the descendants of diasporic Asian emigrants travel to their ancestral home countries for the first time. In this second category, a trip does actually place, but, as a first-time visit to a new country, it is only symbolically a return. By contrast, anthropologists Lynelleyn D. Long and Ellen Oxfeld focus their collection *Coming Home? Refugees, Migrants, and Those Who Stayed Behind* on first-generation return migration of the former type (*actual* returns), intentionally excluding *symbolic* returns (of later generations to their ancestral homelands), and *virtual* returns, "connections facilitated by computer networks and other types of media" (Long and Oxfeld 4). They see return migration as a complex process that takes extended periods of time and may involve three stages: *imagined returns*, in which returnees prepare to return by exploring their options; *provisional returns*, in which emigrants visit their home countries, perhaps settling temporarily, to test the waters for a permanent return; and *repatriated* or *permanent returns*, which include "both organized *and* individual returns, as well as returns that are both forced *and* voluntary" (11). While repatriated returnees may view their resettlement as permanent, Long and Oxfeld caution that such permanence is a "commitment," more aspiration than "assured reality," since in their survey they have found that "there are no guarantees of permanency" (11). Each type of return involves complex social negotiations, which are thoroughly explored in their essay collection as well as in its anthropological intertexts.[13]

As a result of Asian American literature's bias toward English texts, symbolic returns by second- or latter-generation Asian Americans are fairly familiar to readers of this literature. Before discussing them, however, I wish to acknowledge the presence and importance of several types of actual returns in order to suggest the range and richness of these journeys as represented in literary and cultural texts by Asian Americans. These include three kinds of *provisional* returns (*diasporic visits, transnational commutes,* and *adoptee return visits*) and four kinds of *permanent* returns (*postimperial returns, postcolonial returns, expatriate returns,* and *permanent returns* that are read as failures or successes). Finally, *symbolic* returns can be described in terms of purpose (scholarship, job, tourism, family move, or family pilgrimage) as well as duration (a short visit, a longer stay, a series of visits, or permanent residence in the homeland).

The category of *diasporic visits* includes the stories of Asian migrants who visit home countries to maintain ties with family and friends, to transmit familial and cultural ties to their offspring, to tour, and to vacation. Such visits may also nourish roots that include citizenship, ownership of land or a secondary residence, or business relationships. In Monica Sone's 1953 memoir *Nisei Daughter*, the author's *issei* (immigrant) parents, the Itois, bring their children on a final trip "home," around 1924, to see Japan and bid a final farewell to her father's parents before settling permanently in the United States.[14] At the time, the mother and father know, but do not tell their young children, that they will never see Mr. Itoi's parents alive again once the United States passes its new immigration laws. Similarly, in Ronyoung Kim's autobiographical novel *Clay Walls*, the immigrant parents think they are bringing their American children back to Korea in 1931 for a provisional visit to pave the way for a permanent return, but the journey becomes a farewell visit because of the terrible political conditions they observe, with the country under occupation by the Japanese. More recently, Jhumpa Lahiri's novel *The Namesake* depicts an expatriate scholar returning home to meet and marry an Indian bride with whom he will settle in America. In these disparate diasporic visits, the returnees are about to settle in America permanently but make the trips as expressions of the wish to maintain ties to their homeland. Similarly, Asian American writers such as Andrew X. Pham and Michael Ondaatje, immigrants from Vietnam and Sri Lanka, respectively, have written of journeys taken not only for the sake of visiting but also for the sake of giving new form to the past in memoirs of the trips.

Transnational commutes are made by returnees who fit Aihwa Ong's definition of transnational subjects or Haiming Liu's concept of the transpacific family, as summarized by Sau-ling Cynthia Wong:

In view of Asia's vastly superior economic prospects but continued political uncertainty, many middle-class Asian families are splitting their members, sending the children (sometimes accompanied by a parent, sometimes not) to study in U.S. schools and/or gain permanent residency while the breadwinner stays in Asia. Family ties are maintained by frequent visits in either direction. (Hence the Chinese nicknames for such families: *kongzhong feiren*, "trapeze artists," or *taikongren*, "astronauts.") (S. C. Wong, "Denationalization" 7)

Wong suggests a distinction between diasporic families, who settle abroad but maintain psychological ties to the homeland, and transnational or transpacific families, in which members reside in different countries but are prepared to relocate according to the needs of their family enterprises and the changing conditions of the countries where they live and work. Although individuals residing in the United States or Canada may perform a diasporic visit to an Asian homeland, the implications are different for those who see their families as "trapeze artists" suspended between East and West rather than expatriates or immigrants who periodically visit their homelands. In the works I discuss in Chapters 2 and 3, most of the contributors to Khu's collection *Cultural Curiosity* are diasporic narrators, while the families of See and Chong are transpacific in orientation. On the other hand, Wong's point about "transpacific families" is that they blur the distinction between permanent expatriates and temporary residents such as students. In general, it is easiest for first- and second-generation migrants to retain a transpacific orientation; the second and third generations, geographically and linguistically removed from their ancestral homelands, find it more difficult to retain strong roots in their parents' countries but may retain a sense of connection and responsibility to those at home in Asia. Through the writings of second- and third-generation North Americans, this book considers the rhetorical and cultural labor involved in retaining those ties.

By comparison, Korean and other transnational adoptees who return to their motherlands seeking information about their birth families, the circumstances of their relinquishment and adoption, and their birth culture are also return migrants; yet the majority emigrated so young that they have little or no conscious memory of their homeland. Therefore, *adoptee return visits* further pressure the distinction between actual and symbolic returns. In particular, adoptees assimilated into white families resemble second-generation Asian Americans in their first encounters with their Asian homelands. Using the musical term for an interval that is a half-step larger than usual, I call these "augmented first-generation" Asian Americans. (The usual term for

Asian Americans who emigrate before age twenty is "1.5-generation.") When adoptees choose to live in their birth countries for longer periods, they further blur distinctions between provisional and repatriated returns.

When individuals living abroad return to their Asian homelands permanently, the *repatriated return* is often depicted in terms of success or failure, prestige or shame. In *Paper Angels*, Genny Lim's play about the San Francisco immigration facility Angel Island, a woman whose immigration interview is deemed unacceptable and a man who is judged physically unfit to land in the United States both perceive their involuntary repatriations to China as failures. By contrast, Chinese sojourners who return to retire, build houses, buy property, or invest in local schools or businesses, or who have sent money or gifts from abroad to support family members in their Chinese hometowns, are deemed successful (M. Hsu, *Dreaming*; Oxfeld). Yet regardless of financial success, failure can take the form of incomplete assimilation. In Rohinton Mistry's story "Swimming Lessons," a successful Parsi Indian decides that he will leave Canada, regardless of his earning power, if after ten years he has not learned to use a Western-style toilet properly. His eventual self-defined failure is a metaphor for his perception that his Indian body does not fit in North America. Perhaps the best-known Asian American novel of a return caused by *political* failure is Chang-rae Lee's *Native Speaker*, in which New York city councilman John Kwang loses his bid in the mayor's race. Kwang, arguably, is punished (by his political enemies and by the narrative) not only for personal corruption but also for the hubris of aspiring to lead in American politics. In contrast to his media-saturated fall from grace, Kwang's subsequent return migration to Korea is so unmentionable that it is not even dramatized in the novel; it is only mentioned in passing by a real estate agent. Yet this return is like a death, for the tragic memory of Kwang and the lost ideals he embodied haunts Henry Park, the melancholic first-person narrator, at least as much as the actual deaths of his own father and son. For some readers, Kwang's fictional failure may evoke a tragic real-life example of someone who returned to Asia out of political disenchantment: Lily Chin, a Chinese American immigrant who returned to China after the notorious murder of her son, Vincent Chin, chagrined by the U.S. legal system's failure to obtain justice for him (S. Chan, *Asian Americans* 176–178). Chin's return may be viewed not so much as a sign of personal failure or of racial melancholia but as an example of the thesis that some Asian Americans might return to Asia as a response to exclusionary American social practices, such as the failure of the American legal system to guarantee equal justice and protection to Asian Americans.

Fundamentally, the assessment of the migrant's success or failure in these cases rests on the presumption that the initial migration had traditional aims: settlement, assimilation, and the accumulation of cultural and financial capital. However, the same impulse receives a different twist in *postimperial narratives*, by which I mean principally Japanese American narratives of return at the end of World War II: these texts address the end of Japan's ambitions to lead an East Asian empire. A number of Chinese American, Japanese American, and Korean American texts depict the predicaments of Japanese who are caught in China at the time of the Japanese surrender in 1945 (e.g., H. Lee; J. Chang; Keller; C. Lee, *A Gesture Life*), while other authors write about the dislocations of the postwar era in Japan (Chadwick; V. H. Houston; Kuramoto; Tomita [see also Golden; Ishiguro, *Artist*]). Among these, some narratives primarily record the difficulties associated with returning to Japan; my chapter focuses on two novelists who specifically address the problems of imagining private responses to official discourses of that time. Perhaps counterintuitively, I have found that most of these Japanese American narratives of return do not express "postcolonial melancholia," in Paul Gilroy's sense, but actively engage with understanding the circumstances of that era. I would make the same point about Yung's 1909 autobiography, *My Life in China and America*: the text discusses the decline of the Qing Dynasty and appeared in the dynasty's last years, but it counters postcolonial melancholia by recalling many instances of the dynasty's failures.

Closely related to postimperial returns are *postcolonial* and *expatriate returns*. The theme of postcolonial subjects' returns to their homelands recurs in South Asian American literature. In *The Inheritance of Loss*, for instance, Kiran Desai contrasts a cook's son (Biju), who travels to New York City as an undocumented immigrant and returns after years as a restaurant worker, with a local judge (Jemubhai Patel), who rises from poverty to study as a scholarship student at Cambridge, internalizes British racism, and returns to be a harsh judge in the Indian courts as well as an abusive husband to his Indian wife. Patel embodies the colonial subject who is alienated from his heritage and imperfectly Anglicized in the process of being trained to govern on behalf of the British. Desai emphasizes the historical anomaly of the judge's position as a postcolonial subject: having received his office in India from the departed British, he is melancholically unable to distance himself from England and reconceptualize himself as an Indian who combines public power and individual agency with ethnic or national pride or a true call to public service. Biju, on the other hand, experiences the alienation of seeing how global workers and small restaurant owners from around the world, gathered in New York, see him and his countrymen, and he realizes that he is just as unimportant in their eyes as he is as the cook's son at home. In the United States, however, he will not only be poor; he will always be a rootless stranger judged by his nationality and stigmatized by his undocumented immigration status.

For these and other postcolonial returnees, returning to one's homeland requires a postcolonial retuning of their internal moral compass to set aside the dream of inclusion in the British or American middle class. This often results in the claiming of new objectives, such as questioning, activism, or revenge. In the case of Biju, the retuning sounds modest: he realizes he is better off being poor at home, where he can see his devoted father, than being poor and friendless abroad. But for other fictional or biographical characters, the ability or inability to mourn and get over their supposed failures as postcolonial subjects who can never be white, and to refocus on a new worldview such as one of nationalism, may result in vastly different outcomes. As depicted in texts by and about South Asian American writers, colonial education abroad may lead to various ends: postcolonial melancholia in the form of endless self-hatred (Desai), a focus on nationalism expressed in political leadership or journalism (Sara Suleri), or radicalization and conversion to terrorism (Mohsin Hamid). (In the latter cases, the postcolonial subjects—Suleri's father and Hamid's unnamed narrator—are not necessarily melancholic, for they arguably renounce postcolonial mourning and focus on new objects.)

In the context of Filipino literature, Gerald T. Burns has described a particular kind of postcolonial narrative of return, the *novel of expatriate returns*. With José Rizal's classic Spanish-language novel *Noli Me Tangere* and Carlos Bulosan's posthumous revolutionary novel *The Cry and the Dedication* among his examples, Burns shows how such works depict inherent conflict between the never-departed locals and the returnees, who after many years abroad seek to draw on their foreign educations and experiences as resources to lead transformation in their homelands. While foreign education and experience can be perceived as assets, they can also be seen by locals as suspect. In order to lead, the returnees in these novels must demonstrate their commitment and attunement to the needs of those they once left behind (Burns 168–225).[15] Working with a different genre (travel memoirs) and a different ethnic history, Chih-ming Wang has observed that in the autobiographical return narratives of Andrew Lam and Andrew X. Pham, the narrators (expatriate returnees known as Viet Kieu) circle around the themes of economic disparity (between local Vietnamese and the middle-class returnees they perceive as wealthy) and questions of expectations, responsibility, guilt, and the returnees' desire to reconcile past wounds while retaining the advantages they have won through the ordeals of immigration ("Politics of Return").

The narratives I consider include many genres: personal essays, family memoirs, novels, ethnographies, and autobiography. (I have set aside a discussion of Korean adoption narratives, including films, because of space limitations.) These are united by themes of migration out of Asia, return migration, and travel as a trope for understanding one's place in the world.

Like other travel narratives, these works describe the physical conditions of travel, including serendipitous encounters. Many are organized by the literary convention of using a physical journey to Asia to dramatize or perform an introspective psychological journey, as Rocío Davis has remarked (*Relative Histories* 2). And they register awareness of cultural differences, of the process of seeing and being seen by others, of economic differences between Asian American travelers and those they encounter, and of the historical moment of travel and its distance from the pasts they explore.

Most travel narratives are written by voluntary travelers, privileged tourists who combine mobility with freedom. As mentioned above, Asian American travel has often been described in terms of constraint and necessity, in contrast to an Anglophone tradition of travel narration that associates adventure, exploration, recreation, and pilgrimage with white travelers and narrators while discounting the perspectives of their nonwhite companions and staff members (S. C. Wong, *Reading*; Clifford, *Routes* 33; Ty, *Unfastened* xxvi–xxvii). However, Asian Americans often "turn the experience of forced mobility into an educational and liberating journey as well as resistance to oppression," as Su-ching Huang has noted (7, discussing S. C. Wong, *Reading*). Though many of the narratives examined here depict immigrations driven by necessity, I grant primacy to narrators who travel by choice to Asia, combining the aims of commerce, service, education, exploration, and pilgrimage with the privileged status of voluntary travelers.

While in Asia, Asian American travelers must be attuned to their positions as outsiders and their shifting positions in varying contexts, noting the locals' level of acceptance, the significance of local and family histories, and their own linguistic and cultural expertise. The travelers may anticipate linguistic or ethnic affinity rooted in racial likeness yet be perceived as wealthy outsiders. They may be claimed as lost sons or daughters of a family or village yet be unable to meet the expectations of villagers or family members (M. Hsu, *Dreaming*; Khu, *Cultural Curiosity*; Louie, *Chineseness*; Manalansan; Oxfeld). As a group, Asian American authors are acutely aware of Americans' and Westerners' past and current portrayals of Asian countries; their own treatment by Americans and by Asian locals; how they may negotiate with such perceptions, both as writers and as travelers; and how all these factors inform their projects of retrieving family history or their confrontations with its irretrievability. For instance, in his memoir of returning to Vietnam, *Catfish and Mandala*, Pham uses scenes of financial bargaining (haggling, shakedowns, and propositions) to highlight his discomfort as a Viet Kieu being treated as a wealthy American tourist who should be made to feel guilty for leaving the country and now may be exploited as a financial resource (C. Wang, "Politics of Return"). As mentioned above, Ondaatje's memoir

Running in the Family juxtaposes his own vignettes (of interviewing relatives about his parents) with the colonialist writings of European travelers to Sri Lanka. By interleaving family stories and his own poetry with the writings of Sri Lankan dissidents and ancient graffiti poets, he invites readers not to view him as just another orientalist traveler but to place his text within a broad spectrum of local and foreign writing about Sri Lanka.

That said, my study is less concerned with the external conditions of travel than with narrators who come to see themselves as rooted in two or more places and must work to claim their identities, whether as diasporic, transnational, or flexible subjects. These texts are obsessed with the processes of cultural recovery, memory, interpretation, and narration associated with return migration, and these writers fashion personal histories that contest the silences of history. Yung's autobiography rewrites the missionary travel narrative and creates a Chinese sequel to the slave narrative. Minatoya draws on the memoirs of transpacific women writers of Japan, such as Etsu Sugimoto and the Baroness Shidzue Ishimoto. And Ozeki evokes the voices of revolutionaries, kamikaze pilots, and Buddhist nuns who suffered but questioned Japanese imperialism. But despite my efforts to cross disciplines, my work is not fundamentally anthropological, sociological, historical, or properly political. I read these writers as seekers of poetic as well as social justice. Like Renaissance poets, their concern is to create stories of the people and places they love that will outlast the ravages of time, despite—sometimes in the teeth of—the fact that in many cases, those they love are also those they can never know. Faced with what they cannot know, these Chinese Americans and Japanese Americans build countermemories as foundational narratives of origin. In some cases, the fragmented, decentered, nonlinear forms of these countermemories reflect the writers' perceptions of the stories they seek as slippery and multifaceted. Nonetheless, these accounts perform rhetorical work akin to trauma therapy: by narrating the past, they transform it from an unspeakable specter to a usable countermemory that anchors them and memorializes the past in ways that are personally meaningful.

Chapter Overview

Here, then, are the contours of this study. In Chapter 1, I have introduced the topic of narratives of return as a form of literary memorial, explained how the book relates to other studies taking a transnational or global approach to Asian/American studies (by K. Chen; S. G. Lim et al.; Lawrence and Cheung; Srikanth; and Ty, *Unfastened*); and discussed questions of genre, racial melancholia, postcolonial melancholia, types of return migration, and conventions of travel narration. I have introduced the theses that the trope of return is prevalent in and fundamental to Asian American literature; that it is best read in various transnational contexts, including those of transnational trade and educational exchange, postcolonial melancholia, and racial melancholia; and that the authors of Asian American narratives of return seek to address various forms of melancholia through various forms of countermemory.

In Chapter 2, I describe the contemporary narrative of return as I first conceived it, as a kind of pilgrimage in which Asian Americans return to their ancestral homelands. By looking at short personal essays on this theme, written by the children of diasporic Chinese settled around the world and collected and edited by historian Josephine Khu in 2001, I suggest what the form of such a return narrative could be, considering the following: the narrator's family history; his or her location and sense of ethnic and national identity prior to the trip; the reasons for return; the preparations; the meetings with family members and their expectations and perceptions; and the narrator's evolving sense of self, culture, and identity. Taken as a group, the essays reveal the tip of the iceberg of a worldwide Chinese diaspora and also illustrate the cultural labor that second- and later-generation overseas Chinese must undertake in order to be part of what Tu Wei-ming has theorized as the imagined community of "cultural China." Since the narrators articulate legacies and expectations whose powerful affects are not fully understood and grapple with disparities between their own and their families' expectations and realities, I examine one of these stories through the lens of racial melancholia. However, I find that such melancholia takes specific forms for this generation of writers, who symbolically returned to China in the 1980s and 1990s as the country was processing the aftermath of the Cultural Revolution, the death of Mao Zedong, and the establishment of new relations with the West. For this generation, their personal return stories are threads in a large canvas of returns and reunions that crosses time and space.

In Chapter 3, I describe the narrative work Lisa See performs in the multigenerational memoir of her mixed-race family, *On Gold Mountain: The One-Hundred-Year Odyssey of My Chinese-American Family*. First, I assert that even in the Exclusion Era (1882–1943/1965), early Chinese Americans such as See's great-grandfather, Fong See, were transnational subjects: some traveled back and forth many times between China and the United States and had multiple ties to both countries. Second, I find that See combines an unusual depth and range of research with fictionlike narrative tools to bring imagination and insight into her presentation of family members whom she did not know personally, illustrating how an archive in the hands of the right narrator can project a personality (such as Fong See's) in the absence of the subject's written or recorded voice. Third, I argue that given the richness of

See's account, the specific family history merits attention for multiple reasons: the Fong and See relatives exemplify Chinese migration patterns and merchant-class risk and privilege while also providing a model of a mixed-race family who invented new ways to perform and embody Chineseness.

In Chapters 4 and 5, I return to the family memoirs of Denise Chong and of Winberg and May-lee Chai. In regard to Chong's work, I suggest (1) that the model of overseas success illustrated by Fong See, combined with the impossibility of attaining that success, contributed to the racial melancholia of Chong's grandparents, a Chinese Canadian laborer and his concubine, and that this model is exemplified by the trope of the returnee's mansion; (2) that the immigrants' melancholia is accentuated both by gender divisions and by its unacknowledged nature, and is passed on to the immigrants' daughter, Hing; and (3) that the text both registers and combats this melancholia through acts of narration, countermemory, and memorialization.

In the case of Chai and Chai's collaborative, intergenerational biography, a similar dynamic takes place, but with some differences. In contrast to Chong's ancestors, Ruth Chai is educated by missionaries and in 1920 becomes one of the first eight women in China to test into the prestigious National Central University; her husband, Charles Chai, studies law at Northwestern University. Long before they immigrate to the United States, Charles and Ruth Chai come to America as students and return to China, expecting to take an active role in its reform; ultimately, however, they immigrate with their three sons. As elites who studied in America, lived and worked in China, and finally immigrated to the United States, the Chais represent a significant class of Chinese Americans whose stories have received relatively little critical attention thus far. Charles's and Ruth's stories illustrate the influence of American missionaries and study abroad on women's education and the values of Chinese elites, and the postcolonial melancholia that results when the liberal democratic values learned from Americans are inapplicable in China of the 1920s, 1930s, and 1940s. In particular, Ruth's sense of melancholic loss and intergenerational rupture is captured in the tropes of the returnee's mansion and of numerous objects of memory. In one sense, the text demonstrates a typical Asian American literary economy in which the authors use the narrative to pay off their filial duty or debt of recognition of the first generation's struggles. In another, it serves as a countermemory that rhetorically traces and contains the postcolonial melancholia of Ruth and Charles.

Chapter 6 steps back in time to examine the 1909 memoir of Yung Wing, the first Chinese graduate of an American university and a sometime diplomat who organized the first Chinese Educational Mission to send Chinese youth to study in America in the late nineteenth century. Although Yung has published the earliest English-language narrative of return I have found, I deferred the discussion of his text to a later chapter of my book for two reasons. First, I want readers to enter this study as I did, starting with the "curiosity" model of Khu's anthology in which contemporary Asian Americans actually returned to their ancestral homelands, and then to complicate their understanding of this model by examining other intergenerational Chinese narratives of return; Yung's text, a simpler first-person narrative with a global orientation, seemed to belong in a section of its own. Second, I wished to place Yung's text, with its questioning of Qing rule and Western imperialism, into dialogue with Minatoya's and Ozeki's texts rethinking Japanese imperialism and historical memory. Yung's text is included because it arguably provides the best-written English language portrait of an elite Chinese American subject of the late Qing Dynasty, establishes the presence and importance of educational exchange early in Asian American history, and provides an example of an early Chinese American writer who saw himself as belonging to both China and the United States. In opposition to dismissive readings by some scholars, I find that Yung's text should be valued as a deliberate rhetorical performance: Yung presents himself as a global subject through strategies modeled on the travel narratives of missionaries such as Karl Gützlaff and slave narratives such as those of Frederick Douglass and Olaudah Equiano. Far from expressing postcolonial melancholia, a sentiment one might expect of a Chinese nationalist, Yung's text criticizes the failures of the Qing Dynasty, as if performing the task of *deimperialization*—scrutinizing one's inner imperialist—advocated for modern Chinese by Kuan-Hsing Chen. In addition, far from expressing uncritical white supremacist views, as he has been accused of doing, Yung's text contains critiques of missionary collusion with Western imperialism and expresses his support for China's continued independence; hence, his autobiography also performs ideological work akin to Chen's concept of *decolonization*—the practice of questioning habits of mind typical of colonized people. I do not read Yung as aspiring to whiteness but rather as seeking equality with whites for himself and other Chinese. His text is suffused with the melancholia of one who is ultimately denied the freedom and authority of a global subject and who recognizes his kinship with his less fortunate compatriots around the globe.

In Chapter 7, I discuss Japanese North American return narratives, focusing on two novels in which writers respond indirectly to debates about Japanese historical memory. These authors employ their bicultural perspectives to reconsider the period of Japanese imperialism: drawing on extensive research and a form of the focused, sympathetically engaged imagination I call countermemory, they use fiction to imagine the doubts and options of Japanese during the imperialist Showa era as well as to dramatize the complexity of remembering and questioning official narratives of that era in the present moment. I argue that Lydia Minatoya's *The Strangeness of Beauty*, formally an I-novel, draws on Etsu Sugimoto's transpacific memoir *A Daughter of the Samurai* and other sources but also uses imagination to question the agency and responsibility of ordinary Japanese in the 1920s and 1930s. Ruth Ozeki's *A Tale for the Time Being* goes further, drawing on the historical research of Emiko Ohnuki-Tierney and others to create a dialogical text in which a Japanese American narrator reading a Japanese schoolgirl's diary enacts the labor of translating and interpreting texts from the past. Ozeki's young Japanese protagonist embodies another kind of melancholia: that of a returned expatriate to Asia who cannot assimilate into her home culture and must assume a ghostly existence, neither accepted into Japanese society nor released from its gaze. Under this pressure, the girl's ability to understand and interpret her great-uncle's military sacrifice independently is essential to her survival.

2

"Ears Attuned to Two Cultures"

Reconciling Accounts in Josephine Khu's Cultural Curiosity

> In China, I thought I would easily blend in with the crowd because I looked Chinese, but I was wrong, because my thinking, attitudes, reactions, body language, and behavior stood out. Living in China showed me how American I was in most of my ideas and principles. My sense of independence, helping oneself, directing my destiny, and making things happen instead of depending on my family to succeed permeated everything I did. These concepts seemed very strange to my relatives in China.
> —Nancy Work, "Full Circle," 18–19

> It is curious to realize that I have traveled in the reverse direction of my father. Although I am indeed a stranger to China, I feel a strong connection to its people. . . . Even today, after many visits to the mainland, I always have a feeling of inexplicable nostalgia on leaving it.
> —Meilin Chang, "My Father's Land," 110

> [A] visiting Chinese professor . . . commented that my greatest value as a teacher in China would be my ability to look at Chinese history and culture from a Western point of view, and Western history and culture from a Chinese perspective. In fact, I have become a cultural hybrid. . . .
> Having reached the Confucian age when "one's ears are attuned," I have come to realize and accept that my ears are attuned to two cultures.
> —Henry Chan, "Ears Attuned to Two Cultures," 126

THE CONTRIBUTORS to Josephine Khu's *Cultural Curiosity: Thirteen Stories about the Search for Chinese Roots* reflect ambivalence toward the uncanny experience of returning to China after establishing roots in other countries where Chinese are marginalized minorities. In many ways, Maxine Hong Kingston's landmark memoir *The Woman Warrior* dramatized the intense cultural labor required for a diasporic Chinese American to create concepts of China and Chineseness by gathering and interpreting public and private stories of Chinese people and culture while growing up without the opportunity to visit China. Published in 1976, a few years after China reopened doors to the United States, *The Woman Warrior* depicted the author as living in a Chinese American family that was rooted in Cantonese folk culture yet culturally isolated from American culture (by virtue of the parents' limited English) and physically cut off from mainland China.[1] Educated at the University of California at Berkeley in the late 1950s and early 1960s, Kingston recreates in her memoir the historical incoherence of stories and remarks from her immigrant parents as they might have been understood by her teenage self. Khu's book is one of many others in which the writers recall growing up overseas in later decades with an equally unclear or limited sense of what it meant to be Chinese. Through their personal essays, the contributors to *Cultural Curiosity* mark the common points of their journeys of return, in which physical travel is but one aspect of a longer process of education and reflection that enables the diasporic traveler to claim and construct Chineseness.

The collection implicitly invites readers to consider the narrative of return as a genre. Khu, an independent scholar of Chinese history trained at Beijing University and Columbia, was inspired to publish the book by a conversation she had with two former Beijing classmates about the long-term personal influences of their student days in China in the mid- to late 1980s, when China was simultaneously recovering from the Cultural Revolution and reestablishing educational and other ties to the West.[2] All of the contributors to the collection are diasporic Chinese who recount their impressions of visiting China for the first or nearly the first time, and all describe experiences within the period from 1986 through the book's publication date, 2001. One of many studies of diasporic Chinese, Khu's collection provides thirteen stories with similar features. These can serve as an initial prototype for narratives of return, with emphasis on the cultural work involved. She also frames the essays within two paradigms for diasporic or overseas identity formation: the "symbolic universes" delineated by Tu Wei-ming (13) and the "flexible citizenship" model of anthropologist Aihwa Ong (1–2). Following Khu's lead, I begin my discussion of return narratives by reflecting on the cultural work undertaken by the essayists in order to make meaning of their given positions as overseas/diasporic Chinese, work that includes self-education, travel, reflection, and memory. These activities are inherent in the enterprise of entering Tu's third symbolic universe of "cultural China," namely the "symbolic universe" of individuals who "try to understand China intellectually and bring their conceptions of China to their own linguistic communities" (14). Additionally, I argue that these stories cast new light on Ong's model of the transpacific flexible citizen, as the migrations of the contributors' ancestors are marked by ingenious or desperate adaptations to the immigration restrictions that have historically constrained Chinese movements around the globe. Finally, I introduce the concept of racial melancholia in the global context of several of these stories, posing questions that are addressed in subsequent chapters. This chapter, then, provides a prototype for the narrative of return, which I subsequently complicate.

As discussed in my introduction, Chinese American life writing has never been limited to assimilationist immigration narratives patterned after Mary Antin's *The Promised Land* (in which the old world is presented as traditional, patriarchal, and oppressive to minorities while America is modern, egalitarian, and welcoming to immigrants). For political reasons, early Asian American literary histories focused on stories centered in the United States, but in the 1990s scholars began to reframe Asian American literature within studies of postcolonialism, nationalism, and globalization. In Chinese studies, Tu's collection *The Living Tree* opened questions of identity for the diasporic or overseas Chinese by positing the existence of "cultural Chineseness" created by a dialogue among three groups or "symbolic universes": the Chinese residing in nations with predominantly Chinese populations; diasporic Chinese, including the offspring of actual emigrants, who live as minorities in other countries; and intellectuals and businesspeople, Chinese or not, who try "to understand China and share their conceptions of it with others" (Tu 13). In Tu's schema, the first symbolic universe consists of Chinese in Singapore, Taiwan, Hong Kong, and the People's Republic of China (PRC), which he considers but one part of his larger, more global and inclusive concept of China. Those in the second symbolic universe live mostly in countries where they constitute 3 percent or less of the population (with a few exceptions, such as Malaysia [Tu 13]). A second approach, associated with Aihwa Ong and Donald Nonini, depicts diasporic Chinese as fashioning *flexible, transnational citizenship*, described by Khu as "increasingly independent of place, self-consciously postmodern," and "formed out of the strategies for the accumulation of economic, social, cultural, and educational capital as diasporic Chinese travel, settle down, invest in local spaces, and evade state disciplining in multiple sites throughout the Asia Pacific" (*Cultural Curiosity* 227–228). Ong's account of flexible citizenship focuses in part on well-to-do, educated Chinese extended families capable of juggling passports and family members across national borders to build transnational business empires. She also seeks, however, to remedy the erasure of women and gender concerns from many accounts of transnationalism and to point out the unmentioned subtext of exploitation that underlies triumphal celebrations of Chinese values (particularly Confucian Chinese family-work arrangements) as the linchpin of success in late capitalism.

Read as a whole, the collection suggests that for those of Chinese ancestry who have settled and assimilated abroad as minorities, these ideas of diaspora, imagined Chineseness, or belonging to an international Chinese community seem remote. Yet the writers are motivated to reclaim a diasporic Chinese orientation. Because of their persistent reception by others as "Chinese" based on their appearance, and their wish to understand their parents and their heritage more fully, these writers actively seek a deeper understanding of Chinese culture. Their essays attest to the many steps needed to move from Tu's second symbolic universe (minority diasporic Chinese) to the third (observers who write about China). Framed by Khu's editing, their stories present the basic components I claim for a narrative of return: a history of emigration from China, a diasporic location and relationship to Chinese culture and identity, the reasons for return, descriptions of preparations and of meetings with family members, and a narrative arc that, archetypally, traces an evolving sense of self, culture, and identity. I argue that many of these essays are driven by tensions between two forces traced by Khu: the drive to accumulate material capital and the drive to accumulate cultural capital, each of which is typically assigned to a specific generation. However, several essays also describe emotions of loss, distress, or alienation associated with the parents' migrations, emotions that are inherited and registered by these latter-generation narrators; these emotions I consider through the critical lenses of racial melancholia and diasporic Chinese histories.

Becoming Diasporic Chinese

The contributors to *Cultural Curiosity* are indeed dispersed, having settled or been raised in the United States, England, Sri Lanka, Denmark, Colombia, New Zealand, Australia, the Philippines, Indonesia, and Japan. However, prior to visiting China, their degree of identification with China varied greatly. Because Khu defined her search around the experience of visiting China for the first or almost the first time, locating her contributors by Internet and word of mouth, she found writers who were not only geographically dispersed but also removed in other ways from Chinese culture. Nancy Work, born in Taiwan and sent to live with her father in America, was cut off from her divorced Chinese parents early on: when her father died, she was adopted by a white family who forbade her to contact her mother in Taiwan. Maria Tham, Milan Lin-Rodrigo, Richard Chu, and Myra Sidharta report varying degrees of assimilation into local communities in Pakistan, Sri Lanka, the Philippines, and Indonesia. Graziella Hsu and Meilin Ching are raised by European and Colombian mothers, respectively, and by Chinese fathers. Graham Chan, raised in Liverpool by a second-generation Chinese British mother and an immigrant father who spends most of his time working, struggles to find Cantonese classes not designed for children of Cantonese-speaking families. His story begins with a reference to the "silent dummy" routine of Cantonese visitors to his British family, and then works up to his own assumption of the "silent dummy" role when surrounded by Cantonese speakers in Hong Kong (27–28, 36). It captures two themes that run throughout this collection: linguistic alienation and the great difficulty of acquiring Chinese as an adult.

As diasporic Chinese, many of the writers felt inexpert on Chinese culture prior to their journeys, either because they felt the culture belonged to their parents rather than themselves or because they felt their first affinity was to local cultures in their diasporic countries of birth or residence. Tham recalls, for instance, how the Chinese embassy staff in Karachi, Pakistan, attempted to provide Chinese cultural experiences for the locals, speaking in Mandarin—which few local Chinese spoke—and serving the food *after* the cultural programming to induce guests to sit through it (44). Richard Chu, a third-generation Filipino, describes how his mother called him a "stupid foreign barbarian" in Hokkien, their southern Chinese dialect, whenever he spoke Tagalog, the national language of his country, the Philippines (128). Because of his family's strong orientation toward business, he also felt guilty and un-Chinese for participating in Filipino cultural and political activities and for teaching religion in a Jesuit high school instead of becoming a merchant or entrepreneur (136–137).

Many of the writers depict themselves as culturally and discursively isolated in multiple ways. They are cut off from family members and communities in the PRC and the other "first symbolic universe" countries (Taiwan and Hong Kong, in these accounts) and reliant either on their nuclear family members or on very small local communities to establish their sense of Chinese culture and identity. The writers are partially acculturated into their non-Chinese host communities, but many suggest they do not feel accepted socially or integrated politically into their host countries, particularly if they belong to working-class families. A few, like Hsu and Henry Chan, are well established as professionals with European cultural expertise, but they seek to restore ties with their estranged parents by studying Chinese and visiting China. Hsu had split from her father over her choice of dancing as a profession, and Henry Chan from *his* father because he preferred to attend college and eventually to marry a non-Chinese colleague rather than enter the family business and accept a match arranged by his sisters in Hong Kong. Similarly, Chu undertakes his "Guilt Trip to China" (128) to compensate for his refusal to perform Chineseness in the terms his parents preferred: excelling in business. Even though many Chinese families would be pleased by Chu's career as a teacher, Chu's parents are disappointed, so he goes to China to prove that he has not forgotten his Chinese identity, to visit and study his ancestral homeland as a scholar, and to please his mother by learning what it means to be "a true Chinese" (137).

By their concerted efforts to learn Chinese languages, study Chinese culture, and study or work in China, both by living there and visiting, these writers gained the experiences that placed them into Tu's third symbolic universe, that of individuals willing and able to publish their insights on the nation in the public sphere. Yet the difficulties and dedication recorded by the diasporic narrators in moving into the realm of China commentators confirm Tu's and Khu's perceptions that many, perhaps most, diasporic Chinese have little voice in the formation of global discourses on Chinese culture. (To be precise, Khu's contributors are predominantly of Chinese descent rather than being Chinese citizens, but their narratives also describe their parents and other diasporic Chinese—working as merchants, restaurant workers, and housewives—who have little influence over globally shared conceptions of Chinese culture and ethnicity.) As Khu remarks, the nature of her search—conducted in English using the Internet—inevitably resulted in a disproportionate representation of diasporic Chinese privileged with computers, leisure, and funds for travel, as well as the distinctive accretion of cultural capital needed to publish essays (*Cultural Curiosity* 233–234). Tham's account suggests a common element of diasporic existence, the primacy of survival over cultural formation in daily life: "Life in Pakistan was already complicated and harsh enough, and no one had the time, energy, or the tools to differentiate between things [such as people's ethnic origins] too closely" (44). Given the barriers to entering the public realm as commentators, I ask what enabled Khu's contributors to go to China, and what drove them to do so.

Naturally, a trip to China demands material resources. Most of the writers had to work and save money to fund their trips. Their stories also emphasize, however, the process of accumulating *cultural* capital for the trip. Many authors describe how they separated from their parents' expectations or nuclear families' demands in order to claim individual agency and discursive space. Then they describe an ideological apprenticeship: like Maxine Hong Kingston's narrator, they learned to interpret their subjective, idiosyncratic experiences within the frameworks of larger social trends, in some cases after moving to the United States and comparing American discourses about race and identity with those in their home countries. In "Through a Window," Graham Chan, a Chinese Briton raised in Liverpool, describes his alienation both from his hardworking father, an immigrant restaurant worker whose first language was Cantonese, and from British culture, which reflexively constructs even native Chinese Britons like himself as "one of the lesser breeds" (26). He therefore feels that he belongs neither to England nor to Hong Kong (his father's homeland) and can only peer "through a window" at both cultures. While Graham Chan expresses envy of Chinese Americans, who describe themselves confidently as Americans (28), American writer Brad Wong notes the United States' internment of and lingering hostility toward Japanese Americans and the persistent assumptions of foreignness that he faces as a Chinese American (163). Tham, on the other hand, details her family's linguistic isolation from other Chinese Pakistanis, as one of the few newly arrived See-Yip-speaking families in Pakistan, yet claims that within her small village, Chinese Pakistanis were completely accepted as "locals" (44). Upon moving to the United States, however, she developed a new ethnic consciousness and active curiosity about her family origins under the influence of American discourses about race and roots (46–47).

Graham Chan, Lily Wu, and others describe arduous self-created Chinese language apprenticeships; Graziella Hsu and Henry Chan describe Chinese cultural apprenticeships as well. Hsu, for instance, made "Chinese funeral rites and ancestral cults the subject of her first university paper" in Denmark, in anticipation of her father's death, and later dropped her dance career to pursue Chinese studies (83–85). Lily Wu, sent to study in Beijing in 1985, was moved by her classmates' testimonies of hardship in and after the Cultural Revolution (208–211). Henry Chan, a historian of Europe raised and trained in New Zealand, determined to study Chinese after being asked to teach Chinese history, and he moved to London to take a postgraduate degree in that subject (116–117). Yet, as he discovered, a different apprenticeship was needed to bring him into touch with the cultural expectations of his family members in Hong Kong and Guangzhou. Finally, Graham Chan, "physically exhausted and mentally destroyed" (37) by cultural withdrawal after returning from Hong King to England, recovered when he met a creative writing teacher who encouraged him to write, introduced him to other Chinese Britons, and involved him in a succession of workshops and discussion groups. The capacity to write about his experiences and identity, combined with the discovery of a community that could relate to his story, brought him "back to life" (G. Chan 37–38). In short, passing from the second to the third symbolic universe demands not only funds but also the will and stamina to study Chinese language and culture, navigate family expectations, and grapple with discourses of race, ethnicity, and identity. In several cases, that cultural apprenticeship is stimulated by residence and study in the United States or Great Britain. Finally, the authors must create usable narratives to explain the complex experiences of traveling from their diasporic locations to Chinese cities, ranging from Beijing to Hong Kong, as well as ancestral villages. In addition, the writers' trips to China and contacts with Khu as the project's editor signal their entry into a process by which they locate themselves within a global Chinese community of English-speaking writers and readers, an imagined community linked by print and electronic media.

In terms of narration, these writers' journeys to Beijing, Shanghai, Meizhou, Taiwan, Guangzhou, Hong Kong, and their ancestral villages require them to fashion family chronicles reconciling separated branches of their family trees. Like bookkeepers bringing disparate financial records into agreement, these authors reconcile the narrated accounts of separated and estranged family members. Most of their narratives first reconstruct the outward journeys of Chinese emigrant parents or grandparents and describe the relationships among their own families, their host societies, and local Chinese communities as well as their own positioning within these groups; then, when describing their own trips to China, the authors contrast their experiences with those of relatives who remained in China or Hong Kong. At the heart of most of these narratives is a once-in-a-lifetime blind date, the meeting of the narrators with their unknown Chinese relatives. But these meetings can be troubling; to explain why, I invoke the scholarship of Aihwa Ong and her colleagues.

Reconciling Accounts

In *Flexible Citizenship: The Cultural Logics of Transnationality,* Ong contests and complicates scholarship of the 1970s and 1980s that celebrates Chinese entrepreneurship and explains Chinese success in essentializing terms by emphasizing Confucian family values, interpersonal *guanxi* networks, and Chinese work ethics. (*Guanxi* refers both to personal connections and to the networks of favors and obligations they involve.) In her depiction, modern transnational Chinese life is characterized by geographical displacement, family fragmentation, gender difference, and everyday impermanence: in a word, modernity. Describing successful families as placing members strategically in different countries in order to maximize their educational, cultural, locational, and financial capital, she notes the political causes and consequences, costs and benefits, of these families' lack of commitment to particular nations, as well as the personal costs to family members. According to Ong, Hong Kong social scientists use the term "utilitarian familialism" to describe the everyday norms and practices whereby family interests are prioritized over individual interests or wider social concerns:

> One scholar observes that economic interdependency is the basic structuring principle—expressed as "all in the family"—a principle that mobilizes the immediate family and relatives in common interests. An individual's sense of moral worth is based on endurance

and diligence in income-making activities, compliance with parental wishes, and the making of sacrifices and the deferral of gratification, especially on the part of women and children. (Ong 118)

Janet W. Salaff, in her study of Hong Kong factory women, argues that daughters are made to feel that they should repay their inborn debt to their parents by dropping out of school and earning wages, which are often devoted to putting their brothers through college (summarized in Ong 118). In other cases, children, especially sons, are expected to "collect symbolic capital in the form of educational certificates and well-paying jobs that help raise the family class position and prestige" (Ong 118–119). In the wealthiest families, sons are controlled, trained, and groomed to take over the business and assigned non-overlapping geographic territories, while daughters inherit small shares of the family wealth and then have nothing to do with the family estates (126). In many cases of what Ong calls "the Pacific Shuttle" (110), Hong Kong wives and children are placed in Canadian or U.S. locations to accrue educational and locational capital (degrees and real estate) while the "astronaut" fathers continue making money in Asia. Ong describes "parachute kids," teenagers dropped off in California suburbs by Hong Kong or Taiwan parents and deprived of both parents. One such child refers to her absent father as "the ATM machine" (127–128). Ong persuasively insists that what these practices exemplify is not essentialist Chinese values socializing families for success in Western capitalism but rather a new, modern adaptation to global capitalism and the tenuous political situations in states such as Hong Kong, Taiwan, Singapore, Malaysia, and Indonesia.

Within *Cultural Curiosity*, "Ears Attuned to Two Cultures" best depicts the personal costs of familial utilitarianism as retired history professor Henry Chan, who was raised in New Zealand, recounts his story. In a pattern of split migration typical of many Cantonese families (families from Guangdong Province), Henry Chan's great-grandfather was a pioneer who "helped clear the bush" in nineteenth-century Queensland (111). His Chinese-born son, Henry's grandfather, established a country store in Wellington, Australia. Though well established in the Wellington community, the grandfather fathered five sons in Guangdong, three of whom survived into adulthood. Each of these three migrated to Australia or New Zealand, but they purchased homes and started families in Guangzhou (the capital of Guangdong, also known as Canton) with financial help from Henry's grandfather. Henry's father, the eldest of the three sons, was sent as a boy to help the grandfather keep shop in Wellington, but he returned to China, married, and fathered two daughters in his teens. After this, Henry's father was sent, alone, to establish a new branch of the store in Auckland, New Zealand. He returned to China ten years later, at the grandfather's death, to see his family, at which point he fathered Henry. He then returned to his Auckland shop, still alone because New Zealand's laws forbade him to bring his family. In 1940, Chinese residents of New Zealand were temporarily permitted to sponsor relatives to immigrate as war refugees. Fearing the Japanese, the family sent two-year-old Henry and his mother to New Zealand but kept his teenage sisters in China to care for his grandmother. His mother died without seeing either daughter again, and the second daughter died without ever seeing him.

His reunion with his eldest sister, decades later, was fraught with the resentment she had accumulated in the wake of family decisions made in his infancy. Henry had to explain to her that their mother had earnestly tried to sponsor her emigration later but that by that time the sisters, having married, were no longer admissible as his father's dependents under New Zealand law. For his part, Henry had grown up with his father and mother, but he had resented his father's materialism, girlfriends, abuse of his mother, attempts to cut him off from normal friendships and from college, and demand that he accept an arranged marriage and responsibility for the family business. When Henry refused, his father disowned him. Meanwhile, Henry's uncle in Guangzhou ("Fourth Uncle") resented having been sent back to China to look after the family back in the 1930s while Henry's father and youngest uncle ("Fifth Uncle") were expected to work in New Zealand and Australia. It was left to Henry to explain, during his 1984 visit to Fourth Uncle, that both Henry's father and his Fifth Uncle had lived poorly and "died lonely deaths in their fifties and sixties," in contrast to Fourth Uncle, who had lived into his seventies and raised a large, successful family in China (121). In the Chan family's case, the combination of familial utilitarianism and a transpacific business orientation resulted in the separations of husbands from wives, and children from parents, as the family business was prioritized over education and personal preferences throughout the course of three generations. As Henry Chan's account makes clear, not only were his mother and sisters sacrificed; all three brothers in his father's generation also suffered, from both material hardship and incomprehension of their families' nonmaterial needs. However, these separations were not freely chosen in accord with an unchanging sense of Confucian utilitarianism by all, or even by a few: rather, the Chans' decisions over several generations were shaped by economic opportunities, war, and immigration restrictions in Australia and New Zealand.

Ong's insistence on using a global context, rather than essential Chinese values, to define the new flexible citizens echoes many Asian American critics who seek to de-essentialize the conduct of Asian American literary narrators and protagonists by historicizing them. Rather than presenting Chinese culture as fixed, Ong's approach resonates with authors and critics who write and read Asian American stories within the context of exclusion policies or the growing pains of Asian countries negotiating modernity. For instance, Stephen Sumida's classic reading of Milton Murayama's plantation novel *All I Asking for Is My Body* portrays plantation schools in Hawaii as promoting "Confucian" values of endurance and filial piety, primarily to motivate Japanese American laborers' American-born children to assume their parents' unpayable debts to the plantation. However, as Murayama's narrator comes to see, this requirement was not typically Confucian; rather, it was an exceptional demand that emerged in a plantation culture designed to perpetuate a docile, profitably exploited workforce (Sumida 112–137).

Given the popularity of the theme of generational conflict in Asian American family stories, one could conclude that a generational divide is also typical of *Cultural Curiosity*'s reunion narratives: the Chinese relatives and the emigrant generation are charged with the utilitarian demands of survival whose personal costs—political alienation, constant discipline and striving, physical separation and isolation, rivalry, and exploitation—must be set against the benefits of accruing capital. The Westernized, more materially secure descendants then seek to reclaim their roots in a drive to recapture the cultural and emotional capital they have lacked. When the two agendas meet, they may clash. Like other Asian American texts, *Cultural Curiosity* has its share of essays foregrounding this moment of arrival, this collision of agendas and of worlds. However, in the most dramatic instance, described in Lily Wu's personal essay "Coming Home," an Asian American daughter's racial melancholia converges with the struggles of ordinary Chinese to mourn the losses they have suffered in China, and I see the healing power of sharing these kindred griefs.

"Do You Think Your Mother Will Come to See Me?": Melancholia Abroad

In "Coming Home," a story of personal loss and mental illness is implicitly driven by the racial melancholia associated with immigration and mirrored by the multiple shocks of the author's year abroad in Beijing. As an exchange student at Beijing University in 1985–1986, Wu returned to China at a moment when her Chinese peers were struggling to grasp not only their identities as young adults but also their memories of the Cultural Revolution. (Born in Taiwan, Wu had immigrated to New York with her family at age three, in 1966, and grown up there.) Amid this sea of change, Wu's encounter with her mother's favorite sister brought home the similar struggles with mental illness of her mother in the United States and her aunt in China. Noting the sisters' parallel stories, the essay dramatizes how Wu, as a returning overseas

Chinese narrator, rhetorically remembered and resolved her personal grief and racial melancholia. Centering her essay on the shock of this encounter with her aunt, Wu tells a bittersweet story of reconciliation: she could not relieve her mother's or aunt's mental illness, but she gradually resolved her own racial melancholia by moving to China and drawing closer to her uncle, aunt, and cousins.

In considering how the theory of racial melancholia plays into an autobiographical essay such as Wu's, I emphasize that this is not a tool of psychiatric diagnosis but rather a way to think about the social, psychic, and emotional costs associated with immigration and displacement, how these costs may be communicated or inherited within a family, and how the acts of return and narration address these costs rhetorically. I argue that the cultural work done by a traveler such as Wu (to learn and understand Chinese culture as well as the histories of her family members), when combined with the writer's tasks of memory, interpretation, and narration, is an act of agency that seeks to address the demands raised, according to David L. Eng and Shinhee Han, by the losses associated with immigration. As discussed in Chapter 1, such losses must be mourned; however, because of structural discrimination, the minority immigrant typically cannot easily get over them by transferring his or her sense of belonging to the United States, and this strain results in racial melancholia (Eng and Han, "Dialogue"). Wu does not say that at the time of her first trip to China, either she or her parents were specifically melancholic in the psychiatric sense described by Sigmund Freud in his famous essay "Mourning and Melancholia." Rather than suggesting that she or her family were depressed or in mourning, she explains that her mother had begun "talking about incidents and events that seemed increasingly odd and unbelievable" and that her mother's gradual loss of lucidity "marked the onset of her increasingly debilitating mental illness, most likely a form of paranoid schizophrenia" (L. Wu 206). Crafting her essay to the specifications of Khu, a historian, Wu summarizes this medical diagnosis without initially suggesting that she or her family felt grief or loss.

However, when Wu interprets her mother's clinical illness as a response to "the perceived disappointment of her life" (206), she describes a long trajectory of loss and displacement that resonates with scholars' descriptions of racial melancholia as a structure of feeling resulting from the minority immigrant's tenuous social position of being unable to claim belonging in his or her new home (Eng and Han, "Dialogue" 352). First, her mother came from "a family of great wealth, tradition, and heritage" in China, one that was "in the final stages of losing everything by the time she was born" (L. Wu 206). Her grandmother moved to Taiwan in 1948 with her mother and two of her uncles, leaving the rest of their family behind in China. After a long struggle, the Taiwan branch of the family reestablished itself in Taiwan, but Wu's mother married an engineer and in 1966 immigrated with him to New York, where she knew no one but him. Wu describes her parents as mismatched in their class and gender expectations from the start: her mother came from an aristocratic Manchurian family of highly educated, assertive women while her father came from a more traditional Chinese peasant family, in which his sisters had grade-school educations, in the inland province of Anhui. In New York, Wu's father withdrew emotionally from the family, and her mother was principally responsible for raising Wu and her three siblings, which she did in an atmosphere of hostility and silence. Though Wu's mother got a job at the U.S. Customs House, it was "mind-numbingly" dull and discouraging. In response, she withdrew into fantasies of being important, but even in these fantasies she was unrecognized, hounded by the few who knew her true identity, and blocked by others' envy and persecution from "achieving her full potential." After Wu entered college, her mother left her father and filed for divorce in 1984. By 1985, when Wu left for China, her mother was so ill that she no longer admitted that she was Chinese or in any way associated with China (206–207).

Surely, there were many losses to mourn here, and after the move to New York City, Wu's parents seemed too busy working, raising children, fighting, and surviving either to mourn these losses or to provide emotional guidance. While Wu does not insist that her mother's problems were specifically due to her race, she implies that her mother was culturally isolated and unfortunately dependent on her husband for emotional and financial support, and that her fantasies functioned in part to help her transcend her minority status in America. Moreover, one aspect of racial melancholia that corresponds with Freud's construction is that the melancholic person does not know what he or she has lost. In Wu's story, the influence of the model-minority ethos—spurring the father's engineering job and Wu's graduation from the California Institute of Technology (Caltech)—suggests that the family had no language to discuss the pain of displacement from a culturally Chinese country full of similar refugees (Taiwan) to the more isolated position of a Chinese professional family in the East Coast in the 1960s, when Chinese Americans and Japanese Americans were being cast as self-reliant and politically undemanding by mainstream journalists. Already working and raising a family in the late 1970s and early 1980s, Wu's parents might have lacked language to situate their sorrows or grievances in a larger social frame, whether pertaining to their separation from family members in China and Taiwan, their minority status, their gender conflicts, or mental illness. Without such language, their losses became unspeakable, and their characteristic modes of coping were denial, "epic" indifference to surroundings (in Wu's father's case), and working harder (207). Wu herself, for instance, did not consider transferring out of Caltech when she realized, shortly upon arrival, that she did not have the "gift" for understanding science (201); instead, she switched to a less demanding major and stuck it out. Whether or not the family's failed model-minority paradigm and their unspoken griefs are classically melancholic in Freudian terms, it is reasonable to associate the family's dis-ease and disintegration with their double displacement and minority status.

Finally, Eng and Han discuss how immigrant loss and sacrifice can translate into second-generation guilt and depression, but they caution that depression or other intrapsychic experience can be fully understood only as a response to experiences of structural marginalization. Following Freud's account of the melancholic who internalizes the lost object—the person, thing, or ideal being mourned—they summarize how, in certain Asian American literary and biographical texts, Asian American offspring internalize or are haunted by their parents' voices and worldview:

> These daughters have absorbed and been saturated by their mothers' losses. The mothers' voices haunt the daughters. These losses and voices are melancholically displaced from the external world into the internal world of the psyche. The anger that these daughters feel toward the loved object is internalized as depression. (Eng and Han, "Dialogue" 355)

In her account, Wu does not mention personal depression but admits that she arrived in Beijing with unwept tears for her mother's slow withdrawal into mental illness and the dissolution of her family. In addition, she felt shame and secrecy when meeting her uncle, uncle's wife, and cousin because her mother's siblings had never been informed of her mental decline.

The social and cultural isolation depicted indirectly by Wu's short portrait of her parents' marriage in the 1960s–1980s resonates with portrayals of other Chinese and Japanese immigrant families whose parents were scholars or professionals in the midwestern or northeastern United States. (See, for instance, Work, "Full Circle" 1–18; M. Chai; L. Li, *Winged Seed*; Liu; Minatoya, *Talking*; and Jen, *Typical American*, a novel.) None of the fathers depicted in these stories fit Asian American studies' primary model for Asian American identity: farmers, manual laborers, or small business owners who live on the West Coast or in the Pacific Rim. Yet each seems to live in a world where he is constrained by race yet unable to harness the power of collective solidarity or resistance for members of his minority, because he is perceived as a successful, model-minority professional who does not suffer from discrimination and does not need structural remedies. I suggest that, for multiple reasons, with the Civil Rights movement not generally perceived in the American Midwest and Northeast as inclusive of East Asians, the immigrant Chinese and Japanese and their offspring in those regions have been averse to seeking psychological assistance, public financial assistance, or other social services, however much they needed them.

In contrast to her private losses, Wu entered an academic setting (elite Beijing University in the fall of 1985) where the students, by recounting their stories of the Cultural Revolution, were narratively mastering their individual experiences of suffering or isolation and reframing them as part of a shared national trauma. Those admitted to the university in the revolution's aftermath were among the lucky ones who could look forward to fresh opportunities under the new regime. In Wu's words, many were the "rehabilitated victims of political purges," who needed to tell their stories of injustice before they could move forward and who particularly needed to tell their stories to outsiders, who could recognize what they had suffered as "mad" and politically abnormal (210–211). In this sense, their collective mourning for their personal traumas was shared, in contrast to Wu's private sense of loss, which at first she could share with no one. For the Chinese students of that era, telling their stories was the first step in collectively mourning their shared losses and forming identities as leaders of a new era. That process of healing and empowerment, I suggest, culminated in the demonstrations of 1989, only to be brutally suspended by the government's actions in Tiananmen Square and its subsequent censorship of public references to the event.[3] In short, Wu recalls that in 1985, the atmosphere of Beijing University was charged with the raw energy of a generation recounting "the wasted years, the lost lives, and the incredible tragedies" they had survived, haunting stories that "numbered in the millions" but did not come home to her emotionally until she met her mother's favorite sister face to face (220, 211).

For Wu, being introduced to her aunt precipitated the mourning she had suspended for the loss of her mother. The meeting enabled her not only to grieve for her mother's mental illness but also to begin releasing the racial melancholia that she and her mother experienced. Wu's aunt, though born to a well-to-do family in China, had suffered a mental setback, in part as a consequence of facing unwanted romantic or sexual attention from male soldiers or officers during the Chinese Civil War (215), and had been institutionalized, on and off, for about thirty years. The suffering of Wu's aunt, a lifelong Chinese citizen from a privileged family, could hardly be considered a result of racial melancholia; yet meeting her induced Wu to weep uncontrollably, mourning not only the "wasted lives" of her aunt and her mother but also her own loss and her inability to soften these losses by reuniting the sisters. Wu was moved by her aunt's sad circumstances, her physical resemblance to Wu's mother, the realization that the sisters would never see each other again, and recognition of her own submerged grief (218–221). Wu writes:

> I did not know or realize it until much later, but I had, in fact, not come to China in search of my roots. I had come in search of my mother and a deep need to resurrect her being or to get closer to her in any way that I could. I needed to understand why she had left us for her own world. And in fact, I too, had whispered my aunt's prayer and wish to see her again millions of times before. And the answer was no, we none of us, would ever be able to see the woman who was my only sense of family and support as a child. Although her physical being is still here, her person had long ago retreated forever. (221)

Wu discounts her need for "roots" and emphasizes her mourning for her mother as a private, personal loss. However, in returning as an overseas Chinese to Beijing, she also left behind the minority status she bore in the United States; instead, she was recognized as a beloved niece by her Chinese relatives. In the denouement of her essay, she describes how her mother's brother and his wife embraced her as a surrogate daughter: she returned to China after her fellowship year ended and blossomed under their care and attention, which made up for the emotional disengagement of her father and mother.

Wu's story is firmly set in Beijing, and her uncle and his wife serve as not only surrogate parents but also living representatives of her Chinese heritage. For instance, the famous Summer Palace of Beijing had a special meaning for her mother's family. As an expert on its history, architecture, and landscaping, her uncle often depicted the palace and its grounds in watercolors and had worked on projects devoted to its restoration. As a Chinese of Manchurian descent, he took pride and interest in the Summer Palace as part of the cultural legacy of the (Manchurian) Qing Dynasty. Just a week after Wu's first visit to her aunt, her uncle took her to see the Summer Palace and its grounds. There, he revealed that her aunt attempted suicide in the lake on the palace grounds; as they commiserated over the difficult life that followed her aunt's rescue, Wu bonded with her uncle (221–222). That her mother's mental illness linked her more viscerally to her aunt, and through her to her uncle and his wife, meant that for Wu, coming to Beijing helped her see that she and her mother are part of a larger family whose story, in turn, belongs to a complex diasporic history with multiple Chinese roots (in Beijing, her father's home province of Anhui, and Taiwan). The sense of being alone and anomalous, felt in New York (where her parents were isolated Chinese immigrants) and at Caltech (where Wu felt intellectually underqualified and alone in her lack of parental support), was alleviated when she found personal and cultural connections to China. In Wu's case, finding and growing into an extended Chinese family, and knowing and experiencing Chinese history, culture, and geography as her own, ameliorated the melancholy of race experienced by her family in America. In her conclusion, she refers to meeting "countless young overseas Chinese like me" who have grown up in "relative cultural isolation somewhere in the world," and she hopes they find "even a part" of what she found that year in China and are able to "move on" (224). Wu's conclusion points to an ideal scenario for the narrative of return, one in which a Chinese American subject finds relief from the strain of racial melancholia by returning to China. Freud distinguishes mourning from melancholia by the analysand's ability, over time, to recover from depression and invest in a new object of hope and desire. Hence, the sign of the Asian American returnee's relief from racial melancholia might be the ability, in Wu's words, to move on after finding something like Wu's release from racial melancholia, and perhaps, in her case, from personal melancholia as well (224).

The contributors to *Cultural Curiosity* provide a cohesive starting point for modeling Asian American narratives of return and the rhetorical work they perform. To refashion themselves as diasporic Chinese writers of return narratives, the contributors had to articulate their family's histories of migration and their own sense of cultural identity as immigrants or native-born citizens of other nations; they also had to study and understand their ancestral culture, make time and find funds for travel, and meet the expectations and reconcile the divergent stories of estranged family members. Several of the essays, notably Henry Chan's, implicitly evoke Ong's models of flexible citizenship and "utilitarian familialism" (113), in which privileged Hong Kong businessmen not only travel and establish businesses around the Pacific Rim but also divide their family members—sending them to study, work, and live in different countries—with the goal of maximizing the family's cultural and financial capital. Chan's family best illustrates what seems to be a utilitarian strategy of dispersing the family in several locations, yet even they differ from Ong's examples in facing more severe, albeit shifting, constraints on their movements across national borders. It is typical to interpret such transpacific family frictions as generational cultural conflicts; however, most of these narratives also illustrate how families adapt Chinese values in response to shifting conditions associated with globalization, such as changing requirements for manual and professional labor that in turn cause would-be emigrants to scramble for the cultural and financial capital necessary to enter and stay in other countries. Finally, the story of Wu suggests that for diasporic Chinese and their offspring, the stresses of displacement and the experience of racial exclusion may result in racial melancholia, a structure of feeling associated with the lived experiences of racialized minorities. Such melancholia, rooted in the inability either to name and mourn the losses associated with immigration or to transfer one's desires to a vision of belonging to one's new country, may be passed from parents to children; it may also be alleviated by the reestablishment of affective bonds with overseas relatives or by the reclaiming of cultural roots. Return narratives themselves dramatize this process, as the act of narrating one's own and one's family's experiences provides a means for the writers to claim interpretive agency and to enter Tu Wei-ming's third symbolic universe: those who study and write about China.

3

Transpacific Echoes in the Family Memoir

Sojourns and Returns in Lisa See's On Gold Mountain

> Fong See, my great-grandfather, left China in 1871 as a youngster, found prosperity on the Gold Mountain (the Chinese name for the United States), and lived to reach his hundredth birthday. Rising out of a mass of nameless Asian immigrants, he became one of the richest and most prominent Chinese in the country. . . . My family always "knew" that Fong See had two wives. The marriage between Fong See and Letticie Pruett—my Caucasian great-grandmother—would go on to establish the See name. The second . . . family always lived under the name of Fong. Altogether, Fong See sired twelve children—five Eurasian, seven Chinese. . . . This is the story of the Sees and the Fongs and how they assimilated into America.
>
> As a girl, I spent frequent weekends and most of my summer vacations with my paternal grandparents in Chinatown. We would pass through a moon gate guarded by two huge stone lions and enter the dark, cool recesses of our family's Chinese antique store, the F. Suie One Company, a gigantic mercantile museum that contained . . . porcelains taken from the royal kiln[;] . . . altars pillaged from provincial temples; and huge architectural carvings shipped in sections to be reconstructed by Fong See's sons in one of his many warehouses.
>
> —LISA SEE, "Foreword," *On Gold Mountain*, xvii

Generic Innovation, Racial Performance, and the Transpacific Paradigm

OPENING WITH THE PARAGRAPHS ABOVE, Lisa See's family memoir *On Gold Mountain* appears at first to be the kind of book that will provide a typical Chinatown tour, replete with a Chinese patriarch and his multiple wives and children, a Horatio Alger immigration story, and a store full of exotic antiques. As Fong See's great-granddaughter, the author claims the status of a partial insider who will bring the reader along on her search for the real story about her successful, remote great-grandfather and the extended family he founded. However, by the end of the second paragraph, we see a hint of two less orientalizing dimensions of the text. See will claim both families and the landscape of Chinatown, affectively, as her own, and she will describe the nuts and bolts of the family business: the store's exotic goods did not appear by magic but through practical processes of searching, purchasing, transportation, reconstruction, and artful marketing. Additional dimensions of the book are signaled in the first chapter, as both the beginning and the end of the text proper follow the structure of the descendant return narrative I have traced in Josephine Khu's collection. The narrative begins with the movement of See's great-great-grandfather, the immigrant herbalist Fong Dun Shung, from a village on the Pearl River Delta to *Gam Saan*—Gold Mountain, the Chinese name for the United States, around 1866. The final chapter details the author's return to the same village in spring 1991, one year into her research process. There are banquets, reconciliations, and surprises. See's moment of return looks both forward, to the research the author will do to write the book and the relationships that will unfold, and backward, to the family events that preceded her journey, beginning with Fong Dun Shung's first migration to America. But unlike Khu's authors, who typically seek to understand one or two earlier generations, See tells stories from five generations who retain their connections to the home village, in Guangdong Province, while setting down roots in Los Angeles. Although the book is subtitled "The One-Hundred-Year Odyssey of My Chinese-American Family," it has multiple beginning and end points. Does the story begin in 1866, when the herbalist departs for Gold Mountain, or in 1871, when his son Fong See comes to America? Does it end in 1957, with Fong See's death? In 1989, with the birthday party when Lisa See's eighty-year-old great-aunt Sissee asks her to write the book? Or in 1991, when the author returns (symbolically) to the village? The cyclical quality of the chronology, in turn, echoes the repeated crossings by which Fong See's family renewed their ties to his home village and to Los Angeles over many decades. Thus, the theme of returns in this story encompasses several different kinds of events: See's symbolic return to see her ancestral village for the first time echoes the many trips taken by Fong See and his American family to the village and their trips back to Los Angeles. In these instances, the one-time connotation of "return" is admittedly misleading; "transpacific crossings" better conveys the transience of the trips to China and the double roots of the family. The strength of the book is that, at nearly four hundred pages, it takes the space to address the complexity of See's family history, which she interweaves with the story of the Chinese in California, including the Chinatowns of Los Angeles, and a Cantonese view of modern Chinese history. See's choices to combine historical research with techniques of fiction or countermemory and to present a transnational family narrative rather than a linear immigration story make for challenging reading; yet her book holds a unique place in Chinese American letters as the longest English-language family memoir and arguably the most ambitious. *On Gold Mountain* exemplifies many characteristics of a narrative of return:

1. the mixing of genres chosen when authors seek to use traditional historical methods and sources to tell the stories of subjects who are not the traditional subjects of either Chinese or American history (See's memoir draws on techniques and conventions from novels, ethnography, biography, and history)
2. a dense, nuanced expansion of historical knowledge through the author's artful use of a broad archive, placing family stories into a larger context
3. the use of a wide range of literary techniques to tell these stories
4. the theme of ethnic choice and performance as a series of strategies to deal with systemic, race-based exclusion and discrimination, and the exploration of this theme within a mixed-race family
5. the close identification of the patriarch and his family with his business activities, in keeping with Christine So's observations of Asian Americans as economic actors
6. the motif of repeated crossings and reentries, which illustrates both the lived impact of Chinese exclusion laws and the transpacific roots typical of many Chinese American families from the mid-nineteenth century onwards; this motif also contrasts with the immigration-centered model foregrounded by early Asian American literary criticism

Thus, though "narrative of return" may be an overly expansive and porous generic designation, See's book demonstrates that the trope of return, when used to discern and describe a particular thread within the tapestry of Asian North American cultural production, can both transform readers' fundamental paradigm for Asian American immigration (as a one-way journey culminating in assimilation) and demonstrate how Asian American writers fashion narratives that communicate this transformative paradigm.

Generic Crossings: Between Memoir and History

Published in 1995, *On Gold Mountain* was a national bestseller and a *New York Times* Notable Book. The memoir, which launched See's career as a creative writer, inspired exhibitions at the Autry Museum of Western Heritage and the Smithsonian Museum of American History, as well as an opera commissioned by the Los Angeles Opera. See subsequently published nine commercially successful novels, of which one has been made into a feature film (*Snowflower and the Secret Fan*). However, despite the popularity of See's carefully researched novels about Asian and Asian American women, the wide success of *On Gold Mountain*, and the significance of the book's publication in 1995, early in the rise of Asian American studies and multiculturalism, both book and author have been largely overlooked by Asian American cultural critics. I suggest that this is partly due to the book's deviation from the early narratives favored by Asian American literary studies, which focused on immigration and assimilation in the first and second generations and privileged the stories of laborers over those of merchants. The model of the transpacific family, especially one containing multiple wives and children in both America and China, has been slow to emerge in this literature. Finally, Asian American studies has been slow to develop a theoretical structure for interpreting the significance and stories of mixed-race couples and their descendants as so-called authentic Asian Americans. In the absence of early theory affirming mixed-race Asian Americans as central to Asian American concepts of identity or authorship, some scholars may have tacitly viewed Lisa See as another white author writing about Asian women for a popular audience, rather than closely considering how she claims authority to tell this story: by virtue of her descent and family affiliation, cultural awareness, and research. Yet See's text provides one of the most detailed and intimate accounts yet published of a transpacific, Chinese American, mixed-race family. As I have suggested, the book's hybrid form provides a further challenge in institutional contexts with extremely limited discursive space for Chinese American literary texts. The book has been recognized and cited as a historical resource but may have been outpaced in practical contexts, such as Asian American literature courses, by an abundance of more established Chinese American authors whose stories have, until now, been deemed more representative of Chinese American experience.

Structured by See's return to China in search of her roots, *On Gold Mountain* anticipates Khu's 2001 collection of personal essays, *Cultural Curiosity* (discussed in Chapter 2) and most strongly resembles Denise Chong's acclaimed memoir *The Concubine's Children* (published in Canada in 1994 and in the United States in 1995). The latter is set in British Columbia and Guangdong Province and begins approximately one generation after the emigration of See's ancestor, Fong See. Both See's and Chong's texts place the authors within family histories that in turn reflect on larger Chinese migration histories, both depict Chinese North American families as transpacific families and "flexible citizens" in the sense coined by Aihwa Ong (1), and both use the fictionlike techniques and conventions of the memoir to contest the historical authority of traditional biography (as explored by Eleanor Ty in her essay on Chong [*Politics*]). Whereas Chong's book documents a uniquely Chinese Canadian story, See's book is also unique in its setting (Los Angeles), its long chronological range, and its attention to the cultural decisions made by white and mixed-race family members living in the face of Chinese exclusion. As Chapter 4 shows, Chong's book illustrates how the model for successful return migration exemplified by the most successful men of Fong See's generation became part of a gender and family ideology that haunted Chong's grandparents, uneducated manual workers, as they faced exclusion and the Great Depression in Canada and raised children both in British Columbia and in Guangdong Province. Hence, I turn first to See's story, which begins two generations earlier than Chong's.

As a memoir of a Chinese family, See's book enters a tradition of Asian American *life writing* that includes more individualistic works by Pardee Lowe, Edith Eaton (Sui Sin Far), Winnifred Eaton, Helena Kuo, Jade Snow Wong, Maxine Hong Kingston, and others too numerous to list. According to Sidonie Smith and Julia Watson, both "autobiography" and "memoir" refer to self-referential writing, or "life writing." The term "autobiography," coined in the eighteenth century, is associated by some critics with the values of self-interest, self-consciousness, and self-knowledge linked to the Enlightenment. However, the genre is deemed to privilege the autonomous individual and the universalizing life story. Hence, it has been challenged as an exclusionary term in the context of postmodern and postcolonial critiques of the Enlightenment. Characterized as a "master narrative of the 'sovereign self,'" the genre of autobiography, some say, has been defined through the exclusion or marginalization of other types of narratives that have not been deemed "true" autobiography (Smith and Watson 5–6), including slave narratives, narratives of women's domestic lives, coming-of-age narratives, and travel narratives. In U.S. literature, the biographies of minority subjects have generally been defined as not broadly representative of American lives, though a handful of slave narratives and minority texts have arguably become canonical. By contrast, while the term "memoir" also traditionally refers to recollections by public figures chronicling their personal accomplishments, such works sometimes focus on one moment or period of experience and its significance (Smith and Watson 3–4). According to Julie Rak, however, "memoir" may also designate a less exalted form of life writing that focuses on "less acknowledged aspects of people's lives, sometimes considered scandalous or titillating, and often written by the socially marginal" (Rak ix, qtd. in Smith and Watson 4). More recently, the memoir has been described as a text marked by "density of language and self-reflexivity about the writing process, yoking the author's standing as a professional writer with the work's status as an aesthetic object," as well as one that may "capture a dynamic postmodernism in its movement between the 'private and the public, subject and object,' as Nancy K. Miller has observed" (qtd. in Smith and Watson 3–4).

How do these definitions relate to Asian American narratives of return, or to Chinese American family memoirs? For one thing, Asian Americans do not typically write as "exemplary *individuals*" but rather tend to define themselves by describing their place within their families; in many memoirs, including those of See and Chong, the author is a minor figure, at most a narrator or director, whose ancestors take center stage. Moreover, Asian Americans have rarely been considered exemplary in a general sense: they are usually deemed outsiders, rather than typical Americans or Canadians, by publishers, reviewers, and non–Asian American readers. Asian American life writing has most often gained acceptance as exemplary only of minority, immigrant, or third-world experience. Because Asian American perspectives on public events may differ from those of non–Asian American readers, the task of telling personal stories is often overshadowed by the task of introducing these readers to these perspectives, often through discussions of ethnic history, culture, or language. In this context, the choice of the memoir genre (rather than history or biography) can release an Asian American writer—partially—from the encyclopedic burden of rewriting American history by changing the focus to a personal perspective rather than a grand national narrative. Both See and Chong have undertaken to include substantial summaries of Chinese North American public history, notably pertaining to Chinese exclusion from immigration, citizenship, marriage eligibility, and educational and employment opportunities in the United States and Canada; they also present local histories of the Chinatowns of Vancouver, Nanaimo (in British Columbia), and Los Angeles as well as of the Chinese home villages of the Chong and Fong See families. However, since the authors' primary focus is on the stories of their ancestors, the family memoir genre provides a collective subject (the family rather than the individual) that is more manageable and accessible than larger subjects (such as the Chinese Canadian, Chinese American, or Chinatown communities), since they are free to select only the historical information necessary to support their personal narratives. Both See and Chong make abundantly clear the social marginality of their families as a result of their status as Chinese, the See family's mixed race, and the Chong family's poverty, and both authors relate intimate family details that might be deemed scandalous or titillating, such as Fong See's multiple marriages and the fact that Denise Chong's grandmother was her grandfather's concubine. Finally, as I discuss below, both authors demonstrate great self-awareness about the composition of their work and the ways they transgress the norms of biography, history, and other genres.

In choosing the term "family memoir," I draw on Rocío G. Davis's analysis in *Relative Histories: Mediating History in Asian American Family Memoirs*. Davis suggests that the popularity of the genre among "ethnic" American writers is due to the appeal of the "relational model" of life writing, in which the text emphasizes the decisive impact on the autobiographer of "an entire social environment," such as an ethnic community, or of a particular family or set of family members (2–3). (In her introduction, Davis doesn't define "ethnic," but her list of examples includes Americans of African, Jewish, Italian, and Mexican descent [1].) In the case of Asian American writers, she asserts, many Asian Americans "focus explicitly on individual processes of understanding identity," and in these cases, "the narrative centers on an introspective psychological journey—often accompanied by a physical journey to the forebears' homeland" (2). Davis describes four kinds of family memoir. The first, which I call the "family-centered memoir," is the prime focus of her study: it consists of a text that tells the story of at least three generations of one family; emphasizes generational *progression* (among protagonists in the various generations) across the passage of time; highlights intersections between personal and private narratives; supplements relatives' stories with public information; situates family members in their social, cultural, political, and economic contexts; and grants the author's relatives as much space as the author's own story, if not more (3). The second, which I call the "author-centered family memoir," "privileges a poetics of generational *simultaneity*," in which the author as central character "learns about or acknowledges the value of family relationships, incorporating the forebears' influence, lessons, or legacy into her own life" (4). The third, the "narrative of filiation," addresses issues of connection, inheritance, and loss rooted specifically in the author's relations with a parent or parents and includes classics such as Maxine Hong Kingston's *The Woman Warrior* and Sara Suleri's *Meatless Days* (Couser, "Genre " 123, qtd. in Davis, *Relative Histories* 4). And the fourth, the "fraternal narrative," focuses on the author's relations with siblings (Davis, *Relative Histories* 4). Though useful, these categories remain somewhat fluid, as some texts could fit more than one category. However, because of their multigenerational focus, broad historical lenses, and deemphasis of the authors themselves as protagonists, the memoirs of Lisa See and Denise Chong can be classified in the first category—family-centered memoirs—in contrast to more parent- or author-centered memoirs such as *The Woman Warrior* or Winberg and May-lee Chai's *The Girl from Purple Mountain*, which is discussed in Chapter 5.

Finally, before continuing, it may be useful to briefly recap the history of Asian American autobiographical criticism. When Asian American literary studies began, one of the three earliest anthologies (Chin et al., *Aiiieeeee!*) appeared with editorial material criticizing Asian American autobiography as a form not indigenous to Asia (as if this should be a requirement for Asian American Anglophone writing) as well as complicit with the Christian genre of confession and thus inherently tied with conversion to Christianity, the seeking of approval from whites, and the reinforcement of orientalist stereotypes. The editors of the *Aiiieeeee!* anthology were indignant that, according to their research, white publishers, critics, and readers had accorded success and visibility only to Chinese American writers of autobiography (and memoirs) and not to openly imaginative forms such as fiction, poetry, and drama. With time and the evolution of the scholarship, it has become clear that these editors, eager to publish their groundbreaking anthology establishing Asian Americans both as American and as creative artists, invalidated a tradition of insightful work by bilingual Chinese American immigrants whose insights did not suit their agenda. Later, they denied the existence of autobiography as a literary tradition in Chinese and Japanese, ignoring the highly personal and popular I-novel in Japan (Chin, "Come" 11–12). They overlooked at least one highly visible, successful immigrant novelist (C. Y. Lee) and one radical modernist who delved into poetry, plays, and novels (H. T. Tsiang). They discounted numerous others who could provide important bridges with Chinese literature (such as Lin Yutang and Nieh Hualing) because of their editorial biases against educated Chinese immigrants and those who wrote in Chinese. They failed to note complex anticolonial views published by some early writers whom they ignored or dismissed as apologists for white supremacy, such as Yung Wing and Yan Phou Lee. Though Kingston was an avowed Buddhist, they called her a Christian convert. In claiming that all Christian converts despised Chinese culture and advocated white supremacy, they ignored a complex, well-documented history of modernizing Chinese nationalism, and they denied the significant participation of Chinese immigrants in the early Asian American movement, as Chih-ming Wang has shown (Spence, *Search*; C. Wang, *Transpacific* 110–133). In short, their early, strategic choices to exclude writers of non-English texts and reject the intellectual links between immigrant Asian intellectuals and Asian American authors enabled them to create discursive space for the English-language tradition they sought to define as Asian American. Thus they left it to subsequent scholars to investigate the authors and literatures they omitted, in Chinese American and other ethnic traditions.

Later, in his 1985 critique of *The Woman Warrior*, "This Is Not an Autobiography," Frank Chin ignored a growing body of criticism that not only acknowledged the inherent subjectivity of all life writing but also emphasized its selectivity, subjectivity, and craft and distinguished autobiography from memoir. Among the numerous essays contesting the definitions posed by the *Aiiieeeee!* editors, Sau-ling Cynthia Wong's "Autobiography as Guided Chinatown Tour?" lays out the inherent problems of placing special burdens on minority writers to represent their culture and community according to prescribed notions of authenticity. To paraphrase her argument very loosely: she agrees that Asian American writers should portray their communities responsibly, but she argues that when critics attack the same texts for being negative, untruthful, or inauthentic, they set up a constricting double bind in cases where the truth is not wholly positive or happens to resonate with existing stereotypes or misconceptions. To demand that Asian American writers avoid or directly attack stereotypes and remain silent about problems in their own communities would result over time in a pallid image of the community as a model minority. These problems were, of course, exacerbated by the public's preference for Asian American autobiography over overtly imaginative works, which had led to *The Woman Warrior*, Kingston's controversial debut text, being read as autobiography—supposedly a form devoted to a realist presentation of externally verifiable facts—despite its overt postmodernist attention to listening, translating, and storytelling as inherently fictive processes and its designation as a *memoir*, a genre defined by its reflexivity about the fluidity and subjectivity of memory and the elusiveness of the past. Kingston herself published an essay pointing out characteristic misreadings of her first book and suggesting that some critics were wrong to hold her solely responsible for readers' errors and misconceptions ("Cultural Mis-readings"). Despite decades of nuanced criticism and thematically diverse Asian American publications, a 2007 study by critic Jeffrey Partridge still found Asian American writers being assigned to "literary Chinatown" (or the equivalent for their particular ethnic group). He argues that Chinese American literary texts have been judged according to their congruence with formulaic, multicultural norms—basically, the same expectations discussed by the *Aiiieeeee!* editors and Sau-ling Cynthia Wong—for representations of Chinese Americans and that authors have been systematically discouraged from pursuing other subjects and genres. Yet within Asian American studies, as Viet Thanh Nguyen has pointed out, Asian American cultural texts have been judged by their resistance to such stereotypes (*Race* 3–13). Nguyen's argument, that one should instead read Asian American writers as flexible entrepreneurs seeking to publish their ideas in the best form permitted in the context of their particular moment, introduces readings that are more fully historicized as well as more attentive to textual form, irony, and rhetorical nuances. In this chapter, I show that Lisa See departs from the traditional views of autobiography—either as a confession by an Asian American convert seeking white approval or as an objectively verifiable narrative of the life of a great man or woman—by remaking the family memoir in ways that resonate with other Chinese American memoirs but are also unique because of her mixed-race background.

While not all Asian American authors have followed these Asian American or generic critical debates of the 1970s, 1980s, and 1990s closely, or even been aware of them, my analysis presumes that the texts examined here also navigate between the Scylla of orientalist sensationalism and the Charybdis of model-minority boosterism: the very experiences of writing or editing autobiographical essays, or writing family memoirs, force these writers to confront issues of memory; subjectivity; the limits and presumptions of linear, realistic narrative; and the limits of official verification. They must also satisfy the sometimes contradictory requirements of mainstream publishers and readers, on one hand, and critics from their ethnic communities on the other. For writers in the 1990s and 2000s, these conflicting demands may take the form of critics and readers questioning the writers' truthfulness, cultural authority, and research or their taste, judgment, and commitment to the welfare of their communities. While these standards are always present, some critics have argued that minority writers, women writers, and writers of color are not accorded the same presumption of competence, objectivity, and representativeness as their white male peers in the publishing world and that the lack of presumed authority may be seen in the presentation of women's and minority writers' texts. Denise Chong, for instance, has related how fellow authors discounted her painstaking research for *The Concubine's Children* by saying that she lucked out by having a distinctive family story; she has further related how an old family friend found the manuscript so scandalous that she brought suit to try to suppress its publication altogether (Chong, Keynote). In the case of *On Gold Mountain*, the terms of approbation chosen for the first blurb on the back jacket illustrate the publisher's wish to fulfill divergent criteria for excellence: "Astonishing . . . as engagingly readable as any novel . . . comprehensive and exhaustively researched." This brief, anonymous quotation from the *Los Angeles Times Book Review* assures readers that the story, being wondrous, readable, and well-researched, will combine the virtues of fantasy, fiction, and history.

To underscore precisely how See both uses and departs from the norms of history writing, let us turn to a similar book written explicitly as a history. In its detailed descriptions of the family businesses, See's memoir provides a strong precedent for historian Haiming Liu's fascinating 2005 study *The Transnational History of a Chinese Family: Immigrant Letters, Family Business, and Reverse Migration*. Both Liu's and See's subjects were classified as merchant families for immigration purposes, but the two books describe very different families and thereby document the heterogeneity of those classified in this way. The Chang family of Liu's book benefited greatly from the lucrative economic niche of Chinese herbalists in the United States, who drew on an ancient and efficacious Chinese medical tradition to serve both Chinese and white clients. Not licensed to practice as doctors in the United States, Chinese herbalists carefully cultivated their immigration status as merchants who merely sold Chinese herbs, but they quietly dispensed profound medical expertise along with these remedies. Supported by their profitable herbalist practice, the Changs aspired to educate their children in the best available schools and universities of both China and the United States, so that they could find professional work in either country, and even prepared one son to be a Chinese diplomat. By contrast, Fong See, Lisa See's great-grandfather, lacked the education to carry on his father's trade as an herbalist and began his career as a vendor of underwear, which he manufactured covertly to preserve his "merchant" immigration status. All Fong See's children grew up at a time when college education was unusual for the children of Chinatown merchants, and Ticie (Fong See's Caucasian American wife) refused to allow her half-white, American-born children to settle in China; instead, they were raised to be skillful antique dealers and entrepreneurs in Los Angeles' Chinatown.

Liu, as a historian, relies primarily on a traditional paper trail. The core of his research is the bilingual Sam Chang family papers held by the Chinese Historical Society of Los Angeles, supplemented by personal interviews with members of the Chang family, immigration records, and scores of published historical sources. Based on his doctoral dissertation, his book displays a deep knowledge of Asian American studies as well as Chinese and Chinese American history, and it includes family photos, a genealogical chart, endnotes, an index, and a pinyin-character glossary, primarily designed to allow readers to identify the Chinese characters for names and phrases written in pinyin in the text. Like Liu, See draws on published historical studies as well as detailed immigration records that she located. She also uses disparate primary sources, including English and Chinese news publications, marriage and census records, local property and business records, oral histories, and archives in libraries, museums, historical centers, and universities in Oregon and California. However, the heart of her story comes from her many interviews with store customers, relatives, and family friends, supplemented by reminiscences sent by letter and several dozen photographs drawn from immigration records and family collections. Finally, she acknowledges the guidance of her parents, the anthropologist Richard See and the journalist and creative writer Carolyn See. In short, See's research is comparable to Liu's, but her material and narrative approach are shaped by her personal membership in the family she describes, and she writes for a general audience rather than specifically for historians. Her maps further emphasize the personal focus of her book: the map of Kwangtung (Guangdong) Province simply locates the ancestral village Dimtao and neighboring Fatsan (Foshan) in relation to Canton (Guangzhou), Macao, and Hong Kong. A second map marks the various locations of the family stores in Los Angeles, Pasadena, Ocean Park, and Long Beach; a third marks the locations of Los Angeles' Chinatowns and Chinese neighborhoods; and a fourth depicts the close proximity of her great-grandfather's store and the compound of his second family (the Fongs) to her great-grandmother's rival store, above which Ticie lived with her children (the Sees) from 1924 to 1943 (xi–xiii, 143). In lieu of endnotes and a scholarly list of works cited, the author lists her sources by chapter, so that readers can loosely trace the sources for details in each unit; these choices both document her historical research and suggest her wish to reach a general audience.

Both Liu's history and See's memoir go beyond a single family, detail the dire constraints placed on Chinese in California, and describe the perspectives of various family members. But whereas Liu, the historian, stays close to his sources, See, the creative writer, combines research with imagination. Liu cites not only English but also Chinese written and oral sources, emphasizes the historical significance of each event and item discussed, and relies heavily, though not exclusively, on a rich archive of over three thousand letters and other Chang family documents as well as immigration records. Persuasively, he explains that Chinese-language family letters and papers are superior to other sources because of their immediacy (compared to memoirs written down long after events have unfolded), candor (owing to the presumption of privacy), and durability (in contrast to the mutability of memory) and also because they enable scholars "to express and explain the sensibility and perceptions of the Chinese and write history from their perspective" (10–11). Finally, Liu does not belong to the family whose records he examines; he adopts a historian's narrative voice (objective and limited to what can be documented) and organizes his book by chapters examining various aspects of the Chang family's decisions and survival strategies. Presenting his subjects as a typical, if prosperous, transnational family with circular migration patterns, he includes chapters on "Herbal Medicine as a Transplanted Culture," "Asparagus Farming as a Family Business," "Education as a Family Agenda," and "China as a Cultural Home" (vii).

By contrast, See's book draws more heavily on her interviews, arguably incorporates a broader archive of primary sources, emphasizes women's perspectives, uses more novelistic narrative techniques, and more greatly emphasizes the principals' choices and performances of Chineseness in the context of Chinese exclusion. Her chapters are arranged chronologically, with each chapter title identifying a span of years, but her omniscient third-person narrator moves in and out of the minds of her characters and jumps backwards and forwards in time, emphasizing the importance of multiple perspectives and undermining the convention of linear narration. Finally, See narrates two chapters in the first person, fictively assuming the voices of two family friends (artist Tyrus Wong and actress Anna May Wong). Her chapter titles include "The Wonder Time," "Love," "Family Days," "Playboys," "The Kidnapping," and "The Mission Family Gets a Daughter-in-Law." While the chapters' date ranges might suggest a periodized history, their titles emphasize the novelistic focus on family and love stories, and elements such as "wonder" and suspense, as readers are invited to guess who gets kidnapped and who marries whom. My point is not that either book is better but rather that See has done as much research as Liu and has also chosen to combine elements of history with novelistic literary conventions, imaginative interpolations beyond the documented facts, and an orientation toward general readers. Yet, with the exception of Davis (*Relative Histories*), critics have tended to recognize the book's historical research while largely ignoring its literary form: its blending of historical and novelistic conventions to claim the imaginative freedom now associated with memoir, particularly family history memoir.

As discussed above, writers from minority ethnic communities are particularly liable to be read as race representatives and held to arbitrary standards of authenticity. I suggest that additional scrutiny is applied to white or mixed-race authors writing about racial minorities. Like many first books, See's comes with multiple assurances of her qualifications as an author; she also includes several authentications of her Chinese heritage. There are various blurbs; a brief professional history and a personal photo; a dedication to the author's sons, identified as "the great-great grandsons of Letticie and Fong See"; and a quotation from Wallace Stegner, the prestigious writer of the American West whose work crosses genres including history, fiction, and memoir: "Fooling around in the papers of my grandparents . . . I get glimpses of lives close to mine, related to mine in ways I recognize but don't completely comprehend. I'd like to live in their clothes a while" (qtd. in See n.p.). This epigraph from *Angle of Repose*, expressing Stegner's desire to understand his grandparents through acts of imagination, cues the reader to read this book, too, as a memoir using imagination to animate the facts and stories accrued through research. Perhaps See's favorite fictional technique is the retrospective monologue, in which she enters a character's consciousness and reviews personal and historical events from that person's perspective. Through these monologues, See converts pages of research and historical exposition into novelistic narration that sharpens her characters and their stories.

Like many family memoirs, See's text has the structure of a multigenerational novel. A family tree appears in the front matter, and the jacket shows a beautiful black and white photograph of Fong See and Ticie seated amid their children: Ming, Ray, Eddy, Bennie, and Sissee. Many minority autobiographers have published books with forewords or introductions by established authorities who vouch for the authors' authenticity. By contrast, See introduces herself in her foreword. After opening with an abstract of her great-grandfather Fong See's career, See immediately reframes the book by relating her own experiences as a girl spending weekend and summer vacations with her grandparents in Chinatown; she also introduces the family store, F. Suie One Company, which is the central business enterprise of the book. She establishes her grandmother Stella's ethnicity by quoting her statement that "*lo fan* (white people) made all of us Chinese wear buttons so that they would know we weren't Japanese" during World War II and mentioning her five-thousand-year-old way of cooking rice by measuring the water level with the hand (xvii). See recounts how her great-aunt Sissee, the last surviving child of Fong See and Ticie, asked her to write a book about the family in 1989, just two months before Sissee's sudden death at age eighty; the family supported See's efforts out of respect for Sissee, lending her project the support of her great-aunt's wish. (This trope presenting the author as family griot is by no means unique to Chinese American women's writing; the figure of the woman writer urged by others to overcome her modesty and publish a book can be traced through Harriet Jacobs back to the Puritan writer Mary Rowlandson. However, the claim of writing to fulfill a relative's wish to be remembered specifically echoes Amy Tan and tacitly places See into the post–*Joy Luck* club of Chinese American women writing about family stories.) After describing her research and the difficulties of working without knowledge of Mandarin or Cantonese, the author reveals that like Stella, who identified as Chinese despite her red hair, she also thinks of herself as a Chinese member of the Fong See clan. "My grandmother—like my great-grandmother—was Caucasian, but she was Chinese in her heart," she explains. "Though I don't physically look Chinese, like my grandmother, I am Chinese in my heart" (xx). Thus the trope of claiming ethnicity through the performance of everyday acts construed as "Chinese" is introduced.

In what may be another oblique reference to *The Joy Luck Club*, See plays the memoir writer's card in order to preempt the harsh criticism facing books that supposedly convey the Chinese experience: "All I can hope to do is tell *our* story. *On Gold Mountain* doesn't purport to be the whole truth—just *a* truth, one that has been filtered through my heart, my experience, and my research" (xxi). By claiming to describe only her family's story, See sidesteps the responsibility to speak definitively for Chinese Americans and her history, even as she repeatedly purports to do just that—at the many points when she pauses to draw on Chinese American history, or at the end when she makes a case for the increasing importance of Chinese Americans in the present. My point is not to single her out for inconsistency but to suggest that her rhetorical gesture is typical of minority writers who labor under the double burden of articulating *their* experience and making it accessible to readers with other frames of reference while simultaneously negotiating the hazards of minority autobiography sketched above. It also echoes the voices of earlier women writers such as Rowlandson and Jacobs, who, as a Puritan and a former slave, respectively, insist on the individuality of their stories while also purporting to speak for larger groups.

See then problematizes the traditional form of autobiography, which begins with a single protagonist's genealogy and birth. The first chapter's title—"The Wonder Time, 1866–71"—not only provides the requisite mystification of Fong See's legendary origin but also frames the author's interpretation of the multiple versions she has found of the story of Fong See's birth, origins, and immigration. Lacking eyewitness accounts of her great-great-grandfather Fong Dun Shung's life as an herbalist in China and the United States, See relies on historical sources to set forth the conditions of agricultural life in Guangdong Province in the nineteenth century, including the terrible effects of the Opium Wars and the Taiping Rebellion, and also to describe the travel and living conditions for Chinese men and women in California in the years between the Gold Rush and the arrival of her great-grandfather, Fong See, to the state. As a prelude to Fong See's arrival, then, she spins a carefully researched tale about Fong Dun Shung's marriage, emigration, and herbal practice with Chinese railroad workers and prostitutes for patients. Then she admits that the basic facts of Fong See's life are in question: not only his name but also the dates of his birth, first marriage (to a woman in China), and arrival in California are disputable, changing over the years in the stories he himself told to customers, family members, immigration officials, and journalists. (Born as son number four ["See"] of the Fong family, he used the inaccurate surname "See" during his first fifty years in the United States and for his first family and then changed it to "Fong" for his later years and his second family.) Thus from the start the author places Fong See both within and outside official history, loosely framing her book around his (disputed) birth in 1857 and his (well documented) funeral in 1957.

In the long book that follows, See uses the techniques of the novelist to shape several different kinds of stories, each of which seems to resist finding a proper form and outcome. In her story of Ticie's rise as a Chinese matriarch, See insistently demonstrates how Ticie's personal characteristics, including her whiteness, contributed to her initial success as the wife of a merchant, her marriage's end, and her resilience and success in raising her children. In recounting the rise of Fong See, the author provides a detailed ethnographic account of the family businesses and how they eventually came to alienate him from his first family. As foils to the stories of such central figures, additional monologues by the artist Tyrus Wong, Anna May Wong, and Chinatown matriarch Mrs. Leong provide mini-biographies of other Chinese Americans, their careers, and their families (186–192, 225–230, 257–264). Finally, See shows how the family's "return" trips to China, interspersed in these stories, are actually circular, transpacific migrations.

Ticie as Heroine: Setting Scenes through the Retrospective Monologue

Central to the book are three love stories: that of Fong See and his second wife, Letticie Pruett (Ticie); that of Eddy and Stella Copeland See, the author's grandparents; and that of the author's great-aunt Sissee (Florence) See Leong and great-uncle Gilbert Leong. By considering the first of these, readers can see how the author uses the tropes and techniques of historical fiction to engage readers and render Fong See and Ticie memorable. After using Fong Dun Shung and Fong See as nodal points to describe the herbal trade, the railroad strikes, Chinese American prostitution, and Chinese wedding ceremonies in chapter 1, the author introduces Ticie's pioneer heritage in chapter 2, "Exclusion, 1972–93." Citing just one record specific to Ticie's family (John Pruett's registration on October 12, 1872, for the ownership of land in the Rogue River Valley in Oregon) the author sets the scene for Ticie's eventual flight from home by placing Pruett's land claim in the context of the settlement of Oregon by whites from the eastern United States (28). Their movement west is followed by an account of Fong Dun Shung's (westward) return to China and the labors of Chinese of Fong See's generation in Sacramento and elsewhere in California on land, at sea, and in factories; this juxtaposition associates Fong See's generation of Chinese immigrants with white pioneers such as Ticie's parents, John and Luscinda Pruett of Pennsylvania. Pruett's land claim is echoed by the paragraphs in which Fong See registered his first business in Sacramento on June 24, 1874—despite the fact that he had no partners or type of business to declare yet—and had his photo taken in smart clothes (33). From these records, and the family tradition that depicts Fong See as sending money home regularly, the author creates a portrait of him as an ambitious, self-made young man (hypothetically age seventeen in 1874) who saved money, dressed well, and planned ahead:

> In just these few short years [since arriving in 1871, Fong See] had already transformed himself from a brave little peasant boy, who worked for his mother on the streets of Canton, into a young man who eschewed the dress of the poor whites for the elegance of the wealthy ones he had seen on the riverboat. He was training himself not to be a peasant—not just through his clothes and job, but in his mind. He was always thinking, observing, trying to create for himself a context so that he could become a part of the larger world. (35)

Such an interpretive leap—from a few documents into the young man's undocumented frame of mind—can be found in popular historical or biographical writing, but it is fundamentally a fiction writer's tool.

Similarly, the world of John and Luscinda Pruett is evoked from Luscinda's point of view (in close third-person narration) as she lies on her deathbed in April 1877, although the author cites no papers to prove that the biographical Luscinda ever had these thoughts. This kind of retrospective monologue, in which the author imaginatively enters the mind of a historical character to review public and private events, is a hallmark of See's book that lends a novelistic air to the narration, despite the sparsity of dialogue (compared to most novels). This section has Luscinda mentally review the crops, weather, men's and women's labor, family accounts, and her own illness, embellished by references to unusual local events such as the death of a neighbor's son in a vat of boiling soap and the capture of a counterfeiter. These fictionalized details, which Luscinda overhears people discussing, appear to be based on entries in the actual diary of Martin Peterson, the family minister, which the author cites in her source list (384). There can be no source but imagination, however, for the paragraph relating Luscinda's dying thoughts and introducing Ticie, the book's one-year-old heroine:

What about my baby girl? Who will show her how to be a good woman? Who will love her like a mother? Who will teach her about duty, hard work, and religion? Who will make sure she finds a proper husband? If only I could keep Letticie with me. (37)

The omniscient narrator then shifts away from Luscinda's perspective to relate the funeral arrangements, record Luscinda's "future" tomb inscription, and quote Rev. Martin Peterson's diary entry for the funeral day (37–38).

Later, evoking Fong See's start in business, See blends statistics about Chinese women's immigration and employment (primarily as prostitutes in the mid-1860s) with descriptions of Fong See's merchandise and a quoted sales pitch explaining how the firm's products will be particularly useful for his primary customers, prostitutes. Here, See evokes a potentially sensational topic—Chinese women as sexual commodities—but demystifies it by emphasizing the business element, from Fong See's point of view; she also aligns historians' evocations of the sex workers' miserable living conditions and the profits owners made from the trade with the English that Fong See reputedly learned to ply *his* trade as a salesman. Similarly, the tough English phrases See imagines her ancestor memorizing, including "He took it from me by violence" and "He cheated me out of my wages" (40), are direct, unattributed quotations from *An English-Chinese Phrasebook*, issued by Wells Fargo in 1875 (Sam Wong and Assistants, qtd. in Chan et al., 96, 97), which may or may not have been available in Sacramento at the time. (Presumably the book did not include such intimate expressions as "I love you," "I miss you," "I have another wife," or "Let's talk.")

"If You Kill Wong, Who in the Hell Will Do My Laundry?": Personalizing Historical Exposition

Before readers can fully grasp the uniqueness of Fong See's and Ticie's interracial marriage, the author must explain the forces they were defying—recreating a whole history in which two antithetical races came together in the American West—without stopping her story dead in its tracks. She does this like a skilled novelist, reframing her historical exposition as an extension of the thoughts of Fong See and his kinsmen even though it includes facts and events they could not have known. To recreate the ignorance and racism faced by Chinese in the Exclusion Era, See depicts Fong See's kinsmen, working in his small garment factory, as they pause to discuss the hostility of the whites for a few lines; then—as if explaining their concerns—she provides a swift overview of anti-Chinese conduct, news coverage, and legislation, including laws keeping Chinese children out of schools with whites, alien land laws blocking Chinese from owning the land they had worked so hard to render arable, laws forbidding whites from hiring Chinese, and laws singling out Chinese for special taxes. A few words mark these paragraphs as ostensibly voicing the workers' thoughts: "The foreign devils threw eggs and tomatoes. They took their filthy clothes to the Chinese to be cleaned and, when they came back for them, refused to pay" (41). "Filthy," an English word that imbues mere dirt with moral disgust, has historically been used by whites to describe racial others, especially Chinese; here, the author lightly reverses the tourist's gaze and uses the metonymic phrase "filthy clothes" to suggest that Chinese could also look down on whites. She depicts the anti-Chinese caricatures in the California press specifically through Fong See's eyes and ears:

> As [white-demon newsboys] held their newspapers aloft, Fong See saw drawings of Chinese men with their features exaggerated—queues becoming poisonous snakes, beautiful eyes transformed into elongated deformities, teeth rendered as blood-sucking fangs. At night, when he went for noodles, he sat with men who read aloud from the American newspapers in which his countrymen were described as heathens and barbarians—savage, lustful, impure, diseased. (41–42)

Since Fong See is not literate in either English or Cantonese, the author makes a point of imagining how he and his countrymen could have known what was being printed about them. By introducing Fong See's perspective into her summary, she invites readers to imagine what he, a frugal family entrepreneur, would have felt at being called "savage, lustful, impure, [and] diseased" and to inhabit a worldview in which Chinese eyes are normal, even beautiful. Returning to the workshop, See juxtaposes a brief conversation—in which the Chinese men decide whether they will stay—with her account of the depression and high unemployment of the 1870s, as well as the scapegoating of Chinese to win white votes. She asserts that the stereotypical Chinese vices (drinking, stealing, gambling, opium smoking, and brothel use) were common to all races of that time and place and counters them with Chinese stereotypes of whites that ironically mirror white views of Chinese, ending with whites' perceived lack of family values and the huge numbers of whites arriving in California "to take the jobs that the Chinese had fought so hard to develop" (45). Finally, she summarizes the Exclusion Act of 1882, which forbade additional Chinese laborers from entering the United States for ten years, barred the wives of existing immigrants (like most Chinese women) from entry, required Chinese laborers to register and carry residency papers, and rendered them ineligible for citizenship, reserving the privilege of legal entry for Chinese teachers, merchants, students, tourists, and diplomats. Thus See not only recreates the racist environment in which Fong See lived and worked but also explains the importance of his merchant status and implies the legal risk to him of hiring Chinese workers to manufacture goods, a risk that eventually motivates him to stop manufacturing; she explains how these laws drastically reduced Chinese immigration and how the Geary Act of 1892, the first of many renewing and refining Chinese exclusion, entirely stopped Chinese immigration in 1892.

Finally, See introduces the well-documented yet little-known history of anti-Chinese violence in the American West, which arose with the passing of the exclusion laws, as part of Fong See's interior monologue: "In his worst imaginings, Fong See couldn't have envisioned what would happen to the Chinese in the years to come" (45). See's summary of horrifying events of mass violence in six western states in which Chinese were threatened, tortured, terrorized, and forced to move or murdered is both vivid and succinct. (See uses neutral expressions for these events—"the Driving Out," and "what happened to the Chinese" [45, 46]—but Jean Pfaelzer, author of *Driven Out: The Forgotten War against Chinese Americans,* prefers the terms "roundup," "purge," "expulsion," "pogrom," and "ethnic cleansing" [xv–xxix].)[1] See's flair for black humor is reflected in the apocryphal quotation from the one man who "cares" to defend Chinese with his guns during a particular riot, albeit for the wrong reason: "If you kill Wong, who in the hell will do my laundry?" (45). Yet she also concisely evokes the sustained horror and inhumanity of these events. Then she redirects readers' attention at chapter's end to Fong See, whose determination to stay, survive, and succeed in this harsh environment has taken on new meaning.

Throughout the book, See closely interweaves her primary research—using public records, legal and property documents, news clippings, personal diaries and papers, published historical works, and oral history (interviews)—with the imagined dialogue and interior monologues of key characters and the major events of their lives. She links the Boxer Rebellion with the Sees' first trip as a family to Dimtao; World War I with their second trip and the unraveling of their marriage; the Great Depression with Eddy's founding of the Dragon's Den restaurant; and the repeal of the Chinese exclusion laws and a state visit by Madame Chiang Kai-shek with Ticie's death in 1943, even though the events are related only by coincidence (271).

"To Surmount the Odds": Framing Ticie as Heroine of a Chinese Historical Narrative

In relating Fong See and Ticie's love story, See portrays Ticie as a resourceful young woman, a loving and beloved wife and mother, and a shrewd businesswoman: an ideal heroine for a historical novel or a memoir. A runaway orphan from Oregon, Ticie talks her way into a job in Fong See's shop in Sacramento in 1894, when she is eighteen and Fong See is at least thirty-seven (19–20, 25, 35, 50–51). There she bonds with Chinese workers, providing them with guidance on leases and contracts, translation help, advice, empathy, kindness, and the womanly attention they miss in the absence of family (66); she attracts whites as customers and business colleagues; and she pushes Fong See toward success, step by step. Ticie, it seems, goads Fong See to give up manufacturing, move from Sacramento to Los Angeles, jump into the antique business, and cut his queue (56–58, 68, 86). Disregarding their differences in age, language, and culture, they circumvent the law against their interracial marriage by signing a civil marriage contract in 1897 (56). In the wake of the Boxer Rebellion, the couple returns (in the symbolic sense, for Ticie) to China in 1901 to honor Fong See's parents and to search for new merchandise. Visiting Dimtao, Fong See's Cantonese hometown, for the first time with him and their two young sons, Ming (also called Milton) and Ray, Ticie is honored as his "true wife" and "Number One wife" (despite his earlier marriage to a surviving Chinese wife) because of Ticie's sons, her intimacy with Fong See and openness to his Chinese family and community, and her contributions to the family business (69, 71). After surviving smallpox, Ticie joins Fong See in learning about Chinese art and artifacts, returns to California with the family in 1902, and bears three more children (Bennie, Eddy, and Sissee) as Fong See opens branches in Pasadena and Long Beach with the assistance of two brothers (Fong Yun and Fong Quong) from China. Of this period, See quotes her father's cousin Sumoy, the daughter of Fong See's third wife, as saying, "[Ticie] had four boys, and for a Chinese family to have that many sons is a feat in itself. But to surmount the odds—the miscegenation laws and the racist attitudes of Chinese and Caucasians—they must have had a great love" (143).

When the couple splits up, Ticie is portrayed as combining a modern woman's assertiveness and financial acumen with the ideal conduct of a loyal wife and mother. The rift opens in 1919, when the couple return with their brood to Dimtao and Fong See, at age sixty-two, succumbs to the dream of returning one day to his homeland. He decides to purchase land and factories, build a mansion, and open a hotel in China, and he chooses Eddy (then fourteen) to stay behind in Dimtao to tend Fong See's mother and the new enterprises (129–131, 140). When Ticie refuses to cooperate, taking her children back to California, Fong See hires a local widow with a flair for business (Fong Guai King), marries her teenage daughter Ngon Hung, and starts a second family in China (141). Ticie responds by filing for separation. When her marriage is annulled in 1924, Ticie raises and supports the children herself, with only minimal child support. Keeping the store name of F. Suie One, and the best of the merchandise, she opens a shop of her own in competition with Fong See's store, which is henceforth called the Fong See On Company (143). Through the Depression, urban renewal, and personal ups and downs, Ticie is able to keep the family together until all five See children have married. She dies in 1943, shortly after Sissee marries (270).

See's emphasis on Ticie's contributions to the family and business as a means of demonstrating her worth within the family evokes the arguments of Christine So in *Economic Citizens: A Narrative of Asian American Visibility* about the rhetorical functions of Chinese women in what Sau-ling Cynthia Wong has called "Gone with the Wind" epics: family memoirs and family novels set against the backdrop of twentieth-century Chinese history ("Sugar" 200). Wong describes the genre this way: "Virtually all [these texts] involve a multigenerational family saga interwoven with violent historical events . . . as well as a culminating personal odyssey across the ocean to the West, signaling final 'arrival' in both a physical and an ideological sense" ("Sugar" 200). So observes that such narratives, which proliferated in the 1990s and continue to be popular with American and other Anglophone readers, cast Chinese women as both emblems of modernity and guardians of culture, memory, kinship systems, and traditional values. Whereas Ong presents the image of the border-crossing Chinese businessman as a flexible citizen without loyalty to any one nation, these books depict Chinese women both as upholders of family and nation and as skilled family entrepreneurs who express their loyalty by accumulating wealth for the good of the family. These books offer Western readers the opportunity to experience Chinese history vicariously and to enjoy the successes of resourceful female protagonists who combine traditional Chinese and Western values. With "Chinese history" as a major character, heroines who stand at the spatial and chronological junctures of East and West, and plots in which women move from being worth "nothing" to accruing enough financial capital to preserve their families, these stories place women at the center of modern Chinese history, even as the heroines so often end up in the West, and their stories are told by their Chinese American descendants (So 128–129).

Symbolically claiming Chinese women as foremothers of Asian Americans reflects the social reality that, because of Chinese exclusion, Chinese women remained at home, maintaining home and family, while Chinese men lived and worked abroad, as historian Gary Okihiro points out (64–92, qtd. in So 155–156). So concludes:

> The social realities of the transnational family even in the early twentieth century thus continue to support arguments for locating Asian American history outside of U.S. borders. At the same time, however, [such narratives] spurn Asian American history and instead embrace a "global history," in its current postmodern form. They imagine Chinese American women's history not necessarily as a history rooted in the moment of immigration to the United States . . . but instead as one grounded in migration in general. . . . Unlike their male counterparts, they imagine without ever quite realizing a "flexible cultural citizenship," in which their spectacular strength and determination enable their entry into any nation even as that entry is predicated on their personification of China. (155–156)

Finally, So finds that these Chinese heroines' successes in negotiating various levels of economic exchange, "as a means of maintaining intact familial and national ties and establishing Chinese women as 'feminists,' 'modern,'" and tacitly assimilable, positions them as symbols of China's past and of the future of global capitalism (155–156). Reading So's conclusions, one hears her ambivalence toward the opening of the field: it is right to include Chinese women's stories in Asian American literature, she agrees, but she seems concerned that Chinese women's entry into Asian American literature invites readers to look right past contemporary Asian American women to the heroic survivors of modern Chinese history, as if Chinese Americans are interesting only when they are remote in time and space.

Appearing in a flood of memoirs and historical fiction focused on Chinese women, Lisa See's book reflects a sophisticated awareness of Chinese history, of what made Ticie a valuable wife in the eyes of Fong See and his family, and of the theme of repeated, circular migration. At the same time, her primary focus is on the Fongs and Sees in America, and her matriarch,

Ticie, is a Caucasian American from Oregon. See seeks to explain how Ticie became Chinese: in fact, she describes Ticie's complex negotiations as a white woman living as an *honorary* Chinese in the segregated world of Fong See. I discussed above how the author uses the Fongs and the Pruetts to tell the stories of Chinese immigration and of the settlement of the American West in miniature form. While See does recount scenes from Chinese history, she also draws from the history of the Chinese in the West in this period to fulfill her narrative quota of violence, political turmoil, and social instability. Ticie, like her Chinese counterparts, withstands moral pressures and accrues capital that sustains the family: by taking a job with Fong See, she avoids becoming a prostitute and helps improve his fortunes through her hard work, business acumen, and close, kind attention to the needs of family, workers, and business associates. She keeps the books, researches U.S. sources for antiques, and works daily in the store even after the birth of her sons (66). Like a Chinese heroine, she stands at the juncture of East and West, but in her case her flexible cultural citizenship is marked by her brilliant blend of leadership and adaptation in entering a Chinese family and community. In addition to guiding Fong See's business decisions, Ticie becomes a cultural translator whose presence is inviting to white customers. The author writes, "Fong See was a good businessman, but Ticie had heart" (66). Ticie's friend Richard White also claimed that Ticie had been "the brains of the establishment" (See 158). See also cites the immigration record to demonstrate the complexity of Ticie's life as a Caucasian American wife to a Chinese man, as well as her version of flexible citizenship. Having signed a private marriage contract, Ticie is identified as a Chinese merchant's wife, with no designated race, by U.S. immigration officials when traveling to China in 1901; on her second trip there in 1919, she is actively claimed as a citizen by the Republic of China (110). A few years later, her formal marriage is annulled; she never returns to China, yet she lives and works in Chinatown, performing the roles of an honorary Chinese and a white American woman, for the rest of her life.

Chinese women's narratives often dramatize their modernity and Westernization by ending with the women's immigration to America, and Chinese American return narratives typically portray American-born Chinese (ABCs) as discovering their heritage by visiting or returning to China. But Ticie's two return narratives have a different structure: they serve as tests of her ability to negotiate the changing demands of Chinese cultural expectations upon her marriage, which are expressed through the requirements of the family business. On her first journey to China in 1901, Ticie learns about her husband's heritage and family expectations, gains professional knowledge of Chinese art and antiques, and secures her position as a Chinese merchant's favored wife by meeting his family in China. In short, she becomes more deeply embedded in

Fong See's culture, family, and business on this trip. On their second shared trip in 1919, however, Fong See makes clear that he requires sacrifices and commitments to life in China beyond what Ticie is willing to accept, so she and her children separate from him and chart an independent course as a Chinese American family of mixed race. In contrast to Fong See, who in 1919 aspired to settle in China, Ticie sees Los Angeles as her true home, but she never again leaves Chinatown. She remains at the old address for twenty-five years, raising their children and operating her own store under the F. Suie One name, and then moves the store to another Chinatown address. Though her racially liminal identity as the American wife of a Chinese merchant was created through her partnership with and marriage to Fong See, she does everything she can to continue and affirm her and the family's identity as a mixed-race Chinese family, despite their estrangement from her husband. Most importantly, when Ray and Bennie leave the store to found their own manufacturing business, Ticie insists that they contribute to a family pot that supports everyone but Fong See: in this matriarchal yet Confucian arrangement, the mother's and grown children's shared finances express their commitment to their See family identity.

Comparing Ticie to the heroines of Chinese historical narratives reveals that she is presented in ways that parallel them, but See makes clear the differences that derive from Ticie's race and American roots. As the wife of a second-generation, nineteenth-century Chinese pioneer in California, she creates a life on the cusp of Western and Chinese cultures. As the person who enables Fong See to rise above "the mass" of Chinese, in See's favored formulation, she is more than a white mistress or white cultural mentor to Fong See in his process of assimilation: she is a wife and business partner (76). In the classic narrative structure in which female romantic partners represent life options for male protagonists, Ticie, the American wife, represents Westernization and modernity for Fong See and could be deemed a rival to his Chinese wives. Yet See also presents Ticie as doing the work of a Chinese heroine and a diasporic Chinese wife. She is willing to not only marry a Chinese man but also live in Chinatown, visit her husband's homeland, and dedicate her labor and her earnings to their business and their family. By mentioning the chaste nature of Ticie's lifelong friendship with her admirer Richard White, her loneliness, and her constant companionship with Sissee after the annulment, the author establishes that Ticie remained faithful to Fong See, her first and only love, throughout her life.

Symbolically, Ticie differs from the heroines of Chinese narratives whose feats implicitly strengthen the Chinese nation. She does not, for instance, found a famous women's bank in China, or help a family of scholars to emigrate, like the heroines of some Chinese historical memoirs (P. N. Chang; Chai and Chai, *Girl*). However, she and her family also make a distinctive contribution to the preservation of Chinese culture in America and the creation of Chinese American culture. Unable to experience growing up in China or to learn Chinese dialects, Ticie compensates by learning and developing her husband's import business, by studying Chinese art and antiques, and by passing that knowledge to her children (See 126–127). Here, again, her actions link tradition with modernity. See admits that the Sees and Fongs profited from Chinese misfortune by finding and exporting Chinese goods, both cheap commodities and fine art, in hard times. But through their import, promotion, and sale of Chinese art and artifacts, the Sees also contributed materially to Americans' knowledge and love of Chinese art. At one point, See describes how increasing political instability and economic hardship forced Chinese families to liquidate increasingly ancient heirlooms, placing them into the hands of dealers like the Sees. Beginning with the emergence of royal artifacts into the market in 1911, American collectors became interested in older and older artifacts as Chinese families were forced to sell family heirlooms and railroad builders accidentally unearthed graves containing objects dating back to the third century B.C. (234–235). She describes how Fong See and Ming searched for ancient bronzes and bought a huge range of objects, some truly rare and ancient and all likely to appreciate in value, in a buying trip in 1939 (123, 234–236). Since "some of the biggest collectors in the country" visited Fong See, and "many of their collections ended up in museums" (123), See suggests that her ancestors contributed to the preservation of valuable, beautiful, or culturally interesting objects that might otherwise have been lost or destroyed. Over decades, the furniture and props the Sees rented to Hollywood studios also helped filmmakers visualize China for American filmgoers. See describes MGM's elaborate constructions, garnished with props from the See and Fong shops, of a made-to-order Chinese farm in Northridge, California, and a Chinese city on a soundstage for *The Good Earth*. "When the movie premiered," she concludes dryly, "it was hailed as the most authentic view of Chinese life ever filmed" (213). And Grace Nicholson, an art dealer who "learned about Asian art from Fong See when they were neighbors out in Pasadena in the teens and twenties," opened a Chinese-themed art gallery and shop in 1925 that has since become the site of the Pacific Asia Museum in Pasadena (See 87, 317, 356).

Paradoxically, the defining act of Ticie's marriage may be her decision to gather her children and leave China in 1919, to prevent Fong See from separating Eddy from the rest of the family. This decision, compounded by Fong See's third marriage, leads eventually to the annulment of Ticie's marriage in 1924 (131, 143); this sequence breaks up the marriage yet preserves the Sees—Ticie and her children—as a family unit. Dissenting from her husband, traveling independently, and seeking an annulment might be seen as modern, even scandalous gestures (divorce was as remarkable among Chinese as among whites in 1924), yet See also places them within a narrative of family preservation.

Read as a white woman, Ticie plays a traditional role in Asian American letters: she is the figure who enables the Chinese male immigrant to assimilate and succeed, who provides cultural mentoring, and whose sexual availability could arguably serve as a metaphor for the Chinese immigrant's access to symbolic and material membership in the nation. She can be seen as the real embodiment of the "modern" white rival to the "traditional" Chinese wife who appears in Sui Sin Far's short stories of Chinese wives' incomplete assimilation, which I have described elsewhere (Sui, "Wisdom" 42–60, "Americanizing" 83–92, discussed in P. Chu 110–122), or the white woman who chooses to marry a Chinese in Sui Sin Far's other tales (Sui, "Story of One" 66–77, "Chinese Husband" 78–83). But as far as the record shows, Sui Sin Far never imagined an afterlife for these figures. See is the first author to depict in such depth a Chinese American couple of that era in which the wife is white, and she describes the courtships and marriages of three generations of mixed couples: Fong See and Letticie Pruett, her great-grandparents; Eddy See and Stella Copeland, her grandparents; and Richard See and Carolyn Laws, her parents. Whiteness and class intersect, in Ticie's case. After crossing the color line to wed a married man, she could have been depicted as a fallen woman, a concubine, or a de facto divorcée, but she is not remembered as such in the family. Why? Because as a white, American-born citizen, she has money and legal power to separate from Fong See, return to the United States, and negotiate fair terms in annulling the match; she has the command of English, job skills, and capital with which to support herself and her family; and she has the cultural capital—Chinese merchandise, cultural expertise, and interpersonal ties—to live and work in Chinatown. She is an honorary Chinese who retains the privileges of whiteness and U.S. citizenship despite having married a Chinese man. See also portrays Ticie as less submissive than Fong See's other wives. What appears as insubordination from Fong See's perspective could be attributed to Ticie's race and American upbringing; alternately, when compared with the stories of Chinese women who live abroad and embody modernity, it can be read as a sign that Ticie, in See's account, represents both East and West, tradition and modernity, making her more like than unlike her immigrant Chinese contemporaries.

Difference, Desire, and Performance

Racial difference, ethnic performance, and interethnic desire—factors that are present (if sometimes latent) in most Chinese American return narratives—

are addressed overtly throughout See's text, which emphasizes the racially mixed roots of her family. I discussed above how the author carefully situates Fong See and Ticie's successful union in the context of a virulently racist environment. Implicitly, Fong See is able to marry Ticie because of her rock-bottom social status as a runaway orphan, and she is disowned by her brothers when she marries him. In the private matter of interracial desire between Fong See and Ticie, See humanizes her great-grandparents by depicting their relationship as rooted in the practical demands of business and childrearing; transcending stereotypes, it is by turns romantic, subversive, lucrative, fertile, heartbreaking, and enduring. As suggested above, the author uses novelistic conventions, such as describing Ticie's looks through Fong See's point of view, dramatizing their meeting, and describing their working relationship from both Fong See's and Ticie's perspectives (47–58). Rather than address the erotic aspect of their love in a way that exoticizes either partner, however, she naturalizes the match through Ticie's prosaic point of view—"Letticie supposed it was natural that one thing would lead to another. Hard work to success. Loneliness to happiness. Friendship to love. On January 15, 1897, Letticie Pruett of Central Point, Oregon, and Fong See, the fourth son of a Chinese herbalist, were wed"—immediately followed by the legal detail that they had to have a contract marriage to circumvent the state of California's prohibition against their match (56). In this passage, the "naturalness" of the union in Ticie's eyes is juxtaposed with the state's denaturalizing prohibition.

Later, See avoids dwelling on the couple's emotions at the time of their separation, instead relying on eloquent facts, such as the terms of the annulment (the store's name and best stock for Ticie, but only $25 per month in child support) and indirect evidence of the family's suffering, such as Ray's refusal to forgive Fong See for "what he did to us" and Ticie's drinking in later years (143, 148, 173). A short paragraph on Ticie's grief is rapidly supplanted by a discussion of the financial blow the business will take without Fong See, and Ticie's tactics to recover from that setback (145). The breakup is also described from Fong See's point of view as a shock from which *the business* "would never recover" (158). Chinese men of Fong See's generation rarely expressed affection for their wives in public, and the author records no such expressions. See does, however, demonstrate that Fong See still cared about Ticie decades later: he kept his family and business near hers, had his younger children visit her, sent her weekly "tribute meals," stopped to talk with her on walks with his youngest daughter, Sumoy, and ultimately wished to be buried near her in Forest Lawn cemetery (247, 336).

The author details the couple's knowledge of the antique business and their resourceful appropriations of Fong See's ethnicity, including his performances as a "charming Chinaman" (145), as sources of cultural capital. Fong

See and Ticie make an asset of his ethnicity when they renounce laundering and garment manufacturing to become Chinese antique dealers, deploying their "inside" knowledge of Chinese art and artifacts, the networks of sources they cultivate in both California and China, their aura of Chinese exoticism and prosperity, and, finally, their connections with Hollywood studios producing Asian-themed films. While Ticie engages with white customers and advises Fong See on their tastes, Fong See cultivates his mystique as a high-class dealer of Chinese antiques by turning away random tourists and luring select customers into the store's inner sanctum (93, 144–145).

Conversely, the author also tracks Fong See's race and the couple's interracial match as business liabilities. For instance, they must face the arcane legal requirements imposed only on Chinese, which are suggested in the author's analysis of the nearly five hundred pages of immigration-related documents pertaining to Fong See, his associates, and his family. Fong See's presence in the United States, as well as his ability to secure Chinese merchandise, staff members, and partners, is scrutinized closely by U.S. immigration officials before and after the many trips he and his family and workers make to and from China. In 1927, when Fong See's brother, Fong Yun, seeks to return to China to negotiate with kidnappers for the lives of his sons, he and Fong See must submit to months of questions about their private lives before he can do so (161–163). Because Fong See still claimed Ticie as his wife in 1921, when his third wife Ngon Hung bore Jong Oy ("Deep Love"), he resorts to reporting Jong Oy as her mother's daughter by a previous marriage, with the result that the child cannot enter the United States until 1932, five years after her mother and brother emigrate (143–144, 162–163, 177).

Fong See's business and residential decisions are also influenced by California's alien land laws, which forbid Chinese to buy or own land. (Arriving around 1871 as the son of a Chinese herbalist who never sought naturalization, Fong See, like most Chinese in the United States, has been declared an "alien ineligible to citizenship" by a court case in 1878.)[2] Noting, for instance, that Fong See owns three houses in Dimtao in 1810, the author describes how he circumvents California's land laws: he barters rugs for property east of Los Angeles, and merchandise for property near Signal Hill in Long Beach; places both properties in Ticie's name; and builds a store on each property but avoids building houses there (84, 90). Having survived the anti-Chinese purges of the 1880s and 1990s, he may well have considered white neighborhoods too "unpredictable" to live in (90–91). Yet even Chinatown properties are not secure. Fong See will witness the condemnation and dismantling of Chinatown, in two parts, to make way for a new train station, a park, and freeway ramps (178–179, 306–307).

Fong See and Ticie's children have to deal with their mixed race and uncertain class status throughout their working and personal lives. As Fong See's children, they are both privileged and trapped by the family's expectations. Despite their wealth—Fong See buys new cars for each of his grown children as a peace offering in 1934—the See children are not raised with the expectation of college, due both to their parents' limited formal educations (Fong See comes to the United States and enters business in his teens; Ticie has a high school education) and to the lack of professional opportunities for Chinese in the United States in their generation (107, 180, 181). Despite their ethnically ambiguous good looks (shown in photos following p. 234) and their experience working and living in a racially mixed world, See never suggests that they tried to pass as whites. Instead, the eldest son, Ming, was groomed from childhood to run the store, and the other siblings were raised to assist him. Therefore, the boys were expected to help out in the store rather than study after school, and the family's long trips to China were considered more important than formal education. On one trip the older boys were tutored in Mandarin, assessing Chinese art, and bargaining, while Eddy, who rapidly picked up Cantonese, was considered at fourteen as a possible manager for Fong See's new businesses in China. Eventually, Ming would run F. Suie One with Sissee as co-owner (288). Ray, who purportedly hated his father and all things Chinese, married a white woman, lived among whites, and founded a furniture design and manufacturing business that catered to whites, with Bennie as a partner; however, his marketing emphasized his Chinese cultural background (269, 309–310). Eddy entered USC in the 1920s but dropped out of his premed studies and kept company with artists; the high point of his career was his founding of the Dragon's Den (1934–1943), a trendy Chinese restaurant: attracting a diverse clientele including white film actors and filmmakers, homosexuals, and mixed-race couples, it kept the Sees afloat during the Great Depression (168, 214, 271). Sissee dropped out of school to help support the family during the Depression, moved away briefly after marrying the architect Gilbert Leong in 1942, and spent most of her working life at F. Suie One and the Dragon's Den (173). In short, none of Ticie's children completed college. All had careers that combined their parents' skills in business with their interests in Chinese art and design, using their ethnic capital (both cultural and material) to help them negotiate the white-Chinese color line in a generation when few Chinese were able to complete college and find professional careers in the United States. (Though See interviews and quotes the children of Fong See and Ngon Hung, the book does not detail their difficulties in China as the children of a largely absent Gold Mountain sojourner, or in California as the second family of a much older man, expected to fulfill the roles of traditional Chinese children while learning to survive in America. She says even less of the fourth wife, Si Ping.)

See depicts Ticie's sons as initially constrained but resourceful in socializing with whites and defying antimiscegenation laws. As the only Chinese in the 1917 graduating class at Lincoln High School, Ming and Ray had been socially isolated in school. However, after graduating and returning from China, they were seen by whites as wealthy and worldly, and they avoided socializing with the "backward" Chinese of Chinatown (106–107, 136). Ming married Dorothy Hayes, an actress, but the marriage was unhappy and the couple remained childless. When See explains that Ming would say he didn't want children to repeat what he had gone through, it is unclear whether he was referring to his rocky marriage or to his difficulties as a mixed-race Chinese American (165–166). Ray's wife, Leona, is described as very plain, suggesting that he sought out someone different from Dorothy while focusing on his business; however, she was also white (148). Bennie and Eddy married their high school sweethearts, Bertha Weheimer and Stella Copeland (167). Attesting to Ticie's family leadership in Fong See's absence, See describes how deeply Stella, the daughter of a broken home, was attracted by Ticie's kindness, Eddy's Chinese culture, and the closeness and stability of the Sees (153–155). Through Lisa See views Eddy, the most family-centered brother, as the "most Chinese," all four brothers married whites, and all had to go to Mexico to marry, since the State of California considered them racially Chinese and ineligible to marry white women (148, 155, 167, 170).

Sissee, Fong See and Ticie's only daughter, faced the greatest discrimination in her love life. Although Ticie believed that neither Chinese nor whites would marry a mixed-race woman, Fong See wanted Sissee to marry into a good Chinatown family. Sissee chose Gilbert Leong and they began dating, though it was eight years before he proposed because his mother considered Sissee's family inferior (217, 243–244, 261). Gilbert's father, a neighboring restaurant owner, was also a small business owner, but the Leongs were community leaders in Chinatown (261). Mrs. Leong, "a city girl with a city dialect," was a Christian devoted to education (269). For decades, she taught Chinese language classes at the Methodist church, introduced Chinese women and children to Christianity, and supported Gilbert's education as an architect (257–264, 269). According to See, Mrs. Leong looked down on Sissee, despite her modest, hardworking, sweet character, because of Ticie's race and "*fan yin*" ("foreign elements") (257–258, 264). Not only had Fong See and Ticie annulled their marriage and not only did Fong See bring his second, Chinese, family to live near his store; the Sees never bothered to send their children to her Chinese classes, they served alcohol at the Dragon's Den, and, during the war, Fong See refused to join Chinatown's relief drives or stop selling Japanese goods (257–265, 90, 216, 249). These and other stories suggest that, despite their American citizenship and their father's wealth, the See children were never fully accepted, either as white or as Chinese, but had to negotiate their place in every business, academic, social, and family situation. This perennial liminality drove Fong See, alternating between China and America, to forsake three of his four wives and to chart his own course in Chinatown; it drove Ticie to drink; and it drove Ticie's sons to live more wildly, placed as they were on the margins even of Chinatown.

Helping Relatives *and* Making a Profit: Historicizing and Humanizing Fong See

In contrast to the famous precedent set by Maxine Hong Kingston's *China Men*, which combines family lore, historical knowledge, and flights of imagination, See supplements her portrayal of her most elusive subjects, her great-great-grandfather Fong Dun Shung and great-grandfather Fong See, with extensive research about their businesses. Because her central subject, Fong See, passed away in 1957, leaving no personal letters or diaries, and perhaps because the author knew no Chinese languages, See had no direct access to his voice. Instead, she recognized that for this quintessential man of business, the business itself and the memories of family, associates, and customers offered significant testimony to his subaltern subjectivity. Kingston may well have grappled with a dearth of formal documentation for family members who labored in hand laundries, gambling houses, railroads, plantations, or mines, some of whom entered with false papers, before choosing her techniques of active mythmaking in *China Men*. See, by contrast, ingeniously uses the paper trail and oral echoes of Fong See's business career to ground her portrait of him and his life, augmenting historical research with both restraint and imagination. Through her art, Fong See's business and legal papers speak eloquently of his fettered yet brilliant life as an immigrant merchant in the Exclusion Era, telling as much as one can imagine of the inner man without access to his voice. At the same time, See's book could be read as an ethnography of the family businesses, which almost function as characters in themselves. In this light, Christine So's insight that Asians, particularly Chinese, are perceived largely as economic citizens is both suggestive and cautionary (10–14). See goes far indeed in portraying Fong See as an ingenious, resourceful economic agent. But, as So cautions, the tendency to portray Asian Americans as primarily or solely economic agents risks understating their humanity. It is the latter problem that See strives always to address by supplementing her account of the ambitious businessman with her view of Fong See as a complex, flawed family man seeking a full and dignified life (158).

A short summary illustrates how See's ethnographic research into Fong See's business life rivals that of a historian such as Haiming Liu, although her focus is more psychological and interpersonal than Liu's. Like Liu, See periodically widens her lens to provide broader historical overviews, including explanations of Chinese immigration history and the rise and fall of Los Angeles' Chinatowns. As noted earlier, Fong Dun Shung, Fong See's father, is presented as an archetypical Chinese herbalist, though generic details (such as the living conditions of Chinese miners and prostitutes) are supplemented with individual facts (such as the dates of his immigration, marriages, and death). See describes the records filed over decades of Fong See's ever-changing "partners" in the business, explaining that paper "partnership" in Fong See's business established merchant status, and thus exemption from the exclusion laws, for each recorded "partner" (82–84). When the holders of these valuable immigration slots did not actually function as partners, the family still took care to provide sufficient evidence to persuade immigration authorities of their merchant status; for instance, Fong See's brother and "partner" Fong Yun established his merchant status in Hong Kong before applying for entry to the United States (75, 77).

Fong See's marriage to Ticie is also discussed in legal terms, beginning with the fact that, as a Chinese man, he could not marry her, a white woman, in the state of California (or in Arizona, Georgia, Idaho, Louisiana, Mississippi, Missouri, Nebraska, Nevada, South Dakota, Utah, Virginia, or Wyoming [See 85]). To overcome this obstacle, the couple drew up a personal contract, but—whether from personal reticence and caution or from qualms about the legality of his second marriage—Fong See apparently refrained from telling white friends that Ticie was his wife (67–68, 76). This ostensibly legal but actually bigamous arrangement generated legal uncertainty about Ticie's citizenship, and even her race, on their family trips to China in 1901 and 1919 (110–111).[3] In the couple's most serious quarrel, the over-sixty-year-old Fong See, in See's interpretation, expressed his intent to retire in China by establishing a business empire (complete with a mansion, hotel, and factories), and Ticie declined to leave Eddy in China for what she saw as a "business deal" (140, 131). Fong See's subsequent match to the sixteen-year-old Ngon Hung, whose mother (Fong Guai King) became his business manager in China, suggests that he subscribed to a Confucian way of thinking in which family relations and business relations were inseparably intertwined, because only family members could be trusted, and in which it was not unusual for Chinese men to have multiple wives (See 141; M. Hsu, *Dreaming* 95). Finally, the legal and emotional dissolution of the marriage to Ticie was intermixed with the dissolution of their partnership in the store.

Further grounding her portrait of Fong See as a businessman and the business as a subject in its own right, See details the purchases and sales over the years of the various stores; the kinds of merchandise purchased and sold; the keeping of separate books (English and Chinese, official and unofficial); the training of family members as future employees and managers; the differing outcomes as Fong See's partners, brothers, and sons sought to rise in the company or to start their own businesses; and the curation, conservation, and strategic artificial aging of merchandise. She describes how Fong See arranged and presented his merchandise to entice wealthy patrons with the aura of exclusive and exotic merchandise while turning away less wealthy, less discriminating customers. The author frankly reveals that some of Fong See's wares were not intrinsically valuable but became so because the Sees contrived to make them seem ancient, exotic, and precious.

By contrast, the story of Ticie more strongly establishes her business decisions as family choices. Ticie and her grown children survive the Depression by renting furniture and props to Hollywood studios, by opening Ray's furniture business, and by founding and operating the Dragon's Den. See documents the business plan of the restaurant, depicting such particulars as the site selection (the basement of F. Suie One on Los Angeles Street), the menu (cheap but authentic family-style Cantonese food), the striking Chinese landscape mural (designed by Eddy's friend Benji Okubo and painted by art students), and the clientele. Yet these business particulars are interleaved with descriptions of the ambiance of the place and its emotional significance to family members, friends, and former customers. Most importantly, the Dragon's Den is remembered as anchoring the See family partnership. Throughout the Depression years, the family pools the profits of their various businesses; the restaurant and store together supports Ticie, her children, and their growing families; and the family remains close (167). Similarly, See describes Ray's business career in terms of his rebellion against his father, which takes the form of helping his mother keep the family together after the annulment and then founding his own furniture business: designing, manufacturing, distributing, and selling contemporary furniture with Chinese influences (147, 167).

In tracking the family's real estate, See provides both a mini-lesson in Los Angeles' urban development and a riddle about Fong See's heart. Readers may find it strange that, after their bitter annulment, Ticie and Fong See keep their family residences and business premises in close proximity for another twenty-five years, but their personal decisions are also constrained by larger patterns. During hard times, it is cheaper to rent in Chinatown, yet Chinatown and its merchants are always subject to the whims of the white community. Fong See and Ticie leave Sacramento in 1897; searching for a less competitive and racist environment than San Francisco's, they open a store in a white business district a few blocks from Los Angeles' Chinatown, living in the space above the shop (64–65). In 1902, they open a branch in Pasadena (76), move the main store to 510 Los Angeles Street in the "high-class part" of Chinatown in 1906, and open a third branch in Long Beach (80). When they split up in 1924, Fong See keeps the store at 510 Los Angeles Street, renamed as the Fong See On Company, while Ticie opens a new store outside Chinatown with the old store name, F. Suie One (143). After Fong See's nephews in China are kidnapped (and ransomed) in 1927, he and his brother bring their second wives and families from China to a compound near Fong See's store in Los Angeles (164–165). In 1929, Ticie and her sons move her store further out of Chinatown, but in early 1933, as economic conditions worsen, they move the store back to 528 Los Angeles Street, across the street from Fong See's family compound and a few doors down from his store (174). By then, most of Chinatown has been condemned to make way for a new train station; families and businesses are given thirty to seventy-five days' notice to vacate their premises. Those unable to read the English notices are particularly surprised when, a few days before Christmas 1933, the wrecking crews arrive. Since only the two blocks that contain the Fong and See stores are spared, Ticie and her former husband are bound to cross paths often (178–179). The community takes years to recover from the Depression and the razing of Chinatown; not until 1938 do rival developments called China City and New Chinatown open, marking the end of the Depression for Los Angeles' Chinese (222). In 1939, as the economy recovers, Fong See sells out his store and goes to Korea, Japan, and China to stock up on wartime "bargains" before the war closes East Asia to Western commerce (234), but when he returns, he promptly reopens his store at 510 Los Angeles Street and moves with his second family into the space above Ticie's store. Finally, in 1951, even these blocks are condemned and demolished. Only then are Fong See's and Ticie's stores geographically separated: he moves his store to New Chinatown, and she moves hers to New China City (306–307, 316–317). In the matter of Fong See's feeling for Ticie, the author stops short of announcing what the leases say. The record suggests, however, that Ticie's return to the neighborhood was prompted by an instinct to fall back on familiar ground during the Depression but that Fong See deliberately sought premises near Ticie and their children, even after starting another family, because he wanted to remain in their lives.

Returns, Valedictions, and Transnationalism: Flexible Citizenship in the Exclusion Era

Finally, what of the trope of return itself? One of the more poignant moments in the book occurs at the end of the chapter "Fire, 1947–50," when Fong See realizes that his transpacific life must end in America. See uses internal monologues by Ray and Fong See to contrast the resilience of Ray, who rapidly rebounds after a fire destroys his business, to the melancholy thoughts of his exhausted father, who is in his nineties when he is forced to move his store to New Chinatown (280, 307–315). Improbably, Fong See reviews the changing legislative terrain for Chinese in America before turning to the village events of 1949–1950: his Fatsan house has been razed, his hotel has been confiscated by the Communists, his mother-in-law Fong Guai King has been made to kneel on broken glass and confess to class crimes, and even his kind fourth wife, Si Ping, is "occasionally" beaten by farmers from rival villages. Fong See, now deemed an evil landlord despite his contributions to the villages of Fatsan and Dimtao (discussed below), realizes he will not outlast the Communists; will "never be able to return to the home village, recline in his rooftop pavilion, and listen to Enrico Caruso on the Victrola"; and will never be buried in his homeland (314–315). In place of his return, See uses other physical return visits to provide closure to Fong See and Ticie's travels while shifting the book's focus to younger generations. She uses Ticie and Sissee's 1941 visit to Central Point, Oregon, as an occasion to reaffirm Ticie's distance from her origins and her commitment to her Chinatown life and family. Witnessing the neglected homestead and graves of her parents, Ticie avoids searching for her brothers and instead reviews her hopes for Sissee in an internal monologue about Sissee's relationship with Gilbert Leong (241–246). Similarly, See uses Fong See's final visit to Sacramento, the site of his first store and his early years with Ticie, to mark the book's account of his final days (318).

The book's expansive account of Fong See, his four wives, and their many descendants in China and America confounds two narratives common to Asian American studies. See's memoir fits neither the familiar narrative of immigration, assimilation, and upward mobility nor the newer narrative of return I discussed in Chapter 2: the circular travel narrative in which second- or third-generation Asian Americans visit their ancestral homelands to understand their roots and then return to America. Instead, her hundred-year account reveals a more complex story of a transpacific family with multiple roots. For Fong See, a "return" journey may refer to his arrivals in Guangdong Province, his closely documented reentries into America, or his valedictory visit to his second home, Sacramento. For Ticie, as I have discussed, going to China for the first time was not an actual return but a symbolic homecoming, as she was welcomed into the family by Fong See's parents—a homecoming that also served as a test of her cross-cultural skills. Their warm welcome in 1901 contrasts with her angry journey home to California in 1920, as well as with her sadder return to Central Point to bid farewell to her parents' graves in 1941.

Indeed, See's book exemplifies a kind of return narrative that pervades and defines Chinese American history and culture: the narrative of the transpacific family. Though denied the ready mobility of modern global travelers, some sojourners of Fong See's generation could and did travel back and forth even in the long decades of exclusion. Fong See, for instance, circumvented the exclusion laws legally, by filing paperwork and creating a business to establish himself as a merchant. As a merchant, he could bring in relatives, neighbors, and strangers he chose to list as partners in his papers, as long as they were able to answer the skeptical questions of immigration officials. He also brought his American wife and children to China. They were able to return to America both with and without him, although they had to prove their identities each time. Eventually, he brought true and false brothers (Fong Yun, Fong Quong, and a false Fong Lai) into America, as well as his third wife and their children, his brother's wife and children, and others (82–83). Fong See's battles of wits with immigration authorities are described wryly by the author, illustrating the chutzpah and ingenuity needed for Fong See to sustain his transpacific way of living and doing business (162–163).

See also explains, along the way, the history of these interrogations. Citizenship, originally the prerogative of white men, had never been explicitly extended to Chinese, who were categorized racially as "Mongolian" by the courts; in 1878, a U.S circuit court in California specifically identified Chinese as aliens ineligible to citizenship (*In re Ah Yup*, qtd. in I. H. López 163). With Chinese barred from naturalization, politicians seeking the labor vote passed a series of immigration laws singling them out for exclusion from entry, beginning with the Chinese Exclusion Act of 1882.[4] Over time, the laws originally passed with Chinese in mind were extended to bar others of Asian origin from entering as well. Historian Erika Lee has also argued that the system of documentation devised to monitor Chinese in America became the basis for regulating immigration for all others ("Chinese" 144). After a separate legal case (*United States v. Wong Kim Ark*, 1898) had established that all those born in the United States were Americans who could not be stripped of their citizenship, the destruction of municipal records in the San Francisco earthquake and fire of 1905 opened the door for Chinese laborers desiring entry to claim that they had been born in America and were citizens by birth

(S. Chan, *Asian Americans* 92, 194). Returning Chinese Americans, both true and false, would declare upon landing in the United States that they had fathered children, usually sons, in China. Because the United States had passed laws claiming that the children of American fathers were also American citizens regardless of birthplace, these "paper sons" could subsequently claim admission to America (See 81).

Moreover, Chinese American citizens were permitted to bring their wives to America until 1924, when the Immigration Act of 1924 welcomed the wives of European-born immigrants, who were given nonquota status, but decreed that for Chinese Americans, Japanese Americans, and Korean Americans, the foreign-born wives even of U.S. citizens were ineligible for citizenship and entry to the United States (See 143; M. Hsu, *Dreaming* 94–96).[5] Because Chinese merchants retained their right to bring in dependents, paper connections with Chinese Americans of merchant status must have become even more valuable after 1924. With paper sons guaranteed both entry and citizenship, a lucrative trade in false papers arose after the San Francisco earthquake and its fires in 1905 (See 81). Lacking reliable birth and marriage certificates from China, bereft of pre-1905 birth records for Chinese San Franciscans, and mistrustful of photos, U.S. immigration officials after 1905 used detailed interviews to test Chinese immigrants on their identities, under the assumption that most Chinese sought to enter under false names. They questioned migrants closely about their entries and departures as well as personal details about their families and households. Recording those testimonies, they compared them with earlier records and the testimonies of putative relatives, friends, and associates. As a result, U.S. immigration records tracked family births, weddings, deaths, and other details for Chinese who passed in and out of the country during the long decades of exclusion.

In the case of Fong See, who made round trips to China at least six times, bringing family members, merchandise, and business associates to America, the author discovered nearly five hundred pages of immigration records that served as primary sources for her story. She discusses not only Fong See's invention of false stories but also the income, assets, and expenses he reported—and did not report—to immigration officials in 1910 and on other dates (See 84). When considering the symbolic meaning of return in Fong See's case, readers must also consider that each return to China was followed by a return to the United States and that these immigration records, as the author makes clear, are not so much records of facts as records of working stories that the Fongs and Sees used to satisfy the requirements of their interrogators. Hence, the immigration records memorialize not only Fong See's life as a merchant but also the state's scrutiny and control of his private life, which Lisa See describes vividly in individual terms; the records also illuminate the immigration and residence patterns that historians such as Him Mark Lai, Genny Lim, Judy Yung, and Madeline Hsu describe for other Exclusion Era Chinese.

Notwithstanding all these problems, Fong See used his merchant status to attain the Exclusion Era equivalent of flexible citizenship or transnationalism. As a Confucian patriarch who developed a transpacific business empire, he not only built businesses in Fatsan and Los Angeles but also developed a family structure to match his ambitions. Having worked all his life with little or no formal schooling, he lacked literacy and relied on Ticie (until the annulment) to oversee the books in English and his brother Fong Yun to supervise them in Chinese. Perhaps as early as 1914, he aspired to expand his business to four branches (Chinatown, Pasadena, Ocean Park, and Long Beach), one for each son (See 93). Then, in 1919, after purchasing factories, a mansion, and a hotel in Guangdong Province, he wanted to leave fourteen-year-old Eddy, who was just learning Cantonese, in Dimtao to supervise all these operations. When that failed, he found a capable local woman to manage them, but he did not merely hire her; he married her sixteen-year-old daughter, so that once again his properties were managed by a relative. By the end of his life, he had married one wife to care for his parents, a second to strengthen his American business and raise his American children, a third to start a family that would tend to his Chinese businesses, and a fourth for company in China after he brought his third wife and their children to America.

Aihwa Ong's influential study *Flexible Citizenship: The Cultural Logics of Transnationality* usefully questions the celebration of Confucian culture as an ideological model for deploying the energies of the Chinese family to increase the reach and productivity of family-driven businesses. She argues that the practices she describes are not explicable simply as manifestations of Chinese culture. Rather, they are best understood as responses to modern conditions such as the return of Hong Kong to the Chinese government, the instability of other business sites, the increasing openness of national boundaries to trade and travel, and the resulting conditions of global competition. Renaming the Confucian ideology of "filial piety" as "utilitarian familialism" in this context, Ong suggests the need to consider, among other things, the underexamined personal costs to family members, particularly women, of an ideology of individual sacrifice for the good of the family business (118). See's text registers the powerful effects of racism on the family, Fong See's ingenious strategies for responding to the fluctuation of conditions in both China and the United States, and the costs to family members of his decisions. While overtly celebrating Fong See's success, Lisa See cumulatively illustrates the price paid by his family members: she describes the shocking vision of Fong See's first wife in China, prematurely withered by his absence; Ticie's drinking after the annulment of her marriage; the wildness of her sons; and third wife Ngon Hung's dry eyes at Fong See's funeral (See 70, 148, 338). In short, See joins other Asian American writers in challenging the stereotype of the taciturn, endlessly laboring Asian man by candidly tracing her protagonist's problematic but deeply meaningful relations with others. In this, she is joined by many other writers of Chinese family memoirs who seek to humanize the public image of their communities.

At the same time, See also makes clear why Fong See kept his options open in both countries. In America, he outwitted laws against his immigration, residence, and marriage, but he still had to live with threats of violence and deportation; language barriers; barriers to marriage, property ownership, and citizenship; and estrangement from family members in China. When economic conditions were poor in Sacramento or Los Angeles, when Ticie left him, and when the city of Los Angeles condemned his Chinatown property, he had to adjust by closing or moving his stores. Originally sent out of China to seek greater opportunities in America, he found his hope of returning home for a peaceful career and retirement repeatedly disrupted: by kidnappers who acted as a result of harsh political and economic fluctuations, by Japanese invaders, and by Communist ideologues who turned the fruits of his labor into evidence of criminality. These fluctuating conditions, I suggest, frame or significantly shadow numerous Chinese American texts (including those by C. Y. Lee, Jade Snow Wong, Maxine Hong Kingston, and Faye Myenne Ng) and still have analogues for transnational Chinese in the twenty-first century.

Migration scholars know that another element of transnationalism is the flow of remittances from expatriates to home countries. Whereas Ong emphasizes the contingent, unpredictable nature of flexible citizenship—such as the preparations of Hong Kong families to cross borders if political conditions demanded it—an alternative theme that emerges from Chinese family memoirs such as See's is that of the returnees' investments in their home country. Fong See, for instance, acquires factories for paper goods, fireworks, baskets, and kites as well as land on which to build a mansion in Dimtao and a hotel in Fatsan, periodically inviting the villagers to public banquets to create goodwill (See 138–141). In 1933, he donates funds to set up a school and to build a road to Fatsan (209). When the Leong family responds to the Japanese invasion by collecting and distributing relief funds, Fong See rationalizes his refusal to participate—and his flaunting of Japanese goods—by pointing out his personal donations to his home village, which he deems more direct and reliable than relief funds (249–250).

Nicknamed "Gold Mountain See" by his fellow villagers, Fong See is far from unique. He belongs to a long tradition of Chinese from the Pearl River

Delta: arriving and living for decades, even a lifetime, in the United States; sending money to family members back home; and investing in the home village in the hope of eventually retiring there. This peasant tradition is referenced in the fictional works of creative writers such as Kingston (*China Men*), Ng, Sky Lee, and the graffiti poets of Angel Island (see Lai, Lim, and Yung) and in the research of scholars such as Andrea Louie, Madeline Hsu, Him Mark Lai, and Haiming Liu. It places Fong See both within and outside the village as a "Gold Mountain guest" (M. Hsu, *Dreaming* 44) who, despite his long absences, is still claimed as Chinese by the Chinese government. See's text provides evidence of this: the public spectacle of his family's first arrival in Dimtao; his need for bearers, translators, and other attendants to support his buying trips; the threat of kidnappings; and the rise and fall of his local reputation with the vicissitudes of war and Chinese politics. While Lisa See is very direct about discussing U.S. regulation of the Sees' travel and residence, a subtle implication of Fong See's travels is that he and his money are, until the Communist revolution, welcomed by the Qing and Republican governments of China. As historian Madeline Hsu suggests, Fong See's investments in Dimtao and Fatsan had many parallels among other returning Chinese (*Dreaming*).

Within the literature of return, Hsu describes the Exclusion Era conditions that promoted transnationalism, the costs to families, and the traditions of sending home money and investing in the local community among Pearl River Delta Chinese American families. This tradition— which, as discussed below, has a problematic side shown in Denise Chong's family memoir *The Concubine's Children*—also has a modern aspect. In the post-1989 era, overseas Chinese have been welcomed both for their tourist dollars and for their potential to invest in the Chinese economy. Chong, for instance, notes the Chinese government's efficiency in helping her locate her long-lost family members and transporting her to them, and anthropologist Andrea Louie (*Chineseness*) has analyzed how the Chinese government welcomes returning Chinese Americans, hoping to appeal to their residual loyalties to induce them to make future commitments to their ancestral village or country.

In Chapter 2, I discussed how first-time returnees labored to collect the cultural capital necessary to participate in Tu Wei-ming's third circle of global Chinese: that of intellectuals overseas who produce knowledge of China through journalism, scholarship, and other writing. Lisa See is such an intellectual, and the research and narrative techniques I have described provide an extensive example of the kind of intellectual labor that second- or latter-generation Chinese descendants must undertake to enter this circle. (Though See's text has been little noticed by American academics, it has been published in Chinese translation, and she is known in the People's Republic of China and Hong Kong [Lisa See, e-mail to author, September 25, 2014].) I also suggest, however, that the Sees and Fongs participated in the making of global Chinese culture through their extensive investments in Chinese art, antique objects, and everyday objects. Ticie, who did not study Chinese and also discouraged her children from doing so, went through a process of acculturation as she entered Fong See's business and community: first in Sacramento, then in Los Angeles, and then through her visit to her in-laws in Dimtao. In China and America, she studied the Chinese art and antique business with Fong See and, as I argued above, passed that expertise on to her children and collaborated with the family in promoting that knowledge in America. The fact that the Sees often treated common Chinese objects to make them look more valuable may be taken as a metaphor for the creation of Chinese American literature, in which the authors' transformation of stories from Chinese culture and history for the benefit of American readers creates something new and vital. In this memoir, Lisa See transforms her family's raw tales into a remarkable text for the larger community of Chinese Americans and global Chinese, and she replaces the linear narrative of immigration with a more complex form of travel narrative that more fully captures the realities of this community.

4

"The One Who Mediates"

Mimicry, Melancholia, and Countermemory in Denise Chong's The Concubine's Children

> The writer is the one who mediates between the need to remember and the need to move on. . . .
>   One compelling thought that led me to the structure of my book was that my grandparents were already in the grave. They went to the grave taking the privacy of their lives with them. I was about to violate that privacy. My grandparents were buried rows and rows apart. They died penniless in separate rooming houses. . . . [To violate that silence was a serious responsibility. I asked myself,] how do I discharge that responsibility? That led me to the structure of the book, [which was designed] to lay out the truth of their lives. . . .
>   Whatever your history, we all have an innate desire to make sense of our origins. I also feel that we have an innate desire to have a dialogue beyond the grave, in a sense, a dialogue with the dead. . . .
>   In the end the theme I chose was *family*.
> —Denise Chong, keynote address, Homeland, History and Representation: International Symposium on Chinese Canadian and Chinese American Literature in English [paraphrased, from notes]

IN 2010, I had the privilege of speaking with Denise Chong about her writing process after presenting a paper on her family memoir, *The Concubine's Children*, with the author sitting directly in front of me.[1] In my conference paper, I had spoken of her very personal book in relation to the theory of racial melancholia, which argues that Asian American writers register a melancholic structure of feeling rooted in our minority status within U.S. society; I had even suggested that Chong's book implicitly portrayed her family members, working-class Chinese Canadians who endured discrimination similar to that faced by Chinese Americans, as suffering from racial melancholia. During the brief break before her keynote speech, I set aside this provocative hypothesis and asked her the most pressing questions I had as a writer about craft and responsibility. How did she justify breaking her grandparents' silence and publishing their secrets, and how did she find a narrative strategy that converted this exposure into such a deeply respectful, even filial, act of narration? Given the disparate perspectives within her family, how did she determine which side to take, which stories to tell? How did she find the thematic and narrative spine of her story? Chong listened attentively and then excused herself to be photographed and to prepare for her talk. When she returned to deliver her keynote speech, she gave a passionate description—in fact, a defense—of her mission and creative process in writing *The Concubine's Children*. She cited her critics from the Chinese Canadian community, who felt she had minimized the injustices they had suffered or who objected to her publication of family and community secrets; she cited white colleagues, who felt she had just lucked out by having a "good story" and discounted her research and craft; finally, she acknowledged and included the scholars in the room when she said, "This is my reply" (Keynote).

In her speech, Chong did not directly reject the idea of "racial melancholia" as descriptive of her complex, nuanced, and finely wrought family memoir. However, she contested the view of some critics that the Chinese in Canada should be portrayed primarily as "victims of history" (Keynote). (Given that her own parents were able to leave Chinatown, enter the middle class, and provide a secure foundation for her own professional successes as an economist and author, Chong had good reason to provide a less pessimistic interpretation of her family and community history in her book.) She emphasized her own agency in writing a book that would counter the physical contraction or destruction, and the historical erasure, of the Chinatowns in Vancouver and Nanaimo by preserving the memory of those places, those communities, and those people (Chong, *Concubine's Children* 228). And, she said, she wrote the book to counter her mother's profound estrangement and isolation from her family in China, uniting in print the family that could never be united in reality. Chong's speech was a moving reminder of the agency of Asian North American writers, their capacity to inscribe their own theoretical understandings into their work, and the complex rhetorical labor associated with the writing of a narrative of return. Nevertheless, the theory of racial melancholia is useful to sharpen awareness of the inseparability of racial and individual griefs in a story such as hers, to suggest that racial melancholia due to conditions in North America may serve to compound losses suffered in Asia, and to highlight Chong's assertion of her mother's and grandmother's agency in the face of seemingly insurmountable odds.

In Chapter 2, I described a simple paradigm for the narrative of return. The narrators of *Cultural Curiosity* traced a double process: first, of preparing to return and then returning to China, and second, of reflecting on the significance of the trip in the process of writing. The writers were diasporic Chinese who visited China after prolonged absence, or for the first time. They described not only their family members' immigration and settlement in other places around the world but also their own processes of self-education about their ancestral culture, history, and language; their family members' expectations; and their own understanding of the meanings of their trips, particularly in relation to their own evolving sense of culture and identity. I call this the "curiosity" model of return.

In Chapter 3, I showed that, while this paradigm suitably described the experience of Lisa See, an author who traveled to China to understand one hundred years of her family's Chinese American history, her memoir made clear that for her ancestors, the frame of immigration and return was not so simple. See showed that for three generations, family members' returns to China served to maintain longstanding family and business connections on both sides of the Pacific. These patterns reflected both Confucian family structures and the need for her extended family to adapt to shifting, often hostile conditions in both America and China, during and after the Exclusion Era. The biracial merchant family's combination of transpacific travel and settlement—and their inventive melding of business and family, Confucian and American cultures—anticipated and complicated the image of the transnational businessmen described by anthropologists in the 1990s as flexible citizens (Ong and Nonini). In focusing on See's strategies for research and narration and her differences, in focus and technique, from historian Haiming Liu, I suggested that See placed the narrative of her personal search for roots into dialogue with the larger story of Fong See's transnational and biracial Chinese American family. In portraying the elusive consciousness of her great-grandfather, See drew on extensive documentation of her ancestor's business and immigration history, and others' accounts of him, to build a more complex, complete picture of Fong See as a human being. She not only documented his economic skill and success but also used her imagination to trace his family relations and conjure his intimate thoughts.

In this chapter and the next, I argue that like Lisa See, the writers Denise Chong, Winberg Chai, and May-lee Chai use George Lipsitz's technique of countermemory to question official histories from which their family members, and others like them, have been omitted. Lipsitz writes that countermemory, which "starts with the particular and the specific and then builds outward toward a total story," looks for "hidden histories excluded from dominant narratives" but uses those narratives, and their new perspectives, to challenge existing histories (Lipsitz 212–213, qtd. in Davis, *Relative Histories* 16). As Rocío Davis has pointed out, countermemory is closely related to Marianne Hirsch's concept of *postmemory*, which is "distinguished from memory by generational distance and from history by deep personal connection" (Hirsch, *Family* 22, qtd. in Davis, *Relative Histories* 16–17). According to Hirsch, the narratives created by postmemory gain power because they are "mediated not through recollection, but through an imaginative investment and creation" (22). The texts of See, Chong, and the Chais exemplify both countermemory and postmemory. Chong's memoir, *The Concubine's Children: The Story of a Chinese Family Living on Two Sides of the Globe*, provides a Canadian, working-class counterpoint to the story of Fong See and his rise into the merchant class. In the father-daughter memoir *The Girl from Purple Mountain*, Winberg and May-lee Chai use an intergenerational dialogue to tell the story of Winberg's parents, the scholars Charles and Ruth Chai, an American-educated Chinese couple who returned to live in China in the Republican era (1911–1949). All three illustrate conscious efforts at contesting and supplementing official histories with personalized countermemories.

Departures, Returns

In terms of plot structure, Chong shares with other return narrators the entwinement of two narratives: that of the roots pilgrimage, as in *Cultural Curiosity*, and the narrative of a transnational family and its progress. Like the other texts discussed here, *The Concubine's Children* is structured in part around the recitation of a family's transnational crossings, which include the travels of Chong's grandparents, the permanent placement of her mother in Canada and her mother's sisters in China, and Chong's own journeys to China with her mother in search of her grandparents' village and the other half of their family. Opening her story in Chang Gar Bin, a Cantonese village, Chong's omniscient narrator envisions a concubine, Leong May-ying, determining to travel back to Vancouver, where she had previously lived with her husband Chan Sam, so that their third child, the expected son, will be born Canadian. Chan Sam goes back to Canada with her, but they leave their two young daughters in the village to be raised by Chan Sam's primary wife, Huangbo (1). (Huangbo had "replaced" Chan Sam's first wife, who passed away in 1917 [20].) To the parents' disappointment, the "predicted son who came to Canada in the womb" was a girl (1–2). Years later, Chan Sam returns to China see Huangbo and the older children, but May-ying insists that he leave their third child, Hing, with her. In exchange for Hing's presence, May-ying agrees to support Chan Sam's decision to "raise a roof over the family" while in China (1–2). These two trips set the course of May-ying and Hing, who will grow up, rechristen herself "Winnie," and become the author's mother. The couple's decisions mean that Winnie will be raised by her mother in the absence of her father and sisters, and that her mother's modest wages as a tea waitress in Chinatown will be used to support all six family members as well as the construction of a showy brick house in China.

Instead of opening the book with chronologically earlier scenes (such as Chan Sam's initial emigration [11], his arrangement of the match in which May-ying has no say [6–9, 22–23], or May-ying's first arrival in Canada [10]), Chong begins with two life-defining choices that she portrays as May-ying's. Thus, she establishes at the outset May-ying's agency within the severe limits that constrain her as a Chinese woman living in Canada from 1924 to 1967 (9, 228–229).

The foundational scene of the grandparents' bargain is immediately followed by a scene of second- and third-generation return in 1987, a typical roots pilgrimage. The author travels with her mother to meet her uncle Yuen, who was born to Chan Sam and Huangbo in Chang Gar Bin and whom they can identify by his distinctive birth defect: he was born with both feet bent backwards (2). As her aunt Ping and uncle Yuen proudly display the guest room of the house Chan Sam built and "pay homage" to its intended grandeur, Chong and her mother see a storeroom full of junk: through this detail, Chong foreshadows the dissonant views of the family that she seeks to set down and reconcile in her book (2). Although Chong describes Ping's gift of her mother's childhood coat as a symbol of reconciliation between the families, the book that follows will document substantial discrepancies, in experience and perspective, between the Chinese and Canadian sides of the family (2–3). In Chapter 2, I analyzed both bitter and uplifting family reunions recorded in Josephine Khu's essay collection. While Chong and her mother's visit is similarly revelatory, Chong's book paints the larger picture needed to create a sense of reconciliation from the sharply divergent family histories they encounter on that visit.

Mimicry, Racialized Gender Melancholia, and Countermemory: The Mansion at Home, the Poorhouse Abroad

The woes of Chan Sam, Leong May-ying, Winnie, and her siblings are not solely attributable to their race: rather, race, class, and gender are the warp, woof, and weave of the cultural and economic webs that tighten about them as they grow older. Thus, it might seem arbitrary to assess their hardships as strictly *racial* melancholia, but when we acknowledge the intersectionality of their identities and their woes, David L. Eng and Shinhee Han's theory in "A Dialogue on Racial Melancholia" seems particularly resonant with the structure of feeling attributed to Chong's grandparents and mother in these ways:

1. "A Dialogue" raises the question of what losses, real and symbolic, were suffered by Chan Sam, May-ying, Winnie, and their Chinese

Canadian community. These losses did not begin in Canada but were rooted in the desperate conditions of the Pearl River Delta.

2. For Sigmund Freud, melancholia is characterized by the patient's inability "consciously [to] perceive what he has lost." Even if he knows "*whom* he has lost," he may not know "*what* he has lost in him"; this unawareness is combined with an unwillingness to renounce the beloved lost object (a person or an ideal), which is ultimately addressed by psychologically incorporating that object within the mourner's own ego ("Mourning and Melancholia" 245, qtd. in Eng and Han, "Dialogue" 346). According to Eng and Han, the mourner's ambivalent attachment to the lost object can be productive for racial minority subjects, as it can be the foundation of a healthy political imperative to remember the object, whether a person or an ideal, and thus sustain a submerged history needed for survival (363–366). The theory draws attention to the fact that Chan Sam, May-ying, and Winnie were not granted any community or public discourse legitimating their mourning of their losses: prior to Chong's research, their suffering was acknowledged only by family members responding to their personal laments.

3. Applying Homi Bhabha's trope of mimicry to the model-minority stereotype, and to Chan Sam's and May-ying's generation, suggests that Chan Sam and May-ying responded to racial exclusion and poverty not by mimicking *white success* but either by mimicking or by melancholically disavowing *Confucian standards particular to overseas Chinese*. Recognizing that immigrant Chinese did not directly internalize white standards of conduct and culture in the United States and Canada but created their own models for gender identity and success, I argue that the definitions of mimicry and racial melancholia set forth by Bhabha, Eng, and Han understate the capacity of Asian American immigrants (and by extension other minority groups) to adapt and sustain their own ideals. Both Chan Sam and May-ying mourn and express melancholic attachments to their own community's gender ideals; I call their ambivalent attachments "racialized gender melancholia."[2]

4. Adapting Eng and Han's theory, I find that Chong's treatment of her mother's memories illustrates how racialized gender melancholia can be passed on from the first to the second generation as well as how it can also be resisted and contained, both rhetorically and in fact.

5. Finally, I find that, since part of racial melancholia is the mourner's inability to name what has been lost, Chong's writing serves as an

act of countermemory that addresses her foremothers' losses, their melancholia, and their solutions, addressing Eng and Han's imperative of melancholic resistance.

As noted in Chapter 1, Anne Anlin Cheng has written that racial melancholia in the United States arises from a social structure paradoxically defined both by the historical exclusion of minorities and by their inclusion in the democratic ideal. For the white majority, the result is an ambivalent attachment to a ghostly minority presence whose exclusion helps to define the norm, a presence Toni Morrison has called "the ghost in the machine" of American culture (Morrison, "Unspeakable" 11, qtd. in Cheng, "Melancholy" 51). For the "abjected" minority, which "hover[s] on the edges of the dominant progressive narrative as objects at once ungrieved and unrelinquished," the contradictory task of identifying with the inclusive ideal of America while also negotiating with exclusionary realities produces a social dis-ease that Cheng and other theorists have described as "racial melancholia" (Cheng, "Melancholy" 49–51). Cheng's argument, somewhat simplified, is that racial melancholia in the United States is induced by living in the shadow of an ideal of white success and inclusion that is actually unattainable. Chan Sam's family members suffer from a similar, Canadian specter of white success, starting with his father, whose successful sojourn in California began before the passage of the Chinese exclusion laws in 1882. In the year of Chan Sam's birth (1888), Congress revoked Chinese immigrants' certificates of return, so that his father, who was in China at the time, lost the option of returning to America. Unable to follow his father's footsteps to the United States, Chan Sam was one of thousands of Chinese who sought their fortunes in Canada instead, only to encounter racial stereotypes; discrimination in housing, employment, and education; and Canada's own Chinese Immigration Act, which barred most Chinese from entering Canada and charged newly arrived Chinese a hefty $500 head tax (Chong, *Concubine's Children* 14–15, 18). Decades later, Winnie would find her entry into white, middle-class security blocked by her parents' poverty and poor health, which forced her to give up her dream of college and drop out of high school and then business college, first to assist her godmother in her restaurant business and then to support her mother and her adopted younger brother, Gok-leng (Leonard). When she sought certification as a psychiatric nurse, she would be the first Chinese in the program and the only Chinese in her cohort. Her white supervisor would haze her, initially by extending her probation beyond the norm and later by assigning her to work with violent patients just when she needed to recover from surgery.

Moreover, the Chans were also undone by another shadow, the diasporic ideal of sending home wealth from "Gold Mountain" to buy land, build a house, and generally support the family and village at home. The modern legacy of this ideal, most typically passed down in villages along China's Pearl River Delta in Guangdong Province, has been discussed by historian Madeline Hsu (*Dreaming*) and anthropologist Andrea Louie (*Chineseness*), and it animates Lisa See's memoir. In the nineteenth century, Chan Sam's own father had not only supported his family but also raised funds from abroad to help build an ancestral hall at home (Chong, *Concubine's Children* 12–13). Chong documents how, in the early twentieth century, Chan Sam was unable to realize this ideal both because of his lack of business sense (83–84) and because the conditions in Canada and China became so harsh. In China, the fallen Qing Dynasty was succeeded by civil wars, corrupt landlords, and Japanese invasion in the period from 1911 to 1949, and by land reform hostile to landowning peasants such as Chan Sam in the 1950s. A distinguished economist who served on Canadian prime minister Justin Trudeau's Council of Economic Advisors, Chong writes precisely about the felt effects of economic fluctuations in China, discriminatory pay in Canada, and the contracting Canadian economy on Chinatown businesses and their employees, particularly during the Great Depression. She is sometimes amazingly specific about macroeconomic conditions in both Canada and China. Speaking of Depression-era Canada, she introduces her analysis with the inauspicious metaphor "The Chinese sank like stones to the bottom of the labor pool," remarking that 80 percent of Vancouver's thirteen thousand Chinatown residents were unemployed (49). She explains how, from 1930 to 1933, the U.S. currency devaluation and silver price manipulation resulted in economic collapses in the urban economy of China and drastic declines in the sojourners' remittances (60). To set the scene for Chan Sam's homebuilding in 1935–1937, she notes the Chinese villagers' "gloom" during the worldwide Depression: many were defaulting on their loans because they had to pay 30–40 percent interest per year. She notes that the price of high-grade rice fell below the level needed for peasant villagers to pay their rent and the rapidly proliferating taxes, which she lists (69). As Chan Sam's neighbors lost their rice seedlings, pigs, furniture, and tools, a few even sold their unmarried daughters to retain their precious land.

Yet Chong asserts that the villagers all viewed Chan Sam's grand construction plans with pride and approval:

> Among the men of Chan Sam's time, not one in ten who'd gone abroad had managed to send enough to keep their families intact and alive; most returned broken and became a charge upon those left behind. That was not Chan Sam's way, said the villagers of Chang Gar Bin. He had earned face by having the good moral character to worry and care for the family left behind. (70)

Typically for Chong, the passage works on several levels. The economic facts of soaring interest and proliferating taxes lead to the loss of objects, livestock, daughters—and land. Over 90 percent of the sojourners of Chan Sam's generation have failed to support themselves and their families. In the face of this misery—spelled out in all its macroeconomic glory—the narrator seemingly withholds judgment and asserts that the villagers all reveled in Chan Sam's success. However, by introducing the construction chapter this way and then detailing how Chan Sam drove up the cost of the family house while May-ying entered financial jeopardy to meet his monetary demands, Chong invites the reader to judge Chan Sam more harshly and to wonder who exactly was voicing the final, celebratory sentence just quoted. Moreover, Chong suggests that the prestigious house symbolically compensated for Sam Chan's actual business failures. Begun before he and Huangbo conceived his only son and completed after the boy Yuen's birth, the house and its adjoining lands represented the "peasant's dream of soil underfoot and tiles overhead" (75). Contrary to the narrator's praise, Chong's distinctive interleaving of precise Depression-era economic patterns with local research tacitly indicts Chan Sam's willful, costly naiveté.[3] Although the condition of using a transnational family situation to combat economic hardship goes beyond the strict definition of racial melancholia, Chan Sam's unrealistic vision of success, culturally inherited within a specific moment in the global economy, weighed heavily on May-ying as she worked longer hours, took out loans, gambled, and called in favors to meet Chan Sam's demands for payments.

Looking at the situation another way, readers could speculate that Chan Sam was melancholically attached to the dream of "soil underfoot and tiles overhead" in China; refusing to be dissuaded from reclaiming this "lost object" by mere economic realities, he passed from China to Canada in pursuit of the money for this dream. As decades passed and success and domesticity eluded him in Canada, he held even more tightly to his dream. He counteracted the gloomy conditions on both sides of the ocean in the traditional Confucian fashion, by building a grand house and fathering a son, both of which represented his hopes for the future. Out of pride, he kept his financial failures secret and never acknowledged his debt to his concubine (188–189). Yet, because of his son's unusual birth defect—born with his feet bent backwards—and the stigma of owning property under Communism, Chan Sam died without either personal wealth and comfort in Canada or the knowledge that, in his lifetime, he had successfully provided for the future of his family in China (87). (Starting in 1950, the Communists confiscated most of his land and barred his son from further schooling [184–189].) The lost object, the dream of a secure, prestigious life in his village, eluded and haunted him to the end, when he died as a pauper in Canada. Melancholically, he could neither relinquish this dream nor share his mourning with his Canadian family or his fellow villagers. He deepest fears and laments were restricted to his letters to a faraway wife and son.

May-ying also had much to mourn when she arrived in Canada. Sold into service at age four, she had lost her family and childhood. Resold at seventeen as a concubine to Chan Sam, she lost her home country, her honor, and her dreams of married life all at once (6–7). Entering Canada with false papers to evade Canada's strict anti-Chinese exclusion laws, claiming to be the Canadian-born daughter of a Chinese stranger, and living without a formal marriage certificate, she became a "paper daughter" living under a stranger's name as well (10, 22). Scholars of racial melancholia point to the elusiveness of assimilation, but for sojourners like May-ying and Chan Sam, the dream of assimilation into the Canadian middle class was so remote as to be almost irrelevant. Instead, May-ying sought to substitute for a proper marriage the closest things she could seek: respectability, as a tea waitress and a mother in Canada, and the hope of reunion with her first two children and inclusion in Chan Sam's household in China. By the time she made her second journey to Chang Gar Bin, however, one daughter had died and the other had grown attached to her rival, Chan Sam's wife Huangbo. She herself was incompatible with Chan Sam and Huangbo, bored and depressed by life in their village. To her credit, May-ying got herself and her unborn third child back to Canada just in time for Winnie to be born there, establishing the baby as a legal Canadian citizen. But the record of Winnie's lonely childhood, to which I return below, is also the record of May-ying's moral and physical collapse, as she lost the hope of a home and family in China and fruitlessly searched for another aim or object in Canada.

Chong is particularly incisive in tracing the effect of Chan Sam's financial demands on May-ying's life and her future during the building of the house. In order to satisfy Chan Sam's demands, keep him in China, and retain her freedom from his domination, she not only worked long hours at the teahouse (typically nine-hour shifts, six or seven days a week [27]) but also sold lottery tickets on commission, borrowed from friends, gambled, and occasionally "weakened" and gave in to the sexual demands of her admirers, who gave her financial gifts or loans to assist her (79–84). May-ying's psychological transition, as she gave up on ever living with Chan Sam but also gave up most of her earnings and her potential to establish financial stability or security for herself in the future, could be deemed melancholic. Chong asks readers to see May-ying's settling into the common pastimes of her class—gambling and drinking—as a response to the impossible standard for female Confucian virtue that pressed down on her, which she could neither fulfill nor renounce (79). May-ying was unable to mourn her losses or even to recognize what she was really losing: both her financial future and the future love and respect of her remaining daughter. The jaunty earrings and jade pendant May-ying inherited from her mother, which she repeatedly pawned and redeemed and which Winnie ultimately inherited, were emblems of the lost object she could neither attain nor relinquish: the cherished hope that her femininity, wit, intellectual gifts, and endless labor could bring about a true home and family (128–129, 232–233).

In "A Dialogue on Racial Melancholia," Eng and Han explore racial melancholia as an outcome, in the North American context, of postcolonial theorist Homi Bhabha's concept of colonial mimicry, which "describes the ways in which a colonial regime impels the colonized subject to mimic Western ideals of whiteness" (Eng and Han 349). In Bhabha's words, "Colonial mimicry is the desire for a reformed, recognizable Other, as *a subject of a difference that is almost the same, but not quite . . . [a]lmost the same, but not white*" (Bhabha 126, 130, qtd. in Eng and Han, "Dialogue" 349, emphasis Bhabha's). Eng and Han compare the ambivalent social demand of colonialism with Americans' ambivalence toward minority assimilation, specifically focusing on American praise of the model-minority stereotype for Asian Americans. "Asian Americans," the authors write, "are forced to mimic the model minority stereotype of economic success in order to be recognized by mainstream society—in order *to be* at all"; yet because the stereotype is limited to economic achievement, conforming to it only "comes to mask [Asian Americans'] lack of political and cultural presentation" (350). Of course, the model-minority ideal arose in the 1960s, long after Chan Sam's time. As both See and Chong show, the double bind associated with model-minority success resonated only partially for early sojourners like Fong See and Chan Sam: regardless of their economic success or actual conduct, their humanity was hardly recognized by the North American laws under which they lived (See 41–56; Chong *Concubine's Children* 14–15). Nor does the model of colonial mimicry exactly fit for the early Chinese North Americans: the peasant and merchant sojourners of Fong See's and Chong Sam's generations were not expected by whites to be like them or to assimilate; rather, U.S. and Canadian legislation insisted that Chinese were neither white nor assimilable. Eventually, as discussed in Chapter 3, even the exceptionally ambitious Fong See recognized this, invested in his home village, and replaced his mixed-race family with a Chinese one. In short, the early Chinese immigrants typically responded to their blatant exclusion in North America by developing a Confucian ideal of sojourning abroad to support a family at home. Their resulting practice in North America of relying on family, clan, and community associations rather than trusting U.S. or Canadian laws or officials to aid or protect them planted the seeds of the model-minority stereotype.

Reflecting these aspirations, Chan Sam's house in Chang Gar Bin exemplified a kind of secondary mimicry, as the model of the overseas Chinese businessman displaced any desire to emulate whites. Unable to afford the walled compound of a very rich Chinese man, or the large house of a returning merchant, Chan Sam instead modeled his smaller house after his observation that the houses of other, wealthier returnees incorporated Western architectural touches such as balustrades, porticos, balconies, high ceilings, glass windows with wrought-iron gratings, and extra stories (Chong, *Concubine's Children* 73–74). While his home did contain traditional Chinese ornamentation, Chan Sam also commissioned special murals to evoke Gold Mountain connections and an idyll of American luxury that he had not actually experienced. In addition to landscapes of the sojourner's first sights upon arriving in San Francisco (tacitly commemorating his father's journey there) and in Vancouver, he ordered a mural depicting a couple in an open convertible roadster driving along a palm-tree-lined boulevard past a coral-colored mansion (86). He supplemented his design by importing Western furniture and knick-knacks such as clocks. These Western touches were his way of distinguishing his house and himself from the rest of the village, even though he could neither assimilate in Canada nor achieve the kinds of success attained by merchants like Fong See or his own father before him. In building his two-story house, he evoked the colonial architecture of earlier, richer returnees in a form of secondary mimicry that falsely proclaimed his success—not as a Canadian but as an overseas Chinese.

Similarly, Chong portrays May-ying as performing two kinds of mimicry and experiencing racialized gender melancholia. To circumvent the laws against bringing Chinese women into Canada, Chan Sam purchased and sent to May-ying the false papers of a dead Chinese Canadian woman, whose identity she assumed upon entry (22). Her marriage to Chan Sam may never have been formalized, for among married Chinese men bringing concubines to Canada, "few saw the need" to apply for a Western marriage certificate (22). Even May-ying's death was recorded under her false name (264). Thus, May-ying was "almost the same" as a Canadian citizen, but only nominally (Bhabha 89). Actually, she was a paper daughter with few rights or privileges, who had to elude detection by avoiding contact with Canadian officials whenever possible Thus, May-ying assumed the spectral presence in the public imagination that Cheng assigned to Asian American and other minority subjects in her discussion of racial melancholia (Cheng, "Melancholy" 50–51). Chong does not suggest that May-ying ever expected to assimilate culturally or legally as a middle-class Canadian, or that she consciously mourned that she could not do so. Rather, May-ying seemed to mourn her loss of Chinese identity and her inability to gain her community's recognition as a proper Confucian wife and mother (29), an impossible ideal to which she was melancholically attached. For years she mimicked Confucian ideals of female virtue by working hard, refraining from drinking and gambling, fending off other men, giving most of her money to Chan Sam to support the family, allowing her first two daughters to be raised by Huangbo in China, and raising Winnie in Canada with the strictness she might have endured as a child servant, the strictness that she imagined would constitute good parenting. However, since she herself had lost her family at four and been raised as a servant, and because she was a tea waitress and single mother, she was unable to provide the material care, financial stability, love, and flexibility of an ideal mother. Because she was a concubine, her needs and desires were not recognized, her children and earnings were expropriated for a distant household, and her local community expected her to fail as a wife and mother (29). Like a colonial discourse, the community seemingly imposed on May-ying the demand for perfect gender performance (diligence, frugality, chastity, sacrifice, and submission) combined with a refusal to credit her for her contributions. To paraphrase Bhabha, she was *almost the same, but not a wife.*

In rebellion, she imitated the independence of the Chinese men around her. She got her own jobs, had her own affairs, smoked, drank, gambled, and pursued a man more to her liking, the suave gambler Chow Guen. Yet her mimicry of his masculine individualism, embodied in the tailored pantsuit she ordered and enjoyed wearing, was also undermined by her continued bonds to Chan Sam and her children, for whose sake she continued to turn her earnings over to Chan Sam (123–124). By the terms of her own community, then, she could gain full recognition neither as a woman nor as a man. I interpret her conduct, therefore, as an expression of racialized gender melancholia.

Eng and Han discuss several ways in which immigrants may transmit their sense of loss to their children. If the immigrants cannot mourn their losses and resolve them in the process of assimilation, their melancholia can be transferred to the second generation. Yet the hope of assimilation (the replacement object of desire) can also be transferred. If this occurs, the members of the second generation will replicate their parents' negotiation between mourning (acknowledging their losses) and melancholia (being unable to resolve their losses through assimilation). In such cases, they suggest, the offspring may internalize the emotions, the voices, or even the traumatic memories of their parents ("Dialogue" 352–355). Whereas Freud suggests that melancholics internalize the lost object, making it part of their own psyches, Eng and Han caution against defining racial melancholia strictly as an "intrapsychic" phenomenon, since they observe that dejected Asian American students are processing issues that have a significant *political* dimension (355). To address the root causes of these students' problems, they argue, a more politically inclusive public sphere is needed in which the *causes* of immigrant mourning and racial melancholia can be publicly acknowledged (355–356).

As the third child of Chan Sam and May-ying, Winnie inherited an intensely conflicted set of attachments and ideals from her parents. Arriving a few years before the passage of Canada's exclusion laws in 1923, Chan Sam lived most of his life as an alien resident ineligible for naturalization, tolerated but relegated to the worst jobs and housing and unable to bring his Chinese family members to live with him. He responded by focusing on the Confucian ideal of "soil underfoot and tiles overhead," sending his two first daughters, his concubine's earnings, and his own love home to Chang Gar Bin. Only in 1947 was he able and willing to apply for naturalization (154). By then, Winnie was seventeen and had nearly completed her childhood, with little guidance from him about how to survive or envision her future in Canada. Similarly, May-ying's marginal position as a paper daughter and the concubine of a sojourner led her at first, from her arrival in Canada in 1924 until Winnie's birth in 1930, to follow Chinese custom and focus on a future in China. From 1930 to about 1939, May-ying lived mostly apart from Chan Sam but still gave him most of her wages, which he used to support the family, buy land, and build in Chang Gar Bin. Around 1939, she also stopped funding Chan Sam, both because she fell for Chow Guen, the gambler, and because it became difficult to send money to China during and after World War II. Though May-ying's wages no longer went primarily to China, her new vision focused on the dream of creating a home in Canada with Chow Guen and raising Leonard, the adopted son who would provide security for her future in Canada. With her father mostly absent and her mother working most evenings, Winnie spent her childhood in rented rooms, teahouses, and gambling houses, as well as many evenings at the Chinese opera. Her adolescence was more of the same except that her mother left her in boarding houses for three years, she had to help raise Leonard, and she began to worry about supporting the three of them.

In short, Winnie inherited severally racially melancholic conditions from her parents: as Chinese in Canada, they occupied a liminal position in the Canadian culture and economy; in compensation, they sought to live out Confucian norms for masculine success and female virtue among the overseas Chinese, but they could neither do so nor relinquish those norms in time to provide substantial support or guidance to Winnie and her adopted brother. In addition, May-ying passed on unattainable ideals of Chinese womanhood to Winnie, whom she resented for not being a son (90–91) and then raised with a combination of neglect and exaggerated strictness, leaving her with no clear educational path and with unrealistic ideas about how she should meet boys and look for a husband. As the first native Canadian in her family, Winnie was encouraged to study hard and look beyond Chinatown for her livelihood, but the mixed messages she received in the course of her education were also conducive to racial melancholia: she had to reconcile the imperative to study hard and sacrifice for the family with the reality that in Canada, her community had been unable to transform education into opportunity. Despite her excellent grades, she gave up the dream of college for want of financial support, she dropped out of high school to prepare to support her family, she dropped out of her business certificate program to help her godmother resolve an employment crisis, and she faced overt racial discrimination in training to become a psychiatric nurse (161–164, 177). In short, the dream of inclusion in the middle class seemed all but unattainable, both because of her race and because of the race-related poverty and instability of her parents. Chong repeatedly records how these conditions caused her mother to express dejection later in life. For instance, Chong mentions that her mother's family memories generally ended in tears and the motto "I had no one," and she describes her mother's involuntary weeping whenever she saw Chan Sam's naturalization photo. Unknown to Winnie, it was taken in 1947: the year she dropped out of tenth grade, giving up her dream of college, to prepare for May-ying's imminent collapse and the need to support her family (154, 161–164, 219, 229). Such signs of lingering sadness over losses she could not explain are expressions of Winnie's experience of racial melancholia, induced by all the contradictions of being ostensibly included but practically excluded from her society's norms, for complex reasons rooted in her intersectional identity as a Chinese Canadian woman of working-class background.

To give a balanced account of this topic, however, one must recall Chong's own assertion that ultimately she did not see the Chinese in Canada as "victims of history"; her self-claimed task was to publicly acknowledge her mother's losses and resolve them through her writing. This was a deliberate act of countermemory, which draws on "the particular and the specific" and builds toward a larger story, looking for "hidden histories" that then challenge existing histories (Chong, Keynote; Lipsitz 212–213, qtd. in Davis, *Relative Histories* 16). (Chong's book also exemplifies Marianne Hirsch's concept of postmemory, in the sense that Chong is generationally removed yet personally invested in the events she describes, and the narrative is mediated by her "imaginative investment and creation" [Hirsch, *Family* 22]. However, Chong makes fewer flights of fancy than either See or Chai and Chai, so I focus on Chong's countermemorial intent to challenge existing histories.) On one hand, Chong seeks to soften her mother's account of herself as a person without family by recreating a largely forgotten world in which Chan Sam and Mayying were deeply connected to each other, to her, and to the family members in China. However flawed, both of Chong's grandparents are depicted not merely as sickly and impoverished elders but also as vital human beings doing their best to live up to the standards of their community in impossible conditions. On the other hand, Chong seeks to correct her Chinese relatives' one-sided devotion to her grandfather at the expense of her grandmother, whom they know only as the unreasonable concubine who gambled, drank, and made their grandfather miserable. Finally, by telling her mother's own story, Chong grants it a compassionate hearing and places it at the center of a world that would otherwise be forgotten.

In frankly setting forth all that went wrong, Chong balances her grandparents' personal shortcomings with a full account of their suffering and their disadvantages, as well as their positive traits and their moments of agency. She recounts May-ying's beauty, wit, social intelligence, and diligence before she became an alcoholic; Chan Sam's and May-ying's grief at their second daughter's death; the brief periods of domestic harmony when the family ate suppers at home together, sometimes including Chow Guen; and Chan Sam's return to give legal approval for Winnie's emergency surgery and her engagement to John Chong (*Concubine's Children* 179). Continuing to her mother's generation, Chong notes the successes of her mother and uncle: she recalls how Winnie took responsibility for Leonard and how he was able to complete the nurse's training she had not; Leonard also became engaged to another Asian American, a nurse, despite his difficult childhood.

Most importantly, Chong sets a narrative boundary that challenges my critical imposition of the model of racial melancholia on her family's story. As May-ying's fortunes declined and Winnie, still a teenager, encountered her supervisor's opposition at the psychiatric hospital, Chong's future father, John Chong, began to court Winnie and proposed marriage. This offered another path into adulthood for Winnie, one that enabled her to quit her hospital job and marry John in 1950 (180). Lured north when John got a steady federal job as a radio operator in the airport town of Prince George, the young couple left Vancouver and their troublesome in-laws and made a new beginning on Christmas Eve, 1958, which Chong describes as an idyllic contrast to her mother's childhood in a series of contrasting images:

> Mother grew up within the walls of rooming houses, smoke-filled mah-jongg parlors and dank alleyways. My siblings and I had country lanes to ride our bicycles on, snowbanks piled like mountain ranges to frolic in, a backyard that Father and Mother flooded in winter for us to skate on. Mother had no brothers or sisters to play with; we four were inseparable. She was punished if she played too much; we were allowed to play to our hearts' content. (218)

Details like the below-thirty-degree weather, the airport noise, and the initial anti-Chinese teasing, which soon subsided, are subordinated to the celebration of the family's entry, at last, into the Canadian middle class, a traditional endpoint for assimilation narratives.

However, Chong continues beyond this point in two ways. As she relates additional events pertaining to racial discrimination as well as instances of resistance and success, such as the family's progress, legal changes in Canada, and the perennially broken pipe in Vancouver's Chinatown (234–235), the book suggests that assimilation remained an ongoing practice. In addition, she relates how, in the five years after her family moved to Prince George, she began to ask her mother for stories about her life in Chinatown and to try to understand her own identity as a Chinese Canadian, posing questions that would culminate decades later in her publication of *The Concubine's Children*. Chong ends her book with the same statement of purpose she later brought to her conference talk, first evoking her collaboration with her mother to seek out and understand Winnie's past and then concluding with a highly filial visit to her grandparents' graves:

> I owed it to Mother, and to Chan Sam and May-ying, to find the good among the bad, and pride among the shame of their past. The lost history that Mother and I recovered gave the past new meaning, perhaps enough to be a compass to provide some bearings when her grandchildren chart their own course....
>
> If they could hear from the grave, I would tell my grandfather and my grandmother that I have seen, for their dead eyes, the fruits of their labors. I would tell them they can now close their eyes in sleep. (266)

In Chong's book, her mother's luck changed when Winnie married and left Vancouver, putting geographic distance between herself and her unpredictable parents. The move enabled Winnie and John to complete their task of assimilation, handing on to Denise and her siblings the possibility of true Canadian citizenship and belonging—further strengthened by the passage of the new immigration laws in 1967 (234). With the new object of assimilation within reach, Winnie could have bidden farewell to the state of suspended belonging that characterizes racial melancholia. However, her lingering sadness provides one impetus for Chong's strenuous efforts to recreate the past. For, as Eng and Han relate, racial melancholia exists in the "productive gap" wherein Asian Americans negotiate daily with issues such as "immigration, assimilation, and racialization; mimicry, ambivalence, and the stereotype; sacrifice, loss, and reinstatement" ("Dialogue" 364). For them the racial melancholic's refusal to "get over" loss may be interpreted as a productive expression of loyal remembrance, one that can serve to counter social threats to the minority self and community (365). Thus readers can fairly interpret Denise Chong's first book as *both* an act of countermemory (designed to memorialize her ancestors, set their record straight, and reconnect her mother symbolically to her family) *and* an expression of racial melancholia, defined not as personal or familial pathology but as the structure of feeling captured by Chong's literary evocation and tribute to her parents' and grandparents' struggles to survive and claim places in China and Canada.

5

Working through Diasporic Melancholia

Winberg and May-lee Chai's The Girl from Purple Mountain

> I wiped my eyes and looked in the mirror. I was surprised at what I saw. I was strong. I was pure. I had genuine thoughts inside that no one could see, that no one could ever take away from me. . . .
> I made a promise to myself: I would always remember my parents' wishes, but I would never forget myself.
> —Amy Tan, *The Joy Luck Club*, 58

> The last time we argued, we were writing a book together, a book about my grandmother. He had envisioned it as heroic, triumphant, how Nai-nai had saved the family during World War II in China; but I added conflict, the family fights, the bitterness that lingered long after the war had ended, all the elements that I had been taught in college make literature great, the things that make us human. My father couldn't fathom what I was trying to do. "You're a negative person," he concluded.
> My father had been raised to believe in the fine art of denial.
> —May-lee Chai, *Hapa Girl*, 158

Chinese Modernity, Diasporic Melancholia, and Filial Mourning

LIKE THE TEXTS of Josephine Khu, Lisa See, and Denise Chong, *The Girl from Purple Mountain: Love, Honor, War, and One Family's Journey from China to America* depicts the return of its Chinese American authors—May-lee Chai and her immigrant father, Winberg Chai—to China in a search for answers about an earlier generation. Unlike See's and Chong's ancestors, May-lee's grandparents, Ruth (Tsao Mei-en) Chai and Charles (Chu) Chai, were distinguished by their academic achievements. Charles received a Boxer Indemnity Scholarship to study in America and earned a bachelor's degree at Stanford and a law degree at Northwestern University (30–31, 56, 69, 70,

73).[1] Ruth was part of the first generation of women to be permitted to attend college in China, becoming in 1920 one of the first eight women to attend the National Central University in Nanjing (Chai and Chai, *Girl* 37). After a brief stint as a teacher, she also won a scholarship to study at Wittenberg College in Ohio. The couple married in Ohio—the first Chinese couple ever to wed in Springfield, Ohio—and returned to China to start their family and to help modernize China. The book can be described as having multiple lines of narration: Ruth seeks to instill in her son Winberg a heroic family story about her efforts to become a modern woman and to create and preserve a modern family in a transitional period of Chinese history; Winberg must move beyond his mother's wishes and his own childhood memories in order to acknowledge his parents' flaws and errors, convey their full humanity, and, I assert, to accept his own fallibility; and May-lee, the couple's granddaughter, researches her family's past with the help of her father, partly to understand her grandparents' lives and her grandmother's choice to be buried apart from her family but also to understand more deeply her own origins. In a reversal of gender norms, the authors subordinate the story of Charles's checkered yet illustrious wartime career in the Republic of China (ROC) to the story of his marriage to Ruth. However, Charles's professional career links readers to a crucial subtext of the family stories: the failures of the Kuomintang-led ROC and the loss of the Chais' ideal of modern China.

In *Economic Citizens: A Narrative of Asian American Visibility*, literary critic Christine So uses *The Girl from Purple Mountain*, along with Adeline Yen Mah's *Falling Leaves: The Memoir of an Unwanted Chinese Daughter* (1997) and Pang-Mei Natasha Chang's *Bound Feet and Western Dress: A Memoir* (1996) to discuss what Sau-ling Cynthia Wong has called the "Gone with the Wind" genre of women's family history ("Sugar" 200, qtd. in So 161n1). Such works trace the trajectory of a modern Chinese woman against the background of China's twentieth-century upheaval, presenting the woman as a modernizing figure whose efforts to preserve her family are emblematic of the nation's efforts to claim modernity. So effectively argues that the heroines of these texts are liminal figures—crossing and reconciling symbolic divisions between East and West, tradition and modernity—and that their claims to personal merit and heroism are crystallized in the texts' tracing of the women's capacity to accumulate capital, which serves the welfare both of their families and of their nation, China (So 126–130, 155–156).

In *Relative Histories: Mediating History in Asian American Family Memoirs*, literary critic Rocío Davis gives a compelling account of May-lee and Winberg Chai's writing process as a work of countermemory and postmemory: as the authors use emotional engagement and imagination to augment family stories and research, they tell a tale that complicates readers' understanding of the Republican era in China. The text is framed by a "mystery" that drives May-lee to search for clues about the character of her grandmother: why did Ruth arrange to be buried among strangers, shunning the adjacent plots she and Charles had previously purchased (Chai and Chai, *Girl* 1)? Davis speculates that May-lee provided the impetus for her father, Winberg, to move beyond his nostalgic memories of his childhood in wartime China in order to revisit the country in 1985 and 1986 and write a fuller account of her parents' struggles there: the text alternates between Winberg's chapters, which are based on his memories and family stories, and May-lee's accounts, in which she frequently supplements the gaps in her father's narrative with information about Chinese history, politics, and culture. When their sources do not suffice, these authors, like Lisa See and Denise Chong, resort to imagination. Davis insists that for the authors, "the history of China acts primarily as a vital contextualizing element against which the family story evolves and personal knowledge may be achieved" (*Relative Histories* 47). I would argue as well for a historical reading: this personal knowledge enables the authors to mourn or work through their grandparents' melancholic attachment to their Chinese ideals.

(However, unlike See and Chong, whose accounts of events they had not witnessed were historically scrupulous and restrained in tone, the Chais more freely dramatize their witnessed and inherited family stories, heightening elements of absurdity, pathos, and comedy. Their mordant humor, somewhat atypical of Chinese American family memoir but familiar in authors such as Grace Paley, Gary Shteyngart, or Frank McCourt, tempers the bitterness found in classic Chinese literature of the 1920s and 1930s [such as Lao She's *Rickshaw* and Lu Hsun's "The Diary of a Madman"] with a somewhat sweeter tone. [By comparison, contemporary immigrant writers such as Yiyun Li or Ha Jin portray China as more overtly savage than the Chais do.])

On a more historical note, Davis also points out that the story highlights "how Ruth's generation was caught between the traditional and the modern" (*Relative Histories* 47–48). At a time when literacy, college, and study abroad were still unusual for all Chinese, but especially women, Ruth's transpacific courtship by Charles was initially mediated by letter writing and the demand that Charles convert to Christianity. Then both studied in the American Midwest, where they married. After they returned to China, Charles "worked for the government, drafted the new Chinese constitution, trained army officers in Hunan province, and became the founding dean of National Chongqing University Law School." Finally, the couple immigrated to the United States, where Charles coauthored nine books about China with Winberg, his son (Davis, *Relative Histories* 47–48). Davis concludes:

> For May-lee and her father, returning to China and then writing the collaborative text become acts of healing as they revisit their family's past and acknowledge the ways in which the personal and the historical blend into a narrative for the present. The trope of countermemory, highlighted here as the juxtaposition of the remembered past and the reality of present evidence, obliges us to reframe the narratives of history attending to developing understanding of a culture and its historical memory. (53)

Whereas Davis aptly describes the authors' work of countermemory and So emphasizes how Chinese family histories position Chinese women as prototypes for the diasporic Chinese subject reconciling tradition and modernity, East and West, I would emphasize that this work of reconciliation consists in part of memorializing not only Ruth Chai's heroic contributions to the family's survival but also her melancholic attachments to lost ideals of Chinese modernity; I describe her ambivalent attachment as *diasporic melancholia*. As missionary- and American-educated elites, both Ruth and Charles belonged to a generation that hoped to make China modern and democratic, but Ruth had the additional burden of seeking gender equality (or at least recognition and agency) for herself within her own and Charles's families. Davis notes that Chinese American literature has "arguably produced the most thematically unified body of fictional and auto/biographic writing in Asian American literature," rendering "the Communist takeover of China and the Cultural Revolution" as "the defining experience of twentieth-century [Chinese] history for Americans and Asian Americans, in a manner similar to the way the Holocaust may be considered the defining experience of modern Jewish history" (*Relative Histories* 34). To her useful insight, I add that "Gone with the Wind" authors of female-centered Chinese family memoirs, such as Adeline Yen Mah, Pang-Mei Natasha Chang, and the Chais, also capture the vicissitudes and failures of the Republican era (1911–1949), including the Japanese invasion of the mainland, without which the narrative of Chinese American origin and identity is incomplete. Davis succinctly describes this era as characterized by the government's failure as a result of "internal divisions, the lack of democratic consciousness of most parts of the ruling class, and external pressure from the Japanese forces" (32). Also pivotal is the May Fourth Movement, which symbolizes Chinese intellectuals' turn toward a Western-inflected modernity, including the adoption of "Western and artistic forms," the use of modern rather than classical Chinese, radical questioning and rejection of Chinese traditions and ways of thought, and the embrace of Western individualism (34–35). Within this framework, these texts prominently register the effects of so much change and instability on elite Chinese women, who had to support tradition, embrace modernity, and negotiate their own places in the new order. By telling stories of this era through contemporary voices, the intergenerational "Gone with the Wind" texts register structures of feeling specific to this long transitional period. In *The Girl from Purple Mountain,* the work of negotiating gender and modernity (politically, materially, and culturally) is the larger subject of the personal story Ruth seeks to transmit to her sons. Whereas Davis emphasizes the Chais' narration as a performance of healing and reconciliation through countermemory, I would also describe it as a form of *trauerarbeit*: mourning or working through historical losses, which in this text are coded as personal ones.[2]

I have argued that the grandparents of Denise Chong strove for unattainable, gendered ideals, with Chan Sam aspiring to be recognized in his home village as a successful Gold Mountain sojourner and May-ying aspiring to be a good Confucian wife; that they passed on their melancholic longings to their children, particularly their Canadian daughter, Winnie; and that her mother's melancholia drove Chong to write a book in which she supplemented extensive research with sympathetic and imaginative engagement with a past she could not experience directly, performing both countermemory and postmemory. In the same way, Ruth Chai has passed her melancholic attachments and aspirations to Winberg and May-lee, who undertake in this book to tell her story as a means of memory, reconciliation, and mourning. For his part, Winberg must reconcile his filial duty to remember and recount Ruth's achievements with the imperative urged by May-lee to develop a less idealized family narrative, inclusive of suffering, betrayal, and bitterness, to render her ancestors more fully human. In order to fulfill these conflicting demands, Winberg must mourn or get over his own memories of China, and in doing so sacrifice his memories of a happy boyhood and a grand home (Ruth's Nanjing mansion) in exchange for a sadder and harsher yet fuller and truer narrative of his own past. May-lee's task of rediscovering the events that spurred her grandmother's outbursts, narratively historicizing them, and understanding their personal significance parallels the labors of other contemporary narrators who, as I have discussed, use strategies such as language study, personal research, and countermemory to understand their ancestors. However, Ruth's unusual educational privilege and Charles's unusual placement close to the Kuomintang leadership render their story particularly revealing about two aspects of Chinese history: the difficulty of changing Chinese thinking about the roles of female education and of women themselves, and Kuomintang corruption. Thus the book also mourns—works through and accepts—the losses caused by these historical problems.

Useful as the term "racial melancholia" is, I would not attribute a minority psychology to the elder Chais (Ruth and Charles) and their generation of transnational Chinese: their fundamental self-image, in my reading, was that of Chinese citizens rather than minorities aspiring to American acceptance or colonized subjects who wanted to be white. Ruth and Charles also saw themselves as elites who returned from America to reform their own country. In their selective embrace of American values and their desire to bring their education back to China, they resembled, but were not, colonial subjects. Despite many humiliations, China had not (and has not) been fully colonized, either by any Western power or by Japan. Some scholars have called China's situation in the nineteenth century "semicolonial," but a discussion of semicolonial melancholia might lead readers to expect me to quantify the degree of colonial mimicry undertaken by the Chais or their peers of the Republican era (1911–1949).[3] Therefore, I prefer to consider Ruth and Charles as exemplars of diasporic melancholia: China and Chinese ideals are the central lost objects to which they were melancholically attached, but their ideal of China was deeply Americanized. To put it another way, Ruth and Charles were colonial subjects in a cultural sense. They belonged to a generation that sought foreign models to modernize China, and their lives were profoundly transformed by the historical presence of American missionaries in China as well the connections that enabled them to study in America and eventually to immigrate to the United States; yet their core sensibilities were Chinese. In this chapter, I argue that, as portrayed in Chai and Chai's text, Ruth and Charles's ambivalent attachment to China—expressed in family stories, cherished objects, and imperatives to remember family grievances—is best described as a diasporic version of melancholia.[4]

Filial Melancholia: Losing a Mother, Keeping a Name

To explore the intergenerational dynamics of diasporic melancholia at play in *The Girl from Purple Mountain*, I focus on the mother-son dynamic of Ruth and her son, Winberg, as depicted by her granddaughter, May-lee Chai, and Winberg himself as coauthor. Here, I must pause to note the novelistic, imaginative flourishes that both authors have added to the biographical armature of their family memoir and to acknowledge that any reading of the family story rests on the research and interpretive work they have already done in fashioning their account. For instance, the first chapter begins with the revelation, through Ruth's will, of her profound alienation from her family, expressed in her purchase of a solitary burial plot (1). The authors never discover definitively why Ruth chose to abandon the double plot intended for her and Charles, and the book never shows her actually forgiving Winberg and his father. However, Winberg ends the book with an anecdote from an earlier part of their lives that provides symbolic healing, reconciliation, and closure. Ruth and Charles, having physically carried a heavy stone sculpture of the head of Guan Yin, the Goddess of Mercy, from an auction straight to their New York apartment, work through her irritation ("You've been cheated. . . . [T]his isn't the Goddess of Mercy; it's Hell's gatekeeper") through unifying laughter and remembrance of their first impressions ("You still can't tell a lie," says Ruth, "But that's why I wanted to marry you. Because you had an honest face") (303). As a symbol of Chinese history and culture, of female forgiveness, and of family reconciliation, the head is both physically and symbolically weighty, yet the couple bears it home, and it brings them together for one last scene in the book. Even better, Winberg remembers, Ruth had insisted on sending it to him when he began his first tenure-track teaching job in California, complete with a note in her calligraphy saying, "For Winberg, Love Mother and Father" (302–303), as if providing the forgiveness (or mercy) she did not actually grant him in her death. This scene of symbolic reconciliation powerfully telegraphs the book's theme of reconciliation through the transmission of cultural memory. It is so effective that readers may forget that Winberg introduces this story with the words "Once upon a time, when they'd first come to the city" and shifts into omniscient third-person narrative to dramatize a story he has heard secondhand, imagined, and embellished (301). The stories of the lost pebble, the Nanjing house, and the Five Fatties, which I discuss below, also exemplify the authors' use of extended metaphors, wit, and elegant narration to mourn and mitigate past sufferings.

To continue the discussion of melancholia and mourning: in the Chais' book, Ruth is presented as the daughter of a late nineteenth-century protofeminist; in childhood, Ruth's mother cries so loudly and persistently that her mother (Ruth's grandmother) decides to stop binding her feet. As a result of missionary influences, Ruth's mother—identified only as Ms. Shao in the text (118)—grows up to be a student and protégé of American missionaries (14–27). With their support, Ms. Shao founds the Chinese Christian Hospital and Modern School for Girls, where Ruth, her mother's only daughter, receives a modern education, including studies of geography, mathematics, the piano, and English. The old government examination system testing rote knowledge of the Confucian classics, from which women have always been barred, is abolished in 1905, around the time of her birth; the new national examination for admission to a national university is not open to women until 1919 (Chai and Chai, *Girl* 36). Instead of the classics, Ruth memorizes the Bible, distinguishing herself at sixteen in a public competition testing and displaying her verbatim recall of Bible verses. In 1920, she becomes one of the first eight women in the country to win admission to "Nanjing's most prestigious school, National Central University" by earning extraordinary scores on the new college entrance exams (20, 32–35, 37). After graduating, she becomes a teacher and then secures a scholarship to study at Wittenberg College, Ohio, where she earns a master's degree in education in 1929 and remains for an additional year to study music. She then marries Charles Chai and moves to Evanston, Illinois, where Charles completes his law degree.

Upon their return to China, the couple receive a series of shocks, which may be read in terms of both literal mourning and diasporic melancholia. Of these, the most serious is the news that Ruth's mother has died after two years of illness and her father has remarried, to his young personal maid, without sending Ruth any news of her mother's serious illness (80). After several months of intense mourning (106–108), Ruth not only refuses to acknowledge her new stepmother but also uses her donations to influence Nanjing ministers to denounce her father's affair and remarriage, in the guise of public prayer for their souls. She moves her own family out of his guesthouse, legally blocks his attempt to sell her mother's property and disown her and her brothers, and takes her inheritance without reconciling with her father (120). Despite these victories, she never forgives her father. She is deeply disconsolate when, after the Japanese leave the country, she cannot not locate a special pebble her mother had given her as a graduation gift (59–61, 231); is moved to tears decades later when, watching *The Sound of Music*, she sees a father figure jilt his fiancée for a younger woman; and in later years fears that Charles will remarry after her death (85, 121, 267). Among Americans, who are familiar with Oedipal myths, Ruth's vendetta against her father might be deemed unfeminine but not unthinkable. But in China—where most women have historically lacked money and education, male polygamy has been tolerated, and filial piety has demanded deference, loyalty, and obedience to elders—it must have been unique.[5]

Here, it is tempting to read Ruth's story as a psychological case history. Readers can readily consider her initial reactions, particularly her rage, in terms of Freud's own observations about mourning and melancholia. In the case of melancholia, Freud interprets anger as part of the complicated, obscure psychological process by which patients negotiate a loss they are loath to accept. Unconsciously, patients may cherish *any* emotion toward the lost object because as long as they are emotionally engaged with the object, that object remains alive in their psyches. However, it can be difficult to perceive or admit that they are angry at a dead person for abandoning them, since such anger might seem both irrational and disloyal. Hence, instead of directing the full force of their rage at the beloved lost object—the person being mourned—patients may internalize that lost object and turn the anger inward, expressing that rage by denigrating themselves (Freud 244–249). Ruth's reactions are within the range of such mourning and melancholic responses, up to a point. Reading between the lines of the Chais' account from Ruth's perspective, the death of Ruth's mother (Ms. Shao) took place not only without her father's loving attendance, but also while Ruth was abroad. Who, then, was to blame for Ruth's own absence from her mother's deathbed? Was it the licentious father, the obedient servants, the craven clergy who obeyed his wishes, the selfless mother who chose not to write so that Ruth would not worry, or Ruth, who went abroad and stayed for an extra two years after finishing her master's degree, studying music, falling in love, and getting married (78, 81)? Since no one told her of her mother's critical illness, Ruth could not rationally blame herself for enjoying those few precious years of happiness, but nonetheless she was deeply stricken. Like Freud's melancholic, who "knows whom he has lost, but not what he has lost in him," Ruth could not account for her grief and anger. But unlike these melancholics, who deflect their anger from the lost object onto themselves, Ruth deflected her anger from her mother *and* herself onto her father. In Winberg's account, Ruth lingered in the hospital for three months after giving birth to him—mourning her mother intensely—then suddenly recovered her will and resolved to avenge her mother's death. Accounting for Ruth's undocumented recovery from grief with literary aplomb, Winberg conjures up for his mother a splendid transformation sequence in which she arose, washed her face with "fresh, clear, water," viewed the mirror, and determined to replace her "dripping wet, half drowned" reflection (the prototypical image of the woman suicide) with a resilient self—"Wide awake, alert. And very much alive"—who would henceforth be dedicated to "avenging her mother's ignoble death," almost as if she were Hamlet and her father had personally poured poison into her mother's ears (107–108). (The scene evokes and contrasts with the dripping ghost of the suicide in Maxine Hong Kingston's *The Woman Warrior*, as well as Lindo Jong's empowering mirror scene in Amy Tan's novel *The Joy Luck Club* [Kingston 16, Tan 58].) However, Ruth alternated between the terrific energy and resolution she got from this self-protective rage (which she later turned against Charles's sister, father, and brother and finally against Charles and Winberg themselves) and the moments of despair that Winberg vividly remembers, such as her breakdown, after the war, when she returned to Nanjing once more and failed to recover the pebble her mother had given her:

> And although she would have witnessed beheadings, murders, executions, children sold for food and as food, elderly parents abandoned on the side of a road, babies abandoned in a blanket in a ditch, nothing would make her cry the way she did now, inexplicably and for three days, when finally she had to admit that the stone was lost forever. (61)

While Winberg situates his mother's emotional collapse in the context of the anti-Japanese war, he suggests that the stone stands for Ms. Shao and the high hopes she passed on to Ruth while she was still alive, and Ruth was hopeful and innocent. With so much loss, he implies, it is no wonder that Ruth periodically reverted to mourning, or that, for all the years of the war, she shielded herself from grief by championing her family against incursions by threatening outsiders.[6]

So far, so psychoanalytic. However, the Chais' narration suggests that Ruth's melancholia—marked by recurrent mourning and enduring anger and mistrust—was not only a personal response to a personal loss but also a structure of feeling typical for women intellectuals of her time. It is associated with the conflicting demands made on her by her modern mother and women teachers, on one hand, and by her traditional nation and other family members on the other. Ms. Shao embodied the subversive belief that, as a brilliant and accomplished student, Ruth could become the equal of her brothers; conversely, her father's unwillingness to honor her mother's memory, even while she was alive, represented deep-rooted patriarchal norms that treated women as readily fungible, so long as they provided sons. Thus Ruth, as a Chinese woman reconciling her Chinese, missionary, and American education with the social contradictions of Republican China, was doomed to mimic bicultural gender ideals that were constantly shifting, both in China and in the United States. As we will see, even the Chais' naming of Ruth's mother reflects their dissent from Confucian norms in a changing era, as well as their taking up of Ruth's abiding concern with being remembered.

In their wartime migrations, Winberg's parents take him and his brothers to pay their respects to their ancestors at the Chai family temple (in Jing Xian, Anhui Province), recently rebuilt by his uncle Huan (148). A faithful Christian, Ruth mitigates this act of "ancestor worship" by placing a small wooden cross on the altar, but she clearly impresses its significance on young Winberg's memory:

> At the altar the names of all the members of the Chai clan since the second century B.C. were recorded, some names carved on the gray stone tablets that lined the wall, others on bamboo. *Since the 1911 revolution ending the Qing dynasty, the names of wives and daughters had also been recorded, including my grandmother and my father's two younger sisters (and their husbands, and their husbands' titles) as well as my mother's name and that of my uncle Huan's wife.* (150, emphasis added)

Since the fall of the Qing and the beginning of the ROC, Winberg notes, the forward-thinking Chai family has included the names and accomplishments of their daughters and daughters-in-law in their family temple. On the next page, he recalls the special effort his uncle Huan has made to record his father's *and mother's* accomplishments, and the prominent blank space that has been left for the future accomplishments of Winberg and his brothers— only to reveal that in fact the Chai family temple would be destroyed, and its record consigned to oblivion, during the Cultural Revolution in the 1960s:

> As it turned out, nothing more would be recorded for our family. The war would scatter us all across China and then across the world, and then in the 1960s the Red Guards would come and destroy the family temple, smashing the statues and the stone steles, setting fire to the bamboo plaques and the rice-paper books recording the history of the Chai family. (151)

Here, Winberg's flash-forward from his boyhood visit conveys a sense of deep loss. The family temple is a metaphor for the ROC itself, the dream that China could adapt the DNA of its imperial history to form a democratic republic. In attacking the temple, the Red Guards symbolically sought to liberate themselves and China from both the Qing and ROC traditions. This reference to the Cultural Revolution is augmented by the shadow of apprehension about the future erasure or forgetting of the Chai family history. Such a sense of loss can hardly be distinguished from the regret that, from a Chinese historical perspective, the moment for women's inclusion in the temple records has been brief: a scant fifty years out of over two millennia of recorded history, and already over. When this and other family losses are recounted retrospectively by May-lee and Winberg, their shadow seems to underlie Ruth's anger at the time of her mother's death, and to be augmented by the fragility of women's names and stories in public history and family memory.

Even Chinese naming practices favor the erasure of Chinese women from genealogical memory. In traditional China, when men were around age twenty, or when they entered school, they received what was known as a "courtesy name" to be used by peers in lieu of their given name: this appeared in public records, while their given name was reserved for family use. Women, who often did not go to school, were more likely to receive a courtesy name when they married, but they were just as likely *not* to receive a courtesy name and to be addressed respectfully by their family title rather than their given name. Within the family, a woman might be addressed only as "Elder Sister," "Younger Sister," "Daughter-in-Law" or "Mother" (depending on the speaker's relationship to her) once married, and official papers might use only her maiden name followed by the title *"shi."* In *China from A to Z*, May-lee and

Winberg Chai note that married Chinese women use their maiden names rather than taking their husbands' surnames. The use of the title *shi* (also spelled *shee*) in lieu of given names may well be the basis for references to the "No Name Woman" in Kingston's *Woman Warrior* (1–16) and "no-name girl[s]" in See's *On Gold Mountain* (30, 72, 104), as well as historian Jonathan Spence's seemingly impersonal naming of the eponymous murder victim in his book *The Death of Woman Wang*.

The Chais, however, reject such distancing translations when it comes to their own kinswoman. In describing the scandalous advertisement Ruth and her brothers bought in the *Central Daily News* of August 18, 1833, to discourage everyone from participating in her father's attempt to sell and pocket her mother's property, Winberg quotes (or recalls) and translates the actual wording, which begins with the full names of Ruth (Tsao Mei-en) and her brothers. He then translates the names of the property, emphasizing the moral high ground claimed by the siblings on their mother's behalf, and reveals how they saw the property and their mother:

> Tsao Chou-tao, Tsao Shou-li, and Tsao Mei-en announce:
> Regarding the Nanjing properties—Envisioning Virtue Hall and Establishing Righteousness Hall—the majority belonged to our late mother, Ms. Shao, as the fruit of her lifelong labor and management. (118)

Breaking with the Confucian customs that treat a woman's labor and its fruits as the property of *her husband*, the Tsao siblings publicly announce that most of the properties are the product of their mother's "lifelong labor" and thus *her* rightful property, and they warn others from seeking to buy it while the exact division of the property is under dispute. The authors avoid calling this important figure "Woman Shao" or "No Name Shao" in English. Instead, they name Ruth's mother "Ms. Shao," using the anachronistic American title "Ms." to emphasize her autonomy from her husband (which the document asserts) and to memorialize her (in keeping with Christine So's observations) as *a woman who proved her worth by amassing capital for her family*. In this moment of countermemory they memorialize Ruth's mother, who was born in the nineteenth century, and whose life might otherwise be forgotten.

Lost Ideals

Previously, I argued that Denise Chong's grandparents were melancholically attached to two modern, transpacific versions of Confucian ideals that were not attainable but that they could and did mimic, at a high cost to themselves:

the masculine ideal of the prosperous overseas sojourner, symbolized by the building of a two-story house with Western features, and the feminine ideal of a virtuous wife and mother. Failing to attain those ideals in reality, Chan Sam and Leong May-ying passed on to Chong's mother, Winnie Chan Chong, the melancholic response to those failures, combined with the impetus to aspire to the Canadian middle class without the immediate means to overcome the family's poverty and Canadian racial discrimination. While the first and second generations of the Chan family represented versions of the ongoing difficulty of assimilation and the racially related melancholia that resulted, the third-generation author herself (Chong) created a countermemory—her book—to humanize and memorialize their stories, including failures and successes. Similarly, the Chais portray Ruth as mourning for not only her mother (Ms. Shao) but also the ideals her mother passed on to her, which are arguably more elite and Westernized than the ideals of Lisa See's and Denise Chong's merchant and working-class ancestors. Thus the Chais' new family home in Nanjing, built with the proceeds from Ruth's maternal inheritance, epitomizes both Ruth's inheritance of her mother's personal hopes and the hope of bringing American (or Western) social ideals to China. For Ruth, the salient features of such modernity were Christianity, English, women's education, and women's empowerment through such means as the reform of marriage (exemplified in her egalitarian, companionate marriage to Charles) and the ability of women to control and transmit their own earnings and property (exemplified in her negotiations with her father). For Charles, a lawyer by training, modernity also included a new legal system in which cases would be resolved impartially under the law, rather than by bribery and connections, and a new state, which would over time be defined through the writing of a new constitution and new laws. To the extent that these ideals were not realized during their years in China (1932–1949), we can view them as political lost objects whose absence haunts the story of the Chais' interpersonal struggles with family members (Chai and Chai, *Girl* 94–96, 243).

The Ruined House: "China Must Modernize"

One could read the memoir purely as a version of the triumphal family tale Winberg first envisioned (embellished by May-lee with moments of strife and failure), but the authors insist on interlacing their story with historical facts and references to the prominent people and institutions that defined their family; thus, they imply, the family's personal stories are representative of the nation's struggles to modernize. For instance, they describe Ruth's house in Nanjing as built in the image of her American college dorm, just as Charles's legal practice, constitutional drafts, and law school leadership in

China are shaped by his American legal training. (No mere imitator, Charles is not content merely to import Anglo-American legal expertise to China: for his dissertation, he and a colleague document judicial practices in Chicago's Cantonese community [Chai and Chai, *Girl* 81].) Almost as soon as the house is completed, they are forced to flee as Chiang Kai-shek gives up the wartime capital, and the house is occupied by the invading Japanese. By burying her mother's gifts—a Yixing teapot and a special Nanjing pebble—in the yard, Ruth expresses her expectation of returning to the house. When the Japanese do depart, Ruth's brother rents it to a Russian, who establishes a brothel there. Returning in 1945, Charles and his law students, armed with signs bearing nationalist slogans, evict the pimp and prostitutes (123). But after a short period of residence and repairs—during which Ruth recovers the pot but not the pebble, and has the three-day breakdown described above—she again rents the house, this time to Americans. After she and Charles flee China in 1949, they never see the house again. When Winberg and May-lee finally return in 1985, they find the house reduced from the grandeur of Winberg's memory to a dowdy brick house in a rundown neighborhood, surrounded by "tin-roofed shanties and squatters' shacks" (122–123). Seized again with a sense of deep grief and loss, Winberg cries out, "'You've ruined everything! Everything is dirt! Everything is poor! The country is poor! You've ruined China! The Communists have ruined everything!" (123). Thus the authors frame the house, designed with American influences, as an allegorical image for China's struggles with Japanese invasion, Russian exploitation, American advisors who eventually withdrew, and Communist neglect (see also Davis, *Relative Histories* 48–49). Once again, readers could interpret Winberg's grief about the house as purely personal, but bound up with loss of the idealized house is the loss of another idealized object, the political vision of China as a modern, democratic republic; this ideal is in turn bound up with the dreams Ruth receives from her mother, symbolized in the stone Ruth buries and loses in the yard and the teapot she salvages and later passes on to Winberg. The loss of these ideals, combined with the shock of returning after decades of absence, may explain why Winberg specifically blames the *Communists* for ruining not so much his parents' lives—since his family managed to reestablish itself in America—but "everything," which I take to mean China itself. (At the time of Winberg's visit in 1985, China was still recovering politically from the Cultural Revolution and had not yet become the economic powerhouse it is today; the shacks and shanties surrounding the house then reflected the nation's need to rebuild.)

It is not only Ruth's house that carries this national-allegorical weight, however. The story itself can be read as a testimony to the failure of the Kuomintang government (the ROC) to fulfill its promises of democracy, modernity, and good government through its effects on this particular family. Charles Chai's inability to apply his American legal education to the creation of a just legal practice or an American-style, modern constitutional republic—because of Kuomintang infighting and backstabbing, the Japanese invasion, civil war, and finally the Communist revolution—is translated, narratively, into a series of tragicomic ordeals as he and Ruth are alienated from relative after relative until finally, like the Kuomintang itself, they are compelled to leave China. To cast Ruth as symbolically triumphing over feudal family relations, the authors show her treating her father as if he had taken a concubine and stolen his wife's property. In depicting Ruth rejecting her in-laws' attempts to subordinate her, and Charles sending his own father packing from their home, the Chais imagine Charles defending Ruth from their efforts to impose authority over her with the argument, "China must modernize. . . . His wife could not be treated like a daughter-in-law" (131). Charles's attempt to win his first legal case on the basis of strong scholarship and legal argument rather than bribery is presented as a comic character sketch, but it nonetheless indicts the existing system as untenable; indeed, Winberg explains that the Chinese legal system was historically notorious as the excuse for Western powers to introduce extraterritoriality to Chinese soil in the nineteenth century (110–111). When Charles is recruited by a classmate to head Chiang Kai-shek's new military academy in Changsha, the capital of Hunan Province, his job is to reeducate the officers to prevent incidents of looting, rape, and theft from Chinese villages that had given the Kuomintang a bad reputation in contrast to the relatively disciplined populist ethos of the Chinese Communists. (Ever the scholar, Charles plans to address these problems by teaching Sun Yat-sen's American-inspired "Principles of the People" and Chinese and American legal theory to Kuomintang officers.) Later, the book shows Charles, now a colonel at the military academy, threatened by drunken soldiers and their obscene local folksongs; May-lee situates the anecdote in a discussion of Chiang Kai-shek's inability to control both his own officers and the warlords who served as his local allies (170–171, 182–188). Behind its humor and affection, the Chais' account highlights the Kuomintang's problematic ambivalence toward modern ideals: under pressure from the Communists and the Japanese, the leaders cannot not give up their bad old feudal ways and conduct the war and the government in a modern, fair, populist fashion.

The Screens of Memory

In chapter 13, "Fleeing the Japanese Army," the Chais juxtapose historical facts about Kuomintang military failures with May-lee's insistence that her father look beyond his sheltered boyhood memories of those years. The Chais sum up some of the worst events of the war as blunders, or ruthless military tactics, of Generalissimo Chiang and of Chang Chih-chung—then governor of Hunan Province, one of Chiang's most influential warlords, and Charles's boss. (May-lee explains that Chang was one of many key figures who served during this period as both generals and governors, on whom Chiang Kai-shek relied; she identifies such figures as "warlords" [188].) In 1937, Chiang Kai-shek withdraws without warning from Nanjing, which notoriously falls to the Japanese; in a failed attempt to prevent the Japanese from capturing a key rail line, he dynamites dikes on the Yellow River, flooding over four thousand villages; and in November 1938, Changsha is burned in a misguided attempt to "save" it from Japanese capture (171, 175–176). The last is presented as "allegedly" ordered by General Chang, who is replaced by another warlord shortly thereafter (176–177).[7]

In an authorial interlude, Winberg recalls the fire and smoke he witnessed from the safe distance of his village home *outside* Changsha, which his mother had selected out of fear that Changsha would be taken. He remembers his parents' tension but also recalls "racing crickets with boys in the village," watching cockfights and New Year's fireworks, going to market each morning, and feeling "rich and safe" (180). Only when May-lee shows him a bleak wartime family photograph (166) does he admit the gravity of their situation in Changsha. Addressing readers as he summarizes this crucial change of perspective, he writes, "I must think like an adult, not remember like a child. Things must have been very difficult for my parents. They protected me, my brothers, sheltered us from their worries" (180). Accordingly, Winberg reveals that his parents were full of fear, that they quarreled, and that when the Japanese bombed Changsha, Ruth reassured the children about Charles's safety while she was actually uncertain; these and other facts humanize rather than detract from the story of the parents' courage. Winberg's memories have functioned as what Marianne Hirsch describes in "The Generation of Postmemory" as "screen memories":

> The images already imprinted on our brains, the tropes and structures we bring from the present to the past, hoping to find them there and to have our questions answered, may be screen memories—screens on which we project present or timeless needs and desires and which thus mask other images and other concerns. The familial aspects of postmemory that make it so powerful and problematically open to affiliation contain many of these preformed screen images. (120)

Hirsch proposes that for the offspring of trauma survivors, "the screens of gender and of familiality and the images that mediate them . . . function as screens that absorb the shock, filter and diffuse the impact of trauma, diminish harm. . . . [P]aradoxically, they actually reinforce the *living* connection between past and present, between the generation of witnesses and survivors and the generation after" (125). Whereas Hirsch specifically analyzes photographic images, I suggest that Winberg's childhood memories, as well as some of the upbeat stories the authors include in the book, have served to screen him from realizing how close to death his family came and how fallible and vulnerable his parents were, as well as how badly the war was going and how ruthless and desperate the leaders were. The screen memories kept intact his boyhood confidence in his parents' sound judgment and power to protect him and his brothers, a feeling that kept the family close for decades. In terms of history, setting aside Winberg's boyhood feelings of security enables him and May-lee to work through or mourn the dark aspects of the Kuomintang record. In terms of family understanding, setting aside the happy screen memories enables the authors to understand and communicate why, years later, Winberg is not to blame for his inability to reconcile a wartime rift (discussed below) that arises between his parents. Truthfully mourning Ruth's and Charles's suffering, and celebrating their survival and subsequent successes, entails working through both the familial and the historical records in a way that is not only thorough and objective but also open to "hidden histories excluded from dominant narratives" and characterized by "deep personal connection," imaginative investment, and the creativity of postmemory (Lipsitz 212–213; Hirsch, *Family* 22, qtd. in Davis, *Relative Histories* 16–17).

Fraternal Betrayals

Rhetorically, the Chais' stories about Charles's relationship with his brother Huan serve multiple functions in their tasks of memorializing Ruth and mourning her lost ideals: they link Huan with a utilitarian Confucian family system that disregards mother-child bonds and oppresses women; they justify Ruth's profound anger, later in life, when Charles reconciles with Huan by sending Winberg to Huan's deathbed to declare himself Huan's "son" (217–223); and they associate Huan's personal selfishness with the wartime corruption of the Kuomintang. The husband-wife rift begins during the war, when Charles, mistakenly believing Ruth does not want her third son, promises to let his childless brother Huan adopt the newborn if it survives its premature birth. This fraternal adoption plan, made without consulting Ruth, is not so much an emblem of Kuomintang corruption as it is a throwback to Confucian traditions of pooling resources within the extended family, traditions Ruth seeks to displace with Christian ideology and Western marriage ideals (158–162). Charles's bargain is reminiscent of Fong See's wish to leave his fourteen-year-old son Eddy to manage the family properties in China, or May-ying's agreement to have her two eldest children raised in China by Sam Chan's wife Huangbo (See; Chong, *Concubine's Children*). In each case, when the father places the family's needs over the mother-child bond, he tests the mother's willingness to submit to the family, and each case is the point at which the marriage begins to unravel. But whereas Ticie returns to America without her husband, and May-ying returns to Canada with just one of three daughters, Ruth refuses the adoption, forces Charles to break with Huan, and keeps her three sons with her until they all leave together for Taiwan (Chai and Chai, *Girl* 164, 250). I would argue that the fathers' claiming a child for family use functions as a severe test of maternal power in these stories, while the will to resist those claims and keep their children (and husband) close is an expression of the mothers' modernity and agency. It is easy to see why a mother would be indignant toward a husband who plans behind her back to give away their baby. However, Ruth's outrage can also be understood in the context of China's struggle for modernity in the 1920s and 1930s, when highly educated women were still urged to devote themselves to raising well-educated sons for the nation—a goal she has clearly taken to heart—as well as in the specific context of her marriage. From the beginning, she has sought to establish her preeminence in Charles's heart, if necessary by vanquishing his family's competing claims, precisely because tradition decrees that those claims come first. Why else would the authors have Charles defend his wife against his relatives with the motto "China must modernize"?

Finally, the Zhou Enlai incident justifies both the couple's break from Huan and their eventual disengagement from the Kuomintang-led ROC. When they are both living in Chongqing, Huan, a Kuomintang officer, asks Charles, a law school dean, to recruit Zhou Enlai, Mao Zedong's right-hand man, to join the Kuomintang. Charles instantly knows that Zhou would never switch sides and that if Chiang Kai-shek hears that he, Charles, was even in contact with Zhou, Chiang would have Charles killed. Yet, because food is scarce, Charles agrees to establish contact so that Huan will provide enough food for his family to eat. To build a relationship, and maximize the period when his brother would feed his family, Charles does not pop the question instantly to Zhou but rather invites him to give a series of lectures at his law school, taking care never to be present during Zhou's visits to campus. Ultimately, however, recognizing his lack of a good exit strategy, he confides in Ruth, who denounces Huan (again) as an opportunistic traitor, has Charles denounce the Communists in faculty meetings for good measure, and insists that they never speak with Huan again. Recognizing Charles's ruse, Huan cancels the lectures and the food (208–214). This episode is more than simply another instance of Ruth's insistence on a modern marriage and her superior political judgment: it takes place in the shadow of the famous event when Chiang's own generals kidnapped him and forced him to take a vow to stop attacking the Communists and to present a unified front against the Japanese (188). Thus Huan's appalling conduct—withholding food to which he has access, in order to coerce his own brother to undertake a suicidal mission he himself will not risk—is not merely a personal betrayal; it also illustrates Chiang's loss of authority, his officers' desperation, and the moral bankruptcy of man and master.

As for Charles, the Chais present him as making a rash political choice for the honorable purpose of feeding his family. The authors establish the scarcity of food through a series of anecdotes. In one, Charles gives away milk intended for his children to a begging classmate, an overly generous error for which Ruth reproaches him bitterly for the rest of their lives (192–194). In another, Ruth is asked to serve as the interpreter for Lady Mountbatten; startled at the extravagance of the banquets prepared for the American guests, she smuggles food home for her hungry family, parceling it out over three days and eating none herself (206–207). These and other stories linger in the mind when the Chais present the clearly cherished family story of Ruth and the Five Fatties, a fine example of the countermemorial work of their writing.

The Five Fatties: Suffering Contained, Corruption Revealed

In the story, it is 1942. The family members have left fertile Hunan Province and moved to war-ridden Chongqing (Chungking), where they are perennially hungry despite Charles's appointment as the founding dean of the law school at National Chongqing University. Housed on campus, they are required to eat rationed food at the university canteen, where each table must seat six and may receive only a few bowls of vegetables and rice per meal. The dining hall is haunted by a greedy family, dubbed by the Chais "the Five Fatties," whose young children, compared by the Chais to "a cloud of locusts" despite their modest number, have been trained to sit at separate tables and then seize and swallow food so rapidly that their tablemates are left hungry (191). Inevitably, Ruth must defend the family when a hungry Fatty sits at their table, lending it the Darwinian air of a wartime Hunger Game in Winberg's recollection:

> His tiny eyes barely visible in his doughy face, he stared with a wolf's concentration at the empty tabletop, licking his dumpling lips, ready

to pounce when the food came. My brothers started to cry. We were all very hungry. There was barely enough to eat when everyone ate like a normal person. (191–192)

When the dinner is served, Ruth seizes the interloper by the earlobe and insists that no one at the table can eat until they say grace. While Charles prays, Ruth divides the food evenly. The child cries; the Chai family eats. Afterward, the child's father complains, Ruth invokes God's will, the Fatties give up, and the Chais never have to eat with those children again. For good measure, Ruth discusses grace, God, and Jesus with everyone else who sits with them, until no one wants to sit there anymore and the Chais can eat the whole allotment themselves at every meal (191). In the story, wily Ruth deploys her Christian education to defend her children's survival. The bare steel of her refusal to allow another child to take food belonging to her own is thinly sheathed in Christian rhetoric, but who can criticize? The Chais' neat admission of Ruth's tactics renders the story amusing, innocuous. Since the interloper is *fat*, he or she (the omitted gender pronouns render the child more abstract) must be less malnourished than the Chais and in any case deserves no more than his or her share. We may laugh and continue reading, but fundamentally, the children cry and the parents bicker because there is not enough food. The five fatties no longer exist except on the page, so no one can say whether or not they were *really* fat, but even within the memoir, the child cries, and Winberg, pressed by May-lee, admits that his memory is unreliable. In short, the story takes a period of hunger and anxiety, and through wit distills those anxious meals into a harmless triumph for Ruth, a (screen) memory to bond and reassure the family. Where the Kuomintang has failed, Ruth has prevailed. Such is the Chais' work of countermemory. Through wit, imagination, and literary skill, they insulate themselves from the full misery of this period yet also convey the undercurrent of hardship and uncertainty. Within the larger story, the accumulated effect of the stories of privation, paranoia, and treachery is to explain why Ruth and Charles have not only broken off contact with so many family members but also left China altogether.

Ultimately, Ruth's rejection of deceptive conduct—by her father as well as by Charles's sister, father, and brother—works as a political allegory for Ruth and Charles's rejection of traditional Confucian customs and the failures of the Kuomintang, which May-lee and Winberg make clear. "By October of 1932," writes May-lee, "all the forces that would destroy the dream of reforming China as a republic—the coming war with Japan and the civil war between the Nationalists (Kuomintang) and the Communists—were already present when my grandparents arrived in China" (96). A justification is in process: with her many letters and mealtime outbursts in America, Ruth has insisted that Winberg remember why she had to break with these terrible family members. Though the action was necessary, it is painful to remember and even more difficult to remember and explain with fairness. Despite their family background, Charles's honorable service rewriting the ROC constitution and leading the National Chongqing University Law School, their many connections with the military, and their authentic efforts to serve China while preserving their family, the Chais' family memoir aligns them not with the Kuomintang but with the Americans. The family's necessary abandonment of their Chinese relatives mimics the departure of the Americans from China, the American disillusionment with Chiang and the Kuomintang that history has justified.

Reclaiming Diasporic Loss and Melancholia

If *The Girl from Purple Mountain* registers the deep malaise that arises between Ruth and Charles Chai, the elite immigrant couple who renounce their dream of reforming China into a democratic republic that would be legally just and sexually egalitarian, it also demonstrates how the Chais absorb deeply American ideals. Charles fails to reform the Chinese constitution and legal system, but after bringing his family to America (using his transliterated Chinese name "Chu Chai"), he and Winberg coauthor nine books explaining Chinese politics, history, and culture to American readers (Chai and Chai, *Girl*, page facing title page, 260); Winberg also publishes additional texts about modern China, its place in Asia, and its relations with the United States. Thus, Charles and Winberg find success as academics, China experts, in America. When May-lee grows up, she has many questions about the outbursts and silences in her family, which lead her to learn Chinese, study in China, and work with Winberg on this memoir (x–xi). The story of Ruth and Charles's departure from China, like the other family stories that are handed down, denied, recalled, and recreated in *The Girl from Purple Mountain*, comprises emotional material that is managed by Winberg and May-lee through acts of countermemory and postmemory in this double-voiced memoir.

The Chais' memoir depicts China as an object of love and loss in the memories of Ruth, Charles, and their son Winberg, and as an object of curiosity and desire in the imagination of their granddaughter May-lee; America is a positive alternative, but it is not idealized as it is, for instance, in Mary Antin's immigrant memoir *The Promised Land*. This may be because Winberg, though a brilliant scholar, experienced grave professional difficulties (despite his impressive publications) in his academic career, problems linked with his race and his interracial marriage in 1966 to Carolyn Everett, an Irish American artist. (As May-lee notes, her parents' marriage occurred just two years after the Civil Rights Act of 1964 and one year before the U.S. Supreme Court affirmed the constitutionality of interracial marriage in *Loving v. Virginia*, 388 U.S. 1 [1967] [M. Chai 9, 26].) Detailed in May-lee's own family memoir, *Hapa Girl*, Winberg's professional travails included being stereotyped as a right-wing Chinese and targeted for removal by radical demonstrators at City College of New York (36–47); being harassed, fired, and threatened with physical violence after moving to the Midwest to work at the University of South Dakota; and later, having his applications for jobs elsewhere undermined by colleagues' malicious references labeling him a left-wing troublemaker (114–116). May-lee reports that, in addition to the racialized sexual harassment she experienced as a young woman, she and her brother were threatened, her brother was assaulted by teammates at their high school, and local authorities declined to investigate the regular drive-by shootings at their house, though the shooters killed their dogs on three occasions (160–165, 180–182). The banks even refused to make mortgage loans to potential buyers of their house, so that they could not sell it when they wanted to leave (115). Under these circumstances, May-lee explains, her own adolescence was marked not only by fear and tension but also by a feeling of freakishness that was not relieved until she lived and studied in China, where she observed how Chinese viewed outsiders with just as much suspicion as Americans did but where, for the first time in her life, she was accepted as who she was—a mixed-race American (183–194).

Though informed by this traumatic family history, *The Girl from Purple Mountain* does not focus on the elder and younger Chais' struggles to assimilate in the United States but rather on Ruth and Charles's inability to bring American values to China and their undying regret for this failure. Within this book, China, not the United States, is the object of the grandparents' aspirations and mourning and the narrators' desire for recuperative knowledge. Even in the book's American scenes, the lost dream of a modern, democratic Chinese homeland informs Ruth's melancholic outbursts throughout the family gatherings of May-lee's childhood, Ruth's insistence on pricking Winberg's memory and passing on her letters and stories, and Ruth's ultimate rejection of her husband, through the mechanism of a separate burial plot, after he attempts to reconcile with her old enemy, his brother (216–223).[8] The centrality of the diasporic homeland, in this text and in others, is an aspect of racial melancholia that is systematically understudied when scholars focus on the theme of claiming America, but it becomes more obvious when one focuses on return narratives by and about the immigrant generation. However, this text exemplifies a structure of feeling pervasive in Asian American narratives of return in which a family's imagination remains rooted in the homeland rather than in the new world: diasporic melancholia.

6

"A Being... from a Different World"

Yung Wing and the Making of a Global Subjectivity

> The sixth chapter [of this book] begins with my reentrance into the Chinese world, after an absence of eight years. Would it not be strange, if an Occidental education, continually exemplified by an Occidental civilization, had not wrought upon an Oriental such a metamorphosis in his inward nature as to make him feel and act as though he were a being coming from a different world, when he confronted one so diametrically different? This was precisely my case, and yet neither my patriotism nor the love of my fellow-countrymen had been weakened. On the contrary, they had increased in strength from sympathy.
> —YUNG WING, "Preface," *My Life in China and America*, iii

> The encroachment of foreign powers upon the independent sovereignty of China has always been watched by me with the most intense interest.
> —YUNG WING, *My Life in China and America*, 174

Global Subjectivity and Racial Melancholia of *My Life in China and America*

THIS CHAPTER ADDRESSES the extraordinary autobiography of Yung Wing, who was born a peasant near the port of Macao during the Qing Dynasty and rose to become a key figure in the field of Sino-American educational exchange and one of the earliest, most historically influential writers in the Asian North American tradition. I argue that Yung's 1909 autobiography, *My Life in China and America*, has not been fully appreciated—either as a literary text, by historians of Sino-American relations, or as a historical text, by Asian American cultural critics. Belonging to the genre of autobiography, Yung's book must be both historicized *and* read as a literary text shaped by the author with specific rhetorical aims.[1] As an author, Yung modeled his text after travel narratives and slave narratives; consideration of these intertexts,

I argue, reveals *My Life* to be a fascinating record of the author's attempt to fashion and claim a global subjectivity while also bearing witness to the historical vulnerability of Chinese Americans around the globe.

My interpretation of Yung's autobiography rests on three critical terms: "global subjectivity," "racial melancholia," and "narrative of return." The simplest of these may be "narrative of return," the term I use to describe stories in which Asian North American (and Asian diasporic) writers return to their ancestral homelands to seek greater understanding of their familial and cultural roots. Such roots journeys have long been documented by second-generation Asian diasporic writers of fact and fiction, as well as by first-generation (immigrant) writers writing about their own returns to revisit their homelands.[2] As earlier chapters have explored, many narratives of return recount the experiences of writers or protagonists based elsewhere as they seek and discover roots in Asia, but there is a substantial group of texts that reveal different patterns. For example, writers may depict recurrent crossings and returns across the Pacific and Atlantic oceans, emphasizing the multiple roots of the protagonists and their repeated returns to renew and develop connections in multiple sites. Yung's text is, to my knowledge, the earliest that belongs to this second group.

As discussed in Chapter 1, scholars of Asian American studies use "racial melancholia" to describe a structure of feeling that Asian Americans experience as a result of being unable to mourn losses associated with immigration and to assimilate completely in their host countries (such as the United States or Canada).[3] The term refers to the malaise and ambivalence that arises from adapting to the contradictory situation of inhabiting countries that are nominally egalitarian and inclusive but in practice rife with barriers to full belonging. Yung's 1909 autobiography predates Sigmund Freud's 1915 essay "Mourning and Melancholia" as well as recent publications on racial melancholia; yet the text reveals a similarly ambivalent structure of feeling. Through the act of writing *My Life in China and America*—the first true autobiography by a Chinese American and the first full-length, English-language Asian American narrative of return—Yung seeks to resolve the contradictions inherent in his discursive attempt to claim a global subjectivity and his inability to secure that subjectivity rhetorically.

Finally, I use "global subjectivity" to describe how Yung saw himself. Writing before the terms "Chinese American" and "Asian American" were in use, Yung sought to affirm his deep connections both to China and to the United States. Yet, in modeling his writing after the works of global explorers and slave narrators, he also sought to enter literary traditions in which authors transcended national affiliations and wrote with a global consciousness. In what sense might Yung, a naturalized Chinese American who devoted his autobiography to recounting his service to China, have aspired to a global subjectivity? In their survey of the historical subjects of the genre in *Reading Autobiography*, Sidonie Smith and Julia Watson describe two kinds of autobiographical subjects who provide relevant models for Yung. First, beginning with *The Travels of Marco Polo* (published in 1271), travel narratives portrayed secular, educated European male adventurers and explorers as "global or planetary subject[s]" who viewed the world through a "planetary consciousness" (as noted by Mary Louise Pratt) and defined themselves through narratives of "migration, encounter, conquest, and transformation" (Pratt 20, 29–30; Smith and Watson 109). (Pratt's views may also be considered in light of other scholars' critiques of travel narratives as linked with European imperialism, as discussed in Chapter 1.) I consider how the model of explorers as "global subjects" informs Yung's portrayal of his journey to America and his return to China. Second, René Descartes in the seventeenth century introduced the Enlightenment subject of autobiography, defined by Smith and Watson as the "sovereign philosophical self, the cogito": an isolated, individuated self who contemplates experience in abstract terms (110–111). Drawing on Pratt, Smith and Watson assert that the Enlightenment ideal of the "sovereign philosophical self," the rational thinker in pursuit of objectivity and universal knowledge, motivated men to set off on "sustained journeys into interiors of continents, as scientific journeys superseded journeys of conquest"—journeys in which these scientific authors "presented themselves as benign agents of reason and order" (111). Though not a scientist, Yung strove through his autobiography to position himself as such a subject, objectively recording and assessing the various forms of social and political turmoil he found in China, Peru, and the transpacific Chinese Educational Mission he founded. In doing so, Yung had to resist and appropriate a genre that had, in effect, been invented by European traders and missionaries to describe encounters with other peoples whom they saw as primitives needing civilization. In particular, Yung's text evokes and contests the travel narratives of Western missionaries to China.

My Life also draws on the genre of the slave narrative to evoke the racially melancholic position of the racialized subject who cannot complete his emancipation. In *The Intimacies of Four Continents*, Lisa Lowe uses Olaudah Equiano's *Interesting Narrative of the Life of Olaudah Equiano, Written by Himself with Related Documents* (1789) to describe how the genre of the slave narrative fulfilled readers' desire to see the free and educated ex-slave as a subject attaining "individual rights and democratic freedoms" through "ethical education and civilization" (L. Lowe, *Intimacies* 46–47). As an autobiography," Lowe asserts, "*The Interesting Narrative* exemplifies the liberal imperative that the 'life' emplot the transition from slavery to freedom, and in this way, it attests to the power of political emancipation, and Christian redemption" (57–58). At the same time, by citing other slave narratives as well as his own experiences, Equiano also suggested that former slaves could neither be fully recompensed for what they had lost nor fully attain freedom as long as slavery not only remained legal but also suffused the race consciousness of people on the "four continents" (Europe, Africa, the Americas, and Asia) of Lowe's book title (L. Lowe, *Intimacies* 17–20). Thus, Lowe finds, the genres of autobiography and the novel "did some of the important work of mediating and resolving liberalism's contradictions" and provided "aesthetic form[s]" for narrating the "imperatives and privileges of the liberal subjects" (46–47, 56–57). While Yung's text does not quote Equiano, it does echo the *Narrative of the Life of Frederick Douglass* and its concerns; through Douglass's text, I argue, Yung as autobiographer drew on the literary tradition of the slave narrative in his efforts to reconcile the numerous contradictions of his own position as a racialized subject aspiring to claim or perform a global subjectivity through the writing of an autobiography. Just as Equiano portrayed himself as a freedman "continuously threatened by the possibility of abduction and reenslavement" (L. Lowe, *Intimacies* 13), Yung's text displays its author's awareness that despite his conversion, naturalization, American education, and record of distinguished translatlantic service to the Qing and to diasporic Chinese, he could never gain the complete acceptance of either China or America. Moreover, his text also testifies, briefly but memorably, to the more severe sufferings of Chinese contemporaries outside the United States (including Cantonese citizens oppressed by the Qing and coolie laborers in Peru and Cuba) and his own unstable belongings as a naturalized Chinese American. In portraying himself as a global subject who remained restless and aware of the suffering of less privileged Chinese, Yung drew on the tradition of slave narrators such as Equiano and Douglass, who lived and wrote in the shadow of slavery; like these writers, Yung used autobiography to manage, symbolically, the problem of being unable to complete the process of becoming a global subject who could rely on the same rights and freedoms as white imperial travelers or white U.S. citizens. Through Yung, readers can see the Asian American narrative of return, also, as managing the contradictions of combining global subjectivity with Asian birth or ethnicity in the modern era, and as registering a racially melancholic structure of feeling that results from the instability of this process.

Yung Wing may well have begun writing his text in 1902, after he returned from China for the last time to attend the graduation of his second son, Bartlett, from Yale.[4] Born on November 17, 1828, Yung was seventy-four years old at Bartlett's graduation. Yung's dedication, "To my devoted sons, Morrison Brown and Bartlett Golden Yung, these reminiscences are affectionately dedicated," suggests that he wrote specifically to leave them a full account of his public accomplishments—an account they could find nowhere else—that might serve as a model for their own lives as mixed-race Chinese American men. Therefore, though his term "reminiscences" marks the text as a memoir, Yung in writing it followed certain conventions of autobiography, offering a linear, chronological narrative focused on his professional accomplishments and their historical significance. Yung presents himself as a patriotic public servant and strives to present the disparate stages of his career as a coherent, logical progression unified by his goal of public service, while elements that do not support this cohesive vision of his life are omitted, subordinated, or left unexplained. Moreover, he writes as a "sovereign philosophical subject" surveying his life and actions, and others' actions, from a somewhat impersonal, critical distance that some have found stilted. However, at the heart of Yung's text are a series of unspoken paradoxes that evoke the complexity of being a transnational Chinese American, writing as a global subject, in the late nineteenth century. First, he was an illustrious pupil of missionaries, to whom he owed everything; yet he considered missionaries complicit with Western imperialism, which he sought to resist. Second, he became a U.S. citizen, married an American, and raised his sons as Americans, but his career consisted primarily of service to China. Third, his memoir celebrates his lifelong service to the Qing Dynasty, yet as the narrator, he repeatedly criticizes the Qing, and as a historical person, Yung sought first to reform and ultimately to overthrow the dynasty (F. Cheung, "Early Chinese" 34–35). Finally and most poignantly, when Yung fled China in 1902 under the threat of execution, he learned that he had also been stripped of his U.S. citizenship. In his memoir, he symbolically claims for himself two countries that have rejected him, and records a lifetime of service to both. Together, these contradictions convey the complexity of Yung's ambivalent performance of belonging, alienation, and global subjectivity.

A Critical Introduction

Before continuing my argument, I want to provide an introduction to Yung's story and the existing critical conversations about him. *My Life in China and America* is the earliest full-length narrative of return in the Asian American literary tradition. Born in 1828 in Nanping, China (now part of Zhuhai, in Guangdong Province), near the Portuguese port of Macao, Yung was educated in Macao and Hong Kong by missionaries, who then sent him to study in the United States for about eight years. He converted to Christianity, became a U.S. citizen, graduated from Yale in 1854 (becoming the first Chinese graduate of an American college or university), and returned to China. There, in my view, Yung's early career experiences in the port cities of Macao, Canton, Hong

Kong, and Shanghai led him to question missionaries, foreign traders and diplomats, and the integrity of the Qing Dynasty itself. Eventually, however, he persuaded the Qing government, as part of its efforts at modernization, to send 120 Chinese boys to the United States for education, thereby creating the first formal educational exchange program between China and the United States: the Chinese Educational Mission (CEM), for which Yung served as associate commissioner.[5] The CEM boys began to arrive in the United States in 1872 and were called back prematurely, for diverse political reasons, in 1881. Though handicapped by their inability to complete their college educations in the United States, they eventually advanced and made significant contributions to China's efforts to modernize. (Among these students, Yan Phou Lee, who returned to the United States in 1884, became a journalist and published *When I Was a Boy in China*, an early collection of essays sometimes described as the first Chinese American autobiography. Another student, Liang Cheng, became a diplomat and shaped discussions that led the United States to remit and dedicate the Boxer Indemnity funds to the promotion of educational exchanges between China and the United States, with the result that thousands of Chinese were funded to study in the United States, Qinghua Preparatory School and University were founded, and many Chinese have since chosen to attend American schools.)[6] During Yung's time as associate commissioner of the CEM, he married an American, Mary Louise Kellogg, with whom he raised two American sons; investigated and helped block the coolie trade between Macao and Peru; proposed other schemes to support and develop China; joined the reform movement of 1898; fled China to avoid arrest; lost his U.S. citizenship; returned to Connecticut; completed his autobiography; and died in 1912, just months after the Republican revolution in China.

Yung's autobiography is not entirely obscure, but it has been read principally as a historical document and marginalized as a literary text. It was reviewed in the *New York Times*, published in Chinese in 1915, studied in China and the United States in the 1930s and 1940s, commemorated at Yale in 1954, translated into Chinese again and published in 1961, thoughtfully historicized in 1965, and mentioned in the earliest anthologies of Asian American literature (Kawakami; C. Wang, *Transpacific* 33; Wan 1–7; LaFargue; Hu; Worthy; Hsu and Palubinskas; Chin et al.). However, as Chih-ming Wang has shown, Yung's text has been largely ignored by Chinese scholars of modernism and autobiography in China (*Transpacific* 32–35). The English version languished out of print until Arno Press reissued it in 1978 (Yin 81n43); after being labeled a white supremacist text (Chin et al.) and unfavorably compared with the writings of the Eaton sisters (Ling, "Reading Her/stories" 54–67), it was not noticed by Asian American cultural critics until it was reclaimed as an Asian American New England text by Amy Nelson Bangerter (*Chinese Youth*;

"New Englandization") and restored to its place in Chinese American cultural history by K. Scott Wong (K. S. Wong 201–232). More recently, Yung has been feted at Yale, studied by historians of the Qing era, and memorialized online with his own websites. Ning Qian, a contemporary Chinese scholar of Sino-American educational exchange, calls Yung a "trailblazer who quietly devoted his entire life to open[ing] a door for Chinese youth to see the world outside," arguing that despite his modest profile, "only a few people in modern China could claim to have had a comparable impact on China." Calling Yung "China's Columbus," Qian asserts that he "discovered" America, enabling the Chinese to see the outside world "with neither arrogant ignorance nor an inferiority complex," and showed the Chinese people that "there existed other cultures that nurtured brilliant human thought outside of traditional Chinese culture" (14).

Aside from those who wish to celebrate Yung's contributions, China historians have read the autobiography largely as a transparent historical document: verifying its accuracy, accepting portions deemed reliable, and mining the text for information about Yung's era, Chinese attitudes toward America, or diplomatic relations between China and the United States (see, for instance, Spence, *Search*; K. S. Wong). Historians have assessed Yung's work primarily on the basis of its truthfulness, the significance of his life's work, and, more recently, the quality of his observations about America. However, reading Asian American autobiographies strictly as historical documents can lead historians to argue that if these authors write artfully, with specific rhetorical aims, they are untrustworthy. For instance, Peter Pei-de Wan presents Yung in his dissertation as a complex figure whose accomplishments were tarnished by his shadow life, which included an unmentioned first wife in China, an artfully concealed thirst for personal gain, and his supposed concealment of his naturalization as a U.S. citizen (mentioned only in the appendix by Yung's friend Joseph Twichell [Twichell 256]). For Wan, Yung's selective, self-aggrandizing narration is a sign that his self-portrait fails to meet an implicit ideal of truthfulness, objectivity, and full disclosure in an autobiographer. Despite Wan's admirable research, his interpretation (which ignores theories of autobiography as an inherently self-dramatizing, rhetorical genre) has not been widely influential. Yet some literary critics have also dismissed Yung as a white supremacist, an assimilationist, an elitist indifferent to working-class Chinese woes in America, and (most wounding to his literary reputation) an autobiographer lacking in candor, expressiveness, and complex interiority (Chin et al.; Ling, "Reading Her/stories"). The story of the book's fluctuating significance and recent recuperation also exemplifies the limits of early Asian American literary studies. Yung is paradigmatic of two classes of subjects that are crucial to Asian America and to Sino-American diplomatic history: he was the first of over a million Chinese students who have studied abroad, most in the United States, and the second of numerous educated Chinese who have published books in English (Rhoads 1). However, until the mid-1990s, when Asian American studies adopted more global paradigms, Yung was recognized only as a Chinese American or Asian American writer of minor historical importance, not as a transnational or global writer. His text has been critically marginalized within Asian American studies because of the field's formative biases in favor of working-class subjects, stories set in America, and texts focusing on twentieth-century issues of identity and Americanization.[7] In 1972, the groundbreaking anthologists Kai-yu Hsu and Helen Palubinskas defined Asian American literature as constituted by second-generation (American-born) authors grappling with identity issues, and they included a chronology of Chinese American labor and immigration history that omitted mention of educated Chinese such as Hsu himself. Frank Chin and his coeditors, first anthologized by Hsu and Palubinskas, soon published the first *Aiiieeeee!* anthology. There, they attacked Lin Yutang and C. Y. Lee, educated Chinese immigrants publishing best-sellers in English, as reinforcing stereotypes of Chinese as "good, loyal, obedient, passive, law-abiding, [and] cultured" (Chin et al. xiv). Lest readers mistake these model-minority traits as positive, they also attacked the publications of Chinese government officials for depicting Chinese as subservient and inferior, singling out Yung Wing as "the outstanding example of early yellow white supremacy" (xvi). Overlooking the fundamental point that Yung's book delineates his efforts to defend China against Western imperialism, as well as the obvious example of Sun Yat-sen (a Christian who founded the Republic of China), Chin and his colleagues dismissed all Chinese Christians as "converts to white supremacy" (xi). Working independently, yet focused on a working-class agenda, Elaine H. Kim omitted Yung entirely from her influential study *Asian American Literature*, and she criticized the English writings of Chinese intellectuals, including Yan Phou Lee, for emphasizing Chinese culture rather than the hardships faced by Asians in the United States (24–32). In 1991, the *Aiiieeeee!* editors again deemed Chinese Christian writers "fake," insulted Yung while ignoring most of his book's content and context, and attacked Chinese modernizers Sun Yat-sen and Hu Shi for wanting to "Europeanize" China (Chan et al. 11–12). Forcefully cutting Asian American literature off from its roots in Chinese culture and history, these early studies defined Asian American literature as excluding the writings of educated Chinese in America, before anyone in the nascent field had even read them.[8]

Later literary critics have been more sympathetic to Yung's humble origins, modest financial means, and perennial outsider status (which are evident in the text) and have evaluated *My Life* as a literary text—a narrative designed to reveal selected insights gradually and artfully to a specific audience—rather than a catalog of historical events. For instance, Floyd Cheung has shown that, writing at a critical moment in Sino-American relations, Yung modeled his autobiography after strategically written texts by Benjamin Franklin, Frederick Douglass, and Booker T. Washington, while also responding to Theodore Roosevelt's standards of manliness, in order to influence American public opinion about his Chinese countrymen ("Political Resistance" 83–94). Whereas Wan portrays Yung as a manipulative narrator, Cheung shares the postmodernist assumption of autobiography theorists that autobiographers should and do demonstrate literary skill and aim to portray reality in forms that suit their rhetorical aims. In reviewing and challenging the critical history of misreading Yung Wing, I also insist that other early writers, particularly educated Chinese, may now be profitably reread with greater understanding of the historical constraints under which they lived, wrote, and sought an audience. Now let us return—to Yung's ambivalent performance of belonging, alienation, and global subjectivity.

The Trouble with Missionaries: Decolonizing Yung

In Chapter 1, I noted that Kuan-Hsing Chen defines decolonizing in the modern world as "the attempt of the previously colonized to reflectively work out a historical relation with the former colonizer, culturally, politically and economically" (3). Though Yung Wing's homeland was not actually colonized by Western missionaries, he was converted, and his life was transformed by them. Hence, one could say that Yung's text does a version of decolonizing, as he uses it to work out his personal relationship with Western versions of colonizers in nineteenth-century China—missionaries and others who advocated personal conversion to Christianity and the conversion of China and other nations to "free trade imperialism" (K. Chen 3; L. Lowe, *Intimacies* chap. 4). He does this by acknowledging at length both his debt and his distance from his missionary mentors.

Yung makes no secret of his debt to American missionaries, or his Christianity. Born in Guangdong Province, near the Westernized port of Macao, he was schooled by missionaries from age seven onward, with a brief interlude of studying Chinese and helping to support his family after his father's death. In 1941 he returned to the "first English school" in China, named for Dr. Robert Morrison, the first English missionary to China, who left London in 1807, authored the first Anglo-Chinese dictionary, translated the Bible into Chinese, and died in 1834 (Yung 14). The school's first teacher, Samuel R. Brown, returned home to America in 1846, bringing with him Yung Wing and two other Chinese pupils, who were sponsored by American and Scottish patrons.

Dr. Brown's wife was the daughter of a congregational minister in East Windsor, Connecticut, the Reverend Shubael Bartlett. When they entered Monson Academy, in Massachusetts, the boys boarded with Brown's mother, Mrs. Phoebe Brown. Yung commemorated his lifelong intimacy with the Brown-Bartlett clan by naming his sons Morrison Brown and Bartlett Golden Yung.

Yung expresses his Christianity in other ways as well. He had joined the Church of Christ while at Yale, and renewed that membership in 1877, but does not mention this in his autobiography (Rhoads 152). Instead, the book includes a biographical sketch of Yung delivered as a speech by the Reverend Joseph H. Twichell, Yung's close lifelong friend and pastor of the Asylum Hill Congregational Church in Hartford (Twichell 247–273). Twichell notes that Yung had converted to Christianity even before college, during his Monson Academy days with Mrs. Brown (1847–1849), and had told Twichell that in 1871, when he finally received authorization and funding to begin his educational mission, he "walked on air and worshipped God" for two days, because "heaven had at last granted his prayer" (Yung 211; Twichell 252, 268). In 1874, sent to Peru to investigate the coolie trade on behalf of the Qing government, Yung brought along two Americans, his brother-in-law Dr. E. W. Kellogg and Rev. Joseph Twichell, as his right-hand men (Yung 194; Stewart 201). In the course of his book, Yung compares himself with the Biblical figures of Ruth, Esau, and Samson in highly original images (10, 36, 177). And, most importantly, he got the idea of starting his own Chinese Educational *Mission* from his own Christian education.

Yet Yung could also be discriminating and critical of Christian influences in China. In 1849, he recalls, when he wanted to remain in the United States for college study, he declined a full scholarship that was offered him on condition that he pledge to return to China after college as a missionary, lest it "handicap and circumscribe his usefulness" (35). Anticipating that there would be other ways to "do the greatest good to China" (35), he found other sponsors and worked his way through Yale. In recounting this choice, he nominally lauds the power of Christian intentions but primarily prides himself on refusing to "barter away my inward convictions of duty for a temporary mess of pottage" (35–36), suggesting that such a requirement, rather than a calling to serve God, was an imposition on his poverty and on his true mission of serving China, akin to Jacob's swindling of Esau (Genesis 25:29–34).

Acutely aware of the missionaries' close and problematic links with Western imperialism, Yung pointedly disavows his ties with them, even as he records his connections to the influential missionaries Karl Gützlaff, Issachar Roberts, and Peter Parker. His very first Western teacher, Mary Wanstall Gützlaff, was the second wife of the Reverend Karl (Charles) Gützlaff. Historian

John R. Haddad relates how Gützlaff, a Prussian-born missionary initially sponsored by the Dutch Missionary Society, zealously ignored missionary protocol and entered the interior of China without official authorization in the 1830s by serving as an interpreter to illegal trading expeditions, ostensibly in order to distribute Christian tracts:

> Driven by economic concerns, these expeditions attempted to gauge Chinese demand for English textiles, access the secrets of tea production, or sell opium directly to coastal populations. Gützlaff joined them for one reason only: they offered effective vehicles for evangelical penetration. Of course, his employers paid him to communicate with the Chinese, not distribute tracts. Specifically, his job was to pacify, bribe, or intimidate suspicious Chinese officials. (95)

Gützlaff became notorious among missionaries, who debated whether his opium-funded tract-distribution expeditions were an enterprising new model for evangelism or a pact with the devil (Haddad 93–98). Haddad speculates that Edwin Stevens, one of Gützlaff's protégés, was "almost certainly" the man who "infiltrated Canton" and distributed tracts to civil service examinees, including the failed scholar Hong Huoxiu (Hung Siu Chune), who subsequently dreamt that he was the brother of Jesus Christ and started "the bloodiest civil war in human history—the Taiping Rebellion (1850–1864)" (184). The tracts were authored by Liang Afa (Leang Afah), a Chinese convert of Dr. Morrison (Yung 115; Haddad 186–187). A second Gützlaff protégé, the rogue missionary Issachar Roberts of Tennessee (called Icabod by Yung [114]), met with Hong in 1847 and, according to Haddad, joined the Taiping rebels from 1860 to 1862 in the mistaken belief that he could guide them back to a more correct version of Christianity and use them to evangelize to those whose territory they controlled (196). In the fall of 1859, when Yung visited the Taiping headquarters in Nanjing, he recognized Roberts but spent as little time as possible in his presence (Haddad 192–200; Yung 115, 107). Despite the discrepancy in dates, Yung's description of Roberts's shabby looks and uncertain role otherwise fits Haddad's account, though Yung seems unaware that Roberts left the rebels in 1862 (Yung 107; Haddad 198–200). During his 1859 visit to the Taiping leaders, Yung himself suggested that they needed fundamental government reforms and courteously declined to join them. In his account of their rise and fall, Yung delineates the influence of Christian missionaries on the movement, its corruption and decline, and its failure to introduce either Christianity or new political ideas for a new government (chaps. 10–11). "The only good that resulted from the Taiping Rebellion," Yung concludes, "was that God made use of it as a dynamic power to break up the stagnancy of a great nation and wake up its consciousness for a new national life" (122).

During his missionary schooling in Macao and Hong Kong, from 1835 through 1846, Yung had also witnessed firsthand some of the changes wrought by the Treaty of Nanjing in 1842, including the opening of five ports to British trade (Shanghai, Ningbo, Fuzhou, Xiamen [Amoy], and Canton [Guangzhou]) and the rendering of Hong Kong to British possession "in perpetuity" (Spence, *Search* 158–160). Shanghai, where Yung worked briefly in the Imperial Customs Translating Department, had been opened as a "treaty port" to the British in 1842, in the aftermath of the first Opium War, with regular tariffs on all the major imports and the principle of extraterritoriality negotiated in 1844 (Yung 63–65; Spence, *Search* 159–160; W. Cohen 8). Similar rights were also extended to the United States and France in 1844, with all three countries demanding "most favored nation" status, which meant that anything granted to one of the three had to be granted to the other two as well.[9] In *The Foreign Relations of the People's Republic of China*, Winberg Chai sums up how, in the hundred years following the 1844 treaties, other nations (including Japan) seized control of China's ports, coasts, maritime customs, postal service, waterways, railway rights, and outlying possessions (in Manchuria, Mongolia, Annam [Indochina], Burma, Macao, the Ryukyu Islands, and Taiwan [Formosa]), and then began to partition China itself into spheres of influence, "with Russia in Manchuria, Germany in Shantung, and Great Britain in the Yangtze Valley." He concludes, "The complete disintegration of China, which seemed to be imminent, was checked [only] by the bitter rivalries among the powers themselves" (4–5). As an erstwhile subject and official of the Qing, Yung knew only too well how deeply Christianity was entwined with Western imperialism.

His brief treatment of Dr. Peter Parker, his first post-college employer, illustrates how the demands of autobiography—to produce a linear, cohesive, progressive narrative—caused Yung to skirt the central contradiction between his appreciation for his own Christian education and his intimate personal ties with Christian clergy and missionaries, on one hand, and his resentment of Western imperialism on the other. Parker was a medical missionary who in 1839 had assisted Viceroy Lin Zexu in his efforts to counteract the opium trade (Haddad 126–127, 135) and had then been instrumental as a cultural translator in negotiating the first U.S. treaty with the Chinese, the 1844 Treaty of Wangxia (Wang-hsia, now a part of Macao [Yung 58–59; W. Cohen 10–12]). Presumably influenced by Parker and other missionaries present during these negotiations, the 1844 treaty also gave Americans the right to rent sites for the construction of "hospitals, churches, and cemeteries" and "to employ scholars and people of any part of China . . . to teach any of the languages of the Empire" (Spence, *Search* 161; Haddad 136–140, 147–154). The first American missionaries arriving in the 1830s had risked death by strangulation for "propagating Christianity" (W. Cohen 5), and Chinese rulers had long tried to prevent foreigners from becoming fluent in Chinese (Spence, *Search* 161), so these were major concessions giving American missionaries further opportunities to participate in Westernizing China. Extraterritoriality—the principle that foreigners accused of crimes would be tried by their own consuls—was also extended to the Americans, with the result that, since the American consuls for the first ten years were themselves merchants, and there were no American jails, Americans became particularly infamous for misbehaving with impunity, as Yung illustrates with colorful anecdotes in his memoir (Spence, *Search* 161; W. Cohen 8–13; Yung 67–73). In short, the Treaty of Wangxia, for which Parker was known, was a diplomatic coup for the United States and a disaster for China.

As for Yung's connection to Parker, the latter had become commissioner to China in 1856, when Yung worked for him, but Yung left the job after only three months, ostensibly finding Parker unable to introduce him to useful Chinese officials (Yung 58–59; W. Cohen 10–15). In fact, historian Warren I. Cohen records that Chinese officials had "with cause, taken an intense dislike to Parker, classing him with the more arrogant and intractable British officials of their experience" because of his preference for "firmness" and "force" in dealings with the Qing (13). Parker had suggested that the United States occupy Formosa in emulation of the British foothold in Hong Kong as well as build coaling stations and expand offshore naval operations in the region; fortunately, the U.S. government of the time declined to pursue these ideas (W. Cohen 15). Yung, who expresses hope that "the grasping ambition of the West will let the territorial integrity and the independent sovereignty of China remain intact," must have known of Parker's participation in the 1844 treaty negotiations, but his book says nothing about their ideological differences (84). Rather, he says only that Parker gave him no work, had nothing to teach him, and provided no useful contacts, leading Yung to give up being Parker's private secretary after those few months. Yung even specifies that he was not paid enough to be seduced (or "spoiled") by Parker or his diplomatic agenda: "I was with him only three months. My salary was $15 a month (not large enough to spoil me at any rate)" (59). One might think Yung is namedropping, but these details suggest the opposite: a disavowal. Though he once worked for Parker, Yung implies, he remained ideologically independent. Yet, as a former Qing official writing for American readers, Yung codes his disavowal in terms that become clear only when one reads on and realizes how deeply he hated foreign imperialism in China.

Similarly, critics have ignored the anticlerical tone of Yung's proposal to reduce the legal powers of all missionaries in China, another instance of hiding in plain view his antagonism to missionary incursions. In 1868, Yung recounts, having finally found a suitable time and place to submit his cherished Chinese Educational Mission proposal to Beijing, he placed it in a memorial (a policy proposal) "chaperoned" by three other proposals (175). The fourth proposal began on a specifically anti-Catholic note but rapidly shifted to criticize all kinds of missionaries for usurping "temporal power" in China. As recalled and summarized by Yung, the proposal read as follows:

> The encroachment of foreign powers upon the independent sovereignty of China has always been watched by me with the most intense interest. No one who is at all acquainted with Roman Catholicism can fail to be impressed with the unwarranted pretensions and assumptions of the Romish church in China. She claims civil jurisdiction over her proselytes, and takes civil and criminal cases out of Chinese courts. In order to put a stop to such insidious and crafty workings to gain temporal power in China, I put forth this proposition: to prohibit missionaries *of any religious sect or denomination* from exercising any kind of jurisdiction over their converts, in either civil or criminal cases. (Yung 174–175, emphasis mine)

Macao, where Yung Wing had received his primary education, was the seat of the oldest European settlement in Asia. A port city near Hong Kong, Macao "had been occupied by the Portuguese with China's tacit consent since the 1550s," had remained a base of Portuguese trade, and was formally ceded to Portugal in 1887 (Spence, *Search* 19; W. Chai 5). The Protestant missionaries who followed Morrison's arrival in 1807 were relative newcomers when compared to their Catholic rivals, who could trace their presence in China back to Matteo Ricci's arrival in Macao in 1583 (Spence, *Search* 132). No wonder Yung, the missionary protégé, observed the activities of the foreigners there with "the most intense interest."[10] By smoothly equating encroaching foreigners and the Roman Catholic church with "any religious sect or denomination" that sought to exercise "any kind of jurisdiction" over its converts, Yung implies that he considered the legal similarity and insidiousness of the three groups obvious to not only him and other Chinese but also his American readers. Thus, Yung's book depicts China's relations with Christian missionaries as inherently antagonistic, and himself as navigating with some care in these troubled waters. In doing so, Yung's text anticipates and performs a version of Kuan-Hsing Chen's call for Asian intellectuals to decolonize, by working out on a personal level his historic relation to the missionary community that made him a global citizen.

Writing as a Global Citizen

Yung also owed a complex literary debt to the legacies of European travel writers who defined themselves as "global or planetary subjects," explorers who wrote about "migration, encounter, conquest, and transformation," or scientists who "presented themselves as benign agents of reason and order" among nonwhite peoples, whom they depicted as less rational, less civilized, and less fit for self-government (Said; Smith and Watson 100–111). Within this long tradition, the writings of nineteenth-century missionaries about their travels in China were particularly important for Yung, the student of missionaries. Within Yung's text, the missionary travel narrative seems to shape his global frame of reference, the importance he gives to his sea and inland journeys, his preference for objectivity and authority over emotional self-expression, his attention to geographic and ethnographic reportage, his efforts to distinguish himself as a global subject from common Chinese, and his pointed distancing of himself from missionaries.

As an example, I turn to the work of Karl Friedrich August Gützlaff, the Prussian-born missionary whose career exemplified the close entwinement of missionary work, trade, and British imperialism in East Asia. According to historian Jessie Gregory Lutz, Gützlaff began working as a comprador (translator) for representatives of the British East India Company in 1832 and soon gained renown for his officially forbidden forays into the Chinese interior (66). As a comprador, he not only translated but also cajoled and bullied local officials into receiving communications, overlooking illegal activities, and establishing ties for future commerce with himself and his company; along the way, he distributed religious tracts and books, provided medical treatments and supplies to Chinese locals, and surveyed the coast and fortifications of China, later providing navigational information for British ships in the Opium War of 1840–1842 (Lutz 82, 100). The companies he initially worked with were also involved in selling opium, as was William Jardine, Gützlaff's erstwhile employer and sponsor. A brilliant linguist whose mastery of multiple Chinese dialects was priceless during wartime, Gützlaff translated for the British during and after the 1840–1842 conflict; ever the missionary, he even gave copies of the New Testament to Chinese negotiators at the signing of the Treaty of Nanjing in 1842 (Lutz 99–104). Thereafter, he served as Chinese Secretary for the Hong Kong government until his death in 1851 (Lutz 116). As a travel writer, Gützlaff championed the idea that Westerners gained nothing by accepting demeaning Qing protocols but would win greater respect if they simply entered the ports they chose without permission and refused to leave until their demands were met, and he identified key ports that were later selected to be treaty ports; moreover, as a translator, he promulgated the British doctrine that the Chinese, not the British, were responsible for curbing the opium trade (Gützlaff, *Journal* 197–251; Lutz 103).

Yung knew Gützlaff's reputation, not only because of the latter's prominence in the coastal missionary community that nurtured Yung but also because Mary Wanstall Gützlaff, Gützlaff's second wife, was the first English person Yung ever met. In fact, Yung begins his memoir with his account of their first meeting in 1835, when his father took him, then seven years old, to be a pupil at the boarding school she opened in the Gützlaff home in Macao (Yung 3; Lutz 61). In what Lutz calls "perhaps the best picture of her" that survives, Yung recounts her strikingly foreign appearance and dress, and he describes how his fear gave way to trust as she won him over with "kindness and sympathy" and became like a mother to him: "For really, a new world had dawned on me," he admits (Lutz 61; Yung 4). Indeed, this meeting was the start of his conversion from a poor Chinese peasant boy to a global citizen.

In addition, Yung may well have read Gützlaff's works while at Yale: at least four Gützlaff publications appear in the 1846 catalogue of "Brothers in Unity," the debating society for which Yung served as assistant librarian at the university (ca. 1852–1854) (Yung 39; "Catalogue"). Among these titles, Gützlaff's *Journal of Three Voyages along the Coast of China, in 1831, 1832, and 1833, with Notices of Siam, Corea, and the Loo-choo* [Ryūkyū] *Islands* documents Gützlaff's passion for distributing religious publications to Asians from Siam [Thailand] to Korea, as well as the close entwinement of Gützlaff's evangelism and British trade.[11] Published in book form in 1834, *Journal* includes a detailed map of East Asia, stretching from Siam to Korea, informed by his surveys during these voyages. The introduction by the Reverend William Ellis, a colleague, gives an overview of China's history, culture, and language; population statistics from 1813; and opinions on Chinese education and character that are relatively positive. By contrast, Ellis describes the people of Siam as "filthy, indolent," and "servile" and their government as "imperious," "vain," ignorant, impotent, and given to "barbarous" torture and "sanguinary" punishments, tacitly asserting that country's need for foreign civilization (Gützlaff, *Journal* xliv–xlv). Ellis then recounts a history of Protestant missionaries in China, culminating in a recitation of Gützlaff's gifts and heroic conduct in this field. This prologue, along with Gützlaff's own chapters on Chinese religions and Christian missionaries in China, may well have been key sources for Yung's summaries of China's missionary history (Yung 13–18, 114–115).

Gützlaff's *Journal* details each town he and his men visited; the layout of land, sea, and fortifications; the reception they encountered; and their negotiations with the officials and the local people. The "mandarins" regularly refused to receive the traders or their letters, told them not to enter towns, sent armed guards ostensibly to protect them, demanded they leave, and punished local officers who accepted gifts, traded with them, or failed to send them packing on time. But Gützlaff and his employers were shameless: they went where they pleased and tried to befriend, trade with, and evangelize locals, all the while insisting that they were there only to trade, not to invade or convert. As a global citizen and a Christian, Gützlaff claimed that the Qing government had no right to withhold from its citizens contact with the outside world and exposure to Christianity:

> All mankind are created and upheld by the same God, descended from the same parents, subject to the same changes, are living under the same canopy of heaven, upon the same planet, and [influenced by the same] benevolence, which is equally binding upon all the nations of the earth. (1–2)

Gützlaff's doctrine of a natural right for all men to claim fellowship with other nations fits well with the British push in the nineteenth century to extend the country's trading powers around the world, which Lisa Lowe calls "free trade imperialism" (*Intimacies* 74). The possibility that the traders' and missionaries' ostensibly friendly and high-minded overtures resulted in personal wealth, profits from opium, and the violent imposition of Western trade on China is never admitted in Gützlaff's *Journal*. Gützlaff emphasizes the local people's friendliness, openness to trade, desire for Western medicines, and interest in religious materials; yet he admits that official Chinese hostility and countermeasures escalated as he proceeded, as if the Chinese, for their part, were also sizing up the foreigners and concluding that they required a firm hand.

To be fair, Gützlaff's genuine fascination with Chinese culture is amply documented. For instance, he published *A Sketch of Chinese History, Ancient and Modern: Comprising a Retrospect of the Foreign Intercourse and Trade with China* in 1834, the same year as his *Journal*. Published in two volumes, *A Sketch* outlines Chinese history from the "Mythological Era" (predating the first historical dynasty beginning in 2207 B.C.) through the Qing Dynasty (57). However, the links between the author's interest in Chinese culture and his appeal to readers' financial interests are evident. Published just as the East India Company's monopoly on the Indian-Chinese trade was ending, *A Sketch* provides a detailed map of China, based on Jesuit maps updated with the results of Gützlaff's firsthand research—a handy tool for armed or mercantile visitors. Similarly, the second volume concludes with tables itemizing the trade carried on in Canton by major economic interests in the region: the East India Company (1813–1828), private ships flying the British flag (1818–1828), Americans (1804–1833), and British ships (1828–1834) (Gützlaff, *Sketch* 2:455, app. 2–11).[12] Gützlaff's appendices not only document his detailed knowledge of British and American trading and the profits associated with opium sales; they suggest an open appeal to the mercenary interests of his Western readers.

While Gützlaff was far from the only missionary travel writer to record his impressions of China, he was one of the more ambitious and influential. His *Journal* was widely circulated, reprinted, and favorably reviewed, stimulating interest in China and attracting funding for additional publications (Lutz 128). Though his writing demonstrates deep knowledge and increasing respect over time for Chinese culture and people, his publications, estimated at 188 works and appearing in multiple languages, also questioned earlier, romanticized versions of China. Combined with others' reports, Gützlaff's writings helped to establish the new view of China as "a corrupt and tradition-bound oligarchy sustained by oppressed, impoverished peasants," militarily and politically weak; such publications guided Westerners from what historian Harold Isaacs called the "Age of Respect" for China to the "Age of Contempt," 1840 through 1904 (Isaacs, qtd. in Lutz 124–126). It was Yung's misfortune that his career coincided with this period.

Opening with his education at Mrs. Gützlaff's school and his subsequent recruitment into Morrison School, Yung's autobiography establishes him as a latter-day version of an ideal colonial subject: a "Chinese student educated in America," "a naturalized citizen of the United States," a Chinese civil servant, and a person with a global awareness, both implicated in and detached from the Qing and British empires (Yung 75, 158). In describing his early years, Yung takes pains to situate his own experiences within the history of international mission work in China, with Christian literary references (chaps. 1–2). He identifies his early teachers, Mrs. Gützlaff's cousins, as "the Misses Parkes"—the sisters of Sir Harry Parkes, who was later knighted for his role in the second Opium War (7); he taught Mrs. Gützlaff's blind students to read "on raised letters till they could read from the Bible and *Pilgrim's Progress*" (8); he states that his father died during the first Opium War (8); he compares himself, rewarded for reciting English in the rice field with "sheaves of golden rice," to the biblical figure of Ruth (10); and he describes the missionary world in which he moved from childhood onward as peopled by global travelers and merchants.

Moreover, Yung pointedly describes himself as an educated, elite global traveler. Throughout the book, Yung is attentive to the details of his travels, as is Gützlaff in his *Journal*. Recounting his first journey to America, Yung gives a description of an electrical storm at sea that captures his own youthful joy and wonder on the voyage: "The night was pitch dark and the electric balls dancing on the tips of the yards and tops of the masts, back and forth and from side to side like so many infernal lanterns in the black night, presented a spectacle never to be forgotten by me" (21). Like Gützlaff or other travel writers, he describes his experiences—the winds, the route, the Island of St. Helena, New York, and the people he meets—with literary touches: for instance, his reference to the transplanting of "a few twigs" from a tree at Napoleon's grave to Auburn, New York, where they grew into "fine, handsome trees," augurs well for his and his classmates' education in New England (22–23). By contrast, the bleak description of his voyage back to China in 1854 in the dead of winter, on the *Eureka*, a ship without cargo, tacitly conveys his reluctance to return. Yung conceived a dislike for his captain (whose involuntary twitches, convulsions, and cursing suggest that he may have had an early, undiagnosed case of Tourette syndrome) after the captain offended him by referring to him as a "Jonah on board" (47). Yung claimed that he himself could navigate better. Since Yung does not mention ever having studied navigation, his remark makes no sense unless read intertextually. His irritation, recalled decades later, suggests that he took the captain's allusion to mean he was a disposable racial outsider; he responded by symbolically claiming the navigational expertise of a world traveler. Readers might even conjecture that Yung took "Jonah," the Biblical prophet thrown overboard to calm a storm at sea, as a coded reference associating him with African slaves, such as those thrown overboard and claimed as lost cargo in the notorious Zong massacre of 1781.[13] Conversely, to claim maritime skill is to equate himself with Olaudah Equiano, whose narrative cited his maritime skill in order to establish him as a "liberal subject," or Gützlaff, who mapped the coastline and helped British pilots during the Opium War (L. Lowe, *Intimacies* 48). When Yung reports that, outside Hong Kong, he lacked the words to translate the Philadelphia skipper's navigational question to a Chinese pilot, he again marks himself as an English-speaking, global traveler who, like a Western missionary, had to recover his Chinese language skills (48). A few years later, Yung dealt with an incident of rudeness to his Chinese servant on the way home from a prayer meeting in Shanghai. Discovering that one of the offending American revelers was a sailor on the same ship, the *Eureka* (now consigned to Yung's employer, a shipping firm), he summoned the man and delivered the avuncular advice that Americans in China must uphold their good reputation among the Chinese; in relating this episode, Yung reverses the usual roles of whites and Chinese in colonial Shanghai of that time, casting himself as the enlightened representative of the ship's employers and the first mate as an employee who deserved discipline but received advice and a handshake (67–69).

Yung's *Life* most strongly resembles Gützlaff's *Journal* in chapters 9 through 12, where Yung depicts his voyages to the tea districts and his parleys with the Taiping rebels. Gützlaff published his *Journal* just after his journeys, providing information about a country still unknown to the many Western readers contemplating trade, diplomacy, or evangelism. By contrast, Yung, writing in 1902, is describing a journey long past. Since his travel conditions are no longer strategically useful, he writes to record his part in history. This is why chapter 9, in which Yung follows Gützlaff's manner in detailing the geography and conditions of his first trip to the tea districts, now seems dry. However, Yung departs from the model of Gützlaff's *Journal* in one important aspect: whereas Gützlaff asserted the right of Westerners to penetrate the Chinese interior in the name of "free trade" (L. Lowe, *Intimacies* 15–16) and the ostensibly free exchange of ideas, Yung interrupts his own account to plead with his readers to respect Chinese sovereignty:

> The opening of the Yangtze River . . . presents a spectacle of unbounded possibilities for the amelioration of nearly a third of the human race, if only the grasping ambition of the West will let the territorial integrity and the independent sovereignty of China remain intact. Give the people of China a fair chance to work out the problems of their own salvation. (84)

Chapters 10–11, in which Yung describes his reception by, impressions of, and negotiations with the Taiping rebels and assesses their influence, provide a portrait of the Taiping leaders and the desolation of Taiping-governed lands in 1859, the year of Yung's visit. In his historical reflections, Yung establishes his objectivity as an observer, writing, "My object in going was to find out for my own satisfaction the character of the Taipings; whether or not they were the men fitted to set up a new government in the place of the Manchu Dynasty" (96). As he emphasizes, he refused to get involved: he pointedly avoided greeting the missionary Issachar Roberts, whom he recognized at the headquarters of Hung Jin, the rebel leader's kinsman, and then declined the seal of office ("the tempting bauble") offered to him (107, 111). Chapter 11, "Reflections on the Taiping Rebellion," seems, once more, to draw on the historical studies of figures such as Gützlaff, both in the offhand references to China's long history of revolutions (which Gützlaff had described as taking place over "at least twenty-four dynasties" [*Sketch* 75–116]) and in its summary of the missionary influence on Hong Huoxiu (Hung Siu Chune), the rebel leader. Yung's commentary on the Taiping Rebellion's decadent final days is pointedly critical of the movement's Christian pretensions, yet he avoids the trap of orientalist sensationalism: he cites the reputation of three captured cities ("Yang Chow, Suchau, and Hangchau") for "their great wealth [and] their beautiful women" as hastening the rebels' end without providing lurid details (121–122).

In relating the final tea expedition, Yung still describes the business side of things (including routes, cargo, and hazards) but plays up the danger, echoing Gützlaff's more exciting narration. One evening, he and his men observed the signs of bandits across the river and discussed how, hopelessly unnumbered, they should defend their cargo. While the expedition's (tall, white) doctor recommended surrender, Yung persuaded the men to defend their honor, if the robbers discovered them in their hiding place, by allowing him to "spring forth" and, armed mainly with his Taiping-issued passport and tacit threats of Taiping retaliation, "check their determination to plunder" with eloquence alone (132). Though the bandits passed without seeing them, Yung's story pointedly asserts *his* masculinity and leadership over those of his white colleague. Yet by the standards of his time, his descriptions of even the bandits remain respectful and humanizing. In contrast to the type of lurid imagery exemplified in Joseph Conrad's 1899 colonial African fantasy, *Heart of Darkness*, Yung's writing never portrays the Chinese bandits as savages, damned and faceless bodies, or cannibals. He describes only the sight of torches moving slowly and regularly down the river, as the "marauding horde" embarks in boats along the opposite shore and floats downstream in silence (133).[14] In Yung's narration, even marauders need sleep.

Reading *My Life* through Slave Narratives

To claim Frederick Douglass's work and the slave narrative genre as intertexts for Yung's narrative of return may seem forced at first, as Yung seems both to inhabit a different place in the American racial imagination and to be personally privileged and exceptional. However, Asians and Africans were linked in the global economy and in Western thinking. During the nineteenth century, even as the purportedly free Chinese and Indian contract laborer replaced unfree slaves in the liberal imagination of progress, Chinese coolies took the place of African slaves as an exploited labor force in Peru and Cuba, as well as other places in the Caribbean (see L. Lowe, *Intimacies*; K. López; Stewart 183–203; Wilson; and note 10 of this chapter). Just as Equiano, Douglass, and other freed slave narrators spoke as global citizens for the concerns of enslaved Africans everywhere, Yung presents himself to liberal white readers as both a global citizen and an elite, American-educated Chinese who seeks to improve the fates of less fortunate Chinese. Yung's autobiography, in which the author makes rhetorical gestures analogous to those of slave narrators, is also driven by the inability to claim full global subjectivity that some readers find in the slave narrators (L. Lowe, *Intimacies*). Thus the contradictions of Yung's writing, analogous to the double voice of slave narratives, suggest that Yung's racial melancholia as a narrator unable to secure his global subjectivity is analogous to that of slave narrators who found their freedom, and that of fellow Africans throughout the world, to be tenuous. Hence, it is unsurprising that Yung shared with Douglass and other male slave narrators the imperative to demonstrate cultural mastery and Western masculinity, the need to bridge cultural differences from both English and American readers, an awareness of responsibility for less privileged members of the author's race, and a continuing vulnerability at the time of writing.

In discussing the travel narrative, I have already suggested a parallel between Equiano—who, as Lisa Lowe has shown, aspired to an "imperial" or global subjectivity and demonstrated this subjectivity through numerous proofs of his civilized sensibility—and Yung, who sought through his narration to assume the role of a global traveler (L. Lowe, *Intimacies* 43–72). In addition, Yung shared with male slave narrators a need to prove his masculinity in appropriately physical terms. Whereas Douglass demonstrated his manhood by recounting and justifying his psychological and physical battle with the brutal Mr. Covey (chap. 9), Yung asserts his manhood rhetorically (as in the two *Eureka* incidents and the bandit sighting discussed above) and through descriptions of physical action, as in the case when he punched and castigated an insolent American at the Shanghai auction house, or the moment when he jumped into a shallow riverbed to deepen the path for his boats (Yung 46–47, 67–69, 131–132, 70–71, 134; F. Cheung, "Political Resistance").

Equiano, Douglass, and Yung all demonstrate their personal industry and mastery of economic markets despite racial discrimination. Equiano learned such skills as barbering, trade, navigation, and bartering for wages, overcoming obstacles posed by white theft and unreliability. Yung, for his part, earned money as a translator, fundraiser, tea agent, and gun dealer; in addition, his proposal to fund his educational program using revenues from the lucrative Shanghai Customs office was approved (Yung 74–76, 136, 173, 191–192). Douglass's experiences of race-based barriers to professional work include an incident in which he was attacked by white apprentices at the Baltimore shipyard where he worked, and one in which whites declined to work with or to hire him as a caulker in New Bedford (67–68, 79). Such instances provide literary antecedents to Yung's early experiences in Hong Kong—where white attorneys "banded together" against him and he was driven out of legal work—and in Shanghai, where he resigned from the Imperial Customs Office after learning that Chinese could never rise to the level of inspectors (60–62, 64).

In writing about women, Yung's formality may be seen in his use of genre norms: he subordinates revelations of his inner emotional life to the ideal of an objective, global narrator and the rhetorical aim of claiming a global subjectivity. Typically, white global travel narrators such as Gützlaff said little about their romantic lives, focusing instead on their intellectual or other discoveries; male slave narrators also took this disembodying approach. (By contrast, Harriet Jacobs's *Incidents in the Life of a Slave Girl* illustrated why black women slave narrators could not readily portray themselves as disembodied intellectuals.) Douglass, for instance, mentions his marriage to Anna Murray, a free black woman, but says little else about her in his 1845 *Narrative*, minimizing mention of his own sexuality in order to maintain the objective voice needed to expose the sexualized vices of slaveholders (76). Yung is likewise strategically reticent about his marriages. He says nothing of a Chinese marriage recorded in a Rong (Yung) family genealogy. Moreover, his autobiography never names his American wife or her family background, describes their courtship, or mentions that she hosted and tutored students of his Chinese Educational Mission (Rhoads 23n20, 60–61, 157). This discretion, typical in male slave narratives and Victorian travel writing, helps the author to project the image of a desexualized, objective, global traveler and to sidestep readers' potential objections to interracial sexual contact.

Moreover, both Douglass and Yung are careful to demonstrate their respect and appreciation for their own mothers as well as kindly white women. Douglass takes the opportunity to discuss the slaveholders' systemic alienation of mothers from children, as well as the injustice and exploitation arising from interracial unions between slave owners and their slaves. (He points out that the institution of slavery entitles white male slaveholders to have sexual access to their female slaves, and that the children produced by such unions, as well as their mothers, remain the property of the fathers unless legally freed by them. According to Douglass, slave mothers and children are liable to incur the wrath of their owners' wives and to be singled out for harsh punishments, including being sold and separated from each other [14–15]). For his part, Yung emphasizes his affectionate reunion with his mother and his care for her upon his return to China in 1854 (49–52). Douglass uses his portrait of Mrs. Sophia Auld as an example of a kind woman whose fundamental humanity toward blacks became warped by the institution of slavery (30–34), while Yung, as mentioned above, begins his story with a distinctive description of Mrs. Mary Wanstall Gützlaff, who, he writes, had prominent, "assertive" features, "thin lips" and "a square chin . . . indicative of firmness of authority." According to Yung, her features "taken collectively indicated great determination and will power," but she was also kindly and sympathetic (3–4). This unusual portrait suggests respect for Mrs. Gützlaff's extraordinary yet proper and feminine character and, by extension, Yung's respect for other white women.

In the slave narrative, as in Yung's text, Christianity is regarded ambivalently. In Equiano's account, his conversion, baptism, Bible ownership, and trust in God form key aspects of his claim to a civilized, global subjectivity that for many English readers would have been synonymous with Christianity. Douglass also presents himself as a Christian writing to Christian readers, as in passages such as his remembrance of his Sabbath prayers for freedom as he gazed at the ships in Chesapeake Bay (49–50, chap. 10). However, in his appendix, he takes pains to distinguish true Christianity from "the Christianity of this land" of slaveholders, which he indicts at length for hypocrisy (80–86, app.). In short, Yung's text shares with the genre of the slave narrative a healthy awareness of the close entwinement, in many cases, of religion with economic self-interest, and the will to describe those links unflinchingly.

Yung's text most strongly echoes Douglass's when he invokes the trope of education as a painful awakening to collective responsibility. Douglass recounts that as a boy, he taught himself to read in spite of the warnings of his master, Hugh Auld, that literacy would make him restless and dissatisfied. In particular, he recounts how his discovery of the oratorical collection "The Columbian Orator" (Bingham) and Richard Sheridan's denunciation of slavery and "vindication of human rights" helped him articulate his own critique of slavery but also brought on the "painful" difficulty of making him "abhor and detest" his "enslavers" as the "meanest" and "most wicked" of men:[15]

> As I read and contemplated the subject, behold! that very discontentment which Master Hugh had predicted would follow my learning to read had already come, to torment and sting my soul to unutterable anguish. As I writhed under it, I would at times feel that learning to read had been a curse rather than a blessing. It had given me a view of my wretched condition, without the remedy. It opened my eyes to the horrible pit, but to no ladder upon which to get out. . . . The silver trump of freedom had roused my soul to eternal wakefulness. (35–36)

Douglass's description captures the pain inherent in seeing his condition, and that of his fellow slaves, simultaneously from within, as a slave, and from without, as the object of white men's analyses. It was painful to recognize how his suffering accorded with that of others; he gained the power to understand how deeply slavery was woven into the fabric of his society and how difficult it would be to overturn it. Similarly, Yung grieved while a student at Yale College, not only because of personal isolation (as the only Chinese student there) and family difficulties but also because he felt the responsibility to save, or help, China, without any means to do so (Worthy 272–274). Throughout his college years (1850–1854), he writes,

> the lamentable condition of China was before my mind constantly and weighed on my spirits. In my despondency, I often wished I had never been educated, as education had unmistakably enlarged my mental and moral horizon, and revealed to me responsibilities which the sealed eye of ignorance can never see, and sufferings and wrongs of humanity to which an uncultivated and callous nature can never be made sensitive. The more one knows, the more he suffers and is consequently less happy; the less one knows, the less he suffers, and hence is more happy. (40–41)

Douglass responded to his newfound responsibility by working to educate other slaves, fleeing north to claim freedom, giving abolitionist speeches, and publishing his narrative. Yung, for his part, claims that he responded to his own "despondency" by resolving to provide for "the rising generation" of Chinese the "same educational advantages [he] had enjoyed, that through western education China might be regenerated, become enlightened and powerful" (41). Calling this aim "the guiding star of his ambition" (41), Yung designates his Chinese Educational Mission (CEM) the climax of his career, so that later, when he writes that the CEM closed prematurely, the reader shares Yung's frustration. Just as the global status of abolition remained unresolved at the times of Equiano's and Douglass's first publications, the CEM's untimely end underscores the fact that the vast experiment of making Western education (in America and elsewhere) available to Chinese was still in progress as Yung wrote.[16]

Lowe argues that Equiano's text, as an exemplary slave narrative, performs two opposed rhetorical operations. On one hand, it gratifies liberal readers by performing his ascent to freedom; on the other, it reminds readers that no black person could be truly free as long as slavery existed, since blacks could be captured and sold into slavery at any time (L. Lowe, *Intimacies* 48–50). Yung's text performs analogous functions. It presents Yung Wing as an outstanding missionary pupil who sought to better China and promote East-West understanding: a Chinese convert who became a global subject. Conversely, it demonstrates that as long as the Chinese government was weak and corrupt and diasporic Chinese were subject to the whims of foreign immigration and citizenship policies, the global citizenship of even an exceptional Chinese like Yung would remain precarious. However, Yung's critique is both oblique and multilayered: he comments on not only Western imperialism within China (as discussed above) but also the coolie trade, through which the conditions of diasporic Chinese are rendered most slavelike, and finally on the failure and corruption of the Qing Dynasty.[17]

Building their case for abolition, Equiano and Douglass describe how, in the West Indies and the American South, slavery was augmented by labor abuses and atrocities, including the withholding of slaves' food, the theft of their earnings, harsh punishments, incarceration, capture, rape, sexual exploitation, and the separation of families. However, each author is mindful of his audience. Equiano flatters his liberal English readers, and Douglass writes more mildly of racism in the North. Similarly, Yung does not directly attack Chinese exclusion or white racism in New England, focusing instead on British colonialism in China, the coolie trade, and the American government's violation of the Burlingame Treaty in refusing to admit Chinese students to American military and naval academies.

Whereas slave narratives were typically published to support abolition and therefore described in detail the conditions of slavery, enumerating its atrocities, Yung's text was written after the abolition of the coolie trade, from the perspective of a native Chinese observer and a diplomatic champion against the practice. In a few pages, he summarizes its greatest injustices, which he had recited to the Peruvian commissioner in Tianjin in the spring of 1873; his first sighting, in Macao in 1855, of "poor Chinese coolies tied to each other by their cues and led into one of the barracoons like abject slaves"; his arrest and punishment of agents in Canton; his trip to Peru to document the abysmal working conditions, which the commissioner had denied; and the two dozen photos he secretly captured of the laborers' lacerated backs in order to "tell a tale of cruelty and inhumanity perpetrated by the owners of the haciendas, which would be beyond cavil and dispute" (192–195). The discussion of the coolie trade is succinct but memorable, clearly inviting comparison between these workers and the African slaves, as further shown in this excerpt describing the "middle passage" of Chinese who had been "inveigled," kidnapped, and forced to board ships and sign labor contracts:

> On landing at their destination, they were then sold to the highest bidder, and made to sign another contract with their new masters, who took special care to have the contract renewed at the end of every term, practically making slaves of them for life. Then I told [the commissioner] something about the horrors of the middle passage between Macao and Cuba or Peru: how whole cargoes of them revolted in mid-ocean, and either committed wholesale suicide by

jumping into the ocean or else overpowered the captain and crew, killed them and threw them overboard, and then took their chances in the drifting of the vessel. (192–193)

Compared to the abolitionist slave narrators, Yung might seem personally to have been in a safer position, for the coolie trade had ended, but the continuing problem of the failing Qing Dynasty, and its limited ability to defend and protect Chinese around the world, remains prominent in the text. In fact, at the time of his autobiography's initial composition, Yung himself had fled China to escape execution as a traitor and had been informed by the State Department that, "due to the enforcement of the 1878 *In re Ah Yup* decision, which declared Chinese immigrants ineligible for citizenship," his U.S. citizenship had been revoked and he was stateless (Yung 239–242; C. Wang, *Transpacific* 35; Sherman; Wan 6.134–6.135).[18] The latter predicament, a consequence of the Qing Dynasty's inability to enforce the Burlingame Treaty of 1868, was so sensitive that Yung does not mention it in his published autobiography. Instead, he diverts readers from thinking about his immigration status with a dramatic but seemingly arbitrary conclusion in which, for reasons he never explains, he depicts a visit he paid to the Japanese governor of Formosa (Taiwan) in 1901. The governor questioned Yung about his past anti-Japanese activities, magnanimously decided not to turn him in to the Chinese government (which was offering a reward for his arrest), invited him to meet the Japanese emperor in Tokyo (an invitation Yung declined), and assigned him a bodyguard (who, presumably, also functioned as a minder to keep him out of mischief) while he was in Formosa (241–246). The Qing failure, manifested as injustice and instability in China and a lack of protection of Chinese abroad, informs Yung's emphatic text and its abrupt, grandiose ending with an unspoken uncertainty and vulnerability. This gap—between Yung's bold narrative voice as a global subject, on one hand, and the reality of his precarious status on the other—is arguably a characteristic literary expression of racial melancholia, found both in slave narratives and in other Asian American texts.[19]

Whereas Douglass says little about African Americans abusing each other, Equiano takes a global view of slavery, including the facts that Africans capture, enslave, and sell other Africans and that his own duties as a slave included the oversight of other slaves. For his part, Yung generally speaks respectfully of his fellow Chinese, except when he turns his criticism back on Qing officials. Perhaps the most important yet unstated contradiction that drives the book is Yung's deep ambivalence toward the Qing Dynasty, which at different times of his life he despised, served loyally, and sought to overthrow. On his title page, Yung signed his name as "Yung Wing, A. B., LL.D.

(Yale), Commissioner of the Chinese Educational Commission, Associate Chinese Minister in Washington, Expectant Tao-Tai of Kiang Su." Despite the Qing appointments, and the love of China announced in his preface, Yung's relationship to the Chinese government of his time was deeply troubled from the outset. His autobiography, published just two years before the fall of the Qing in 1911, reflects and implicitly justifies that deep alienation. Yung signals his critical distance from the Qing early on, by describing his visits to the Canton execution grounds and the Taiping rebels in the 1850s. His account of the Chinese Education Mission (CEM) makes clear that his support of the Qing government was mixed. As he relates his career, he gives ample evidence throughout of the conservatism and pervasive corruption that led to the fall of the Qing, so that his eventual support for the Reformers of 1898 and, later, for anti-Qing revolutionary movements seems not arbitrary or self-serving but deeply rooted in his experiences (Yung 239–241; F. Cheung, "Early Chinese" 31–36). However, because Yung as autobiographer seems to impose a unified form on his life story by emphasizing his service to the Qing, readers have failed to observe that the actual shape of his life was more complex than his rhetorical framing communicates. When read as a would-be triumphal narrative of Yung's loyal service to the Qing, the book seems episodic, incoherent, and full of his personal failures (as history scholar Peter Pei-de Wan suggests). But when read as a memoir of service and disillusionment, the book is a powerful record of his subjective experience of the failure of the Qing.

As an initial critique of the conduct of members of his own race, Yung's rhetorical equivalent to Equiano's description of his capture and sale by fellow Africans might well be his description of the Canton execution grounds he visited in 1855, the year of his return to China. During the first six months after his arrival, Yung reports, Guangdong (Kwangtung) Province was thrown into disarray by a local insurrection that, he says, was unrelated to the Taiping rebellion in the interior.[20] To suppress the rebellion, Viceroy Ye Mingchen (Yeh Ming Hsin) had seventy-five thousand people executed in the summer of 1855. Yung, living with a missionary half a mile from the execution grounds in Canton while brushing up his Chinese language skills, visited the execution grounds. He recalls the sickening smell, the blood-soaked ground, the heaps of decapitated corpses that lay unburied in ninety-degree temperatures for two days, and his indignation that the ruthless Ye had not "deign[ed] to give them even the semblance of a trial, but hurried them from life to death like packs of cattle to the shambles" (54–56). Upon his return from the execution grounds, Yung felt "faint-hearted," "depressed in spirit," and unable to eat or sleep; he deemed the Taiping rebels justified in their attempt to overthrow the Qing Dynasty, which he identified as foreign ("the

Manchu regime"), and briefly considered joining the rebels before returning to his original plan to relearn Cantonese and seek "logical" means, such as educational exchanges, to accomplish his aim (56–57). Truly, Yung must have been not only physically horrified but also ideologically appalled by this evidence of the Qing's neglect, corruption, violence, and injustice. In his text, he charges Ye with seeking vengeance on the region for being the home of the Taiping rebels, who had earlier destroyed Ye's home, and also with extorting money from those threatened with execution, who were said to be largely innocent. Thus Yung introduces a little-discussed but central theme of his text: his own alienation from the Qing rulers. His description of the 1855 atrocities is not mere sensational reportage: it lays the groundwork for rationalizing Yung's eventual rebellion against the Qing, just as Benjamin Franklin's autobiography tacitly justified his alienation from the British by describing the arrogance and incompetence of General Braddock, and Douglass's autobiography dwelled on plantation atrocities to justify his flight from slavery and support for abolition.

Yung's visit to the Taiping rebels, in which he considered whether they were appropriate successors to the Qing, turned down a seal of office, and received a passport, was not only unorthodox but also treasonous, so much so that upon receiving a letter from Viceroy Zeng Guofan, Yung at first feared he would be executed (138). Though critical of the Taiping and the missionaries, Yung also uses these chapters to blame the Qing Dynasty, blaming not only the Taiping but also the "imperialists"—Qing forces—for causing the people to abandon the countryside, and official graft, exploitation, "fraud," and "falsehood" for driving common Chinese to support the rebels (100, 119).

In discussing the complex causes of the CEM's premature closure, Yung foregrounds the U.S. government's refusal to accept CEM applications to West Point and Annapolis but primarily criticizes the "malicious misrepresentations and other falsehoods" of his conservative colleagues, who reported that the students lacked rigor in Chinese studies and were becoming too Americanized (205, 209). In fact, the failure of the CEM was rooted in the government's perception of Yung himself as a useful but Westernized outsider, as well as the conservative Chinese perception that Christianity, U.S. citizenship, and interest in Western culture were antithetical to true Chineseness. From this perspective, Yung's American studies and friends, his conversion to Christianity, his U.S. naturalization in 1852, and his marriage to an American in 1874 were proofs of Yung's unreliability.

While the Qing officials envisioned that the students would root their acquired learning of Western technology within the soil of Chinese culture to contribute to China's "self-strengthening," they also chose to create conditions that would make it almost impossible for the boys not to be deeply influenced by their American surroundings (Spence, *Search* 197–199). Sent as teenagers for a long period of tutelage and separation from their families and home country, they were placed into the homes of American host families and enrolled in American schools. Despite the Qing government's recognition that Yung was indispensable to the project, it signaled a lack of full confidence in him as its representative by pairing him with traditionally educated Chinese who were placed nominally at the head of the CEM, despite the fact that the first two leaders knew no English at all and were dependent on the aid of official translators and, of course, of Yung himself, whose true title was always "Assistant Commissioner," not co-commissioner as he claimed in his autobiography (Yung 181–183, 196–204; Rhoads; Wan). Moreover, the government imposed detailed, somewhat contradictory requirements to ensure that the boys would fully absorb American culture while retaining their loyalty and cultural identifications with China.[21] As Edward Rhoads describes in some detail, these conditions proved difficult to sustain: the boys were young and impressionable; close affective ties naturally sprung up between the boys and their hosts, who acted as surrogate parents as well as cultural teachers to them; and it was extremely difficult to replicate or sustain Chinese culture in white, Anglo-Saxon, Protestant New England. It did not help that Yung himself was an avowed Christian and U.S. citizen—who married Mary Louise Kellogg, a volunteer hosting two of his charges.

Most of these contradictions, fundamental to Yung's story, are directly addressed in his autobiography through his account of his fellow commissioners' efforts to undermine the mission (chap. 19). Rhoads's painstaking research documents Yung's care in enforcing most of these requirements, his deliberate equivocation on the issues of Christianity (he encouraged the students' contact with Twichell and other Christian clergy and tolerated their formation of Christian-Chinese societies but warned them against formal membership in any church), and his deep sympathy with the boys' responsiveness to American culture, including the sports in which they excelled but which were so alien to the training of traditional elite men in China. Despite Yung's effort to conceal his involvement, his behind-the-scenes encouragement of two boys to run away instead of being sent home for intolerable infractions (religious conversion and cutting their queues) may well have contributed to the third commissioner's impression that Yung was a bad influence who was letting the boys run wild. Both Yung and Rhoads explain that the individual failures of the boys were not the direct cause of the mission's early end: rather, the deciding factors were the pervasive Chinese hostility to Western culture, expressed by Yung's conservative partners and the negative reports they sent home; the unexpected expense of the mission; and American hostility to the Chinese. The U.S. government refused to allow the boys to apply for naval and military academies, in violation of the Burlingame Treaty; it ratified in 1881 the unfavorable Angell Treaty, which paved the way for new immigration restrictions; and it imposed those restrictions in the Immigration Act of 1882 (Yung chap. 19; Rhoads 172).

Within this complexity, Yung devotes most of his space to emphasizing the conservatism of his fellow commissioners' pernicious reports and describing his protests of the decision to end the mission. The CEM's closure, followed by the failure of various other schemes Yung proposed for the Chinese government, alienated him, leading him to decry the pervasive corruption of this government. As the book describes, Yung eventually lent his support to the reformers of 1898, who were dispersed and executed by the Empress Dowager, and returned to the United States to see his son graduate from Yale.[22] Writing at the ebb of the dynasty's power, an ebb that in turn lowered the status of Chinese in America, Yung did not challenge the Chinese exclusion laws directly in his autobiography. Rather, beneath the façade of simply recounting his career and achievements, he wrote a testament to the need for a regime change in China—which was in fact imminent but unpredictable—and demanded sovereignty for the country and respect for himself and the other Chinese dispersed around the globe. Written with this profound uncertainty as well as the sure knowledge of his mortality, Yung's autobiography does contrast with slave narratives, which focus less on the validity of specific African regimes than on the injustice of a global economic system dependent on slavery. Nonetheless, Yung's work shows the influence of those double-voiced autobiographies that use one life to register both the uncertain status of many and the racial melancholia that arises from living with that uncertainty. His autobiography sought to contain numerous contradictions—between Yung's debt to his missionary mentors and his rejection of their imperialist goals in China, his lifelong service to China and his claiming of U.S. citizenship and roots, his service to the Qing government and his alienation from it, his binational loyalty and his statelessness. Through this writing, Yung endeavored to claim symbolic citizenship in China and the United States and to address elite and ordinary Americans alike as a fellow global traveler. The contradictions that he found inherent in his position—as a profoundly assimilated American whom the U.S. government had stripped of citizenship due to his race (Sherman)—and that he sought to manage in his autobiography would also haunt the lives of other Chinese migrants and their returning descendants. Yung's text, which combined hopes and fears for China, disillusionment with the Qing Dynasty, and love for America, may not have spoken for many Chinese Americans of his generation (he had, after all, been born in 1828), but by the time it was published in 1909 the anticolonial, anti-Qing sentiments he expressed must have resonated for the generation that overthrew the Qing, created the Republic of China, and installed another American-educated Chinese, Sun Yatsen, as its leader. Thus, Yung's narrative stands at the very beginning of a tradition of narratives of return, in which themes of memory, family history, and ambivalent belonging inform racially melancholic structures of feeling. Furthermore, although many Asian American texts have been read in terms of nationalism and assimilation, Yung's text illustrates how, from the beginning, Asian American writers have also drawn on disparate traditions, such as white travel narratives and black slave narratives, to fashion and claim their own form of global subjectivity.

7

"To Bring the Dead to Life"

Countermemories in Lydia Minatoya's
The Strangeness of Beauty *and Ruth Ozeki's*
A Tale for the Time Being

> Where do words come from? . . . They come from the dead. We inherit them. Borrow them. Use them for a time to bring the dead to life. . . . The ancient Greeks believed that when you read aloud, it was actually the dead, borrowing your tongue, in order to speak again.
> —Ruth Ozeki, *A Tale for the Time Being*, 346

> Postmodern fiction suggests that to re-write or to re-orient the past in fiction and in history is, in both cases, to open it up to the present, to prevent it from being conclusive and teleological.
> —Linda Hutcheon, *A Poetics of Postmodernism*, 110

> Since Asian immigrants began arriving in large numbers in the 19th century, other Americans had not seen them as part of an American imagined community. Against this exclusion and erasure from dominant memory, Asian Americans engaged in practices of countermemory. . . . Countermemory is oppositional memory, the memory of the subordinated and the marginalized, memory from below versus memory from above. Much of Asian American memory is an exercise of countermemory, one engaged in recovering what has been forgotten about and forgotten by Asian Americans.
> —Viet Thanh Nguyen, "Memory," 154

> Unless I see her life branching into mine, she gives me no ancestral help.
> —Maxine Hong Kingston, *The Woman Warrior*, 8

THIS CHAPTER ASKS how Japanese American writers of return narratives engage with the history of the Japanese imperial era and its aftermath, focusing on two novels that range in setting from the 1920s to 2012: Lydia Minatoya's *The Strangeness of Beauty* (1992) and Ruth Ozeki's *A Tale for the Time Being* (2013). Drawing on the work of Ian Buruma as well as historical debates of the 1990s, both of which informed Minatoya's novel, I turn first to the questions posed by Buruma, historians, and others of whether, how, and why Japan suffers from postcolonial melancholia, defined as an inability to mourn and examine its wartime history. I raise the question neither to revive past grievances nor to resolve these debates but rather to acknowledge and describe the historiographic issues that loom over contemporary Japanese American writers who seek to write narratives of return, much as the Holocaust would loom over a contemporary writer looking back to World War II Europe. In "Writing the Pacific War in the Twenty-First Century," Theodore Goossen has suggested that it was necessary for Japanese Canadian writers to be circumspect in scrutinizing Japanese Canadian wartime history during the era of the Redress Movement in Canada, which sought restitution for the internment of Japanese Canadians (63); the same is true of Japanese Americans. As a result, Japanese North American literature from roughly 1953 to 1988 emphasized the internment and other North American experiences while remaining reticent about the complex Japanese politics of World War II. Since 1988 (when both the Canadian and the U.S. redress movements were successfully concluded), the new popularity of Asian American writing, debates about how to remember World War II, and the rise of a new generation of authors have contributed to Japanese North American publications that examine this history from less constrained perspectives ("Japanese American Redress"; see also "Redress Movement"). Because of space constraints, I have chosen two representative texts that combine historical intelligence, literary artistry, and Asian American consciousness; for both authors, fiction provides freedom to speculate on unknowable realities and comment on the processes of writing and interpreting the past. These novels are, respectively, Japanese North American literature's earliest and most recent fictional narratives of return that contribute to a "countermemory" of this period, providing nuanced representations of Japanese responses to the pressures of militarization and war. Although it does not claim to be autobiographical, Minatoya's novel *The Strangeness of Beauty* performs the functions of "postmemory" as defined by Marianne Hirsch. It is set in places and times experienced by Minatoya's relatives, draws on her understanding of her family's history, and generates narratives that are "mediated not through recollection, but through an imaginative investment and creation" while also incorporating historical influences, including a tradition of transpacific women's literature that notably includes Etsu Sugimoto's memoir, *A Daughter of the Samurai* (Hirsch, *Family* 22). *Strangeness* is also historiographic metafiction: it foregrounds the complexities of textual creation and political speech, and it reframes events from the perspectives of ordinary people, exploring their responses and their political efforts to resist and question Japan's militarization (Hutcheon). Ozeki's novel, *A Tale for the Time Being*, is more explicitly historiographic metafiction. Its plot turns on the interpretation of a series of personal documents left by a World War II pilot as they are read by his great-niece, as well as by a stranger in Canada, who stands in for the novel's readers. In both novels, the circumstance of Japanese characters returning to live in Japan becomes the occasion to address questions of historical memory and representation. Ultimately, I argue that both novels avoid postcolonial melancholia—eschewing nostalgia, they actively question Japan's official rationales for war—and that this refusal is typical of Japanese American writing about wartime Japan.

How Should Japan Mourn Its History?

This chapter looks back briefly to the early 1990s—when World War II commemorations provoked much discussion about how events in Europe and Asia were to be remembered in museums, memorials, history textbooks, literature, and popular culture—in order to consider how Japanese American narratives of return enter into dialogue with these discussions about Japanese history and memory. In Washington, D.C., the Holocaust Museum opened in 1993; Congress designated December 7 as National Pearl Harbor Remembrance Day on August 23, 1994; and the *Enola Gay* exhibit at the Smithsonian was criticized, censored, canceled, reconceptualized, and ultimately moved to the Air and Space Museum in early 1995.[1]

In 1995, the Dutch writer Ian Buruma's *The Wages of Guilt: Memories of War in Germany and Japan* compared the two countries' historical memories of World War II. The book argued that both Germans and Japanese had examined and debated their pasts but that Japan's acceptance of responsibility for its wartime history was less complete than Germany's, due not so much to culture as to differences in the two countries' postwar circumstances. Buruma focuses on the two countries' performance of memory work or *trauerarbeit*, the work of mourning their historical failures. This term was coined in the 1960s by German psychoanalysts Alexander and Margarete Mitscherlich, who argued in their influential book *The Inability to Mourn* that Germans needed to fully confront their guilt over their own and their country's wartime history in order to complete the work of mourning the Nazi era (qtd. in Buruma, *Wages* 21–22). In the early 1990s, Buruma argued that in the wake of the Mitscherlichs' book, many Germans appeared to have honored this obligation (*Wages* 21–22). In Japan, however, he found greater ambivalence about the obligation to take full responsibility for the harsher aspects of the nation's wartime conduct—even though much of the history being debated has been documented by Japanese themselves.

John Dower explains the paradox of Japan's pacifist modern identity and its lingering postwar stigma in *Ways of Forgetting, Ways of Remembering: Japan in the Modern World*: "It is fashionable among foreigners to say that 'the Japanese' have sanitized the past and failed to acknowledge their wartime aggression and atrocities," he explains, because of both official denials and the popularity of "victim consciousness," the powerful memories of wartime suffering and loss that pervade Japan ("Aptitude" 105–106). Dower acknowledges conservative politicians' provocative denials of such key actions as the Nanjing invasion; official visits to the Yasukuni Shrine where war criminals as well as ordinary war veterans are memorialized; attempts to censor Japanese textbooks; and denials of responsibility for the military's enslavement of so-called comfort women for soldiers in wartime. In the realm of victim consciousness, he notes the importance of the Peace Memorial Museum and other memorials to Japanese suffering in the public eye (104–105). Yet, he insists, Japan has produced its share of rigorous scholarship, books, and museum exhibitions devoted to Nanjing, the comfort women, and other aspects of the war such as medical experiments on POWs; moreover, neither victim consciousness nor historical whitewashing is unique to Japan (106).[2] Like other U.S. historians, he acknowledges America's own historiographic failures and omissions: citing the censored 1995 *Enola Gay* exhibit and the lack of historical memory and clarity about Vietnam, he writes that for Americans to overlook these while questioning Japan's self-awareness would be "hypocritical" (106; see also Heinrichs; Loewen). Yet despite Japan's democratization, postwar prosperity, and commitment to peace, Japan is more likely than Germany to be criticized, both by Western and Asian countries, for refusing to confront its wartime responsibility: "On this particular issue," Dower asserts, Japan's *unbeliebtheit* or "aptitude for being mistrusted and unloved is truly singular" (108). Japanese conservatives who feel that self-critique has led to loss of national pride have argued that the primary purpose of historical writing and education is, rather than promoting critical self-awareness, to instill pride in the nation. Yet Japanese cabinet and Diet (parliament) members descended from "the same conservative party lineage since 1949" speak for conservatives but not for the entire population; polls have shown that most Japanese agree with the view that Japan was the aggressor in the war that, for Japan and China, began in Manchuria in 1931 (Dower 111). Dower then devotes an essay to explaining how and why Japan has retained its "aptitude for being unloved" (105–135).[3] After examining the causes of Japan's vexed relationship to the work of mourning the war, Dower suggests that the current situation in Japan, which "does not really seem exceptional," is one of ongoing discussions stimulated by the ongoing need to balance national and security needs—to define a viable military presence, for instance—with the need to establish trust and cooperation with other nations by establishing a credible national narrative of the period (134).

Japanese North American Responses

Given that the Japanese themselves have not agreed about how to incorporate their harsh wartime actions into their contemporary narrative of Japan as a uniquely peace-loving nation, outsiders, including Japanese North American writers, must approach this period with caution. Is attention to Japanese suffering and loss necessarily synonymous with historical whitewashing? Or is there a just middle ground where historical acknowledgment of Japanese aggression and war crimes can coexist with space to acknowledge inherited legacies of loss and suffering, contemporary Japan's love of peace, and other, new stories? Finally, how do Japanese North Americans write stories that engage with this history without being discursively overwhelmed by it? Writers like Minatoya and Ozeki have their own tales to tell, and their tales are not limited to North American experiences of internment and assimilation but also engage with twentieth-century Japan and its vexed imperial period.

As we move forward, and Japan and its neighbors grapple with these historical debates, I argue that Japanese American narratives of return complement stories more familiar to Americans, such as those of Japanese internment, Pearl Harbor, and Hiroshima and Nagasaki, by entering into dialogue with these globalized questions of history and responsibility. In both fiction and nonfiction, Japanese Americans also seek to tell the personal stories that are *not* being told by historians.

Whereas Chinese American narratives of return can be strongly linked to the urge to reclaim a Chinese past in the wake of the cold war, the Cultural Revolution, and the warming of Sino-American relations, Japanese American narratives of return include a subset that deal with the 1937–1945 period and its immediate aftermath. Within the Japanese North American literary tradition, I have found, the kind of postcolonial melancholia described by Paul Gilroy, Buruma, and the Mitscherlichs is rare. Rather, Japanese American writers, particularly women, are displaced by gender, class, generation, geography, and choice from celebrating or waxing nostalgic or proud of Japan's military might in the early twentieth century. These authors are deeply mindful of both their responsibility to connect with North American readers and the difficulty of balancing between contrasting rhetorical imperatives: they celebrate Japanese humanity and modernity, on one hand, and critique Japanese militarism, public passivity, and insularity on the other. In published memoirs and personal papers, war survivors Mary K. Tomita and Kazuko Kuramoto both criticize Japanese callousness and humanize readers' understanding of the Japanese in wartime. In fiction, Minatoya and Ozeki perform countermemory work similar to that of Chinese American authors such as Lisa See, Denise Chong, and Winberg and May-lee Chai. Informed by memoirs, diaries, and letters published in English or in English translation by Japanese subjects, novelists such as Minatoya and Ozeki provide alternative personal stories that serve to portray Japanese as loving family members, pacifists, dissidents, and reluctant and questioning participants in wartime acts of nationalism.[4]

Beyond the Family: An I-Story with Questions

In the wake of the World War II history debates, Lydia Minatoya's novel *The Strangeness of Beauty* was the first narrative of return to depict Japan in the 1920s and 1930s. Minatoya, a sansei (or third-generation Japanese American) writer, models her novel after the Japanese form of the I-story (also called the I-novel), a genre that blends elements of fiction and life writing.[5] Within this highly personal form, she chooses for her primary narrator a young Japanese widow, Etsuko Sone, who raises her motherless niece, Hanae Shinoda, in Seattle. Born in Seattle in 1921, Hanae is returned, so to speak, to Japan in 1928; her father hopes that a Japanese education will help her overcome her minority status, diffidence, and loneliness in America. When Hanae's father sends her to Kobe to be educated in the house of her maternal grandmother, Chie Fuji, Etsuko returns with her. The novel combines two thematic threads. Many scenes instruct readers on aspects of Japanese culture such as attunement to nature, use of indirect social cues, reliance on *kata* or form to negotiate social rituals, and blending tradition with modernity; simultaneously, the novel explores ordinary Japanese people's struggles to respond to Japan's militarization and rising imperial ambitions. Rather than end with a death or a marriage, the novel concludes with Hanae's high school graduation and a brief, harmonious family outing in the spring of 1939, before she is to return to her father in Seattle. In terms of form, the originality of Minatoya's novel may be described in terms of the dissonance between her chosen genre—the episodic, diary-like Japanese I-story—and her wish, expressed explicitly by Etsuko as narrator and implied by the bibliography of historical sources, to write a personal, domestic novel that reflects on the rise of Japanese imperialism in the years 1922–1939 (375–376).

Though the story is primarily about the double return and *bildung* of Etsuko and Hanae, it also portrays Etsuko as a feminist peace activist. The novel, which emphasizes Japan's interest in modernity, America, and European culture, poses the historical question of how educated Japanese understood and supported Japanese imperialism. Minatoya's answer is both provocative and complex. She portrays Japanese moderates in the military and pacifists in the ordinary population as being unable to stem the tide of imperialism led by (largely unnamed) military hawks; however, she also provides repeated instances of individuals following, questioning, or resisting the imperialist line. Summarized schematically, her novel might seem inconsistent: at some moments, it sympathetically views ordinary citizens who (willingly or not) conform to the imperialist public climate; at others, it holds individuals strictly accountable for their thoughts, speech, and actions. However, these contradictions accumulate into a vision of society in which overt political acts and statements must be understood within the larger context of the novel. Within this world, the actions of Etsuko and her mother, Chie Fuji, are effective not so much through their direct impact on the decisions of political elites as through their indirect effects on the ordinary people they meet and educate, particularly Hanae. The novel does not exactly argue that the personal is political. Instead, it conveys that the political is but one aspect of the personal and the everyday. For Etsuko and for the novel, political events, interpersonal relations, nature, the narrator's intellectual formation, and aesthetic expression all combine into a larger form of ethical expression: the novel registers the narrator's slow formation, throughout these imperialist years, of a multilayered ethical consciousness.

As a first-time novelist, Minatoya may have begun the novel as a filial act of postmemory, a way "to fill in imaginatively what the parent could not express" and imagine "stories my parent(s) never told me," as Goossen puts it in his study of Japanese Canadian novels about this period (Goossen 66). Her memoir, *Talking to High Monks in the Snow* (1992), provides context for this work through features readers may recognize from return narratives. The author uses her stint as a visiting scholar in Japan, combined with family stories, to tell the story of her identity formation, not only as a Japanese American but also as a transnational citizen with an Asian American political consciousness. Her firsthand impressions of Japan include the story of her reunion with her Japanese relatives, which effects a reconciliation in the wake of a bitter divorce. Minatoya reveals that her own grandmother, a picture bride, separated from her husband in America, returned to Japan with their four children, and was divorced five years later. When the divorce occurred, the children were cut off from their mother and her kin and supported, but not fully acknowledged, by their father's parents (*Talking* 5–8). After many years, the children were permitted to rejoin their father in America. Minatoya's mother hesitates to introduce her to their Japanese family members because of the sad circumstances of the divorce, which sundered ties between the mother's and father's clans, but the author's eventual meeting with family members in Japan turns out happily.

As a *kibei* (a Japanese American sent to Japan to be educated) Minatoya's mother provides a biographical antecedent for Hanae, the younger heroine of *Strangeness*. Minatoya's grandmother, who returned to Japan after marrying and beginning a family in America, provides a prototype for the novel's narrator, Etsuko. However, illustrating the novel's function as a work of postmemory in Goossen's sense, Minatoya creates new characters rather than replicating her relatives. Unlike Minatoya's grandmother, Hanae's mother Naomi marries for love, emigrates to rejoin her sweetheart in Seattle, and dies in childbirth. Also unlike the grandmother, Etsuko marries for love and is widowed, with no children. The settings of the novel (Seattle and Kobe, 1921–1939) enable Minatoya both to imagine the era of her mother's birth in America and, turning to Japan, to raise broader questions about the conduct of individuals in that troubled time. However, in contrast to historical accounts centered on political or military elites, Minatoya's focus on the private lives of a family of samurai women leaves space for the traditional subject matter of the Western domestic novel—the interiority of the bourgeois domestic woman—and of the Japanese I-story, detailing the narrator's interior and everyday life. The novel may be seen as a work of postmemory not because the protagonists replicate Minatoya's family stories but because she uses her imagination, anchored in research, to provide a glimpse for American readers of Japanese life in that period.

Reimagining Japanese Femininity

To underscore the novel's literary status, Minatoya emphasizes her characters' roots in transpacific, Japanese American women's autobiographies, but she also uses her freedom as a novelist to stress her heroines' development of the values of individualism, self-determination, and political dissent. Etsuko's surname, Sone, alludes to the Japanese American author and psychologist Monica Sone, who published her groundbreaking internment memoir *Nisei Daughter* in 1953 (*Strangeness* 51). "Etsuko" is a feminized version of the given name of Etsu Inagaki Sugimoto, whose transpacific autobiography *A Daughter of the Samurai* was first published in 1926 (Sugimoto xv).[6] Similarly, the names "Chie" and "Hanae" are reminiscent of the names of Sugimoto's daughters, Hanano and Chiyo (Sugimoto 219, 239). Minatoya draws on Sugimoto's text for many memorable details about samurai life, such as the use of "friendship ribbons" during dockside parting, wedding clothing and rituals, kimonos, New Year celebrations, the annual ritual of airing family heirlooms, and bilevel kitchens; both also tell the story of a samurai wife who, after the loss of a battle, must hide the family and servants and burn down the family mansion (Sugimoto 5, 7, 252–253, 282–283, 305, 311; Minatoya, *Strangeness* 223). The motif of Etsuko being raised by farmers, resulting in a humble self-image and mixed feelings toward her aristocratic mother, Chie, may be rooted in the story of Minatoya's mother being raised under the shadow of her mother's divorce in Japan. However, it may also have been inspired by a detail in Sugimoto's autobiography: when her father was captured and her family concealed, the author's sister stayed with a farmer's family (Sugimoto 284–285). In another echo, Etsuko imagines Chie's parents reasserting their mutual commitment when they learn that his samurai status is officially ended (Minatoya, *Strangeness* 174–176). This traumatic historical transition is treated at greater length by Sugimoto in her accounts of the declining fortunes of Mr. Toda (a former samurai) and her own father (27–32, 35–41). Minatoya's fictional scene captures the feeling of the young samurai couple's shock but omits the grim details included in Sugimoto's family history, choosing instead to foreground the couple's unspoken romantic passion. The novel's terse, oblique references to death, such as the sudden deaths of Etsuko's parents in Japan and her husband in America (*Strangeness* 33), echo Sugimoto's compressed treatment of her father's death in Japan and her husband's in America (41, 240–241).

When newly widowed and returned to Japan, Sugimoto worries about pleasing her Japanese in-laws because they have the power to separate her from her own children (Sugimoto 242–245); similarly, Minatoya's Japanese returnee, Etsuko, is wary of her mother's judgment and fearful of having her niece Hanae separated from her. Sugimoto is stung when her mother compliments her resemblance to her father, because "no Japanese woman likes to be told that her walk suggests that of a man" (269). Similarly, Etsuko receives a mixed compliment from her mother when Chie praises her for being like her father ("patient, generous, wise") but adds that, like her contemplative father, Etsuko meanders like a turtle: lost in thought, with hands behind the back and neck stretched forward (Minatoya, *Strangeness* 269). Whereas Sugimoto's recollection underscores her and her daughters' efforts to perform Japanese femininity, Minatoya's narrator is more concerned with finding a means to model the (implicitly samurai) virtues of "integrity, commitment, and valor" for Hanae (*Strangeness* 249).

For all the turmoil in Sugimoto's family of origin (the Inagaki family), she finds her most poignant moments in observing her daughters' homesickness for America. In particular, her older daughter Hanano is too intelligent and physically restless to please Sugimoto's mother, Mrs. Inagaki, who comes to stay with them. After two years, Mrs. Inagaki says approvingly that Hanano is "growing gentle and graceful," but Sugimoto herself wonders whether her daughter is "ever really happy anymore," for she has lost her "joyous eagerness to see, to learn, to do." In Sugimoto's eyes, her "American girl, so full of vivid interest," has been subdued like the family's potted dwarf pine, whose roots are perpetually bound; she worries that neither it, nor Hanano, "will *ever* be free!" (271–272). Though Hanano is a young child, her loneliness and sense of loss seem to inform Minatoya's portrait of Hanae as a child who is lonely in both Seattle and Kobe (*Strangeness* 34, 253). Sugimoto overhears little Hanano telling her smaller sister Chiyo that their Mama—the author—is the "only treasure [they] have left" now that their father has died and they have lost their home in America (Sugimoto 260). In a fictional variation on this mournful scene, Hanae, in Kobe, tells Etsuko that she has "lost everything she's ever valued. Father, Mari, even school! There's not a single thing left that I love!" (Minatoya, *Strangeness* 253).

Despite their superficial narrative similarities, the two books' endings project contrasting values. Sugimoto gains leave to return with her American-born children to America, and Minatoya ends her novel with the understanding that Hanae will return to her father in America while Etsuko remains in Japan.⁷ However, Sugimoto's memoir ends with a description of her trip to her family's hometown, where her daughters hear more about their grandmother's courageous compliance with tradition, and a gentle plea to readers for transpacific understanding. By contrast, Minatoya's novel culminates with a dramatic scene in which Hanae violates Japanese norms of behavior by giving an impromptu graduation speech asking listeners to question the war:

> Now we are engaged in a broadening war that we say is to benefit Asia. . . .
> What I ask tonight is that each of us, in our personal and national decisions, consider our motives for acting. (*Strangeness* 367)

Sugimoto depicts her mother as subtly training Hanano to suppress her individual spirit; by contrast, Minatoya depicts Chie as guiding Hanae to internalize and express individualist values such as wartime pacifism, critical thinking, and freedom of speech. This theme is exemplified by Hanae's commencement speech and Chie's shouting out a quotation from Abraham Lincoln: "To remain silent when they should speak makes cowards out of men!" (364).

Both authors use the familiar trope of the valiant, resourceful Asian matriarch who preserves the family and combines respect for tradition with the capacity to adapt to changing times, but while Sugimoto's mother, Mrs. Inagaki, proves fundamentally too traditional for the narrator, Minatoya's matriarch, Chie Fuji, is modern at heart (So 127–130). Mrs. Inagaki is the intrepid samurai woman who, upon her husband's capture, burned down the house but kept all the family members alive and hidden until the family could be reunited (Sugimoto 280–285). Yet, having saved the life of their firstborn son, she and her husband later disown him for declining an arranged match while in love with another woman (55–58). (Shortly thereafter, Sugimoto's education becomes more masculine, and she receives the masculine nickname Etsu-*bo,* as if being groomed to be the replacement heir.) Years later, when Mrs. Inagaki joins Etsu's Japanese household, she is overtly gentle and positive yet subtly disapproving of her granddaughters' nontraditional studies. Having formerly explained to American friends that "beneath all the gentle meekness, Japanese women are like . . . volcanos," Sugimoto feels immense relief when permitted to return with her daughters to America (202). By contrast, Minatoya envisions Chie, the haughty matriarch of the House of Fuji, as combining aristocratic judgment and hauteur with the fundamental modernity that Christine So has identified as typical of Chinese women in Chinese American family history narratives (So 127–130). Like Mrs. Inagaki, Chie also disowns a child for choosing the wrong romantic partner. However, as a young woman Chie breaks matchmaking protocol (*kata*) to glare at a suitor and then accept his wedding proposal face to face (Minatoya, *Strangeness* 89–90); later admonishes Etsuko to teach Hanae integrity, commitment, and valor (172); sells family heirlooms rather than collecting rents, evicting tenants, and driving local farmers' sons to join the army (283); sports an anti-imperialist kimono (203–204); introduces Hanae to subversive ideas about female autonomy and self-determination via "Western Masterpieces in Translation" (235); and publicly supports Hanae's graduation address by shouting Lincoln's words as an antiwar slogan (365). As this list suggests, the novel gradually converts Chie from the embodiment of tradition to a model for individualism, pacifism, dissent, and covert action—or, in the novel's words, "integrity, commitment, [and] valor" (172). Minatoya seems well aware of Sugimoto's artful combination of feminism and 1920s apologetics for Japanese culture, and she mines Sugimoto's transpacific, feminist text for historical detail and rhetorical strategy.[8] Her own novel, written to scrutinize and understand Japanese imperialism from a later vantage point, imagines its protagonists as mentally freer but politically still quite constrained.

Searching for Dissent

In its historical reasoning, Minatoya's novel seems caught between a wish to explain or understand those who supported the war and the wish to affirm the importance of individual conscience and action. In an indirect response to public questions about the responsibility of individual Japanese for the war, she depicts the social conditions arising from the economic and political situation. For instance, the rise of official xenophobia in December 1933 is signaled by the withdrawal of local boys from the English-language school of the sincere, respected American missionary, Miss Langley (193–194). Etsuko then inserts a historical digression tracing the rise of Japanese militarism back to the massive Tokyo earthquake of 1923, which leads not only to the introduction of modern amenities in the course of rebuilding but also to a financial panic and an enduring economic collapse in 1927, forcing young men to join the army. The press is muzzled by the Peace Preservation Law on 1925, young officers express their rage by assassinating those in power, and heroic newsreels are released to promote the war effort (198–201). In this context, she demonstrates how New Year's visits in the community are rendered awkward, as guilty parents apologize to Miss Langley for their sons' withdrawal from her English school, and Etsuko cannot express her political views without offending Hanae's anti-American headmaster (206–210).

In *Strangeness*, the limits of the novel's action reflect limits on the political agency of educated women—a proxy for all ordinary people—in Showa-era Japan. Despite her rank, Chie has so little real political power that she can shrug off the headmaster's threat to have her arrested after the graduation: "I'm nearly seventy years old. No one would seriously consider jailing an old woman whose crime is quoting Abraham Lincoln" (368). Similarly, Minatoya portrays Etsuko as laboring to find a way to protest and resist the war, in a fictional world where few women are politically active. After the departure of Miss Langley in 1934, Etsuko joins a women's protest group that starts to publish an antiwar newsletter (223, 239). However, the tightening of press censorship is dramatized when the police destroy the group's mimeograph machine and search for their mailing list on February 26, 1936; this is also the date of "a wide-scale plan for the assassination of statesmen and senior officers" by 1400 soldiers and "a cadre of fanatical young officers," later dramatized in the story of the attack on Admiral Sato (274–275, 298). Though the near-coup fails and representative government briefly flourishes, the prime minister is too weak to reverse Japan's declaration of war on China in 1937. "War wasn't the will of the people," Etsuko narrates. "Prime Minister Konoye made a mild protestation . . . but by that time the government was largely controlled by the military and he was overruled" (276). Her group resorts to circulating news found in foreign language women's magazines. However, Etsuko acknowledges the futility of such efforts upon learning of the invasion of Nanjing (316).

Minatoya uses the trajectory of Tatsuo Tanida, a filmmaker who visits Etsuko's pacifist group, to sketch a second form of civilian resistance to Japanese militarism. Etsuko explains that Tanida's samurai films, like the American films being supplanted by propaganda, "had served the sly purpose of advocating ideas of individual conscience and social resistance" (289). Anticipating the rise of propaganda films, Tanida takes a job as a newsreel photographer, hoping to provide "an alternative point of view" (289). Though Tanida aims "to confront complacency by depicting the horrors of war," he quits when he sees that his images are so terrible that they have the power of pornography (309–310). Arrested, tortured, and released, Tanida is forced to give a public speech voicing support for the war and is then confined to house arrest (313). Despite his public humiliation, Etsuko insists on visiting him. For her sake, he rebuffs her—refusing to see her and sending word not to visit again. Minatoya portrays Tanida as nobly questioning the war, unable to produce images that adequately resist the government's master narrative and severely punished for his refusal to comply. Yet she gives hope that his questioning spirit has survived. Etsuko interprets his parting gift, a book of Basho's life journey poems, as a sign that, like Basho, Tanida will survive through contact with art and the ordinary pleasures of everyday life (318).

Similarly, Minatoya portrays Lt. Matsunaga, a decorated veteran of Nanjing hired to teach military drills at Hanae's school, as a troubled pacifist; this unexpected characterization undermines both traditional notions of military heroism and negative American stereotypes of Japanese soldiers as mindlessly self-sacrificing or brutal. At school, Matsunaga converts military drills to first aid practice and then instructs students to question the Japanese cause; outside his workplace, he joins Etsuko's antiwar discussion group (277, 280). By recalling how Matsunaga's enlistment was resisted by his parents, who discussed techniques to secure a medical draft exemption for him, Minatoya suggests that Japanese people did not uniformly celebrate the ideal of patriotic sacrifice for this war (285–286). Later, pressed by Hanae to explain how he became a war hero, Matsunaga describes his actions in Nanjing, his first battle after officer training. Nauseated by the officers' violent initiation ritual, he fled: seizing an army vehicle, he picked up women who had been raped and injured, administered first aid, and tried to return them to their homes and families until he realized that those homes and families no longer existed. For resisting military police, he was shot, arrested, and hospitalized, losing a foot to gangrene and amputation. Unsuited for command, he nonetheless received an honorable discharge and an award when his superiors were recalled in disgrace. He considers himself lucky to have escaped "the self-hatred, the horror, the loss of all hope that [he sees] in the veteran troops' eyes" (340–348). When Hanae tries to affirm his resistance as heroic, he criticizes his "heroic fantasy" of joining a brotherhood of war martyrs whose deaths, like falling cherry blossoms, "would transform the world with blinding beauty," but he voices respect for other enlisted men who had no utopian illusions but "loved their families and wanted them to be proud" (345). Thus

Matsunaga's story both undercuts official Japanese military rhetoric and counters essentialist stereotypes of Japanese soldiers as violent and unfeeling by nature. It reinforces the historical reality that individuals, in the absence of good leadership, could do little to resist the momentum of the war. By telling a story of Nanjing through the eyes of one insistently self-deprecating soldier who perceives all the soldiers as brutalized by their training and wartime duties, Minatoya reaffirms the humanity and constraints on the soldiers while stopping short of condoning the results.

Halfway through the book—as Minatoya delineates the efforts of the Japanese government to demonize and expel foreign people and influences, Hanae's mourning of her Japanese American friend's return to the United States, and the contraction of her education to numbing versions of military propaganda—Chie voices the novel's central philosophy of faith in the power of everyday rituals. Speaking in 1934, she argues that ordinary Japanese prefer "small gentle pleasures like baseball" to glory (216). To clarify her point, she compares the slow rituals of baseball to those of the traditional Japanese tea ceremony. Because people are driven by "small," "powerful" things such as familiar tastes and the touch of loved ones, she hopes that the love of everyday pleasures such as "movies [and] fashion" will motivate them both to resist those who would drive Japan to war out of greed and ambition and to keep the country engaged with the outside world through peaceful means (216–217). Though love of Western culture did not, historically, prevent Japan's military escalation in the Pacific War, Chie's speech foregrounds the novel's celebration of everyday beauty, including its strangeness, as a grounding for moral clarity, curiosity, and freshness of vision even in wartime. The novel's climax, in which Chie and Hanae break *kata* (form) to denounce the war, is followed by a symbolic homecoming (similar to the homecoming near the end of Sugimoto's text), in which Chie takes Etsuko and Hanae to visit the family gravesite. In a custom found in the original I-novels, Etsuko completes a poem initiated by Chie:

> *[Chie:] Family reunion!*
> *Kites spin skyward with diamond hope!*
> *[Etsuko:] Near the graveyard, snow flowers bloom.*
> *Morning rises from shadow. (372)*

While Chie's lines juxtapose their present "reunion" and Hanae's anticipated return to America, Etsuko's lines also evoke a distant future when the Fuji family will recover from the difficult times to come. Through Etsuko and her choice of the I-novel format, Minatoya demonstrates how a gracefully indirect novel can provoke American readers to return with a fresh eye to a painful historical period. She humanizes the Japanese by depicting their everyday joys and fears in nuanced fashion, yet also poses serious questions about citizens' responsibilities in a time of war and limited political agency.

Ozeki's *Tale*: Mourning History, Countermemory, Postmemory, and Historiographic Metafiction

In her award-winning novel *A Tale for the Time Being* (2013), Japanese American author Ruth Ozeki uses magical realism to comment on the difficulty of recovering historical truth from traditional sources and suggest the corresponding need to activate one's compassionate imagination. As *A Tale* addresses the work of mourning history (*trauerarbeit*), Ozeki mobilizes the narrative of return, here in novel form, to illustrate how a searching and flexible reading of history can enrich both the returnee and the book's readers. As a work of fiction that brings to its readers' attention the writings of real Japanese Buddhists, anarchists, and military pilots, Ozeki's novel participates in the construction of a collective Asian American *countermemory*. Through her portrayals of a nun and a World War II pilot, she counters the anti-Japanese tropes of American popular memory by portraying both characters as intellectually voracious, cosmopolitan, spiritual, brave, and decent. Earlier, I quoted Viet Thanh Nguyen's definition of countermemory as the "oppositional memory . . . of the subordinated and the marginalized, memory from below versus memory from above" (154). This builds on George Lipsitz's earlier definition of countermemory as a narrative that "starts with the particular and the specific and then builds outward toward a total story" and uses "hidden histories excluded from dominant narratives" to challenge existing histories (212–213, qtd. in Davis, *Relative Histories* 16).[9] In addition, the novel's portrayal of its protagonists' imaginative journeys exemplifies Marianne Hirsch's formulation of *postmemory*, which is "distinguished from memory by generational distance and from history by deep personal connection" and generates narratives that are "mediated not through recollection, but through an imaginative investment and creation" (Hirsch, *Family* 22). The protagonist, Nao, resolves her melancholic mourning of migration-related losses through acts of postmemory. When focused on the difficulties of interpreting historical documents, *A Tale for the Time Being* also exemplifies *historiographic metafiction*. It draws on the final words of World War II pilots in order to subvert conventional representations of them, questions the project of revisiting the past, focuses on marginal figures rather than historically representative types, portrays the details or supposed facts of history as both compelling and slippery, and foregrounds the labor of assimilating or interpreting these facts.

In the novel, a Japanese American writer (Ruth) reads and interprets the diary of a Japanese schoolgirl (Naoko "Nao" Yasutani), which she finds on the beach near her home on the rustic Canadian island of Whaletown, British Columbia, along with a watch, a set of letters in Japanese, and a diary in French. Much of the novel consists of Ruth's efforts to translate and interpret Nao's diary and then to respond to what she perceives as Nao's urgent need for supportive intervention from her imagined reader—Ruth herself. Ruth, a struggling writer, stands in both for Ruth Ozeki, the author of the novel, and for the novel's readers. As Ruth the character imaginatively follows and ultimately intervenes in the story of Nao, who is a both a writer and a reader, Ozeki the author provides a double model for readerly acts of postmemory. The novel also refers to the 9/11 attacks on the World Trade Center and the United States' subsequent attacks on targets in Iraq and Afghanistan, introducing a contemporary frame of U.S. global politics for Nao's and Ruth's interpretations of World War II documents.

The theme of time, signaled in the novel's title, is reinforced by the artifacts, references to Marcel Proust's novel *In Search of Past Time,* and the diary author's name, which puns on the word "now." She also introduces herself as a "time being," "someone who lives in time," and includes her imagined reader(s) as time beings as well (1). Nao's diary records a period in which her family, having returned to Japan after her father was laid off from a Silicon Valley computer programming job, grapples with questions of meaning that could determine whether she chooses to live or die. Disheartened by vicious bullying at school, her father's unemployment, and his suicide attempts, Nao turns for inspiration and encouragement to her ancestors. Her father, whom she calls "Haruki #2," is the namesake of his uncle ("Haruki #1"), a pilot who died in a suicide mission in World War II. Despite the official honor Haruki #1 gained for his service in the kamikaze or *tokkōtai* forces, his mother, Jiko Yasutani, embraced Buddhism and pacifism and became a nun in the wake of his death.[10] Though contemplating suicide, Nao plans to live long enough to tell the story of her great-grandmother Jiko, whom she admires and affectionately calls "my old Jiko" and "Granny" (17–18). As Nao gets to know her great-grandmother, she draws strength from Jiko's compassion and steadfast faith in human nature, but these lessons in Zen fail to defend her from schoolmates' violent attacks, psychological cruelty, and cyberbullying. Hence, Nao is attracted to the story of Haruku #1's life and death as a suicide bomber, which she interprets in various ways. At first, she idolizes him as a heroic ancestor whose patriotic sacrifice contrasts with her father's failure to provide for the family or to protect her at school. When Nao learns that Haruki was *not* a zealous suicide bomber but rather a conscripted pacifist who died to provide for his family, she still idealizes his willingness to die bravely, and with this understanding she and her father lean further toward suicide, as Jiko's life also draws near to its natural end. However, after a magical-realist episode in which Ruth dreams that she is able to warn Nao's father of Nao's suicidal thoughts, and deliver Haruki #1's true diary to Nao, the father-daughter suicides are averted. Nao learns that, in the end, Haruki #1 resolved not to kill at all; she regains her father's support in embracing Jiko's affirmation of life and finally learns and appreciates that he lost his job through an exercise of conscience.

At the start of the novel, Nao and her father are suffering from a structure of feeling akin to *racial melancholia*, in which migrants to America cannot mourn the losses associated with immigration. However, as the Yasutanis are repatriated Japanese citizens, their failure to assimilate consists of mourning the losses they experience upon *reverse* migration, which I call "repatriate melancholia." Otherwise, Nao's story follows the patterns described by Anne Anlin Cheng, David L. Eng, and Shinhee Han for racial melancholia (Cheng, *Melancholy*; Eng, "Melancholia," "Transnational Adoption"; Eng and Han, "Desegregating," "Dialogue"). Cheng describes racial melancholia in terms of social marginalization or abjection, while Eng and Han describe it in terms of individual, migration-related loss and the inability to compensate by assimilating into one's new host country. Cheng argues that American society relies on the presence of racial outsiders in order to reaffirm the centrality of whites as the nation's racial insiders. As a result, whites retain a "melancholic" attachment to minorities, whose presence they require (to maintain their own status) but do not acknowledge. This view draws on Toni Morrison's argument in *Playing in the Dark* that American literature depends on the presence of African Americans as a "ghostly presence" (Cheng, *Melancholy* 133). According to Cheng, while whites are melancholically attached to racial minorities, the minorities experience racial melancholia because they have to deal with the demand to be present but excluded and unrecognized. In addition, Eng and Han argue that immigration necessarily incurs the loss of treasured elements of culture, language, and identity that America's utopian discourses of assimilation do not acknowledge. The minority immigrant must therefore mourn these losses in private, and must perform assent to assimilation while frequently being reminded that, in fact, he or she may not assimilate. This generates a complex psychic structure, or structure of feeling, as the immigrant can neither return nor go forward and can neither recover nor mourn the lost identity, nor substitute a secure sense of belonging in America. This ambivalent structure of feeling, called "racial melancholia," is structural, not a sign of individual pathology. Whereas all immigrants are liable to experience migration-related losses, Eng and Han suggest that racial melancholia will be particularly strong for those who are structurally excluded by reason of race from actual and symbolic citizenship. For Asian Americans, cultural exclusion has historically been rooted in the laws that labeled Asian immigrants as "aliens ineligible to citizenship" (L. Lowe, *Immigrant Acts* 7) on the grounds that they were culturally unassimilable and prevented most Asian immigrants from entering or naturalizing for six decades, called the Exclusion Era, from 1882 through 1943.

Now, let us return to the novel. In returning to Japan from America, Nao and her father experience multiple losses. Some pertain to migration itself, such as the loss of their place, language, culture, community, and identity in California, and others pertain to Nao's father's unemployment and his corresponding fall in social status. The two characters are unable to mourn and get over their losses, however, because within the world of the novel, neither American nor Japanese discourses provide affirmative means to express migration-related loss. Instead, father and daughter are abjected from work and school, structurally blocked from assimilating into their own country, and threatened with cultural erasure. As the daughter of a Silicon Valley computer software designer, Nao was successful and accepted by her peers at her school in Sunnyvale, California, but as the Americanized daughter of an unemployed Japanese returnee she is subject to violent, cruel, degrading, and officially sanctioned bullying at her school in Tokyo. In particular, she is simultaneously required to be visible as a target at school and unacknowledged as a member of her community. After escalating Nao's ostracism to the point of pretending they cannot see or hear her, the class even conducts a mock funeral for her. Thus, Nao experiences in full force the Japanese version of U.S. discrimination against outsiders; however, Nao is singled out not because of race but because she is Americanized. As others, including the lowly substitute teacher, bond and raise their own status by ostracizing her, harmony and group cohesion in this Japanese school are revealed to be built on the arbitrary designation of outsiders to be abjected, simultaneously denied belonging and retained on the community's margins. The status of Nao's father as an unemployed professional is similar: he feels obliged to simulate employment and perform the role of a salaryman by dressing up for work, spending the day away from home, and trying to raise funds by gambling. Like U.S. minorities, who lack full legal and cultural citizenship but whose presence helps define the limits of the nation, Mr. Yasutani can neither enter the Japanese economy nor escape its conventions and his family's expectations; nor can Nao easily evade the requirement to fill the role of school pariah. Internalizing this abjection, Nao and her father express anger, self-blame, and dejection; they are unable, at the outset, to settle on new objects of hope and desire. This is why I read their mental state as melancholic. Recall that in Freud's classic essay "Mourning and Melancholia," mourning is a normal period of processing one's losses, a process that gradually ends when the mourner gives up his or her attachment to the lost object of desire. However, when the mourner refuses to give up mourning for the lost object, cannot get over the loss, and can find no new object of desire, that person is displaying melancholia. In short, mourning is transient; melancholia is chronic. Although Nao's and her father's blocked, hopeless mental condition could be read simply as personal melancholia or depression, I find it is also a structure of feeling rooted in their position as returnees unable to assimilate.

Thus, Nao's narrative of return depicts a return-related form of racial melancholia. Let us say that the family's lives in Sunnyvale are the lost objects mourned by Nao and her father. Let us also say that the stories of Haruki #1 and Jiko, the pilot and the nun, are new objects to which Nao becomes attached in her search for a new object of desire to replace her migration-related losses. In this case, since these two figures represent, respectively, Japan's wartime history and its aftermath, Nao's choice of them as new objects may represent a choice to resolve her personal losses by engaging in a more public form of mourning: *trauerarbeit*, or the work of processing Japan's wartime history. Because Nao does so through the critical, pacifist, Buddhist perspective of her great-grandmother Jiko, the novel challenges conventional views of the tokkōtai sacrifices as necessary, meaningful, and patriotic. Through her efforts to comprehend their stories, Nao also parallels ongoing public discussions about Japan's need to counter its historical melancholia and come to terms with its past by fully examining its wartime history: the novel comments on this debate. Born in Japan in peacetime but raised primarily in the United States, Nao may serve as a proxy for any modern person who seeks to understand this period, particularly for Japanese Americans for whom the war is an important but elusive part of their heritage. In pursuing the stories of Jiko and Haruki #1, Nao finds a new object to replace her losses and resolves her melancholia through acts of postmemory. However, to survive this process, she must reach an understanding of Haruki #1's story that promotes life, not sacrifice or suicide.

Moreover, Ozeki uses magical realism to do the work of *historiographic metafiction*—fiction that, as explained by Linda Hutcheon, foregrounds the processes of writing and interpreting history as a set of discursive conventions (Hutcheon 5, 110, 113–114). At no point does the novel presume directly to dramatize the events of Haruki #1's life and death through the eye of an omniscient narrator; rather, Haruki's tale is seen indirectly, through Nao's retelling of her encounters with his words—his literary remains—and Ruth's reading, with the help of her husband Oliver and others in Whaletown, of Nao's account. The implication of Ozeki's choice to use nested first-person narratives to approach Haruki #1's story is that as latter-generation spectators, neither authors nor their readers can know or definitively document the final actions and mental experiences of those who died in war. Rather, the novel dramatizes the process by which Nao uses primary sources and artifacts (Jiko's oral accounts and Haruki #1's picture, watch, beads, letters, and diary) to imagine and interpret her great-uncle's life and death. However, the novel reaches its crisis when Nao develops a conventional view of her great-uncle as a patriotic martyr. This view, which seemingly accords with official Japanese interpretations of the tokkōtai deaths, leads Nao to conclude that suicide, as an exercise of courage and resolution, may be the last remaining means for her and her father to claim agency in lives they see as futile and meaningless.

This interpretive crisis is marked by the sudden disappearance of all words from the last pages of Nao's previously full diary, which implies not only that she and her father may have died before she could finish writing but also that Ruth and Oliver, the "time beings" for whom Nao writes, are also existentially at risk: after all, they are defined in this novel primarily by their roles as Nao's readers. The risk that they will also vanish is theorized by Oliver and implied by the disappearance of both the words at the end of Nao's diary and Oliver's cat (Ozeki 341–344). Indeed, Ruth and her fellow Canadians stand in for Nao's North American readers, and Ruth's active engagement with Nao's and Haruki #1's texts implicitly models an ethics of reading that is tested at the novel's climax. The novel portrays Ruth as seeking help with translations of Nao's diary and Haruki #1's letters and secret French diary, discussing the materials with Oliver and others, consulting the Internet, and finally searching for information about Nao's family with the hope of intervening in her story, despite the fact that her discovery of the diary postdates its composition by many years. Ruth's response to the threatened extinctions of Nao, her father, her grandma, the diary, and herself is therefore critical to the novel's comment on readers' obligations to the stories they receive through others.

The novel's resolution, which requires Ruth to intervene in Nao's story by magical-realist means, implies that merely reading the historical record is not enough: the reader must employ an active and sympathetic imagination to create an alternate story, a form of postmemory. As a naively patriotic reader, Nao has doubly misread Haruki #1's life. First, she has misinterpreted his character—as understood by Jiko, the person who knew him best, and legible in and between the lines of his official final letters. Second, Nao's reading provides poor guidance for her own life: she thinks she should emulate his code of conduct by committing suicide. However, Ozeki's novel suggests another solution. Through postmemory, Ruth—as Nao's reader and a stand-in for the novel's readers—can discern an alternate interpretation of Haruki #1's life for which, logically, no textual evidence should remain. However, her imaginative desire and her attunement to the clues provided by Nao's historical documents—Haruki #1's letters and diary—give her access to his real words, his real heart, his real actions, and the interpretation that Nao needs to survive. Within the novel, Ruth's imaginative intervention produces outcomes—including a physical diary that others read—that enable Nao and her father not only to survive and properly mourn the deaths of Haruku #1 and Jiko, who dies at that juncture, but also to reevaluate Nao's father's idealistic career choice, reconcile, and create new futures for them both. Thus, the novel implies that it is both necessary and historically valid to seek the ethical and psychological meaning of past events and to question official accounts of events themselves through the imaginative work of postmemory.[11]

Textual Remains

On one level, *A Tale for the Time Being* engages with historiographic issues by drawing on new research by the anthropologist Emiko Ohnuki-Tierney on the writings of the students who served as tokkōtai in the last days of World War II. Fundamentally, as discussed in her book *Kamikaze Diaries: Reflections of Japanese Student Soldiers*, this research shows that one-quarter (about one thousand out of four thousand) of the Japanese tokkōtai, whom Americans imagined to be the most fanatical and fearsome patriots, were in fact university students, whose writings reveal complex inner lives: love of country, family, and life; fear and horror; and doubt and cynicism about the war and their missions. (The other three thousand were young teenagers who left little writing behind.) Ozeki's character Haruki #1 is apparently inspired by the literary remains of the college-educated tokkōtai, as transcribed, edited, and translated by Ohnuki-Tierney, whose work is cited in Ozeki's bibliography (Ozeki 420). However, the novel is highly self-conscious about the centrality and limits of textual evidence in the writing of history. In poststructuralist fashion, Ozeki emphasizes the textuality of Haruki #1 by emphasizing the material processes by which his story travels to Nao and her interpretive efforts as she receives the information.

The first account of Haruki #1's life is Jiko's oral recollection, which emphasizes that he was a Tokyo University student of philosophy and French literature when drafted. Employing countermemory, Nao speculates how this felt for Haruki, given that he was just a few years older than she is. She also distinguishes between her own thoughts of voluntary suicide and Haruki #1's feelings at being compelled to die for the state, observing, "Being annihilated in a great big ball of fire was not Haruki #1's choice, and . . . he was also a cheerful, optimistic boy who actually liked being alive, which is not at all the situation with me or my dad" (Ozeki 179). As Ohnuki-Tierney points out, the so-called voluntary suicide bombers of the tokkōtai were actually conscripted young men who were required to die in the service of their country (6–9). Jiko frames this account of her son's death with her comments that she also wanted to commit suicide but remained alive for the sake of her fifteen-year-old daughter, Ema (Nao's grandmother), and decided to become a nun and devote her life to teaching others how to live in peace (Ozeki 180). According to Nao, this teaching requires young people like her to understand that, although Japan is now a peaceful nation, the war has shaped the entire course of their lives (180).

Within the first portion of the novel, the ghost of Haruki #1 also makes visitations to Nao, which readers may understand as occurring when she is mentally prepared for the next level of understanding his story. When the ghost first appears to Nao at the gate of Jiko's temple, she has been preparing for her ancestral spirits to visit during Obon, staying up late to await them (211).[12] Their brief encounter leads Nao to locate Haruki #1's last official letter to his mother, stored behind his portrait. In this letter, he declares he is calm, looks forward to providing a good pension for her and his sisters, and insists, "There are so many things I cannot express or send to you. It is too late. By the time you read this, I will be dead, but I will die believing that you know my heart and will not judge me harshly. I am not a warlike man, and everything I do will be in accordance with the love of peace that you have taught me. . . . Empty words, but my heart is full of love" (217–218). Though purporting to be the final letter, this letter gestures toward additional meanings that cannot be conveyed in words, not only because the feelings are too complex or powerful to articulate but also, as readers will learn, because Haruki's real thoughts, if discovered, could undo his goal of providing a posthumous pension for his family.

Shortly after reading this letter, Nao receives a second visit from Haruki's ghost, who recalls that the officers began the recruits' training by teaching them how to kill themselves if facing defeat—to die rather than surrender or be captured (239–240). This detail is Ozeki's subtle way of conveying Ohnuki-Tierney's explicit point that, once drafted and assigned to the tokkōtai, the recruits were designated for death and had no hope of survival. When Nao tells Jiko of this visit, Jiko confirms that officers bullied the university recruits and remarks that Haruki #1's letter "was just for show." Actually, Jiko says, he hated war, fascism, the government, its "bullying politics of imperialism and capitalism and exploitation," and "the idea of killing people he could not hate," but he served because he was drafted (245). She recalls the government's farewell pageant without admiration, noting that another boy, who made a patriotic speech that day, survived and returns to the temple to apologize each year: not, apparently, for surviving, but for the speech. Jiko remembers that she wept for joy when, after the war, the prime minister Tojo Hideki was hanged but says that she has since vowed to stop hating

(245–246). She explains that the box that was supposed to contain Haruki #1's remains held nothing but a government-issued slip of paper that said "remains," a fine joke that her son, a writer, would have enjoyed. Jiko gives Haruki's watch and his final, official letters to Nao but enjoins her to remember that these are also not his last words (248–249). The letters, which Ruth gets translated into English and transcribes into her own narrative in the novel, cover dates from December 10, 1943, two months from the ceremony celebrating the recruits ("that ceremony of sad puppets in the cold and bitter rain"), to March 27, 1945, a few days before Haruki #1's death in the Battle of Okinawa. They reveal that the recruits were instructed to "switch off their hearts and minds completely," and that Haruki had been singled out for bullying by their squadron leader, "F," a noncommissioned officer whose training methods resembled those of "that brilliant French soldier, the Marquis de Sade"; the literary reference served as a code incomprehensible to Haruki's less educated commanders (252–253). The letters are deeply sad and loving. Knowing he was assigned to die one way or another, Haruki #1 volunteered for accelerated training for the tokkōtai in order to maximize his pension and claim a measure of freedom; he asked his mother not to be sad about his death, which was inevitable, and to realize that the official letter she would receive would not be his last words, for "there are other words and other worlds" (251–258). Reading them, Nao becomes even more critical of herself and her father, considering their own everyday efforts insignificant compared to Haruki #1's brave sacrifice. Unwittingly or not, she seems to admonish her father to shape up and do a better job of committing suicide: "He didn't want to fight in a war but when the time came, he faced his fate. . . . He wasn't a coward. He flew his plane into the enemy's battleship to protect his homeland. You should really be more like him!" (264).

In an apparent interruption, Ozeki follows this with Nao's description of the 9/11 attacks on the World Trade Center, after which Nao's father becomes obsessed with the figure of the man who jumped from the towers, whom she calls "Falling Man." Nao imagines her father mentally questioning Falling Man about his experience: *"What made you decide to do it? Did you have to decide or did your body just know? . . . Do you feel alive or dead? Do you feel free now?"* (268). Here, Nao understandably fails to use postmemory to enter Falling Man's story. She knows nothing about the man to begin with, and her empathy is less pronounced than her curiosity about the process of suicide. However, she does express sympathetic concern for the mental state of her father, whom she observes replaying the recording of the event, as she tries to understand what he is thinking and feeling. She also meditates on suicide methods and thinks wishfully about dying in the sea, where her flesh would be eaten by jellyfish and her soul would be with Haruki #1 "forever"

(268–269). Through this juxtaposition, Ozeki provides an implicit critique of suicide bombers from the perspective of the bombed. She also establishes that Nao sees suicide as a way to express affinity with her father and uncle. Indeed, Nao later describes their shared obsession as "Our last project. Our suicide project" (368).

Haruki #1's final document, his secret French diary, is translated at Ruth's request by Benoit, a local Canadian (317–328). In keeping with Haruki's letters, his secret diary opens on January 10, 1943; its last dated entry is August 3, 1944, but the final entry marks Haruki's final flight as part of the Battle of Okinawa, probably in early April 1945.[13] To evade the sudden inspections of critical officers, he wrote this diary by moonlight, when others were sleeping, in French, so that he could articulate his true feelings while keeping them concealed. The truth was that F had singled Haruki out not only for beatings but also for sexual humiliation, that Haruki came to hate and then to pity him, and that Haruki's senior schoolmate, K, could not bear to watch the Haruki's "training" (which consisted of beatings and humiliations) ran away, and was killed (254–255, 319). With his own death approaching, Haruki came to understand time as a series of moments in which both life and death manifest, ceaselessly and simultaneously, as expressed by the Buddhist writer Dōgen Zenji (324; Dōgen, *Shōbōgenzō* or *Treasury*, qtd. in Ozeki 30, 259; Dōgen, *Shōbōgenzō* chap. 86, qtd. in Ozeki 62). Consequently, each moment provides a fresh opportunity "to choose, and to turn the course of our action either toward the attainment of truth or away from it. Each instant is utterly critical to the whole world" (Ozeki 324). He did not aspire to any particular afterlife but only to attain truth in the crucial moment when he had to decide whether to attack an American target. In the end, his practice of using his prayer beads to count "one for every thing on earth I love, on and on, in a circle without end" led him to choose to fly into the sea without killing anyone other than himself (326). In this way he could "give [his] life for his country" while resisting the "capitalist greed and imperialist hubris" that motivated the war and "the depravity with which it has been waged" (328). He thereby reclaimed a small measure of truth and choice at the moment of his death. Though addressed to Jiko, the diary gave no indication that it would ever be delivered to her. Logically, the diary should have been lost at sea with Haruki's remains, and the novel never shows Jiko reading this diary; yet Jiko's earlier words to Nao suggest she is indeed familiar with its contents (Ozeki 245). Readers may surmise that she did not need to receive the secret diary. She knew her son so well, and contemplated his death so deeply, that through her practice of countermemory she understood what he did not say.

By incorporating this material, inspired by Ohnuki-Tierney's research, Ozeki extends the anthropologist's dual critique of common representations:

both writers challenge conventional Japanese portrayals of the pilots as willing patriots who volunteered to die for their emperor, as well as American stereotyping of them as fanatical patriots with no identity other than their mission. Ohnuki-Tierney specifies that when a Japanese navy vice-admiral (Ōnishi Takijirō) conceived, as a last-ditch defense, the idea of attack forces who would be unable to return alive, it was part of a culture in which Japanese soldiers, once drafted, were expected only to die for their leader. Facing imminent defeat, Ōnishi sought to stay the inevitable by using what was thought to be Japan's unique strength: its willingness to sacrifice its men's lives in self-defense. "Whereas German soldiers were told to *kill*," Ohnuki-Tierney writes, "Japanese soldiers were told to *die*" (1, 4). In contrast to American military justice, which generally judges and punishes the individual, she notes, punishments in the samurai tradition could be imposed on a person's extended family, including those connected by marriage, for up to five generations. Thus, individuals were discouraged from taking risks that could place their families in danger. As for the tokkōtai, they were taught how to kill themselves to avoid capture or surrender, as Ozeki relates. In addition, no provision was made for conscientious objectors; officers could, with impunity, shoot and kill soldiers for minor acts of disobedience; and those who ran away and were caught were executed (Ohnuki-Tierney 4). Once assigned to the special attack forces, no one was permitted to return, even if they could not find a target; one pilot who was unable to locate an enemy to attack was shot to death upon his ninth return (10). When the operation was first instituted in October 1944, not a single officer trained at the military academies volunteered, because the career officers knew the missions would be fatal and futile (1). Instead, the government drafted or otherwise coerced three thousand teenagers and one thousand university students for these special, lethal missions while claiming that they were volunteers (6–9). In her study, Ohnuki-Tierney is particularly detailed in describing the university students' immersion in Western and Eastern philosophy, to which they turned for answers in facing their impending deaths, and in Western culture and literature. Having exhausted its manpower, Japan resorted to drafting the nation's most brilliant students and its adolescent boys for this final, desperate mission. While the younger teenagers left little writing behind them, the university students left extensive records of their wide-ranging reading and their private agony as they contemplated their own and others' slaughter. Ozeki draws on this research, portraying Haruki #1 as one of these exceptional students—young, brilliant, sincere in his love of peace, and drawing on German philosophy and Buddhist teaching in his search for meaning, truth, and freedom within his constricted final days. By working this material into her novel, Ozeki joins the tradition of transpacific, feminist, and pacifist scrutiny and critique of the Japanese government's actions of that time while also humanizing the figure of Haruki #1.

"To Bring the Dead to Life": Inherited Words and Postmemory

Thickening this historiographic metafictional commentary on the project of looking back in history for present-day inspiration, Ozeki has Nao acquire Haruki #1's secret diary by fantastic means. Ruth first receives it when it washes up on the shore along with Nao's diary and Haruki #1's official letters, implying that the materials were stored or jettisoned together, but the novel never explains how the family originally received the diary. On the contrary, the diary itself suggests Haruki #1 died without mailing it, and readers learn that Jiko received only his watch, beads, and official letters as well as the box containing the word "remains" (247–249). Haruki has written:

> Perhaps I will burn [this diary] tonight when I'm drunk, or take it with me to the bottom of the sea. It has been my consolation, and without being overly fanciful, I truly believe that although you have not laid eyes on these pages, still you have read every word I have written. You, dear Mother, know my true heart. (328)

If Haruki took the diary with him on his last day, why was it not destroyed by the sea? Who put it into its handy late twentieth-century freezer bag? The diary provides a necessary confirmation of Jiko's assertion that the other letters are "not his last words" and Haruki #1's assertions that his mother "ha[s] always known [his] heart" (218, 255) without being told. She even echoes his words about hating capitalism, imperialism, and killing those he cannot hate (244, 324–325, 328); yet nowhere in the novel does Jiko receive, handle, or give away her son's secret diary.

At the climax of the novel, Ruth responds to the alarming appearance of blank pages in Nao's previously full diary by conducting a symbolic journey to the dead, which not only draws on a classic trope of myth and fantasy but also dramatizes the concept of postmemory, which is mediated "not through recollection but through an imaginative investment and creation" (Hirsch, *Family* 22).[14] Ruth's husband cues this journey by urging her to seek the missing words by delving into her own unconscious. Oliver proposes both that people's words are borrowed or inherited from the dead and that the dead speak again when the living read their words. "Where do words come from?" he asks. "They come from the dead. We inherit them. Borrow them. Use them for a time to bring the dead to life. . . . The ancient Greeks believed that when you read aloud, it was actually the dead, borrowing your tongue, in order to speak again" (Ozeki 346). As a writer, he insists, Ruth has the privilege and responsibility to find Nao's words, to complete her story even when she seems unable to know how it ends. At this point, neither Ruth nor the novel's readers know whether the blank pages signify that Nao has refused to continue writing out of concern for her father, or whether she herself has ceased to exist. As long as the possibility of Nao's own death remains unspoken, Ruth and the readers retain the sense that, somewhat like Schrödinger's theoretical cat (and like Oliver's cat, who goes missing at this point, Nao is neither definitively alive nor dead; her condition is open until the end of the story is discovered (as Ozeki explains in appendix E, "Schrödinger's Cat," 413–414). When Oliver extinguishes the light that night, promising to find Ruth if she gets lost in her dreams, Ruth's sleeping body remains in her Canadian home, while her mind moves through a dark, dreamlike state to the various sites connected with Nao's story. She encounters Jiko, who hands Ruth her glasses, but Ruth decides in a very authorial way to use her limited dream time to skip Jiko's story and focus on Nao's (348). Ruth therefore leaves Jiko, finds Nao's father, dissuades him from suicide, and sends him to find Nao, who had last described herself as waiting alone at Sendai for the train to Jiko's temple, but apparently could not travel or write further without knowing whether her father would choose to live (341). Ruth, too, has been unable to contemplate his end: not only does she retain hope for his and Nao's survival, but the pages that might have described his decision have gone blank. To return to Ruth's dream-journey: after Ruth scolds him for neglecting his daughter, Nao's father forsakes suicide and joins his daughter on the way to Jiko's deathbed, making it possible for Nao to continue her journey and, one hopes, her narration. Though physically still asleep at home and seeming to dream, Ruth is "blown back" to the temple graveyard, where she finds Haruki #1's secret diary in her hands once more. From there, she intentionally walks to Jiko's temple, places the diary in the "remains" box for Nao to find, meets Jiko again, falls into the nun's arms, and reenters the silence and darkness of sleep (353–354).[15]

Informed by Ohnuki-Tierney, Ozeki the author has imagined the secret last words of her fictional tokkōtai pilot for Ruth to read. However, in order for Nao to understand her uncle and her father fully, she needs these words as well, and she requires Ruth's unconventional intervention—the transmission of a diary by dream-mail, across space and backward in time—to complete the *trauerarbeit*, the work of understanding the past, on which her story depends.[16] When Oliver directs Ruth to search for Nao's words in sleep, the implication is that the diary represents a truth one cannot reach or verify by conventional material means, a truth one can find only by searching one's understanding in an act of postmemory. Ruth's dream journey is a metaphor for consulting the dead by activating one's empathy, imagination, and intuition. Within the novel, such postmemory work has, tacitly, been performed by Jiko. Through the superpower of her insight and compassion she has understood what Haruki's deepest values were and all that he did not say in his official correspondence. But Ruth, who is not only Nao's reader but also an avatar for Nao's creator, Ozeki, exceeds the normal bounds of postmemory by acting to *change* the story she is observing. Whereas ordinary postmemory requires one to imagine the past, Ruth's postmemory-like dream permits her to guide Nao and her father to what is, for them, a different future.

Just as Nao sees the ghost of Haruki #1 only when she is prepared to face a new truth, Haruki's secret diary is deposited in the "remains" box just before Nao and her father arrive at the temple and receive Jiko's last message, a single word she sits up to write just before dying: "LIVE" (362).[17] Readers' access to these events is also textually mediated, narrated by the new entries that appear in Nao's diary directly after Ruth's dream intervention. Nao and her father know Jiko's message is for them: it is an imperative to give up their flirtations with suicide. For the reader who has already seen Haruki #1's secret diary, Jiko's last word also restates the central theme of his writing, life, and death. Even in dying, he sought to live by protecting the living: not only his own family but also the American troops who were supposed to be his enemies. Only when primed by these events to understand Haruki #1's secret diary do Nao and her father find it in his "remains" box. Thereafter, the shared task of translating the diary will replace their former family project of suicide and bring them into the future.

When Nao learns that Haruki #1 refused to fulfill his orders to kill and chose instead to fly directly into the sea, she is finally ready to understand her father's seeming professional failure: Haruki #2's decision to risk his career arose from a deep philosophical struggle with his conscience that, in fact, echoes the conflicted thoughts of his uncle, Haruki #1. As a programmer employed in Silicon Valley after 9/11, Nao's father had refused to create computer interfaces that would make it fun or easy for U.S. pilots to bomb military targets without considering the death and destruction they would cause. Implicitly, he anticipated and protested the U.S. attacks on Iraq and Afghanistan. By following his conscience, he lost his job, ended his career, and plunged his family into the seas of unemployment and despair in Japan. However, when Nao understands and affirms his choices, this renews their mutual bond and will to live.

The novel's denouement suggests one other essential aspect of postmemory. Like historical memory and the emotional processes of mourning and remembrance, postmemory is necessarily selective. Freud theorized that the mourner cannot get over the grief of loss without symbolically and psychically letting go of the lost object and turning to a new object. David Eng and Shinhee Han, on the other hand, have suggested that melancholic remembrance of one's losses, as a form of countermemory that resists official erasure of one's history or one's loss, can be a vital element of a minority person's or community's survival and mental health ("Dialogue," 363–365). Theorists of postcolonial melancholia, similarly, have argued that it is essential for a postimperial nation to question and recall the full, if negative, consequences of empire and its aspirations. By contrast, Ozeki's ending asks readers to contemplate what postmemory can and should do about a shameful act of violence committed and rendered public as a form of humiliation and disavowal by others. While the direct reference is to an act of cyberbullying in which Nao's classmates post a video online of them victimizing her, the incident poses larger questions about historical memory and countermemory. In the same imaginary conversation where dream-Ruth warns Haruki #2 to desist from suicide and rejoin his daughter, she unwittingly plants the seed of his professional renaissance by telling him that she could find no traces of his family on the Internet (352). Haruki #2 is thus inspired to create programs that protect people's privacy retrospectively, by permitting them to erase unwanted postings and references to themselves, as well as prospectively, by shielding them from unwanted future postings. The first person he uses his program for is Nao, as he erases the humiliating video from the Internet. Thus freed from an unauthorized public portrayal of herself as victim, Ruth imagines, Nao is freed to get over her victimization, to depart from Japan and redefine herself in her own terms (381–383). In this case, I argue, the novel suggests that postmemory can also include an empathetic use of imagination to erase and pass beyond a traumatic event or events whose random return has power to wound anew; postmemory may also allow the abjected to forget and be forgotten, to be free of the majority's melancholic requirements for their continued silence, suffering, and sacrifice.

To summarize: Among narratives of return, the transnational novels of Lydia Minatoya and Ruth Ozeki frame a period in which Japanese American writers have turned to examine the history of Japan's twentieth-century imperialism, engaging with questions raised by scholars of Japanese history and historical memory. For some time, scholars and observers have debated whether Japan has deeply and properly examined its wartime history, doing the work of self-examination and mourning called *trauerbeit*, or whether Japanese people, in both official and private capacities, have contained the nation's sense of historical guilt by distancing themselves from the terrible wartime acts of Japan's military. Paul Gilroy and Ian Buruma argue that the failure to examine and acknowledge individual and collective responsibility can result from and perpetuate a euphemized sense of history—recalling colonial power without its violence—and a lingering wish for an idealized past that Gilroy terms "postcolonial melancholia"; I ask how these Japanese American narratives of return, which are also novels, engage with the work of mourning or processing Japan's imperial past and to what extent they register, resist, or avoid the structure of feeling Gilroy describes. In *The Strangeness of Beauty*, Minatoya imagines Japanese life in Kobe as characterized by a balance between tradition and modernity; a search for social harmony in the face of increasing material hardship, xenophobia, and patriotic chauvinism; and the active efforts of a small minority of citizens to comprehend, contest, and resist the nation's wartime mentality. Though Minatoya seeks to provide a nuanced portrait of Kobe that transcends U.S. stereotypes and emphasizes the lives of ordinary people rather than combatants, her novel engages with historical debates by questioning the extent of civilian knowledge and responsibility and suggesting that the foremost responsibility of ordinary Japanese is to understand and question their country's actions. This imperative, I argue, challenges the attachment to a false ideal of empire that, according to Gilroy, characterizes postcolonial melancholia. In addition, I find that this novel can be seen as a *historiographic metafiction*: on one hand, it can be read as a creative re-vision of Etsu Sugimoto's 1926 memoir *A Daughter of the Samurai* and a larger transpacific, feminist tradition of women's writing; on the other hand, Minatoya's narrator comments continually on the processes of textual production and interpretation involved in interpreting events and producing an I-novel. Within the novel, Etsuko's narration foregrounds the empathy, imagination, and personal investment that characterize *countermemory* as she imagines personal events she could not have experienced; at the same time, Minatoya employs the same techniques to fashion her novel from the historical sources she cites in her bibliography, including Sugimoto's memoir.

In *A Tale for the Time Being*, Ozeki deploys the techniques of countermemory and historiographic metafiction to question the notion of history as a received text with a fixed meaning. Ozeki refuses to represent either Japanese history or Yasutani family history as a linear master narrative, written according to scholarly conventions for verification and presentation and tracing the unidirectional progress of the Japanese nation or a family that may represent it. Instead, the history she presents is mediated by a Japanese schoolgirl's diary: subjective, episodic, in need of translation, incomplete, and uncertain in meaning and direction. By emphasizing Ruth's historianlike labors in recovering and interpreting Nao's texts and story, and Nao's similar labors in recovering and interpreting the texts and story of her great-uncle Haruki, Ozeki foregrounds both the slipperiness of historical meaning and the creativity, imagination, and empathy inherent in writing a historiographic metafiction that does the work of countermemory. As a historiographic metafiction, her novel models and questions the processes of writing and interpreting history, throws into question the authority of traditional historical sources, and tells alternative stories that give voice to persons otherwise occluded from official history. Like *The Strangeness of Beauty*, *A Tale for the Time Being* is not driven by and does not express the nostalgia for imperial greatness Gilroy associates with postcolonial melancholia: rather, it challenges official efforts to frame the death of Haruki #1 as a meaningful patriotic sacrifice.

In addition, my reading of these novels clarifies that just as racial melancholia characterizes the experiences of minorities in the United States, a similar melancholia due to displacement may propel some narratives of return. Overall, *The Strangeness of Beauty* is not driven by racial melancholia: Etsuko's voice is rarely mournful, despite her losses and displacements. (Granted, the character of Hanae, dejected and displaced in both Seattle and Kobe, has many losses to mourn, but she recovers in time to join the peace movement and give her valedictory speech.) In *A Tale for the Time Being*, I find a vivid portrayal of what might be called "repatriate melancholia." As I have suggested, Ozeki portrays Nao and her father as outsiders in Tokyo society, paralyzed and rendered suicidal for much of the story by their isolation and their mourning for their losses; although their melancholia during this time is not due to racial discrimination in Japan, it is rooted in comparable issues of displacement and inability to assimilate into their home country.

Finally, I note that Minatoya and Ozeki are not the only Japanese American authors engaging with questions of history, memory, and Japanese imperialism. Most other Japanese American return narratives share these writers' sense of belonging elsewhere rather than being rooted in Japan, and thus they seem free to record and question the pro-war, pro-empire ideology of the day while describing the conditions of Japanese life from the perspectives of outsiders. Kazuko Kuramoto's *Manchurian Legacy*, Gene Oishi's *Fox Drum Bebop*, Kerri Sakamoto's *One Hundred Million Hearts*, Mary K. Tomita's *Dear Miye*, Yuko Taniguchi's *The Ocean in the Closet*, and Jim Yoshida's *The Two Worlds of Jim Yoshida* are among the Japanese American return narratives that view Japan from outsider perspectives opposed to postimperial melancholia; in particular, Sakamoto's novel questions the vexed process of memorializing the war. On the basis of these and other texts, I suggest that Minatoya and Ozeki are typical of an emerging tradition of Japanese American narratives, including narratives of return, that forgo postcolonial melancholia, instead bringing active skepticism and empathetic techniques of countermemory to bear on the topic of Japan's wartime record while opening readers' understanding with fresh, uniquely North American stories.

Coda

AT THE END OF HIS 2006 BOOK *Oracle Bones*, Peter Hessler recalls his meeting in Arlington, Virginia, with Wu Ningkun, an American-trained English-literature scholar who, like Ruth and Charles Chai, returned to China after his studies to help modernize the country. Wu, who abandoned his doctoral dissertation on T. S. Eliot to return after the revolution in 1949, survived years in a labor camp and then wrote about his experiences in his own narrative of return, *A Single Tear: A Family's Persecution, Love, and Endurance in Communist China*. Wu did not regret his choice: he told Hessler that if he had not been persecuted in the Anti-Rightist campaign and the Cultural Revolution, he might have been a better scholar and produced good books about English or American literature: "But so what? There are already so many books. *A Single Tear* might be more important" (qtd. in Hessler 456).

At the University of Chicago, Wu had a classmate, Lucy Chao, who also returned to China and married a great scholar, Chen Mengjia. Chen had used his time in America to document Americans' holdings of ancient Chinese bronzes. Though he committed suicide during the Cultural Revolution, his manuscript, published by the Chinese Institute of Archaeology (Kaogusuo) as *Our Country's Shang and Zhou Bronzes Looted by American Imperialists*, became a seminal text in its field (Kaogusuo, qtd. in Hessler 221, 462). Chao not only survived but also published the first Chinese translation of Whitman's *Leaves of Grass*. These Chinese works are not proper narratives of return, but they are nonetheless products of the tradition of study abroad pioneered by Yung Wing and discussed in his narrative of return. Hessler's book is both a meditation on modern China and a story of the shadows cast by Wu's generation—both the returnees from America and the others who lived through the Cultural Revolution. Hessler closes his book with two quotations, the first his own translation from Chao's translation of Whitman's "Out of the Cradle, Endlessly Rocking." The speaker has become one who unites songs of the past with "this life and the next," adding what seems to my ear a Chinese, intergenerational note to Whitman's poem:

> *I, the singer of painful and joyous songs, the uniter of this life and the next,*
> *Receiving all silent signs, using them all, but then leaping across them at full speed,*
> Sing of the past. (Whitman, qtd. in Hessler 458)

In the second quotation, Hessler cites scholar David N. Keightley about the imaginative labor of interpreting oracle bone inscriptions: "Those are the notes. We have to provide the music ourselves" (Hessler 250, 458).

My own parents belonged to the generation of these three scholars—Wu Ningkun, Lucy Chao, and Chen Mengjia. During the course of writing this book, I established contact with the family members my parents had left in China when they came to America to study after the end of World War II. Warmly and generously, my relatives have also provided stories of their lives, but I find that I am not yet able to make music of the notes they have given me. In fact, Hessler writes of the failed attempts of modern scholars to replicate the ancient Chinese methods of cracking the oracle bones, as the ancients did to attain the revelations that inspired their inscriptions (256–257). As I picture these scholars in their labs boiling and searing their uncrackable beef T-bones (why not add scallions and garlic?), I also have tried to boil down the multiple complexities of narratives of return. But my critical aim is not to read against the books, nor to boil them down to repetitive plot structures. I am looking for the music: the intertextual conversation that emerges in personal essays, family history memoirs, an autobiography, and novels about the experience of returning to one's own or one's ancestors' homeland, both physically and through the channels of research, memory, and imagination. This is why I have focused this study on the themes of loss, mourning, and the intergenerational communication of racial melancholia, which I find eloquently expressed throughout this literature. My aim has been not to psychoanalyze but to test the usefulness of critical language to articulate the structure of feeling that drives and unites these disparate texts. However, I have also focused on the form, technique, agency, and intentions of the authors: frequently describing their literary refutations, re-creations, and emotionally engaged inventions with the past as "countermemory" and "postmemory," I emphasize the authors' use of empathy and imagination to enliven their factual research and convey their intellectual ideas.

As a writer, critic, and Asian American, I do not believe that Asian American authors should be limited to writing about traditional ethnic themes such as intergenerational communication, migration, assimilation, hybridity, and interethnic contact and exchange; nor should we be required always to be expositors of Asian history. But narratives of return have a place in my heart, and a place in the culture, because of what they can tell readers about all these issues, as well as about the processes of cultural loss, transmission, and remaking. Here are some of the things I have learned.

From Josephine Khu, Lily Wu, and other contributors to *Cultural Curiosity*, I learned that, as a second-generation Chinese American, I was not alone in my wish and hope to understand China; that such complex cultural understanding cannot be gained merely by visiting once; that, as with any travel but particularly journeys of symbolic return to ancestral homelands, there can be a lifelong cultural apprenticeship; and that errors and silences are just as important as the obvious successes. I also learned the power of the editor to shape the writers' narratives and to give an intentional form to this process. Wu's essay in that volume, "Coming Home," provides a structurally elegant example of a return narrative in which living and studying in Beijing, and meeting relatives there, resulted in a powerful internalization of Chinese and family history that enabled her to resolve personal issues of mourning, melancholia, and alienation. However, other essays in the collection provide examples of return narratives that, while similarly structured, are instructive in their lack of such powerful resolutions.

Though Lisa See's *On Gold Mountain* ends with her journey to her great-grandfather Fong See's home village, the book as a whole prompts readers to see the author's return as the coda of a multigenerational family story driven by repeated transpacific journeys between California and the Cantonese villages of Fatsan and Dimtao. See is only one-eighth Chinese and unversed in any Chinese dialect, but her use of English archival sources, immigration documentation, and personal interviews, along with her imagination and storytelling skills, establish her authority to tell her Chinese family's story. As the story of a family business and of a biracial family, See's family history memoir extends readers' historical knowledge of early Chinese Americans of an underexamined class. It also raises awareness of hybridity within Chinese America—in a textured, deeply personal, and memorable way. At the same time, it illustrates how material research can become a family history memoir, rather than a history book or hagiography, if the author focuses on novelistic themes of personal development, romantic decisions, and family formation;

uses storytelling techniques such as invented interior monologues to counter the remoteness of a character who has left no written voice in either Chinese or English; and skillfully marries personal anecdote to the material traces of a family business to push the story beyond the economic into the realm of family, survival, and feeling. Her book, in which archival research and personal interviews are enlivened by her imaginative engagement, provides a strong example of the use of countermemory in narratives of return.

Similarly, Denise Chong's *The Concubine's Children* pushes beyond an anecdotal account of her immigrant grandparents' economic struggles before, during, and after the Great Depression in Vancouver, and beyond the family stories of her grandmother's bad character and conduct. Instead she tells a transpacific tale of an extended clan both united by economic interest and Confucian family ideology and blasted by racism and economic and political pressures in China and Canada. Chong traces the sources of her grandparents' melancholia to their wish to fulfill Confucian, Chinese gender ideals that were materially unattainable by either grandparent, a situation I call "racialized gender melancholia." Chan Sam sought without success to fulfill the role of the wealthy, successful sojourner able to retire to his home village after making good in Canada. The role that eluded Leong May-ying, his concubine, was that of the virtuous woman who could spin a tea waitress's wages into enough gold to support an extended family, including Chan Sam's relatives and properties in China, without the love or respect due to one serving as wife, mother, and breadwinner. Yet, for Chong, the ultimate meaning of her story lies not in the loneliness and melancholia passed on from her grandparents to her mother but in the reconciliation that her written book makes symbolically between the two alienated halves of the family; the enlargement of her mother's perceptions from her lonely childhood into the larger struggles of Chinese communities in Canada and Guangdong Province; and in the respectful preservation, through countermemory, of these stories and the communities they represent in Chong's book. Because her grandmother was a paper daughter (who eluded Canada's Chinese exclusion laws by claiming a false identity) doubly stigmatized by her official concealment of identity and by her low status within Chinatown as concubine and tea waitress, and because her grandparents died as paupers, their stories would have been forgotten without Chong's intervention. Thus, this book also demonstrates the powerful use of countermemory to memorialize the communities these family members inhabited in Canada and China.

Roughly parallel in time to Chong's stories are those told by the father-daughter team of Winberg and May-lee Chai about Winberg's parents, Charles and Ruth Chai, in *The Girl from Purple Mountain*. Like Maxine Hong Kingston's mythical evocation of the grievances carved on the woman warrior's back, the Chais' story illustrates how the transmission of unresolved traumas can drive writers to look backward, to seek to understand the past. Ruth's angry memories, conveyed in letters, gifts, holiday outbursts, and her secret burial plan, drove her granddaughter May-lee to replicate the pattern of Khu's essayists: to study Chinese language and history, to move to China for a time, and then to question her father, Winberg. To put it another way, Ruth and Charles Chai's stories of family conflicts with victims and heroes, expressed and transmitted what I describe as "diasporic melancholia" in their unresolved mourning for the ideal of a democratic Republic of China, a society that would have been inclusive and affirmative of women, abided by the rule of law, and had a moral force that would have enabled the Nationalists to eject the Japanese and overcome their Communist rivals. I use this term to distinguish the diasporic, Sinocentric focus of Ruth Chai's stories and goals from racial melancholia, which has typically been analyzed in terms of thwarted assimilation and minority feeling, as expressed in texts by and about second- and latter-generation Asian Americans. The book's unusual dialogic structure depicts the two authors' complementary tasks: May-lee situates the family stories within a public narrative of Republican China and its failures, while Winberg confronts the gap between his "screen memories" (Hirsch, "Generation" 120) of a loving and secure family and the evidence of a family and a government in crisis. Their writing, still another form of countermemory, emphasizes the tension between the hagiographic story Ruth wanted to have as her legacy, Winberg's recollections of a childhood sheltered in wartime, and the stories of loss, alienation, and survival carved out by May-lee, with her father's help, through her dogged and empathetic imagination.

Each of these books reveals the combination of public awareness and introspection that makes for an excellent narrative of return. Without the private joys, griefs, secrets and revelations, grievances, lies, and reconciliations these authors narrate, history is a long march through the archives of others, but when the personal stories connect from time to time with those public narratives, they gain an additional significance. And if the stories depart from the archives, as do all three of these, so much the better: they deliberately reveal the limits of official historical sources and contribute to the collective Asian American countermemory. Moreover, they demonstrate the vitality of *postmemory*—a form of memory mediated not through recollection but through an imaginative investment and creation—to augment understanding of experiences that are otherwise unknowable (V. T. Nguyen, "Memory"; Hirsch, *Family* 22).

The authors of family memoirs break taboos and expose stories that risk stigmatizing their ancestors, but all provide symbolic reconciliations at the ends of their books. Lisa See accomplishes this partly by narrating her physical returns to her great-grandparents' places of origin, her first visit with her Chinese relatives, and her last visit to her great-grandmother's American hometown with her great-aunt Sissee. Denise Chong uses the gift of her mother's childhood coat and family photographs to symbolically reunite of the two halves of the family through her narration. And Winberg and May-lee Chai provide closing images of Winberg's reunion with his Chinese cousin, and of Ruth and Charles Chai recovering the head of Guan Yin from an auction and laughing together, to create a sense of reconciliation that Winberg did not actually achieve with his mother. All three books place these symbolic resolutions at the ends of long narratives that lay bare patterns of *multiple transpacific migrations and roots*, as well as the frayed family relations and the many forms of political and cultural alienation and *racial melancholia* the families experienced, leaving it up to readers to decide whether to emphasize the themes of alienation or of reconciliation that coexist in the stories.

In the Yung Wing chapter, I take a different approach. Drawing comparisons with Lisa Lowe's readings of Olaudah Equiano, I argue that Yung sought not only to preserve a record of his career for his sons but also to claim the authority of a *global subject*. Critical of both the Qing Dynasty and Western imperialism, Yung claimed a global orientation such as those of the missionary travel writer Karl Gützlaff and the slave narrator Fredrick Douglass. Unlike Gützlaff, however, he decried Western imperialism in China. Like Douglass, he consciously created a text that would perform an acceptable form of global subjectivity, he registered the ongoing oppression of less privileged people of his own race, and he could not completely claim the subjectivity to which he aspired. For this reason, *My Life in China and America* registers as melancholic. Furthermore, Yung's reiteration of many themes from slave narratives such as Douglass's *Autobiography* and his general rejection of missionaries and Western imperialism in China mark him as the prototype of a postcolonial subject: he blends genuine love of America with awareness of its limits rather than celebrating American imperialism or, as critics have claimed, white supremacy. Thus, I argue for a nuanced reading of Yung's autobiography in order to bring out his struggles to claim global citizenship, which align him with white travel writers as well as diasporic African slave narrators in a multiracial, global economic order. Yung's complex positioning, I argue, makes him a fascinating precedent for the many educated Chinese who would follow him to America, whether they returned to China or settled in the United States, as well as educated migrants to the United States from other Asian countries—whose collective publications have not been fully studied.

In Chapter 1, I introduced Paul Gilroy's term "postcolonial melancholia," which describes a nation failing to mourn or process the negative aspects of its imperial past and thus encouraging some citizens to remain nostalgic for a past era of greatness. Since Gilroy's book is about Great Britain, one would naturally think of Brexit as the most obvious current example, in his country, of postcolonial melancholia. As I thought about the narratives of return I have discussed here, I realized that although these narratives express desires to return to China and Japan, and many register melancholic attachments to these homelands, none of them expresses postcolonial melancholia as defined by Gilroy—either for the Qing imperial era or (in the Japanese texts) for twentieth-century Japanese imperialism. Because this is what scientists call a negative finding, and because it may seem too obvious to discuss, it is not heavily featured in my chapters on Chinese narratives of return. But I am jumping ahead and must return to my point about Yung Wing (the only writer analyzed here who personally experienced the Qing imperial era) and its corollary: written in 1909, Yung Wing's text expresses support for Chinese sovereignty but does not express any Chinese form of postcolonial melancholia. He does not suppress the faults of the Qing Dynasty, for instance, in order to engender nostalgia for a pure Chinese empire. Rather, as the son of a poor Cantonese family, he portrays the Qing empire critically even as he seeks to reform it and to defend his fellow Chinese; his critique is a prototype for what Kuan-Hsing Chen has described as *decolonization*. In his lack of nostalgia for this period of empire, Yung anticipates the powerful desire for change expressed by Chinese intellectuals such as Lu Xun and Ba Jin and also by the generation captured in the "Gone with the Wind" texts celebrating Chinese women as agents of modernity (S. C. Wong, "Sugar" 200). Indeed, there are multiple reasons why one sees little postimperial attachment to traditional China among Chinese American writers, who are or descend from people who left China. Early male sojourners, as discussed earlier, were driven to migrate by hardships at home and opportunities abroad; woman writers emphasize the gender oppression of traditional and sometimes of modern Chinese society; even returning elites of the next generation, such as the elder Chais, were bent on reforming and modernizing China. This is not to say that there is no postimperial nostalgia to be found among Chinese but that, where it concerns the Qing and Republican eras, it is unlikely to be a governing feeling in modern Chinese American texts. It remains to be seen how or whether Gilroy's model applies to current Chinese nationalism, either in Asian American writing or in Sinophone writing.

Though these eighteen authors (See, Chong, the Chais, Yung, and Khu's collected essayists) tell stories spanning almost two centuries, they demonstrate that Chinese American narratives of return share similar structures of feeling, including various kinds of *melancholia*. All tell family stories that are best understood as transpacific or diasporic, with families rooted in multiple sites, rather than in terms of one-way or circular migration. Generally,

Chinese North American return narratives are enriched by study within the specific contexts of Chinese, U.S., and Canadian history, including China's relations with visitors from other nations; Asian American studies is enriched, rather than misdirected, when scholars attend to authors with differing class origins, study cultural hybridity and racially mixed families, and consider Chinese-U.S. narratives in dialogue with Chinese-Canadian stories and global or diasporic Chinese stories. As a group, Chinese North American authors do *not* express postcolonial melancholia in the sense of looking back to an idealized memory of Chinese imperial power. (In terms of Kuan-Hsing Chen's categories—deimperialization, decolonization, and de–cold war—Yung provides a fairly deimperializing and decolonizing account, in my view, and the Chais directly criticize the Republic of China [1911–1949]. Aside from Yung, most of the authors I have considered refer to the experience of arriving in China in the late 1980s and witnessing the aftermath of the Cultural Revolution, but they do not make post-1949 politics the focus of their essays. It remains to be seen how contemporary Chinese American writers who focus on the era after 1989 [the year of the Tiananmen demonstrations] will address the postcolonial questions raised by Chen.)

In Chapter 7, I focus on fictional narratives of return by Lydia Minatoya and Ruth Ozeki. These texts grapple with the responsibility of Japanese Americans to participate in the work of understanding Japan's prewar and wartime history. Here, too, I find that these texts do *not* convey postcolonial melancholia either for Japanese or American imperial powers. On the contrary, these authors engage with Japanese history on multiple levels and tend to work against what Ian Buruma calls Japan's inability to examine the history of this period fully (6–10). Both novels were written after 1988, when the U.S. and Canadian governments had passed redress bills compensating Japanese North Americans for their forced internments in wartime camps, and both reflect the authors' freedom to write more openly, after these bills, about the dual roots of *issei* and *nisei* (immigrant/first-generation and second-generation Japanese American, respectively) before and during the war. Both texts also reflect a willingness to explore Japanese imperialism and engage indirectly with contemporary debates about Japan's official accounts of that time, using countermemory and postmemory—sympathetic, imaginative engagement with events they did not witness—to reimagine and interpret information provided by family history and official histories. In nuanced fashion, Minatoya portrays ordinary Japanese in prewar and wartime Kobe as focused on everyday survival but developing a heightened concern about Japan's actions abroad, although they have a limited capacity to counter the government's decisions. Ozeki, for her part, explores the complexity of historical interpretation, and its costs, in the historiographic elements of her plot. Both novels are historiographic metafictions: using the techniques of postmemory and humor, they engage with difficult questions concerning Japanese historical memory, break the relative silence of Japanese North American literary texts about Japan's wartime history, and comment on the processes of writing, reading, and interpreting history. In both cases, the dramatic and dialogic forms of the novel genre enable the authors to present deeply troubling glimpses of wartime Japanese conduct with insight and compassion, thus engaging indirectly with criticism of Japan as unable to mourn or examine its past. Finally, I find that each novel portrays at least one character as experiencing a form of racial melancholia specific to return narratives, as these figures experience an inability to assimilate upon arriving or returning to Japan.

The theme of return is so deeply embedded in Asian American literature, as it is in literature itself, that no single study to could hope to exhaust this vein of discussion. Beyond its descriptions of narrative arcs, narrative techniques, types of melancholia, the functions of counterememory and postmemory, I hope this book shifts the objects of Asian American literary analysis not only to include different subjects but also to emphasize the agency of Asian American writers as cultural interpreters. I ask how Asian American writers engage with not only the creation of countermemorial books but also the problems of history and public memory, as raised around the globe by writers as diverse as Buruma, Kuan-Hsing Chen, Gilroy, Hirsch, Huyssen, and Lowe—and how they will engage with the problems of the present.

Notes

CHAPTER 1

1. See, for instance, Fei; Kingston, *China Men*, *Broad Margin*; Lam; D. Lee; H. Lee; Mori; Mukherjee, *Desirable Daughters*; Mukherjee and Blaise, *Days and Nights*; V. T. Nguyen, *Sympathizer*; Ondaatje, *Anil's Ghost*, *Running*; Pham; Taniguchi; Thien; and Trenka, *Fugitive, Language*. I use the term "Asian American" primarily to refer to texts by Americans and Canadians of Asian descent, though sometimes this text also discusses works by diasporic Asians around the globe. In this respect, I follow the traditional usage. However, in chapters discussing Asian Canadian texts, I use the term "Asian North American" to highlight the inclusion of Canadian texts.

2. See, e.g., Davis, *Relative Histories*; Jerng; Manalansan; V. T. Nguyen, *Nothing*; and C. Wang, "Politics."

3. See also M. T. Nguyen's *The Gift of Freedom*, Um's *From the Land of Shadows*, and Ngô, Nguyen, and Lam's "Southeast Asian American Studies."

4. Tom Miller, author of *China's Asian Dream: Empire Building along the New Silk Road* (Chicago: University of Chicago Press, 2017), qtd. in Perlez and Huang.

5. For narratives of return reflecting on anti-Japanese stereotyping of the 1980s, see Mura's *Turning Japanese* and Kondo's anthropological study *Crafting Selves*. For narratives of return engaging with issues of history and memory, see Kuramoto, *Manchurian Legacy*; Sakamoto, *One Hundred Million Hearts*; Tomita, *Dear Miye*; and Yoshida, *The Two Worlds of Jim Yoshida*.

6. See, for instance, Chin et al. (11), Ling ("Reading Her/stories" 16), and Zhang (43) on Yung Wing, qtd. in F. Cheung, "Early Chinese," 25.

7. Yanagisako's article specifically addresses the teaching of Asian American history courses at four institutions in the late 1980s (University of California at Berkeley, University of California at Los Angeles, University of Washington, and San Francisco University

[279]), a small but key sampling of influential schools at a moment when Asian American history courses were just being introduced in many universities.

8. These are the stories of Chiang Monlin (M. Chiang 34–48), Sun Yat-sen (Boorman and Howard 3:170–189), Hu Shih (Y. W. Wong; Boorman and Howard 2:167–175), Wen Yiduo or Wen I-to (K. Hsu, *Wen I-to*), Zhang Youyi or Chang Yu-i (P. N. Chang), and Wu Ningkun (N. Wu).

9. For instance, a typical Asian American literature course may well contain numerous references to suicide, especially the suicides of women. Well-known texts featuring the suicides of women and feminized males include works by Chandra; Fenkl; Hwang; Houston, *Tea*, Kingston, *Woman*; Ng; Okada; Pham; Sui, "Smuggling"; Tan; and many more.

10. Williams gives various definitions of "structure of feeling." In *Preface to Film* (1954), he proposed the term to refer to the "*ideas*" or "*general life*" of a community in a particular period portrayed in a film, but he emphasized that the "structure of feeling" is an affective remainder that transcends individual elements of a film and hence defies formal analysis:

> We examine every element as a precipitate, but in the living experience of the time every element was in solution, an inseparable part of a complex whole. . . . [I]t is from such a totality that the artist draws; it is in art, primarily, that the effect of the totality, the dominant structure of feeling, is expressed and embodied . . . but it is a common experience, in analysis, to realize that when one has measured the work against the separable parts, there yet remains some element for which there is no external counterpart. This element . . . is what I have named the *structure of feeling* of a period, and it is only realizable through experience of the work of art itself, as a whole." (Williams, "From *Preface*" 861)

In this early essay, the structure of feeling is something that inheres in "the effect of the totality" in a film and cannot properly be analyzed as an isolated element (861). In *Marxism and Literature* (1977), Williams describes the concept as a shared change in "practical consciousness"—"thought as felt and feeling as thought"—that has not yet been formally recognized; it is "a social experience that is still in process, often indeed not yet recognized as social but taken to be private, idiosyncratic, and even isolating, but which in analysis . . . has its emergent, connecting, and dominant characteristics, indeed its specific hierarchies" (Williams, *Marxism* 130–132).

11. The Dalai Lama has publicly stated that he favors cultural preservation in Tibet rather than separation.

12. However, I salute the excellent publications in Asian American adoption studies by Catherine Ceniza Choy, Sara Dorow, Mark C. Jerng, Eleana J. Kim, Andrea Louie (*How Chinese*), Kimberly McKee, Kim Park Nelson, and others. And I have retained a few adoption-related primary texts—by Dobbs, Dorow, Fenkl, D. Lee, M. M. Lee, Liem (*First Person, Cha Jung Hee*), Prager, K. Robinson, Taniguchi, and Trenka (*Fugitive, Language*)—in my Works Cited and Additional Sources list.

13. I am indebted to Martin Manalansan for sharing with me his keynote address and his wealth of knowledge about the anthropological literature, including Long and Oxfeld.

14. In Japanese American parlance, *issei* refers to the immigrant generation, which is also counted as the first generation. The term *issei* may stand as a singular noun, referring to an individual, or a plural noun, referring to a generational group; it may also function as an adjective. The following generations include *nisei*, the second generation (which some would call the first American-born generation); *sansei*, the third generation; and *yonsei*, the fourth generation. As historian Greg Robinson has noted, at the time of the internment of

Japanese Americans along the Pacific Coast in 1941, "the majority of Japanese Americans confined were native-born U.S. citizens (the 'Nisei'), and their parents, the immigrant generation (the 'Issei'), were long-term residents who were barred from naturalization by racist laws" (57n1).

15. I thank Professor Sharon Delmendo for this intriguing reference.

CHAPTER 2

1. According to travel writer Chiang Yee, visas to China became available in the early 1970s, immediately after President Richard Nixon visited (52).

2. According to various online sources, Khu studied literature at Beijing University while working part time for the *New York Times* from 1986 to 1988. She published an article on the 1989 Chinese Democracy Movement in 1990 and was a visiting scholar at Hong Kong University's Centre of Asian Studies when she published *Cultural Curiosity* in 2001, shortly before completing her doctoral dissertation at Columbia University in 2001. Since then, her scholarship has drawn on sources from Hong Kong, Taiwan, the Philippines, and Fujian Province. She is the daughter of José Khu, a respected community and educational leader in Calgary, Alberta. See Khu, "Student Organization," "The Making of a Frontier," and "Jose Tan Sunco."

3. On Chinese censorship and public memory on the tenth anniversary of the Tiananmen crackdown, see Hessler 57–60. On diasporic representations of Tiananmen, see Kong, *Tiananmen Fictions*.

CHAPTER 3

1. For a thorough yet concise analytical summary of violence, evictions, and other forms of discrimination encountered by Asian Americans, see S. Chan, "Hostility" 48–54.

2. See *In re Ah Yup*, U.S. circuit court in California (qtd. in S. Chan, *Asian Americans* 47). Historian Sucheng Chan argues that the U.S. Supreme Court used ingenious, rather than consistent, criteria, when they ruled in *Ozawa v. United States* (1922) and *United States v. Bhagat Singh Thind* (1923) that Japanese and Asian Indian immigrants were also ineligible for citizenship (*Asian Americans* 47).

3. Ticie's citizenship is complicated by her race, the ambiguity of her marital status, and changes in laws governing married women's citizenship during this period. In 1901, the time of her first trip to China, Ticie traveled without formal documents as the wife of Fong See, a Chinese merchant, despite the ambiguous testimony of Fong's associate, Mr. Conan, and his friend, Richard White, about her marital status (See 67–68). According to Madeline Hsu, the Supreme Court had ruled in 1900 that Chinese merchants' wives were eligible for entry and residence in the United States, but the wives of Chinese laborers were not (*Dreaming*; see note 4 below). In 1919, the Chinese consulate general claimed Ticie as a citizen of the Republic of China, but U.S. immigration officials, confused by the anomaly of an American-born white woman married to a Chinese merchant, designated her the wife of a Chinese merchant without commenting on her race or citizenship (See 67–69, 110–111). According to history writer Marian L. Smith, in 1901 the matter of whether American women who married aliens automatically lost their citizenship had not yet been settled. Under the Expatriation Act of March 2, 1907, all women (alien or American) acquired their husband's nationality (American or alien) upon marriage, but only if the marriage occurred after that date. In 1922, the Cable Act (Married Women's Act) specified that American women lost their citizenship by marrying aliens ineligible for citizenship (Smith).

As Ticie's marriage was contracted in 1897 and annulled in 1924, it is unclear whether this law was ever applied to her. Ticie, it seems, never tested her citizenship status by crossing the U.S. border after she returned in 1920.

4. Following common practice, historian Madeline Hsu defines the Exclusion Era as 1882–1943, the period "when the Exclusion laws legally defined Chinese as being unwelcome in the United States" (*Dreaming* 177). But there was actually a prior history of laws designed to bar or financially penalize Chinese laborers and Chinese women seeking entry, as summarized by Sucheng Chan (*Asian Americans* 54). Perhaps because of her focus on Ticie, See does not discuss the Page Act of 1875, which forbade the entry of "Chinese, Japanese, and Mongolian contract laborers, women for the purpose of prostitution, and felons," and which in practice permitted authorities to prevent most Chinese women from entering the United States (S. Chan, *Asian Americans* 54). In summarizing the Page Act and other bars to Chinese women's entry, Hsu notes:

> By 1900, the only Chinese women who could legally enter the United States were the wives and daughters of merchants, diplomats, and U.S. citizens. In 1900 the Supreme Court ruled in the case of *United States v. Mrs. Gue Lim* that the wives and children of merchants, although citizens of China and not one of the designated classes of acceptable immigrants, were allowed to enter and reside in the United States. That same year, the Supreme Court used the same logic to rule that laborers' wives, although themselves not laborers, acquired their husbands' status and could not enter the United States. Moreover, even those who had the proper status had to lay to rest the suspicions of immigration officials [and prove] that they were not prostitutes. (*Dreaming* 95)

For more on the treatment of Chinese women seeking entry, and other laws pertaining to Chinese women's immigration and citizenship, see M. Hsu, *Dreaming* 92–99.

5. According to Madeleine Hsu, this act's exclusion of Chinese Americans' foreign-born wives was confirmed by the U.S. Supreme Court in *Chang Chan et al. v. John D. Nagle* in 1925. However, the court ruled on the same day in *Cheung Sum Shee et al. v. Nagle* that the Chinese wives and minor children of *merchants* could enter and reside in the United States as nonquota immigrants, though still as aliens ineligible for citizenship (M. Hsu, *Dreaming* 96).

CHAPTER 4

1. For useful essays on Chong, see Quigley; Ty, *Politics*; and Zackodnik. I thank Professor Eleanor Ty for introducing me to Chong's book and for organizing the "Homeland" conference.

2. My account of racialized gender melancholia, in which racialized subjects remain attached to an unattainable gender ideal, is to be distinguished from the gender melancholia that is said to be constitutive of male and female subjects and that Eng and Han trace through Klein, Butler, and Freud (*Butler* 139–140, qtd. in Eng and Han, "Dialogue" 361–362).

3. However, Chong also includes the extenuating information that Chiang Kai-shek's replacement of a silver-based currency with a managed currency in 1935, along with two years of good crops, induced a short-lived bubble of optimism, which helps explain Chan Sam's state of mind during this construction period, just before the arrival of the Japanese army (78–79).

CHAPTER 5

1. Congress established the Boxer Indemnity Scholarships in 1908 in an effort to improve U.S.-Chinese diplomatic relations by promoting educational exchange. China had been required to make large payments to compensate the United States and other Western powers for losses incurred in the Boxer Rebellion, in which anti-foreign rebels attacked Western people and institutions within Chinese borders. After individual claims were settled, the United States moved to return the surplus, in excess of $11 million, to China. To ensure a pro-American use of these funds, Congress stipulated that the money be used to create opportunities for Chinese people to study in the United States. According to historian Stacey Bieler, "The bill assumed that China would continue to pay the Boxer Indemnity to the United States until 1940," but from 1909 through 1940, the United States would annually return $500,000, which was to be used (1) to promote preparatory studies at Qinghua Preparatory School, later Qinghua University, and (2) to send Chinese people to study in the United States (42–45). For more on the roots of U.S.-Chinese educational exchange, see T. K. Chu and Chapter 6 herein.

2. This term comes from Mitscherlich and Mitscherlich's *The Inability to Mourn*. For a fuller discussion, see Chapter 7 herein.

3. *A Dictionary of Sociology* gives the following definition for "semicolonialism": "A term used, classically by Lenin and Mao Zedong . . . to describe states that in the late nineteenth and early twentieth centuries were penetrated by imperial capital, trade, and political influence, but which preserved their juridical independence. Examples include Persia, China, Thailand, Afghanistan, Yemen, and Ethiopia" ("Semicolonialism").

4. The term "postimperial melancholia," introduced in Chapter 1, must also be considered briefly here. Though Ruth and Charles were born near the very end of a great and fallen empire (the Qing Dynasty) whose territorial integrity they wished to restore, their story lacks what Paul Gilroy, in the British context, describes as postimperial melancholia: they were not nostalgic for the Qing Dynasty but rather, as we shall see, eager to leave it behind. In this, they resembled their predecessor, Yung Wing, as Chapter 6 shows.

5. At the risk of overgeneralizing, one could contrast Ruth's conduct toward her own father with a story at the other extreme of female filial piety rendered by another woman of her generation, Chang Yu-i of Pang-Mei Natasha Chang's memoir *Bound Feet and Western Dress*. Chang Yu-i, who continued to care for her ex-husband's parents as their daughter-in-law years after he had divorced and abandoned her, can be considered both personally extraordinary and socially traditional, since she followed a tradition lived out by the unsung first wives of polygamous sojourners such as Fong See and Chan Sam, even as she founded the first women's bank in China (See 69–70; Chong, *Concubine's Children* 17, 20; P. N. Chang 184–191).

6. Here, Winberg's narration echoes the intense emotion of loss conveyed in Tan's *Joy Luck Club*, in which another maternal gift, a swan feather, "comes from afar and carries with it all [the mother's] good intentions" (17). Though critics might consider this novelistic rhetoric too sentimental, I consider it a legitimate expression of the sense of unspeakable loss and trauma suffered by Ruth, whose story corresponds to those of the mothers in Tan's novel.

7. In its article on Chang Chih-chung, the earliest edition of the *Biographical Dictionary of Republican China* gives a more nuanced account of the event (without the term "warlord") but seems indirectly to support the Chais' view that Chang was responsible for the burning. It appears that Chang was still alive in 1967, the time of its publication:

Chang Chih-chung (1891–), military commander and government official, Nationalist general and dean of the Central Military Academy became governor of Hunan in 1937, but lost the position after the misjudged burning of Changsha. . . .

On 12 November 1938 a local report stated that Japanese cavalry had already reached Hsin-ho, a minor market hamlet some 20 miles to the north of Changsha. If that report were true, the enemy might be arriving at any time. Without confirming or investigating the report, the Changsha authorities panicked and issued orders to carry out the destruction. Changsha, which had with the influx of refugees doubled in population to an estimated 800,000, was put to the torch and in four days was consumed in one of the worst conflagrations in modern Chinese history. No Japanese appeared, for the Japanese cavalry had been at Hsin-chiang-ho, on the established Chinese defense line well north of Hsin-ho. As the provincial governor, Chang Chih-chung accepted the blame for the catastrophe. The National Government held an investigation, and three senior Changsha officials were executed. Chang Chih-chung himself was "demoted but retained in office." He resigned the Hunan governorship in January 1939 and proceeded to Chungking. ("Chang Chih-chung" 43)

The article details a long and influential career and ends with the observation, "Since Chang Chih-chung had for years been one of the most trusted military associates of Chiang Kai-shek, his defection to the Communists in 1949 constituted a major psychological loss to the Nationalist cause at a critical hour" (46). It notes that in 1954, Chang was named "a vice chairman of the National Defense Council at Peking" (46).

8. In 1972, learning that Huan is about to die, Charles refuses to break his promise to Ruth openly by visiting his brother in Taiwan. He does, however, send Winberg in secret to reconcile with Huan and to to declare himself Huan's son, so that the old man can die knowing that Charles still cares for him and believing that Winberg will continue his line. According to Buddhist custom, Huan needs a son to remember him, burn spirit money for him, and leave offerings for him at temples, and Winberg promises to fulfill that role. In the minds of Charles and Winberg, it does not matter that the two of them are Christians; what matters is that Charles wishes to heal the rift with his brother, and Winberg to please and obey his father (Chai and Chai, *Girl* 222–223). When Ruth learns of the secret trip, she sends Winberg a long, heartrending letter reminding him of her lifetime of care and sacrifice for him, in contrast to Huan's manipulation and self-interest, and disowning Winberg for his betrayal (223). Clearly, the text implies, Charles's "gift" of his eldest son to Huan is the final act that drives her to buy a separate burial plot (222).

CHAPTER 6

1. Following East Asian practice, Mr. Yung places his surname first. In Mandarin, his name would be Anglicized as Rong Hong. For other well-known figures whose surnames are listed first, see "A Note on Names and Spelling."

2. Second- and third-generation examples include Chong, *Concubine's Children*; Khu, *Cultural Curiosity*; H. Lee; M. M. Lee; Minatoya, *Talking*; Mura; See; and Sone. First-generation examples include Y. Chiang, *China Revisited*; Mukherjee and Blaise; Ondaatje, *Running*; Pham; Tuan; and N. Wu.

3. Borrowing from Sigmund Freud's account of mourning and melancholia, scholars such as Anne Anlin Cheng, David L. Eng, and Shinhee Han have described mourning as a finite process of grieving one's losses, ultimately characterized by the capacity to contain

or get over one's attachment to the lost object of mourning, such as a loved person who has departed, and invest in a new libidinal object, such as a new relationship. Since Freud specified that people may also mourn for places and ideals, scholars have described immigration as a process that calls for mourning what is lost or left behind, implying that the immigrant processing the loss of country, language, culture, family, place, or profession might reasonably grieve such losses. If migration precipitates mourning, the process of assimilation, in which the migrant invests in the new libidinal objects of citizenship and cultural belonging in the new nation, is theoretically linked with the process of getting over the losses associated with immigration (Freud 239–258; Cheng, *Melancholy*; Eng, "Transnational Adoption"; Eng and Han, "Dialogue," "Desegregating"; Williams, *Marxism* 128–135). However, since Asians have historically been unable to assimilate completely into the United States or Canada as a result of legal, economic, and cultural barriers, they are unable to get over the losses of immigration; even if they try to invest fully in the process of assimilation, they cannot assume they will be recognized by the state and by the white majorities of their new countries as legal citizens who culturally belong in North America (S. Chan, *Asian Americans* 45–61; L. Lowe, *Immigrant Acts* 1–36).

4. This timing was suggested by Floyd Cheung in a July 27, 2010, e-mail to the author. Cheung notes that Yung's diary of 1902 mentions purchasing writing supplies and furniture and working on the autobiography. In his *Transpacific Articulations*, Chih-ming Wang dates its composition as between 1900 and 1902 (28).

5. On Yung's official title, see Rhoads 49.

6. On Liang's role in dedicating the Boxer Indemnity funds, see T. K. Chu, vii–xx.

7. On Yung's marginalization, see F. Cheung, "Early Chinese," 24–40; F. Cheung, "Political Resistance" 77–100; and C. Wang, *Transpacific* 35–38.

8. On Yung as a seminal figure in transpacific accounts of study abroad, see C. Wang, *Transpacific* 21–39; for groundbreaking analysis of the transpacific, international roots of the Asian American movement, and its turn toward U.S. nationalism and identity, see C. Wang, *Transpacific* 110–133.

9. Spence, *Search* 160–162. Of the five treaty ports, Shanghai was the most lucrative: the silk trade alone was worth over $20 million by the mid-1850s (Spence, *Search* 162). As the Taiping rebels approached Shanghai in the early 1850s and imperial authority "evaporated," the British and the Americans had taken over responsibility for customs collection and eventually set up the Imperial Maritime Customs Service, "the most reliable source of revenue the Chinese government enjoyed in the last third of the nineteenth century—and perhaps in the first half of the twentieth century as well" (W. Cohen 18). Having arrived in the Shanghai customs office in the fall of 1856, Yung observed the "Imperial Customs Department" being run by foreigners; Chinese workers were limited to ill-paid minor positions, which they supplemented by graft (Yung 63–65). Years later, he made brilliant use of his observations there: he proposed that the Shanghai customs taxes fund his fifteen-year Chinese Educational Mission (Yung 173). According to Edward J. M. Rhoads, the mission was indeed funded by Imperial Maritime Customs: the Shanghai customs house dispersed approximately US$82,000 per year or US$1,644,000 over more than fifteen years (10).

10. Notably, Macao was the seat of the notorious coolie trade to Cuba and Peru, which Yung helped investigate in September 1874 (Stewart 200). Yung devotes a full chapter to the injustices of the trade, his mission to document the abuses of workers in Peru, and his contribution to the cessation of the trade (Yung 191–96). According to Watt Stewart, the coolie trade from Macao was ended by the Portuguese in 1873 under international pressure, effective March 27, 1874 (158–159, 192). When Peru then sought to renegotiate and renew its treaty with China, Yung's investigation helped the Qing document that the coolies'

claims of abuse were well founded (Stewart 183–205, esp. 200). Although the 1874 Treaty of Tientsin with Peru was ratified in 1876, the shipping company contracted to bring additional laborers from China to Peru, the Olyphant Brothers, failed to do so because of Chinese government interventions and subsequently failed as a company in 1878 (Stewart 210–214). (See also Yung 39, on the firm's sponsorship of Yung's college education, and Haddad for more on this firm's activities in China.) Stewart concludes, "Yung's report may well have exerted a determinative effect on later policy of the Chinese government in the matter of the 'new' immigration" to Peru (208).

11. "Loo-choo" refers to the southern islands of present-day Japan, now known as Okinawa. These islands were Chinese tributaries from 1383 to 1872. Their Chinese name, *Liuqui*, was pronounced Ryūkyū in Japanese (Kinoshita and Palevsky 750).

12. According to Gützlaff, the British East Company did not list opium as an export to China from 1813 to 1828, but "Private India Ships Under the British Flag" quadrupled their opium sales from 1817 to 1828 (Gützlaff, *Sketch* 2:455, app. 2 and 3). In appendix 11, "Estimated Statement of the British Trade at the Port of Canton for the Year Ending in the 31st of March, 1834," Canton is listed as receiving opium valued at $11,381,930 and supplementing its exports of tea, silk, and other goods with silver bullion valued at $4,976,841 and gold valued at $375,906 (Gützlaff, *Sketch* 2:455, app. 11).

13. In addition to being reported by Olaudah Equiano, the Zong massacre inspired J.M.W. Turner's 1840 masterpiece *The Slave Ship*, which is owned by Boston's Museum of Fine Arts and discussed in Mark Twain's travel narrative *A Tramp Abroad*. Twain's companion on the trip described in *A Tramp* was Joseph Twichell, Yung's close friend, so it is not unreasonable to expect that Yung, who was so informed about the Chinese coolie trade, also knew of this and other stories about the transatlantic Middle Passage by the time he drafted *My Life*. See "The Slave Ship"; "A Tramp Abroad."

14. *Heart of Darkness* first appeared in *Blackwood's Edinburgh Magazine* in 1899. I cite it only to illustrate the type of exotic stereotyping Yung avoided in representing fellow Chinese. I attribute Yung's dry style to his emulating the genres of missionary travel narrative and colonial novel while avoiding their orientalism.

15. See Bingham, *The Columbian Orator*. Among other short speeches and dramatic pieces, it includes "A Dialogue between a Master and a Slave" (no author, 240–242), and "Extract from a Discourse Delivered before the New York Society for Promoting the Manumission of Slaves," by Rev. Samuel Miller (293–294). Douglass describes the effect of the dialogue and of Sheridan in his *Narrative* (35).

16. For more on Chinese studies abroad, see Y. C. Wang.

17. Yung 192–196; Lopez; Stewart. Yung also worked as a diplomat to help Chinese Americans and as a revolutionary to overthrow the Qing government, but he chose to omit these activities from his autobiography in order to cultivate a more moderate public image. See F. Cheung, "Early Chinese" 31–36.

18. (Wan's dissertation pages are numbered by chapter and page.) Apparently the price on Yung's head was revoked in 1905, after Yung had permanently returned to the United States. See "Bulletin of Yale University" 186.

19. In addition, Yung's text is written with a particularly keen awareness of the conditions of Chinese exclusion in the United States, under which naturalized U.S. citizens like Yung himself were stripped of their U.S. citizenship and American-born Chinese were perceived and treated as aliens. Chang-rae Lee, for instance, has explored a similar gap between a confident narrative performance and a condition of race-related isolation and inability to assimilate in his portrayal of the racial melancholia of Doc Hata in his novel *A Gesture Life*. Similarly, the first-person narration of his *Native Speaker* is infused with racial melancholia

as narrator Henry Park contrasts the brilliant performance of American subjectivity of his idol, Councilman John Kwang, with Kwang's enduring marginalization.

20. According to Peter Pei-de Wan, "This was the repression of the 1855 Guangdong Insurrection by the Heaven and Earth Society, which was a secret society associated with the Taiping rebels" (4.55).

21. Although they were learning English and studying in American schools, the students were criticized for not keeping up their Chinese fluency and for becoming fluent in English. They were required to study Chinese language, including calligraphy and the memorization and interpretation of traditional texts, for an hour each day; to write two pages a day in Chinese; to compete for prizes in Chinese essay competitions; and to attend Chinese classes at the CEM headquarters in Hartford for several weeks every summer. In addition, they were required to attend cultural events instructing them in Chinese values and to perform ritual kowtows to portraits of important figures every so often. They were not to convert to Christianity, and their host families were not to proselytize, but they were to participate in all normal family activities and school activities, including saying grace, attending church services, and attending religious services in their schools. They were also explicitly forbidden to cut their queues, which were legally required as outward signs of their loyalty to the Qing Dynasty, or to apply for naturalized citizenship in the United States (Rhoads 135–165).

22. The cryptic relocations Yung records (from Beijing to the foreign quarter of Shanghai, to British protection in Hong Kong, to temporary Japanese protection in Formosa, to his son's graduation at Yale University) have been linked by history scholar Peter Pei-de Wan to a series of involvements in failed revolutionary movements. According to Wan, the "Deliberative Association of China" is a euphemism for the failed uprising organized by Tang Cai-chang; Tang's execution drove Yung to flee to Hong Kong. En route to Hong Kong, Yung met Sun Yat-sen, with whom he had a private meeting in Japan. In Hong Kong, Yung associated with members of Sun's Tong-meng Hui, the party that eventually founded the Republic of China, but parted ways with them and joined another revolutionary group. By the time Yung arrived in San Francisco to raise support for this new group, in 1902, it had been exposed and destroyed. See Wan 6.135–6.137.

CHAPTER 7

1. According to Waldo Heinrichs, the Smithsonian's attempt to introduce historical debates about the bombings of Hiroshima and Nagaski was widely perceived as conflicting with the imperative that the museum present the *Enola Gay* as a technological breakthrough that saved American lives. In this debate, the Smithsonian's historians learned too late that many viewed the primary mission of the museum as one of commemorating a particular narrative of American achievement rather than of fostering debate or critique of that narrative.

2. See, especially, Nazaki and Inokuchi on the Ienaga textbook case, which also turns on a controversy about the proper purpose of textbook history.

3. Dower identifies typical Japanese rationalizations that minimalize Japanese responsibility and provoke criticism. The most extreme version of "denial," resurrected from wartime propaganda, argues that the military was defending the homeland from the threat of Soviet Communism and establishing a "Greater East Asia Co-prosperity Sphere" to combat European and American imperialism in Asia. Another approach is to repudiate both Marxist analysis of Japanese history (criticizing the authoritarian emperor system, close links between business and government, and similar structural roots of the "domestic repression

and overseas aggression of imperial Japan") and the "victor's history" of the "Tokyo War Crimes Trial" of Japanese war criminals by the allied powers (112–114). Some conservatives, Dower goes on, use "evocations of moral (or immoral) equivalence": in efforts to deny Japan's aggression or to minimize the singularity of Japan's past, they cite reasonable critiques of legal flaws in the Tokyo War Crimes Trial, point to immoral acts and a history of colonial interference by other nations, or emphasize the selective historiography of other countries (114–118). "Victim consciousness" consists of focusing on Japanese suffering and loss rather than the damage caused by Japan to others. Dower argues that the genuine shock many Japanese felt when their country's atrocities were revealed in the War Crimes Trial was blunted by their intense suffering and defeat and that historical self-scrutiny was also blocked by Japan's Cold War alliance with the United States, which many Japanese now consider oppressively unequal (118–123). During its occupation of Japan, the United States "concealed the true nature and full enormity of Japanese war crimes" in order to make it a viable Cold War ally in the shortest possible time, thus forestalling proper *trauerarbeit*—particularly concerning the responsibility of Emperor Hirohito, military and political head of the nation—until after Hirohito's death in 1989. Since so many acts were committed in the emperor's name, his exoneration from responsibility made it difficult for ordinary Japanese to acknowledge responsibility for their own acts taken on his behalf, let alone those of the nation (123–129). For additional perspectives, see Buruma on the Ienaga textbook case, 1952–1992 (*Wages* 189–201), Onishi, Oi, and Kotler.

4. As discussed in Chapter 1, note 14, Japanese Americans count immigrants to America as the first generation: *issei*. Subsequent generations include the *nisei* (second), *sansei* (third), and *yonsei* (fourth). At the time of the internment of Japanese Americans in 1941, the majority of those interned were *nisei*, American citizens by birth. Other intriguing treatments of this period with a return motif, or Japanese American characters participating in East-West cultural contact in Japan, include *nisei* Jim Yoshida's memoir of coerced wartime service with the Japanese army, *The Two Worlds of Jim Yoshida* (1972), coauthored with Bill Hosokawa; Kerri Sakamoto's story of a Japanese Canadian who learns her father was a "kamikaze" pilot, *One Hundred Million Hearts* (2003); Yuko Taniguchi's adoption-themed novel of return, *The Ocean in the Closet* (2007); Gene Oishi's autobiographical short-story cycle, *Fox Drum Bebop* (2014), which contrasts a return to Japan with a family's search for a final home for one member's ashes; and Lynn Kutsukake's novel of the occupation, *The Translation of Love* (2016). Because of space constraints, I focus on Minatoya's and Ozeki's novels as closely related projects of feminist, transpacific countermemory. This is not a comprehensive list. See also P. Chu, "Asian American Narratives"; and Goossen.

5. Minatoya's narrator, Etsuko Sone, describes the "*shi-shosetsu*" as the "I-story" and suggests that "the autobiographical novel is an ancient art" though it has gained new popularity in modern Japan (*Strangeness* 11). By contrast, Ruth Ozeki inserts a fictitious academic article into *A Tale for the Time Being* that defines "*shishōsetsu*" as "a genre of Japanese autobiographical fiction, commonly translated into English as 'I-novel,'" that "flourished during the brief period of sociopolitical liberalization of the Taishō Democracy (1912–1926)" and continues to influence contemporary Japanese literature (149). Ozeki's fictive article foregrounds debates about this genre, which is touted for "its 'confessional' style, its 'transparency' of text, and the 'sincerity' and 'authenticity' of its authorial voice," yet raises "issues of truthfulness and fabrication, highlighting the tension between self-revelatory, self-concealing, and self-effacing acts" (149). However, Minatoya's premise is that her narrator is a literary novice whose personal narration has the sincerity of a journal, and who is crafting these notes into her own "I-story." Since Minatoya refers throughout to the "I-story," I use that term in discussing her novel, but the term "I-novel" elsewhere.

6. Hiroko Kugisima asserts that *A Daughter of the Samurai* also draws on the experiences of Florence Mills Wilson, a close American friend who lived with Sugimoto all her life and secretly helped her with her writing; however, to strengthen their protest of the passage of anti-immigration laws in 1924, the friends decided to present Wilson's observations as part of Sugimoto's autobiography, first in magazine publications and then in the book. Wilson declined to be listed as a coauthor. As a foreign missionary from America sharing a household with a Japanese woman, Wilson might also be seen as an archetype for the character of Miss Langley in *Strangeness*. Since my focus is on Minatoya, however, I discuss *Daughter* as a single-author autobiography, the fact that some of the details have been fictionalized notwithstanding. Of the sources listed in Minatoya's bibliography, Sugimoto seems to be the primary source for Minatoya's portrayal of her novel's female characters. For some readers, *Strangeness* may also be reminiscent of two early novels of Japanese British author Kazuo Ishiguro, *An Artist of the Floating World* (about an artist who places his art at the service of Japanese militarism) and *A Pale View of Hills* (narrated by another mother named Etsuko).

7. Etsuko describes her decision to stay in terms of social norms; Minatoya does not mention the legal conditions that, in real life, would have required Etsuko to remain in Japan (*Strangeness* 215). After 1924, ordinary Japanese citizens were barred from legal entry into the United States. Since Japanese could not be naturalized as U.S. citizens until 1965, Etsuko would have been a Japanese citizen, while Hanae would have been American or held dual citizenship by virtue of her American birth to Japanese parents. In *A Daughter of the Samurai*, Sugimoto presents her decision to bring her American daughters back to the United States as hinging on the consent of her in-laws. Behind the scenes, however, she may have arranged a teaching job and a scholar's exemption from the exclusion laws in order to return to the United States with them. According to Kugisima, Sugimoto first entered the United States on a student's visa, married a Japanese businessman in 1898, and was teaching at Columbia University in 1925, when the book was published (Kugisima 141–144; Sugimoto lists 1926 as the book's initial publication date [*Daughter* xi]). Minatoya follows Sugimoto in minimizing references to these barriers to foreground the need for transpacific, cross-cultural understanding.

8. For a transpacific feminist reading of Sugimoto, see K. Kuo.

9. Also, Viet Thanh Nguyen writes that countermemory is "oppositional memory, the memory of the subordinated and the marginalized, memory from below versus memory from above. Much of Asian American memory is an exercise of countermemory, one engaged in recovering what has been forgotten about and forgotten by Asian Americans" ("Memory" 154).

10. Jiko is introduced as a Japanese New Woman of the Taisho era (1912–1926), an anarchist, a novelist, and an admirer of the anarchist author Kanno Sugako, but the novel ends up focusing primarily on her Buddhism (Ozeki 69). In *Kamikaze Diaries: Reflections of Japanese Student Soldiers*, Emiko Ohnuki-Tierney disputes American stereotypes of the World War II kamikaze pilots, particularly the popular equation of them with the 9/11 terrorists. Since most of the kamikaze pilots were drafted or coerced into enlisting and wanted to live, she argues, they were not suicide bombers. And since they performed state-sponsored acts of war against military targets, she argues that they were military combatants, not terrorists. I follow her use of *tokkōtai* to minimize the sensational connotations of "kamikaze pilots," although *Kamikaze Diaries* is the title of her book (Ohnuki-Tierney xiii–xvii).

11. Technically, since Haruki #1's secret diary arrives on the beach alongside Nao's and is translated by Benoit, it preexists Ruth's readerly desires to understand his and Nao's

stories. But just as the need arises for Ruth to know Haruki #1's final words, Benoit invites her to retrieve his completed translation of the secret diary, with its message about Haruki #1's decision not to kill others (315, 328). When Ruth needs to convey this message to Nao, she passes backward in time and across the ocean in her dream; Ruth's dream-self finds the secret diary in her hands and delivers it to the empty "box containing Haruki #1's remains-that-were-not-truly-remains" in Jiko's study (353–354), where it stays and is discovered by Nao and her father, who agree to continue living and to translate it together (as Nao reports in the new entry that appears in her diary the morning after Ruth's dream [366–369]). I would therefore argue that in this novel, Haruki's secret diary is not only a historical artifact but also a symbol of the sympathetic understanding of his life and death that is produced by efforts of postmemory, efforts that are shared by Jiko, Ruth, Nao, and Haruki #2.

12. In *The Strangeness of Beauty*, Bon or Obon is described by the narrator as "Japan's midsummer festival," "a day when the dead return for public rejoicing," "with no private rituals" and with "roots in ancient wonder of nature rather than in Buddhism––less a religious observance than a ritualized community party" for the Japanese American community in Seattle, circa 1928 (Minatoya, *Strangeness* 48). In *A Tale for the Time Being*, Obon is similarly described as a festival to remember the dead; it is a "party" for ghosts as well as for the community, for which Jiko and her fellow nun Muji prepare the monastery (210). However, Nao also describes the festival as commemorating a disciple of Buddha who was instructed to make special offerings of food to help bring his mother's ghost out of Buddhist hell (210). Caught up in the planning, Nao is thus prepared to receive a visitation from Haruki #1.

13. According to *Wikipedia* ("Battle of Okinawa"), the Battle of Okinawa began on April 1 and lasted eighty-two days. Seven major *tokkōtai* attacks were sent out from April 1 through May 25.

14. Famous heroes who gain new insight or power upon returning from the land of the dead include Odysseus, Harry Potter, Lyra Belacqua (in Philip Pullman's *His Dark Materials* trilogy), and Brave Orchid (Kingston, *Woman Warrior* 72–23). For an influential discussion of this motif in myth, see Campbell 97–109.

15. For a simile linking books to cemeteries, see Marcel Proust, *Le Temps Retrouvé*, qtd. in Ozeki 357.

16. Despite the illusion of simultaneity promoted by reading, Nao's crisis takes place years before the diary arrives on the shores of Canada and reaches Ruth.

17. In keeping with the convention-breaking aspect of historiographic metafiction, Jiko's final act of writing is itself an instance of citing a convention—that of a Zen teacher writing a last poem before dying—only to subvert it, in this case by writing only a last word.

Works Cited and Additional Sources

Sources preceded by an asterisk (*) are primary texts with a scene or theme of return.

Antin, Mary. *The Promised Land.* 1969; repr., Princeton, NJ: Princeton University Press, 1985.
*Aslam, Nadeem. *Maps for Lost Lovers: A Novel.* New York: Vintage International, 2004.
*Bacho, Peter. *Cebu.* Seattle: University of Washington Press, 1991.
Backer, Sara. *American Fuji: A Novel.* New York: Berkeley–Penguin, 2001.
Bangerter, Amy Nelson. *Chinese Youth and American Educational Institutions, 1850–1881.* Ph.D. diss., George Washington University, 2005.
———. "The New Englandization of Yung Wing: Family, Nation, Region." In *Asian Americans in New England: Culture and Community.* Ed. Monica Chiu, 42–65. Lebanon, NH: University of New Hampshire Press–University Press of New England, 2009.
"Battle of Okinawa." *Wikipedia.* https://en.wikipedia.org/wiki/Battle_of_Okinawa. Accessed February 21, 2018.
Bhabha, Homi K. "Of Mimicry and Man: The Ambivalence of Colonial Discourse." *October* 28 (Spring 1984): 125–133. Repr. in *The Location of Culture*, 86–92. London: Routledge, 1994.
Bieler, Stacey. *"Patriots" or "Traitors"? A History of American-Educated Chinese Students.* Armonk, NY: M. E. Sharpe, 2004.
Bingham, Caleb (compiler). *The Columbian Orator: Containing a Variety of Original and Selected Pieces Together with Rules, Which Are Calculated to Improve Youth and Others, in the Ornamental and Useful Art of Eloquence.* 1821. Bicentennial ed. Ed. David W. Blight. New York: New York University Press, 1998.
Boorman, Howard L., and Richard C. Howard, eds. *Biographical Dictionary of Republican China.* 3 vols. New York: Columbia University Press, 1967.
Bow, Leslie. *Partly Colored: Asian Americans and Racial Anomaly in the Segregated South.* New York: New York University Press, 2002.

"Bulletin of Yale University: Obituary Record of Yale Graduates." University of New Haven, New Haven, CT, series 8, no. 9, July 1912, 183–186.

*Bulosan, Carlos. *The Cry and the Dedication*. 1946; repr., Philadelphia: Temple University Press, 1995.

Burns, Gerald T. "The Repatriate Theme in Philippine Second-Language Fiction." In *Presenting America: Encountering the Philippines: Fulbright Lectures*, 168–225. Quezon City: University of the Philippines Press, 1992.

Buruma, Ian. *Inventing Japan: 1853–1964*. New York: Modern Library, 2004.

———. *The Wages of Guilt: Memories of War in Germany and Japan*. 1994; repr., London: Atlantic Books: 2009.

Butler, Judith. *The Psychic Life of Power: Theories in Subjectivities*. Stanford, CA: Stanford University Press, 1997.

Campbell, Joseph. *The Hero with a Thousand Faces*. Novato, CA: New World Library, 2008.

Campomanes, Oscar. "Filipinos in the United States and Their Literature of Exile." In *Reading the Literatures of Asian America*. Ed. Shirley Geok-lin Lim and Amy Ling, 49–78. Philadelphia: Temple University Press, 1992.

*Castro, Brian. *Shanghai Dancing*. 2003; repr., New York: Kaya, 2009.

"Catalogue of the Library of the Society of the Brothers in Unity, Yale College, April." New Haven, CT: B. L. Hamlen, 1846. https://archive.org/details/cataloguelibrar22librgoog.

*Cha, Theresa Hak-yung. *Dictee*. New York: Tanam Press, 1982.

*Chadwick, David. *Crooked Cucumber: The Life and Zen Teaching of Shunryu Suzuki*. New York: Broadway Books–Random House, 1999.

*Chai, May-lee. *Hapa Girl: A Memoir*. Philadelphia: Temple University Press, 2007.

*Chai, May-lee, and Winberg Chai. *China from A to Z: Everything You Need to Know to Understand Chinese Customs and Culture*. New York: Plume, 2007.

———. *The Girl from Purple Mountain: Love, Honor, War, and One Family's Journey from China to America*. Hardcover ed. [contains photos not in paperback]. New York: Thomas Dunne–St. Martin's, 2001.

Chai, Winberg. *The Foreign Relations of the People's Republic of China*. New York: Capricorn Books, 1972.

*Chan, Graham. "Through a Window." In Khu, *Cultural Curiosity*, 20–38.

*Chan, Henry. "Ears Attuned to Two Cultures." In Khu, *Cultural Curiosity*, 111–127.

Chan, Jeffery Paul, Frank Chin, Lawson Fusao Inada, and Shawn Wong, eds. *The Big Aiiieeeee! An Anthology of Chinese American and Japanese American Literature*. New York: Meridian–Penguin, 1991.

Chan, Sucheng. *Asian Americans: An Interpretive History*. Woodbridge, CT: Twayne, 1991. Chap. 3, "Hostility and Conflict," repr. in *Asian American Studies: A Reader*. Ed. Jean Yuwen Shen Wu and Min Song, 47–66. New Brunswick: Rutgers University Press, 2000.

———, ed. *Chinese American Transnationalism: The Flow of People, Resources, and Ideas between China and America during the Exclusion Era*. Philadelphia: Temple University Press, 2006.

Chandra, Vikram. *Red Earth and Pouring Rain*. Boston: Little, Brown, 1995.

Chang, Jung. *Wild Swans: Three Daughters of China*. New York: Anchor–Doubleday, 1991.

*Chang, Pang-Mei Natasha. *Bound Feet and Western Dress: A Memoir*. New York: Doubleday, 1996.

"Chang Chih-chung." In Boorman and Howard, *Biographical Dictionary of Republican China*, 1:39–46.

*Chao, Buwei Yang. *Autobiography of a Chinese Woman*. Trans. Yuenren Chao. 1947; repr., Westport, CT: Greenwood Press, 1970.

Chao, Lucy [Zhao Luorui], trans. *Cao Ye Ji* [*Leaves of Grass*]. By Walt Whitman. Shanghai: Yiwen Chubanshe, 1991.
Cheng, Anne Anlin. "The Melancholy of Race." *Kenyon Review* 19, no. 1 (1997): 49–61.
———. *The Melancholy of Race*. Oxford: Oxford University Press, 2001.
Chen Kuan-Hsing. *Asia as Method: Toward Deimperialization*. Durham, NC: Duke University Press, 2010.
Cheung, Floyd. "Early Chinese American Autobiography: Reconsidering the Works of Yan Phou and Yung Wing." In *Recovered Legacies: Authority and Identity in Early Asian American Literature*. Ed. Keith Lawrence and Floyd Cheung, 24–40. Philadelphia: Temple University Press, 2005.
———. "Political Resistance, Cultural Appropriation, and the Performance of Manhood in Yung Wing's *My Life in China and America*." In *Form and Transformation in Asian American Literature*. Ed. Xiaojing Zhou and Samina Najmi, 77–100. Seattle: University of Washington Press, 2005.
Cheung, King-kok. *Articulate Silences: Hisaye Yamamoto, Maxine Hong Kingston, Joy Kogawa*. Ithaca, NY: Cornell University Press, 1993.
*Chiang Monlin. *Tides from the West: A Chinese Autobiography*. New Haven, CT: Yale University Press, 1947.
*Chiang Yee. *China Revisited after Forty-Two Years*. New York: W. W. Norton, 1977.
Chin, Frank. "Come All Ye Asian American Writers of the Real and the Fake." In Chan et al., *The Big Aiiieeeee!* 1–92.
———. "This Is Not an Autobiography." *Genre* 18, no. 2 (1985): 109–130.
Chin, Frank, Jeffery Paul Chan, Lawson Fusao Inada, and Shawn Hsu Wong. *Aiiieeeee! An Anthology of Asian American Writers*. 1974; repr., New York: Mentor–Penguin, 1991.
*Ching, Meilin. "My Father's Land." In Khu, *Cultural Curiosity*, 95–110.
*Chong, Denise. *The Concubine's Children: The Story of a Chinese Family Living on Two Sides of the Globe*. New York: Penguin Books, 1994.
———. Keynote address. Homeland, History and Representation: International Symposium on Chinese Canadian and Chinese American Literature in English. Renison University College and University of Waterloo, Waterloo, Ontario, October 16, 2010.
Chow, Rey. "Translator, Traitor: Translator, Mourner (or, Dreaming of Intercultural Equivalence)." *New Literary History* 37 (2007): 565–580.
Choy, Catherine Ceniza. *Global Families: A History of Asian American Adoption in America*. New York: New York University Press, 2013.
Christian, Barbara. "The Race for Theory." In *Gender and Theory: Dialogues on Feminist Criticism*. Ed. Linda Kauffman, 225–237. Oxford: Basil Blackwell, 1989.
*Chu, Louis. *Eat a Bowl of Tea*. 1961; repr., New York: Lyle Stuart–Kensington, 2002.
Chu, Patricia P. "Asian American Narratives of Return: Nisei Representations of Prewar and Wartime Japan." In *Ethnic Life Writing and Histories: Genres, Performance, and Culture*. Ed. Rocío G. Davis, Jaume Aurell, and Ana Beatriz Delgado, 204–221. Berlin: LIT 2007.
———. *Assimilating Asians: Gendered Strategies of Authorship in Asian America*. Durham, NC: Duke University Press, 2000.
*Chu, Richard. "Guilt Trip to China." In Khu, *Cultural Curiosity*, 128–144.
Chu, T. K. "Translator's Preface." In *Chinese Students Encounter America*. By Ning Qian. Trans. T. K. Chu, vii–xxiii. Seattle: University of Washington Press, 2002.
Clifford, James. *Routes: Travel and Translation in the Late Twentieth Century*. Cambridge, MA: Harvard University Press, 1997.
———. "Traveling Cultures." In *Cultural Studies*. Ed. Lawrence Grossberg, Cary Nelson, and Paula A. Treichler, 96–115. New York: Routledge, 1992.

Cohen, Robin. *Global Diasporas: An Introduction.* Seattle: University of Washington Press, 1997.

Cohen, Warren I. *America's Response to China: A History of Sino-American Relations.* 3rd ed. New York: Columbia University Press, 1990.

Conrad, Joseph. *Heart of Darkness.* Ed. Ross C. Murfin. Boston: Bedford Books, 1996.

Conrad, Sebastian. "Entangled Memories: Versions of the Past in Germany and Japan, 1945–2001." *Journal of Contemporary History* 38, no. 1 (2003): 85–99.

Couser, G. Thomas. "Genre Matters: Form, Force, and Filiation." *Life Writing* 2, no. 2 (2005): 123–140.

Crimp, Douglas. "Mourning and Militancy." *October* 51 (Winter 1989): 3–18.

*Davidson, Cathy. *Thirty-Six Views of Mount Fuji: On Finding Myself in Japan.* Durham, NC: Duke University Press, 2006.

Davidson, Robyn, ed. *The Picador Book of Journeys.* London: Picador, 2000.

Davis, Rocío G. *Begin Here: Reading Asian North American Autobiographies of Childhood.* Honolulu: University of Hawai'i Press, 2007.

———. *Relative Histories: Mediating History in Asian American Family Memoirs.* Honolulu: University of Hawai'i Press, 2011.

*Desai, Kiran. *The Inheritance of Loss.* New York: Grove Press, 2006.

Dirlik, Arif. "Asians on the Rim: Transnational Capital and Local Community in the Making of Contemporary Asian America." In *Asian American Studies Now: A Critical Reader.* Ed. Jean Yu-wen Shen Wu and Thomas C. Chen, 515–539. New Brunswick, NJ: Rutgers University Press, 2010.

———. *The Postcolonial Aura: Third World Criticism in the Age of Global Capitalism.* Boulder, CO: Westview, 1997.

*Dobbs, Jennifer Kwon. *Paper Pavilion.* Buffalo, NY: White Pine Press, 2007.

Dodge, Georgina. "Diasporic Literature and Identity: Autobiography and the I-Novel in Etsu Sugimoto's *Daughter of the Samurai.*" In *Recovered Legacies: Authority and Identity in Early Asian American Literature.* Ed. Keith Lawrence and Floyd Cheung, 60–79. Philadelphia: Temple University Press, 2005.

Dōgen, Eihei. *Shōbōgenzō.* Trans. Gudo Wafu Nishijima and Chodo Cross. Berkeley: Numata Center for Buddhist Translation and Research, 2008.

———. *Treasury of the True Dharma Eye: Zen Master Dogen's Shobo Genzo.* Ed. Kazuaki Tanahashi. Trans. Kazuaki Tanahashi, Peter Levitt, et al. Boston: Shambala Publications, 2011.

Dorow, Sara K., ed. *I Wish for You a Beautiful Life: Letters from the Korean Birth Mothers of Ae Ron Won to Their Children.* St. Paul, MN: Yeong and Yeong, 1999.

———. *Transnational Adoption: A Cultural Economy of Race, Gender, and Kinship.* New York: New York University Press, 2001.

Douglass, Frederick. *Narrative of the Life of Frederick Douglass, An American Slave: Written by Himself.* New Haven, CT: Yale University Press, 2001.

Dower, John. "'An Aptitude for Being Unloved': War and Memory in Japan." 2002; repr. in *Ways of Forgetting, Ways of Remembering: Japan in the Modern World.* By John Dower, 105–135. New York: New Press, 2012.

Eaton, Edith Maude. See Sui Sin Far.

Eaton, Winnifred. *Me: A Book of Remembrance.* 1915; repr., Jackson: University Press of Mississippi, 1997.

Ehrenreich, Barbara, and Arlie Russell Hochschild. *Global Woman: Nannies, Maids, and Sex Workers in the New Economy.* New York: Metropolitan Owl Books, 2003.

Ellis, Rev. W[illiam]. "Introduction: Brief Notice of China and Siam, and of the Labour of Protestant Missionaries in These and the Adjacent Countries; Sketches of Morrison, Milne, Gutzlaff, and Leang Afa." In Gützlaff, *Journal of Three Voyages*, 1–64.

Eng, David L. "Melancholia in the Late Twentieth Century." *Signs: Feminisms at a Millennium* 25, no. 4 (2000): 1275–1281.

———. "Transnational Adoption and Queer Diasporas." *Social Text* 76, no. 21 (2003): 1–37.

Eng, David L., and Shinhee Han. "Desegregating Love: Transnational Adoption, Racial Reparation, and Racial Transitional Objects." *Studies in Gender and Sexuality* 7, no. 2 (2006): 141–172.

———. "A Dialogue on Racial Melancholia." *Psychoanalytic Dialogues* 10, no. 4 (2000): 667–700. Repr. in *Loss: The Politics of Mourning*. Ed. David L. Eng and David Kazanjian, 343–371. Berkeley: University of California Press, 2003.

Equiano, Olaudah. *The Interesting Narrative of the Life of Olaudah Equiano, Written by Himself, with Related Documents*. Ed. Robert J. Allison. 2nd ed. Boston: Bedford–St. Martin's, 2007.

*Fei, Deanna. *A Thread of Sky: A Novel*. New York: Penguin, 2010.

*Fenkl, Heinz Insu. *Memories of My Ghost Brother*. New York: Plume–Penguin, 1997.

Franklin, Benjamin. *The Autobiography of Benjamin Franklin (1771–89)*. 1868. Ed. and with an introduction by William L. Andrews. New York: Mentor–Penguin–Putnam, 1992.

Freud, Sigmund. "Mourning and Melancholia." In *The Standard Edition of the Complete Psychological Works of Sigmund Freud*. Trans. under the general editorship of James Strachey, with Anna Freud, assisted by Alix Strachey and Alan Tyson, 14:239–258. London: Hogarth Press and the Institute of Psychoanalysis, 1957.

*Fukuzawa, Yukichi. *The Autobiography of Yukichi Fukuzawa*. Rev. trans. Eichii Kiyooka. 1899; repr., New York: Schocken Books, 1972.

Gilroy, Paul. *Postcolonial Melancholia*. New York: Columbia University Press, 2005.

Goellnicht, Donald C. "Blurring Boundaries: Asian American Literature as Theory." In *An Interethnic Companion to Asian American Literature*. Ed. King-kok Cheung, 338–365. Cambridge: Cambridge University Press, 1997.

Golden, Arthur. *Memoirs of a Geisha: A Novel*. New York: Vintage, 1997.

Goossen, Theodore. "Writing the Pacific War in the Twenty-First Century: Dennis Bock, Rui Umezawa, and Kerri Sakamoto." *Canadian Literature* 179 (Winter 2003): 56–69.

Gotanda, Neil. "A Critique of 'Our Constitution is Colorblind.'" *Stanford Law Review* 44, no. 1 (1991): 1–68.

Gützlaff, Charles [Karl Friedrich]. *Journal of Three Voyages along the Coast of China, in 1831, 1832, and 1833, with Notices of Siam, Corea, and the Loo-choo* [Ryūkyū] *Islands*. London: Frederick Westley and A. H. Davis, 1834. Repr., Taipei: Ch'eng-wen, 1968.

———. *A Sketch of Chinese History, Ancient and Modern: Comprising a Retrospect of the Foreign Intercourse and Trade with China*. London: Smith, Elder, 1834.

Haddad, John R. *America's First Adventure in China: Trade, Treaties, Opium, and Salvation*. Philadelphia: Temple University Press, 2013.

*Hagedorn, Jessica. *Dogeaters*. New York: Penguin, 1990.

*———. *Dream Jungle*. New York: Penguin, 2003.

Hamid, Mohsin. *The Reluctant Fundamentalist*. Boston: Houghton Mifflin Harcourt, 2007.

*Hayslip, Le Ly, with Jay Wurts. *When Heaven and Earth Changed Places: A Vietnamese Woman's Journey from War to Peace*. New York: Plume–Penguin, 1990.

Heinrichs, Waldo. "The *Enola Gay* and Contested Public Memory." In *The Unpredictability of the Past: Memories of the Asia-Pacific War in U.S.–East Asian Relations*. Ed. Marc S. Gallichio, 201–233. Durham, NC: Duke University Press, 2007.

Hessler, Peter. *Oracle Bones: A Journey through Time in China*. New York: Harper Perennial, 2006.

Hirsch, Marianne. *Family Frames: Photography, Narrative, and Postmemory*. Cambridge, MA: Harvard University Press, 1997.

———. "The Generation of Postmemory." *Poetics Today* 29, no. 1 (2008). doi:10.1215/03335372-2007-019. Accessed February 18, 2017.

Holland, Patrick, and Graham Huggan. *Tourists with Typewriters: Critical Reflections on Contemporary Travel Writing*. Ann Arbor: University of Michigan Press, 1998.

*Hongo, Garrett. *Volcano: A Memoir of Hawai'i*. New York: Vintage–Random House, 1996.

*Hopgood, Mei-ling. *Lucky Girl: A Memoir*. Chapel Hill, NC: Algonquin Books of Chapel Hill, 2009.

Houston, Velina Hasu. *Asa Ga Kimashita (Morning Has Broken)*. In *The Politics of Life: Four Plays by Asian American Women*. Ed. Velina Hasu Houston, 219–274. Philadelphia: Temple University Press, 1993.

———. *Tea*. In *Unbroken Thread: An Anthology of Plays by Asian American Women*. Ed. Roberta Uno, 155–200. Minneapolis: University of Massachusetts Press, 1993.

*Hsu, Graziella. "No Roots, Old Roots." In Khu, *Cultural Curiosity*, 77–96.

Hsu, Kai-yu. *Wen I-to*. Woodbridge, CT: Twayne, 1980.

Hsu, Kai-yu, and Helen Palubinskas, eds. *Asian-American Authors*. Boston: Houghton Mifflin, 1972.

Hsu, Madeline Y[uan-yin]. "Befriending the 'Yellow Peril': Chinese Students and Intellectuals and the Liberalization of U.S. Immigration Laws, 1950–1965." *Journal of American–East Asian Relations* 16, no. 3 (2009): 139–162.

———. "Befriending the Yellow Peril: Student Migration and the Warming of American Attitudes toward Chinese, 1905–1950." In *Trans-Pacific Interactions: The United States and China, 1880–1950*. Ed. Vanessa Künnemann and Ruth Mayer, 105–122. New York: Palgrave Macmillan–St. Martin's Press, 2009.

———. *Dreaming of Gold, Dreaming of Home: Transnationalism and Migration between the United States and South China, 1882–1943*. Stanford, CA: Stanford University Press, 2000.

Huang, Su-ching. *Mobile Homes: Spatial and Cultural Negotiation in Asian American Literature*. London: Routledge, 2006.

Hu Shi. "One Hundred Years after His Graduation." *Chinese Studies in History* 35, no. 3 (1954): 87–95.

"Hu Shih." In Boorman and Howard, *Biographical Dictionary of Republican China*, 2:167–175.

Hutcheon, Linda. *A Poetics of Postmodernism: History, Theory, Fiction*. New York: Routledge, 1988.

Huyssen, Andreas. *Present Pasts: Urban Palimpsests and the Politics of Memory*. Stanford, CA: Stanford University Press, 2003.

*Hwang, Henry David. *M. Butterfly*. New York: Penguin, 1989.

Imbert, Patrick, ed. *Converging Disensus, Cultural Transformations and Corporate Cultures: Canada and the Americas*. Ottawa: University of Ottawa Research Chair with Gauvin Press, 2006.

In re Ah Yup. 5 Sawy. 155; Fed. Cas. No. 104 (1878). *Yes WeScan: The Federal Cases*. https://law.resource.org/pub/us/case/reporter/F.Cas/0001.f.cas/0001.f.cas.0223.pdf. Accessed June 18, 2016. Also qtd. and discussed in López, *White by Law*, 163.

Isaacs, Harold. *Images of Asia: American Views of China and India*. New York: Capricorn Books, 1962.
Ishiguro, Kazuo. *An Artist of the Floating World*. New York: Vintage, 1989.
———. *A Pale View of Hills*. New York: Vintage, 1990.
*Ishimoto, Shidzue Hirota [Shidzue Kato]. *Facing Two Ways: The Story of My Life*. New York: Farrar and Rinehart, 1935.
*Jacobs, Harriet. *Incidents in the Life of a Slave Girl*. Ed. Nellie Y. McKay and Frances Smith Foster. New York: W. W. Norton, 2001.
"Japanese American Redress and Court Cases." *Wikipedia*. www.en.wikipedia.org/wiki/Japanese_American_redress_and_court_cases. Accessed February 21, 2018.
*Jen, Gish. "Duncan in China." In *Who's Irish?* 49–91. New York: Vintage–Random, 1999.
———. *Typical American*. New York: Plume–Penguin, 1992.
Jerng, Mark C. *Claiming Others: Transracial Adoption and National Belonging*. Minneapolis: University of Minnesota Press, 2010.
Jin, Ha. *The Crazed: A Novel*. Vintage–Random House, 2002.
*Kamani, Ginu. "Ciphers." In *Junglee Girl*, 1–14. San Francisco: Aunt Lute Books, 1995.
Kaogusuo [Chen Mengjia]. *Mei Diguo Zhuyi Jieluede Wo Guo Yin Zhou Tongqi Tulu [Our Country's Shang and Zhou Bronzes Looted by American Imperialists]*. Beijing: Kexue Chubanshe, 1962.
Kawakami, Kiyoshi K. "The Life Story of Dr. Yung Wing." *New York Times Saturday Review of Books*, March 12, 1912, BR4.
Keller, Nora Okja. *Comfort Woman*. New York: Penguin, 1997.
*Khu, Josephine [Meihui Tianpo], ed. *Cultural Curiosity: Thirteen Stories about the Search for Chinese Roots*. Berkeley: University of California Press, 2001.
———. "Jose Tan Sunco (Chen Guangchun)." *Forum Kritika: Regional Studies on the Chinese Diaspora in the Philippines* 21/22 (2013–2014): 336–352. Ateneo de Manila University. http://kritikakultura.ateneo.net. Accessed February 14, 2015.
———. "The Making of a Frontier: The Qing Military in Taiwan, 1684–1783." Ph.D. diss., Columbia University, 2001.
———. "Student Organization in the Movement." In *Chinese Democracy and the Crisis of 1989: Chinese and American Reflections*. Ed. Roger V. Des Forge, Ning Lou, and Yen-bo Wu, 161–176. Albany: State University of New York Press, 1992.
Kim, Elaine H. *Asian American Literature: An Introduction to the Writings and Their Social Context*. Philadelphia: Temple University Press, 1982.
———. "Home Is Where the Han Is: A Korean-American Perspective on the Los Angeles Upheavals." In *Asian American Studies: A Reader*. Ed. Jean Yu-wen Shen Wu and Min Song, 270–289. New Brunswick, NJ: Rutgers University Press, 2000.
Kim, Eleana J. *Adopted Territory: Transnational Korean Adoptees and the Politics of Belonging*. Durham, NC: Duke University Press, 2010.
*Kim, Ronyoung. *Clay Walls*. 1986; repr., Seattle: University of Washington Press, 1987.
*Kingston, Maxine Hong. *China Men*. New York: Vintage, 1989.
——— "Cultural Mis-readings by American Reviewers." In *Asian and Western Writers in Dialogue*. Ed. Guy Amirthanayagam, 55–65. London: Macmillan, 1982.
*———. *I Love a Broad Margin to My Life*. New York: Vintage, 2011.
———. *The Woman Warrior: Memoirs of a Girlhood among Ghosts*. 1976; repr., New York: Vintage–Random House, 1977.
Kinoshita, June, and Nicholas Palevsky. *Gateway to Japan*. 3rd ed. Tokyo: Kodansha International, 1998
Klein, Melanie. *The Selected Melanie Klein*. Ed. Juliet Mitchell. New York: Free Press, 1986.

*Kogawa, Joy. *Obasan*. Boston: D. R. Godine, 1981.
*Kondo, Dorinne K. *Crafting Selves: Power, Gender, and Discourse of Identity in a Japanese Workplace*. Chicago: University of Chicago Press, 1990.
Kong, Belinda. *Tiananmen Fictions outside the Square: The Chinese Literary Diaspora and the Politics of Global Culture*. Philadelphia: Temple University Press, 2012.
*Koo, Carolyn. "One Family, Two Fates." In Khu, *Cultural Curiosity*, 173–186.
Kotler, Mindy. "The Comfort Women and Japan's War on Truth." *New York Times*, November 14, 2014. http://nyti.ms/1sOdHOt. Accessed December 2017.
Kugisima, Hiroko. "Dual Images of 'An Ideal Japanese Woman' in a Critical Historical Period—through the Analysis of *A Daughter of the Samurai*." *International Journal of Area Studies* (2010): 141–144.
Kuo, Helena. *I've Come a Long Way*. New York: Appleton, 1942.
Kuo, Karen. "'Japanese Women Are Like Volcanoes': Trans-Pacific Feminist Musings in Etsu I. Sugimoto's *A Daughter of the Samurai*." *Frontiers* 36, no. 1 (2015): 57–86.
*Kuramoto, Kazuko. *Manchurian Legacy: Memoirs of a Japanese Colonist*. East Lansing: Michigan State University Press, 1999.
Kutsukake, Lynn. *The Translation of Love: A Novel*. New York: Doubleday, 2016.
LaFargue, Thomas E. *China's First Hundred: Educational Mission Students in the United States 1872–1881*. 1942; repr., Pullman: Washington State University Press, 1987.
*Lahiri, Jhumpa. *The Namesake*. Boston: Houghton Mifflin, 2003.
Lai, Him Mark, Genny Lim, and Judy Yung. *Island: Poetry and History of Chinese Immigrants on Angel Island*. Seattle: University of Washington Press, 2014.
*Lam, Andrew. *Perfume Dreams: Reflections on the Vietnamese Diaspora*. Berkeley, CA: Heyday Books, 2005.
Lao She [Shu Ch'ing-ch'un]. *Rickshaw: The Novel "Lo-t'o Hsiang Tzu."* 1936–1937. Trans. Jean M. James. Honolulu: University of Hawai'i Press, 1979.
Lawrence, Keith, and Floyd Cheung, eds. *Recovered Legacies: Authority and Identity in Early Asian American Literature*. Philadelphia: Temple University Press, 2005.
Lee, Chang-rae. *A Gesture Life*. New York: Riverhead, 1999.
*———. *Native Speaker*. New York: Riverhead, 1995.
Lee, C. Y. *The Flower Drum Song*. 1957; repr., New York: Penguin, 2002.
*Lee, Don. *Country of Origin: A Novel*. New York: W. W. Norton, 2004.
Lee, Erika. "Asian American Studies in the Midwest: New Questions, Approaches, and Communities." *JAAS: Journal of Asian American Studies* 12, no. 3 (2009): 247–293.
———. "The Chinese Are Coming. How Can We Stop Them? Chinese Exclusion and the Origins of American Gatekeeping." In *Asian American Studies Now: A Critical Reader*. Ed. Jean Yu-wen Shen Wu and Thomas C. Chen, 143–167. New Brunswick, NJ: Rutgers University Press, 2010.
*Lee, Helie. *Still Life with Rice: A Young American Woman Discovers the Life and Legacy of Her Korean Grandmother*. New York: Touchstone–Simon and Schuster, 1996.
*Lee, Marie Myong-Ok. *Somebody's Daughter: A Novel*. Boston: Beacon Press, 2005.
Lee, Sky. *The Disappearing Moon Cafe*. Seattle: Seal Press, 1991.
Lee, Yan Phou. *When I Was a Boy in China*. Boston: Lothrop, 1887.
Leung, Edwin Pak-wah. "China's Decision to Send Students to the West: The Making of a 'Revolutionary' Policy." *Asian Profile* 16, no. 4 (1988): 391–400.
Li, Hongshan. *U.S.-China Educational Exchange: State, Society, and Intercultural Relations, 1905–1950*. New Brunswick, NJ: Rutgers University Press, 2008.
Li, Li-Young. *The Winged Seed: A Remembrance*. New York: Simon and Schuster, 1995.

Li, Yiyun. *The Vagrants: A Novel.* New York: Random House, 2009.
*Liem, Deann Borshay, dir. *First Person Plural.* San Francisco: Center for Asian American Media, 2000.
*———, dir. *In the Matter of Cha Jung Hee.* Harriman, NY: New Day Films, 2010.
*Lim, Genny. *Paper Angels.* In *Unbroken Thread: An Anthology of Plays by Asian American Women.* Ed. Roberta Uno, 11–52. Amherst: University of Massachusetts Press, 1993.
Lim, Shirley Geok-lin, John Blair Gamber, Stephen Hong Sohn, and Gina Valentino. *Transnational Asian American Literature: Sites and Transits.* Philadelphia: Temple University Press, 2006.
Ling, Amy. *Between Worlds: Women Writers of Chinese Ancestry.* New York: Pergamon Press, 1990.
———. "Reading Her/stories against His/stories in Early Chinese American Literature." In *American Realism and the Canon.* Ed. Tom Quirk and Gary Scharnhorst, 69–86. Newark: University of Delaware Press–Associated University Presses, 1994.
*Lin-Rodrigo, Milan L. "In Search of Lin Jia Zhuang." In Khu, *Cultural Curiosity*, 58–76.
Lipsitz, George. *Time Passages: Collective Memory and American Popular Culture.* Minneapolis: University of Minnesota Press, 1990.
Liu, Haiming. *The Transnational History of a Chinese Family: Immigrant Letters, Family Business, and Reverse Migration.* New Brunswick, NJ: Rutgers University Press, 2005.
Loewen, James W. "The Vietnam War in High School American History." In *Censoring History: Citizenship and Memory in Japan, Germany, and the United States.* Ed. Laura Elizabeth Hein and Mark Selden, 150–172. Armonk, NY: M. E. Sharpe, 2000.
Long, Lynellyn D., and Ellen Oxfeld. *Coming Home? Refugees, Migrants, and Those Who Stayed Behind.* Philadelphia: University of Pennsylvania Press, 2004.
López, Ian Haney. *White by Law: The Legal Construction of Race.* 10th ed. New York: New York University Press, 2006.
Lopez, Kathleen. *Chinese Cubans: A Transnational History.* Chapel Hill: University of North Carolina Press, 2013.
Louie, Andrea. *Chineseness across Borders: Renegotiating Chinese Identities in China and the United States.* Durham, NC: Duke University Press, 2004.
———. *How Chinese Are You? Adopted Chinese Youth and Their Families Negotiate Identity and Culture.* New York: New York University Press, 2015.
Lowe, Lisa. *Immigrant Acts: On Asian American Cultural Politics.* Durham, NC: Duke University Press, 1996.
———. *The Intimacies of Four Continents.* Durham, NC: Duke University Press, 2015.
Lowe, Pardee. *Father and Glorious Descendant.* Boston: Little, 1943.
Lu Hsun [Lu Xun]. "A Madman's Diary." In *Selected Stories of Lu Hsun.* Trans. Hsien-yi Yang and Gladys Yang, 7–18. 1960; repr., New York: W. W. Norton, 1977.
Lutz, Jessie Gregory. *Opening China: Karl F. A. Gutzlaff and Sino-Western Relations, 1827–1852.* Grand Rapids, MI: William B. Eerdmans, 2007.
Manalansan, Martin F., IV. "Wayward Erotics: Mediating Queer Diasporic Return." Consuming Asian America: Association for Asian American Studies Conference, New Orleans, May 20, 2011.
*Manjiro, John, and Kawada Shoryo. *Drifting toward the Southeast: A Story of Five Japanese Castaways; A Complete Translation of Hyoson Kiryaku [A Brief Account of Drifting toward the Southeast] as Told to the Court of Lord Yamauchi of Tosa in 1852 by John Manjiro.* Transcr. and illus. Kawada Shoryo. Trans. Junya Nagakuni and Junji Kitadai with foreword by Stuart M. Frank. New Bedford, MA: Spinner Publications, 2003.

McKee, Kimberly. *Disrupting Kinship: Transnational Politics of Korean Adoption in the United States.* Urbana: University of Illinois Press, forthcoming.

Miller, Nancy K. *Bequest and Betrayal: Memoirs of a Parent's Death.* New York: Oxford University Press, 1996.

*Minatoya, Lydia. *The Strangeness of Beauty.* New York: W. W. Norton, 2001.

*———. *Talking to High Monks in the Snow: An Asian American Odyssey.* New York: HarperCollins, 1992.

*Mistry, Rohinton. *Swimming Lessons, and Other Stories from Firozsha Baag.* New York: Vintage, 1997.

Mitscherlich, Alexander, and Margarete Mitscherlich. *The Inability to Mourn: Principles of Collective Behavior.* Trans. Beverley R. Placzek. 1967; repr., New York: Grove Press, 1975.

Miyoshi, Masao. "A Borderless World? From Colonialism to Transnationalism and the Decline of the Nation-State." *Critical Inquiry* 19, no. 4 (1993): 726–751.

*Mori, Kyoko. *The Dream of Water: A Memoir.* New York: Henry Holt, 1995.

Morrison, Toni. *Playing in the Dark: Whiteness and the Literary Imagination.* Cambridge, MA: Harvard University Press, 1992.

———. "Unspeakable Things Unspoken: The Afro-American Presence in American Literature." *Michigan Quarterly Review* 28 (Winter 1989): 1–34.

*Mukherjee, Bharati. *Desirable Daughters.* New York: Theia, 2002.

*Mukherjee, Bharati, with Clark Blaise. *Days and Nights in Calcutta.* New York: Doubleday, 1977.

Muñoz, José Esteban. *Disidentifications: Queers of Color and the Performance of Politics.* Minneapolis: University of Minnesota Press, 1999.

*Mura, David. *Turning Japanese: Memoirs of a Sansei.* New York: Anchor–Doubleday, 1991.

*Murayama, Milton. *All I Asking for Is My Body.* 1975; repr., Honolulu: University of Hawai'i Press, 1988.

Nazaki, Yoshiko, and Hiromitsu Inokuchi. "Japanese Education, Nationalism, and Ienaga Saburo's Textbook Lawsuits." In *Censoring History: Citizenship and Memory in Japan, Germany, and the United States.* Ed. Laura Elizabeth Hein and Mark Selden, 96–126. Armonk, NY: M. E. Sharpe, 2000.

Nelson, Kim Park. *Invisible Asians: Korean American Adoptees, Asian American Experiences, and Racial Exceptionalism.* New Brunswick, NJ: Rutgers University Press, 2016.

Ng, Faye Myenne. *Bone.* New York: Hyperion, 1993.

Ngô, Fiona I. B., Mimi Thi Nguyen, and Mariam B. Lam, eds. "Southeast Asian American Studies." Special issue, *Positions: Asia Critique* 20, no. 3 (2012).

Nguyen, Mimi Thi. *The Gift of Freedom: War, Debt, and Other Refugee Passages.* Durham, NC: Duke University Press, 2012.

Nguyen, Viet Thanh. "Memory." In *Keywords for Asian American Studies.* Ed. Cathy Schlund-Vials, Linda Trinh Võ, and K. Scott Wong, 153–156. New York: New York University Press, 2015.

———. *Nothing Ever Dies: Vietnam and the Memory of War.* Cambridge, MA: Harvard University Press, 2016.

———. *Race and Resistance: Literature and Politics in Asian America.* Oxford: Oxford University Press, 2002.

*———. *The Sympathizer: A Novel.* New York: Grove Press, 2015.

Ohnuki-Tierney, Emiko. *Kamikaze Diaries: Reflections of Japanese Student Soldiers.* Chicago: University of Chicago Press, 2006.

Oi, Mariko. "What Japanese History Lessons Leave Out." *BBC*, March 14, 2013. www.bbc.com/news/magazine-21226068. Accessed July 21, 2017.

*Oishi, Gene. *Fox Drum Bebop*. New York: Kaya Press, 2014.
*Okada, John. *No-No Boy*. 1957; repr., Seattle: University of Washington Press, 1976.
Okihiro, Gary Y. *Margins and Mainstreams: Asians in American History and Culture*. Seattle: University of Washington Press, 1994.
Omi, Michael, and Howard K. Winant. *Racial Formation in the United States: From the 1960s to the 1980s*. New York: Routledge, 1986.
*Ondaatje, Michael. *Anil's Ghost*. New York: Knopf, 2000.
*———. *Running in the Family*. 1982; repr., New York: Vintage, 1993.
Ong, Aihwa. *Flexible Citizenship: The Cultural Logics of Transnationality*. Durham, NC: Duke University Press, 1999.
Ong, Aihwa, and Donald Nonini, eds. *Ungrounded Empires: The Cultural Politics of Modern Chinese Transnationalism*. New York: Routledge, 1997.
Onishi, Notimitsu. "Japan's Textbooks Reflect Revised History." *New York Times*, April 1, 2007.
Oxfeld, Ellen. "Chinese Villagers and the Moral Dilemmas of Return Visits." In *Coming Home? Refugees, Migrants, and Those Who Stayed Behind*. Ed. Lynelleyn D. Long and Ellen Oxfeld, 90–103. Philadelphia: University of Pennsylvania Press, 2004.
*Ozeki, Ruth. *A Tale for the Time Being: A Novel*. New York: Viking–Penguin, 2013.
Partridge, Jeffrey F. L. *Beyond Literary Chinatown*. Seattle: University of Washington Press, 2007.
*Patel, Eboo. *Acts of Faith: The Story of an American Muslim; The Struggle for the Soul of a Generation*. Boston: Beacon Press, 2007.
Perlez, Jane, and Yufan Huang. "Behind China's $1 Trillion Plan to Shake Up the Economic Order." *New York Times*, May 13, 2017. https://nyti.ms/2rc1mKd. Accessed January 31, 2018.
Pfaelzer, Jean. *Driven Out: The Forgotten War against Chinese Americans*. New York: Random House, 2007.
*Pham, Andrew X. *Catfish and Mandala: A Two-Wheeled Voyage through the Landscape and Memory of Vietnam*. New York: Picador–Farrar, Straus and Giroux, 1999.
*Phan, Aimee. "Motherland." In *We Should Never Meet*, 213–243. New York: Picador–St. Martin's, 2004.
*Poeuv, Socheata. *New Year Baby*. New Haven, CT: Broken English Productions, 2006.
Porter, Dennis. *Haunted Journeys: Desire and Transgression in European Travel Writing*. Princeton, NJ: Princeton University Press, 1991.
*Prager, Emily. *Wuhu Diary: On Taking My Adopted Daughter Back to Her Hometown in China*. New York: Random House, 2001.
Pratt, Mary Louise. *Imperial Eyes: Travel Writing and Transculturation*. London: Routledge, 1992.
*Preus, Margi. *Heart of a Samurai: Based on the True Story of Nakahama Manjiro*. New York: Amulet–Abrams Books, 2010.
Price, Tom. "Karl Yoneda: Historical Essay." *The Dispatcher*, May 1999. http://foundsf.org/index.php?ttle-Karl_Yoneda. Accessed December 3, 2014.
Proust, Marcel. *Le Temps Retrouvé* [*Time Regained*]. 2 vols. Paris: Gallimard, 1927.
Qian, Ning. *Chinese Students Encounter America*. Trans. T. K. Chu. University of Washington Press, 2002. (Translation of *Liuxue Meiguo* [Studying in America]. Nanjing, China: Jiangsu Wenyi Chubanshe, 1996.)
Quigley, Ellen. "Unveiling the Ghost: Denise Chong's Feminist Negotiations of Confucian Autobiography in *The Concubine's Children*." *Essays on Canadian Writing* 63 (Spring 1998): 237–253.

Rak, Julie. *Negotiated Memory: Doukhobor Autobiographical Discourse*. Vancouver: University of British Columbia Press, 2004.

"Redress Movement." *SEDAI: The Japanese Canadian Legacy Project*. www.sendai.ca/for-students/history-of-japanese-canadians/redress-movement/. Accessed July 6, 2017.

Rhoads, Edward J. M. *Stepping Forth into the World: The Chinese Educational Mission to the United States, 1872–81*. Hong Kong: Hong Kong University Press, 2011.

*Rizal, José. *The Lost Eden (Noli Me Tangere)*. Trans. León Ma Guerrero. Westport, CT: Greenwood Press, 1968. (Translation of *Noli Me Tangere*. Berlin, 1887.)

Roberts, Neil. "Paul Gilroy's *Postcolonial Melancholia*." *Shibboleths: A Journal of Comparative Theory* 2, no. 2 (2008): 163–166.

Robinson, Greg. "Writing the Internment." In *The Cambridge Companion to Asian American Literature*. Ed Crystal Parikh and Daniel Y. Kim, 45–58. New York: Cambridge University Press, 2015.

*Robinson, Katy. *A Single Square Picture: A Korean Adoptee's Search for Her Roots*. New York: Berkley Books, 2002.

Rossington, Michael, and Anne Whitehead, eds. *Theories of Memory: A Reader*. Baltimore: Johns Hopkins University Press, 2007.

Said, Edward W. *Orientalism*. New York: Pantheon: 1978.

*Sakamoto, Kerri. *One Hundred Million Hearts*. Orlando: Harcourt, 2003.

Salaff, Janet W. *Working Daughters of Hong Kong: Filial Piety or Power in the Family?* Cambridge: Cambridge University Press, 1981.

Schlund-Vials, Cathy J. *War, Genocide, and Justice: Cambodian American Memory Work*. Minneapolis: University of Minnesota Press, 2012.

*See, Lisa. *On Gold Mountain: The One-Hundred-Year Odyssey of My Chinese-American Family*. New York: Vintage, 1995.

Selvadurai, Shyam. *Funny Boy*. Toronto: McClelland and Stewart, 1994.

*———. "Pigs Can't Fly." In Selvadurai, *Funny Boy*, 1–40.

*———. "Radha Aunty." In Selvadurai, *Funny Boy*, 41–100.

*———. "See No Evil, Hear No Evil." In Selvadurai, *Funny Boy*, 101–153.

"Semicolonialism." *A Dictionary of Sociology*. http://www.encyclopedia.com. Accessed June 20, 2018.

*Shang, William. "In My Father's Shadow." In Khu, *Cultural Curiosity*, 187–200.

Sherman, John. "No. 1567 National Archives, Record Group 77: Secretary of State John Sherman to Charles Denby, April 14, 1898." Transcr. Cassandra Bates. Yung Wing Project: Transcribed Texts, 2006.

Sianturi, Dinah Roma. "'From Colonial to Cosmopolitan Visions': Detours in the Theory of Travel." Unpublished paper presented at a workshop in "Travel Writing: Practice, Pedagogy and Theory," Asia Research Institute, National University of Singapore. February 2011.

*Sidharta, Myra. "In Search of My Ancestral Home." In Khu, *Cultural Curiosity*, 145–159.

"The Slave Ship." *Wikipedia*. https://en.wikipedia.org/wiki/The_Slave_Ship. Accessed December 31, 2016.

Smith, Marian L. "'Any Woman Who Is Now or May Hereafter Be Married . . .': Women and Naturalization, ca. 1802–1940." *National Archives: Prologue Magazine* 30, no. 2 (1998): https://www.archives.gov/publications/prologue/1998/summer/women-and-naturalization-1.html. Accessed June 18, 2018.

Smith, Sidonie, and Julia Watson. *Reading Autobiography: A Guide for Interpreting Life Narratives*. 2nd ed. Minneapolis: University of Minnesota Press, 2010.

So, Christine. *Economic Citizens: A Narrative of Asian American Visibility.* Philadelphia: Temple University Press, 2008.
*Sone, Monica. *Nisei Daughter.* 1953; repr., Seattle: University of Washington Press, 1979.
Spence, Jonathan D. *The Death of Woman Wang.* New York: Penguin, 1979.
———. *The Search for Modern China.* New York: W. W. Norton, 1990.
Srikanth, Rajini. *The World Next Door: South Asian American Literature and the Idea of America.* Philadelphia: Temple University Press, 2004.
Stegner, Wallace. *Angle of Repose.* New York: Penguin, 2000.
Stewart, Watt. *Chinese Bondage in Peru: A History of the Chinese Coolie in Peru, 1849–1874.* Durham, NC: Duke University Press, 1951.
*Sugimoto, Etsu Inagaki. *A Daughter of the Samurai.* 1926; repr., Rutland, VT: Charles E. Tuttle, 1966.
Sui Sin Far [Edith Maude Eaton]. "The Americanizing of Pau Tzu." In Sui, *Mrs. Spring Fragrance*, 83–92.
———. "Her Chinese Husband." In Sui, *Mrs. Spring Fragrance*, 78–83.
———. "Leaves from the Mental Portfolio of an Eurasian." In Sui, *Mrs. Spring Fragrance*, 218–230.
*———. *Mrs. Spring Fragrance and Other Writings.* 1909, 1912. Ed. Amy Ling and Annette White-Parks. Urbana: University of Illinois Press, 1995.
———. "The Smuggling of Tie Co." In Sui, *Mrs. Spring Fragrance*, 104–108.
———. "The Story of One White Woman Who Married a Chinese." In Sui, *Mrs. Spring Fragrance*, 66–77.
———. "The Wisdom of the New." In Sui, *Mrs. Spring Fragrance*, 42–61.
*Suleri, Sara. *Meatless Days.* Chicago: University of Chicago Press, 1991.
Sumida, Stephen H. *And the View from the Shore: Literary Traditions of Hawai'i.* Seattle: University of Washington Press, 1991.
"Sun Yat-sen." In *Biographical Dictionary of Republican China.* Ed. Howard L. Boorman and Richard C. Howard, 3:170–189. New York: Columbia University Press, 1967.
*Syjuco, Miguel. *Illustrado.* New York: Farrar, Straus and Giroux, 2010.
*Tamagawa, Kathleen. *Holy Prayers in a Horse's Ear: A Japanese American Memoir.* 1932. Ed. Greg Robinson and Elena Tajima Creef, with Shirley Lim and Floyd Cheung. New Brunswick, NJ: Rutgers University Press, 2008.
*Tan, Amy. *The Joy Luck Club.* 1989; repr., New York: Vintage–Random House, 1991.
*Taniguchi, Yuko. *The Ocean in the Closet.* Minneapolis, MN: Coffee House Press, 2007.
*Terasaki, Gwen. *Bridge to the Sun.* Durham: University of North Carolina Press, 1957.
*Tham, Maria. "Travels Afar." In Khu, *Cultural Curiosity*, 39–57.
*Thien, Madeleine. *Do Not Say We Have Nothing.* New York: W. W. Norton, 2016.
Thompson, Carl. *Travel Writing.* London: Routledge, 2011.
*Tomita, Mary K. *Dear Miye: Letters Home from Japan, 1937–1947.* Ed. Robert G. Lee. Stanford, CA: Stanford University Press, 1995.
"A Tramp Abroad." *Wikipedia.* https://en.wikipedia.org/wiki/Aa_Tramp_Abroad. Accessed December 31, 2016.
*Trenka, Jane Jeong. *Fugitive Visions: An Adoptee's Return to Korea.* St. Paul, MN: Graywolf Press, 2009.
*———. *The Language of Blood: A Memoir.* St. Paul, MN: Graywolf Press, 2008.
Tsuda, Takeyuki. *Diasporic Homecomings: Ethnic Return Migration in Comparative Perspective.* Stanford, CA: Stanford University Press, 2009.
———. *Strangers in the Ethnic Homeland: Japanese Brazilian Return Migration in Transnational Perspective.* New York: Columbia University Press, 2003.

*Tuan Yi-Fu. *Coming Home to China*. Minneapolis: University of Minnesota Press, 2007.
Tu Wei-ming. "Cultural China: The Center as Periphery." In *The Living Tree: The Changing Meaning of Being Chinese Today*. Ed. Tu Wei-ming, 1–34. Stanford, CA: Stanford University Press, 1991.
Twain, Mark. *A Tramp Abroad*. 1880; repr., New York: Modern Library, 2003.
Twitchell, Joseph H. "Appendix: An Address by the Rev. Joseph H. Twitchell, Delivered before the Kent Club of the Yale Law School, April 1878." In *My Life in China and America*. By Yung Wing, 247–273. 1909; repr., Whitefish, MT: Kessinger, 2010.
Ty, Eleanor. *The Politics of the Visible in Asian North American Narratives*. Toronto: University of Toronto Press, 2004.
———. *Unfastened: Globality and Asian North American Narratives*. Minneapolis: University of Minnesota Press, 2010.
Um, Kaatharya. *From the Land of Shadows: War, Revolution, and the Making of the Cambodian Diaspora*. New York: New York University Press, 2015.
*Ung, Loung. *Lucky Child: A Daughter of Cambodia Reunites with the Sister She Left Behind*. New York: Harper Perennial, 2006.
Wan, Peter Pei-de. "Yung Wing, 1928–1912: A Critical Portrait." Ph.D. diss., Harvard University, 1997.
Wang, Chih-ming. "Politics of Return: Homecoming Stories of the Vietnamese Diaspora." *Positions* 21, no. 1 (2013): 161–187.
———. *Transpacific Articulations: Student Migration and the Remaking of Asian America*. Honolulu: University of Hawai'i Press, 2013.
Wang, Y[i] C[hu]. *Chinese Intellectuals and the West, 1872–1949*. Chapel Hill: University of North Carolina Press, 1966.
Wang, Zhuolun, and Hui Wang. "Diplomatic Hat-Trick toward Year End No Accident." *Shanghai Daily News*, January 4, 2017. http://www.shanghaidaily.com/opinion/chinese-perspectives/Diplomatic-hattrick-toward-year-end-no-accident/shdaily.shtml. Accessed July 7, 2017.
White, Jonathan, ed. *Recasting the World: Writing after Colonialism*. Baltimore: Johns Hopkins University Press, 1993.
Whitman, Walt. *Cao Ye Ji* [*Leaves of Grass*]. Trans. Zhao Luorui [Lucy Chao]. Shanghai: Yiwen Chubanshe, 1991.
Williams, Raymond. "From *Preface to Film* (UK, 1954)." In *Film Manifestos and Global Cinema Cultures: A Critical Anthology*. Ed. Scott MacKenzie, 856–865. Berkeley: University of California Press, 2014.
———. *Marxism and Literature*. Oxford: Oxford University Press, 1977.
Wilson, Andrew R., ed. *The Chinese in the Caribbean*. Princeton, NJ: Markus Wiener Publishers, 2004.
*Wong, Brad. "A Yellow American in China." In Khu, *Cultural Curiosity*, 160–172.
Wong, Jade Snow. *Fifth Chinese Daughter*. 1950; repr., Seattle: University of Washington Press, 1989.
*———. *No Chinese Stranger*. New York: Harper and Row 1975.
Wong, K. Scott. "The Transformation of Culture: Three Chinese Views of America." *American Quarterly* 48, no. 2 (1996): 201–232.
Wong, Sau-ling Cynthia. "Autobiography as Guided Chinatown Tour? Maxine Hong Kingston's *The Woman Warrior* and the Chinese American Autobiographical Controversy." In *Multicultural Autobiography*. Ed. James Robert Payne, 248–279. Knoxville: University of Tennessee Press, 1992.

———. "Denationalization Reconsidered: Asian American Literary Criticism at a Theoretical Crossroads." *Amerasia Journal* 21, nos. 1–2 (1995): 1–28.

———. *Reading Asian American Literature: From Necessity to Extravagance*. Princeton, NJ: Princeton University Press, 1993.

———. "'Sugar Sisterhood': Situating the Amy Tan Phenomenon." In *The Ethnic Canon: Histories, Institutions, and Interventions*. Ed. David Palumbo-Liu, 174–212. Minneapolis: University of Minnesota Press, 1995.

Wong, Yoon Wah. "Imagism and Hu Shih's Program for Literary Revolution of 1917." In *Essays on Chinese Literature: A Comparative Approach*, 39–151. Singapore: Singapore University Press, 1988.

Wong Sam and Assistants. "An English-Chinese Phrasebook." In Chan et al., *The Big Aiiieeeee!* 94–110.

*Work, Nancy. "Full Circle." In Khu, *Cultural Curiosity*, 1–19.

Worthy, Edmund H. "Yung Wing in America." *Pacific Historical Review* 34, no. 3 (1965): 265–287.

Wu Jean Yu-wen Shen, and Min Song, eds. *Asian American Studies: A Reader*. New Brunswick, NJ: Rutgers University Press, 2000.

*Wu, Lily. "Coming Home." In Khu, *Cultural Curiosity*, 201–224.

*Wu Ningkun, with Yikai Li. *A Single Tear: A Family's Persecution, Love, and Endurance in Communist China*. New York: Atlantic Monthly Press, 1993.

*Yamashita, Karen Tei. *Circle K Cycles*. Minneapolis, MN: Coffee House Press, 2001.

Yanagisako, Sylvia. "Transforming Orientalism: Gender, Nationality, and Class in Asian American Studies." In *Naturalizing Power: Essays in Feminist Cultural Analysis*. Ed. Sylvia Yanagisako and Carol Delaney, 275–298. New York: Routledge, 1996.

Ye, Weili. "'Nu Liuxuesheng': The Story of American-Educated Chinese Women, 1880s–1920s." *Modern China* 20, no. 3 (1994): 315–346.

Yen Mah, Adeline. *Falling Leaves: The True Story of an Unwanted Chinese Daughter*. New York: Wiley, 1997.

Yin, Xiao-huang. *Chinese American Literature since the 1850s*. Urbana: University of Illinois Press, 2000.

*Yoshida, Jim, with Bill Hosokawa. *The Two Worlds of Jim Yoshida*. New York: William Morrow, 1972.

Youngs, Tim. *The Cambridge Introduction to Travel Writing*. Cambridge: Cambridge University Press, 2013.

*Yung Wing. *My Life in China and America*. 1909; repr., Whitefish, MT: Kessinger, 2007.

Zackodnik, Teresa. "Suggestive Voices from 'the Storeroom of the Past': Photography in Denise Chong's *The Concubine's Children*." *Essays on Canadian Writing* 72 (Winter 2000): 49–78.

Zhang, Qingsong. "The Origins of the Chinese Americanization Movement: Wong Chin Foo and the Chinese Equal Rights League." In *Claiming America: Constructing Chinese American Identities during the Exclusion Era*. Ed. K. Scott Wong and Sucheng Chan, 41–63. Philadelphia: Temple University Press, 1998.

Index

adoptee return visits, 35–36
Angel Island, 36; graffiti poets of, 102
Angell Treaty, 175
Antin, Mary (*The Promised Land*), 47, 143
Anti-Rightist movement (China), 29, 209
Asian American identities, scholarship on, 15–23
Asian American literature: category of, 3–4, 19–22, 69–71, 216; central genres of, 12; as countermemory, 11–12; intellectuals and professionals underrepresented in, 7, 20, 58, 66; life writing as genre of, 67–68
Asian Americans, as model minorities, 57–58, 115
Asians: Africans compared to, 165; stereotypes of, 70–71, 101
assimilation: immigration narratives promoting, 47; incomplete, 36; legal and cultural barriers to, 25, 27; melancholia associated with, 25, 117, 121, 225n3; model minorities and, 115
astronaut fathers, 53
autobiographies: Asian American, 69–70; concept of, 67; subjectivities of, 147; theories of, 5–6, 151, 153. *See also* I-novels

Ba Jin, 215
Bangerter, Amy Nelson, 150

Bartlett, Shubael, 154
Beijing University, 46, 51, 55, 59
Bhabha, Homi, 110, 115, 117
Bow, Leslie, 27
Boxer Indemnity Scholarships, 123, 150, 223n1
Britain, 28, 29, 215
Brown, Phoebe, 154
Brown, Samuel R., 153
bullying, 192, 194, 198–200, 205
Bulosan, Carlos, 15; *The Cry and the Dedication*, 38
Burlingame Treaty, 170–171, 175
Burns, Gerald T., 38
Buruma, Ian, 177–180, 205, 216, 217
business and careers: Chinese expectations concerning, 49, 54; Confucian values and, 94, 100; in See's *On Gold Mountain*, 73, 75–76, 79, 82, 85–87, 89–91, 93–96, 100; unemployment of Chinese Canadians, 112; Yung and, 166–167
Butler, Judith, 23, 26

Campomanes, Oscar, 16, 21
careers. *See* business and careers
CEM. *See* Chinese Educational Mission
Chai, Charles (Chu), 42, 108, 123–144, 213
Chai, Huan, 132–133, 139–141, 224n8

INDEX

Chai, May-lee, 27, 31, 42, 86, 123; *China from A to Z*, 133–134; *The Girl from Purple Mountain*, 69, 108, 123–144, 212–214; *Hapa Girl*, 123, 144
Chai, Ruth (Tsao Mei-en), 42, 108, 123–144, 213; as Tsao Mei-en, 123, 134
Chai, Winberg, 27, 31, 42, 86; *China from A to Z*, 133–134; *The Foreign Relations of the People's Republic of China*, 156; *The Girl from Purple Mountain*, 69, 108, 123–144, 212–214
Chai family, 7, 132–133
Chan, Graham, 48–51
Chan, Henry, 45, 49, 51, 53–54, 61
Chan, Jeffery Paul, 3, 15
Chang, Meilin, 45
Chang, Pang-Mei Natasha, 86, 124, 126; *Bound Feet and Western Dress*, 223n5
Chang Chih-chung, 138, 224n7
Chang family, 72–73
Chan Sam, 108–121, 127, 135, 212
Chao, Lucy, 209–210
Chao Ts'ai Piao, 2, 6
Chen, Kuan-Hsing, 12–14, 28–30, 43, 153, 158, 215, 217
Cheng, Anne Anlin, 23–25, 111, 193
Chen Mengjia, 209–210
Cheung, Floyd, 153; *Recovered Legacies*, 17–20, 225n4, 226n17
Cheung, King-kok, 15
Chiang Kai-shek, 2, 6, 136–138, 140–141
Chiang Kai-shek, Madame, 82
Chin, Frank, 3, 15, 69–70, 152; *Aiiieeeee!* 69–71, 152
Chin, Lily, 36
Chin, Vincent, 36
China: historical memory of, 29; and imperialism, 7, 13–14, 28–29; intellectuals' return to, 19; investments of diasporic Chinese in, 102, 112; modernity and modernization in, 6, 52, 124, 126, 128, 135–137, 140, 150; postcolonial melancholia of, 29–30, 215; Qing Dynasty, 30, 37, 43, 112; Republican period (1911–1949), 6, 124, 126, 132–133, 136–143. *See also* Communism in China
Chinatowns, 90, 92–93, 96, 106
Chinese: heroine model of, 82–88 (see also "Gone with the Wind" genre); stereotypes of, 81, 152; as victims of racism, 80–81, 90, 92–93, 111, 144
Chinese Canadians, 105–106, 112
Chinese Civil War, 59
Chinese Educational Mission (CEM), 42, 147, 150, 154, 158, 167, 169, 172–175, 225n9
Chinese Exclusion Act, 98
Chinese exclusion laws. *See* exclusion policies and laws
Chineseness, 46–47
Ching, Meilin, 48
Chong, Denise, 27, 31, 35, 42, 105, 112; *The Concubine's Children*, 66–68, 72, 102, 105–122, 212, 214
Chong, John, 120–121
Chong, Winnie (Hing), 108–111, 115, 117–121, 135
Chow Guen, 117, 118, 120
Christian, Barbara, 6
Christianity: in Chai and Chai's *The Girl from Purple Mountain*, 125, 129, 132, 135, 139, 142; criticisms of, 69–70, 152, 165; in See's *On Gold Mountain*, 92; in slave narratives, 168; Yung and, 149, 152–159, 168, 174. *See also* missionaries
Chu, Richard, 48–50
Chu Ching-nung (Zhu Jingnong), 2, 6, 7
citizenship, U.S., 94, 98–99, 149–151, 171, 221n3 (chap. 3). *See also* flexible citizenship
Civil Rights movement, 59
Clifford, James, 21
Cohen, Warren I., 157, 225n9
Communism in China, 2, 13–14, 97, 101, 113, 126, 136, 209–210
Confucian values: of business, 94, 100; in educational system, 55, 129; of family, 47, 52, 55, 86, 94, 100, 107, 113, 115, 139, 212; of femininity, 114, 116–118, 127, 134–135; of masculinity, 118, 134–135; of practicality, 54; rejection of, 110, 132, 134, 142
Conrad, Joseph (*Heart of Darkness*), 165
Conrad, Sebastian, 13
coolie trade, 148, 150, 154, 165, 170–171, 225n10
countermemory: Asian American, 4–5, 11–12, 40, 107–108; Chai and Chai's *The Girl from Purple Mountain* and,

124–126, 141–143; Chong's *The Concubine's Children* and, 118–120, 122, 135; defined, 4, 107, 191; and Japanese experience of World War II, 178; melancholia as, 205; Minatoya's *Strangeness of Beauty* and, 182–191, 206; Ozeki's *A Tale for the Time Being* and, 191, 195, 197, 200, 206–207. *See also* postmemory
courtesy names, 133
Crimp, Douglas, 23, 26, 27
critical refugee studies, 10
cultural Chineseness, 46–47
Cultural Revolution, 29, 41, 46, 51, 55, 59, 126, 133, 136, 209–210
cyberbullying, 192, 205

Dalai Lama, 29
Davidson, Robyn, 8–9
Davis, Rocío G., 20, 39, 68–69, 75, 107, 124–127; *Relative Histories*, 5
de-cold war: Asian American return narratives and, 14; concept of, 12–13, 28, 216
decolonization: Asian American return narratives and, 14; concept of, 12–13, 28, 153; Yung and, 30, 43, 158, 215–216. *See also* deimperialization
deimperialization: Asian American return narratives and, 14; Britain and, 28; China and, 13, 29; concept of, 12–13, 28; Japan and, 30; Yung and, 43. *See also* decolonization; imperialism
Depression, 67, 82, 83, 91, 95–96, 112
Desai, Kiran (*The Inheritance of Loss*), 37–38
Descartes, René, 147
Dewey, John, 20
diasporic Chinese, 48–52
diasporic melancholia, 126, 128–135, 143–144, 213
diasporic narratives, 41, 45–62
diasporic visits, 34
Dodge, Georgina, 18–19
double vision, 9
Douglass, Frederick, 43, 148, 153, 165–171, 173, 214, 226n15
Dower, John, 180, 227n3

East India Company, 159, 161–162
Eaton, Edith (Sui Sin Far), 15, 67, 88, 150
Eaton, Winnifred, 67, 150

Ellis, William, 160
Eng, David L., 23, 25–27, 33, 56, 58, 109–111, 115, 117, 121, 193, 205
Enola Gay exhibition, 179, 180, 227n1
Equiano, Olaudah, 43, 147–148, 163, 166, 168–172, 214, 226n13
ethnicity. *See* race/ethnicity
ethnic writers. *See* writers, minority and ethnic
Everett, Carolyn, 143
exclusion policies and laws, 25; Asian American literature in context of, 18, 55, 229n7; Chinese attachments to home country as result of, 115; Chinese Canadians and, 111; circumvention of, 98–99, 114, 116; flexible citizenship in context of, 97–103; gendered effects of, 84; historical era of, 194, 222n4; multiple effects of, 81; racism in the time of, 80–81; transnational travel in context of, 41, 65, 67; Yung's *My Life in China and America* and, 226n19
expatriate return visits, 37

family: Confucian notion of, 47, 52, 55, 86, 94, 100, 107, 113, 115, 139, 212; generational conflict in, 55; modern adaptations by, 53; racial melancholia in, 58; transpacific, 34–35, 66, 98; utilitarian notion of, 52–54, 61, 100
family memoirs, 5, 68–69, 71, 75, 83, 101, 125, 213–214
Fanon, Frantz, 23
flexible citizenship: defined, 47; in *On Gold Mountain*, 85, 97–103; Ong's model of, 46–47, 52, 54, 61, 66, 83, 101. *See also* citizenship, U.S.
Fong Dun Shung, 64, 77–78, 93, 94
Fong Guai King, 83, 94, 97
Fong Lai, 98
Fong Quong, 82, 98
Fong Yun, 82, 90, 94, 98, 100
Franklin, Benjamin, 153, 173
Freud, Sigmund, 23–24, 26, 56–58, 110, 117, 130–131, 146, 194–195, 204–205, 224n3

Gamber, John Blair, 15, 16; *Transnational Asian American Literature*, 20–21
Geary Act, 81

gender. *See* men and masculinity; racialized gender melancholia; women and femininity
George, Henry, 20
Germany, historical memory of, 179
Gilroy, Paul, 28, 37, 205–207, 214–215, 217
global subjectivity, 146–149, 162–171, 175–176, 214
Goellnicht, Donald C., 6
"Gone with the Wind" genre, 83–84, 124, 126–127, 215
The Good Earth (film), 87
Goossen, Theodore, 32, 178, 183
Great Depression, 67, 82, 83, 91, 95–96, 112
guanxi (personal connections/networks), 52
Gützlaff, Karl, 43, 154–155, 159–165, 167, 214; *Journal of Three Voyages,* 160–165; *A Sketch,* 161–162
Gützlaff, Mary Wanstall, 154, 160, 167–168

Haddad, John R., 155
Hamid, Mohsin, 38
Han, Shinhee, 23, 25–26, 56, 58, 109–111, 115, 117, 121, 193, 205
Hayes, Dorothy, 92
herbalists, 72–73
Hessler, Peter (*Oracle Bones*), 209–210
Hirsch, Marianne, 5, 107–108, 118, 138, 178, 191, 217
historiographic metafiction, 191, 195, 206–207, 217
Hitler, Adolf, 28
Holland, Patrick, 8
Hong Huoxiu (Hung Siu Chune), 155, 164
Hsu, Graziella, 48–49, 51
Hsu, Kai-yu, 3, 152
Hsu, Madeline, 100, 102, 112, 222n4
Huang, Su-ching, 39
Huangbo, 108–109, 114, 117
Huggan, Graham, 8
Hung Jin, 164
Hu Shi (Hu Shih), 2, 6, 152
Hutcheon, Linda, 177, 195
Huyssen, Andreas, 10–11, 14, 217

Ibsen, Henrik (*A Doll's House*), 20
immigration: laws on, 25, 34, 54, 81, 90, 111, 175, 222n4; racial melancholia linked to, 193; records associated with, 99–100. *See also* exclusion policies and laws
Immigration Act (1882), 175
Immigration Act (1924), 99
imperialism: Asian states and, 12–14; China and, 7, 28–29; Christianity and missionaries linked to, 154, 156–157; Japan and, 7, 12–13, 30, 32, 43–44, 183, 216. *See also* decolonization; deimperialization
Inada, Lawson Fusao, 3, 15
I-novels, 19, 30, 44, 70, 182, 184, 190, 206, 228n5
In re Ah Yup decision, 171
intellectuals/professionals: in Chai and Chai's *The Girl from Purple Mountain,* 123–126; regarded as atypical of Asian Americans, 7, 20, 58, 66, 152; roles of, in modern China, 6, 124, 126, 128, 135, 137; self-understanding and self-presentation of, 18–19
internment of Japanese North Americans, 21, 32, 51, 178, 181, 216, 220n14, 228n4
Isaacs, Harold, 162
Ishimoto, Baroness Shidzue, 40

Jacobs, Harriet, 76–77, 167
Japan: historical memory of, 179–181, 195, 205–206, 216; and imperialism, 7, 12–13, 30, 32, 43–44, 183, 216; invasion of China by, 126, 130, 136–139; and postcolonial melancholia, 37, 178–179; and World War II, 178–182, 186–205, 216–217, 227n3
Japanese American writers, and Japanese history and memory, 181–182, 207
Jardine, William, 159
Jin, Ha, 125

kamikaze pilots, 32, 192–193, 195–201, 229n10
Keightley, David N., 210
Kellogg, E. W., 154
Kellogg, Mary Louise, 150, 174
Khu, Josephine, 31, 41, 211, 221n2 (chap. 2); *Cultural Curiosity,* 2, 35, 41, 43, 45–62, 66
Kim, Elaine H., 16, 18; *Asian American Literature,* 3, 152
Kim, Ronyoung (*Clay Walls*), 34

Kingston, Maxine Hong, 1, 67, 70, 101, 177, 212; *China Men,* 93, 102; *The Woman Warrior,* 45–46, 50, 69–71, 131, 134
Kondo, Dorinne, 18
Kuo, Helena, 67
Kuomintang, 124, 127, 136–143
Kuramoto, Kazuko, 182, 207

Lahiri, Jhumpa (*The Namesake*), 34
Lai, Him Mark, 100, 102
Lam, Andrew, 38
language, Chinese, 49
Lao She (*Rickshaw*), 125
Lawrence, Keith (*Recovered Legacies*), 17–20
laws: Asian Americans in relation to, 36; on immigration, 25, 34, 54, 81, 90, 111, 175, 222n4. *See also* exclusion policies and laws
Lee, Chang-rae (*Native Speaker*), 36
Lee, C. Y., 70, 101, 152
Lee, Erika, 98
Lee, Sky, 102
Lee, Yan Phou, 18, 70, 150
Leonard (Gok-leng), 111, 118, 120
Leong, Gilbert, 78, 91–92, 97
Leong, Sissee (Florence) See, 75–78, 83, 86, 91–92, 97
Leong May-ying, 108–110, 113–121, 127, 135, 212
Li, Yiyun, 125
Liang Afa (Leang Afah), 155
Liang Cheng, 150, 225n6
life writing, 67–70. *See also* autobiographies; I-novels
Lim, Genny, 100; *Paper Angels,* 36
Lim, Shirley Geok-lin, 15, 16; *Transnational Asian American Literature,* 20–21
Ling, Amy, 16, 21
Lin-Rodrigo, Milan, 48
Lin Yutang, 70, 152
Lin Zexu, 156
Lipsitz, George, 4, 107, 191
Liu, Haiming, 34, 94, 102, 107; *The Transnational History of a Chinese Family,* 72–74
Liu Xiaobo, 29
Long, Lynelleyn D., 33
Louie, Andrea, 102, 112
Lowe, Lisa, 30, 147–148, 161, 166, 169, 214, 217; *Immigrant Acts,* 6

Lowe, Pardee, 67
Lu Hsun (Lu Xun), 215; "The Diary of a Madman," 125
Lutz, Jessie Gregory, 159, 160

Macao (Macau), 156, 158, 225n10
magical realism, 191, 195, 196
Mah, Adeline Yen, 124, 126
Mao Zedong, 29, 41
marriage: citizenship affected by, 94, 221n3 (chap. 3); concubinage and, 116–117; race and, 82–83, 88–89, 92, 94, 143–144
masculinity. *See* men and masculinity
May Fourth Movement, 126
McCourt, Frank, 125
melancholia, 23–31; assimilation associated with, 25, 117, 121, 225n3; Chai and Chai's *The Girl from Purple Mountain* and, 130–132; as countermemory, 205; Freudian theory of, 23–24, 26, 57–58, 110, 117, 130–131, 195; Yung and, 43. *See also* diasporic melancholia; mourning; postcolonial melancholia; postimperial melancholia; racialized gender melancholia; racial melancholia; repatriate melancholia
memoirs, 67, 71. *See also* family memoirs
memory: cultural anxieties associated with, 10–12; narratives of return and, 10–12, 14; screen memories, 138–139. *See also* countermemory; postmemory
memory work. *See* trauerarbeit
men and masculinity: Confucian values relating to, 118, 134–135; naming practices for, 133; role of sons, 53; slaves and, 166; Yung and, 18, 165–166
mental illness, 55–56, 58–60
MGM, 87
Miller, Nancy K., 67
mimicry, 110, 115–116
Minatoya, Lydia, 7, 31, 40, 43; *The Strangeness of Beauty,* 44, 177–179, 182–191, 206–207, 216–217; *Talking to High Monks in the Snow,* 183
minoritarian subjects, 23, 25–27
minority writers. *See* writers, minority and ethnic
miscegenation. *See* marriage: race and
missionaries, 42, 129, 147, 149, 153–161

Mistry, Rohinton ("Swimming Lessons"), 36
Mitscherlich, Alexander and Margarete, 28, 179
model minorities, 57–58, 115, 152
modernity and modernization: in Asia, 12–15; Asian Americans and, 22; in China, 6, 52, 124, 126, 128, 135–137, 140, 150; Chinese women and, 83–88, 124, 126, 140; postcolonial melancholia and, 28–30
Morrison, Robert, 153, 155, 158
Morrison, Toni, 111, 193
mourning: Chai and Chai's *The Girl from Purple Mountain* and, 127, 130–132; Freudian theory of, 23–24, 130, 194–195, 204–205, 224n3; Japan's relationship to World War II and, 179–181; migration linked to, 225n3; post–Cultural Revolution, 59. See also melancholia; *trauerarbeit*
Muñoz, José Esteban, 23, 25, 26
Murayama, Milton (*All I Asking for Is My Body*), 55
My Life in China and America (Yung Wing), 42–43, 145–176, 214; and Chinese exclusion in the United States, 226n19; contradictions of, 149, 171–172, 174–175; genres utilized in, 40, 145, 146–149, 153; and global subjectivity, 146–149, 162–171, 175–176, 214; key aspects of, 146–147; on missionaries, 153–159; as narrative of return, 176; origins of, 148–149; on Qing Dynasty, 30, 37, 43, 149, 170–175, 215; scholarship on and critical reaction to, 149–153; slave narratives in relation to, 147–148, 165–176; travel narratives in relation to, 147, 159–165

naming practices, Chinese, 133–134
narratives of return: Chinese, 31; cultural anxieties associated with, 10–12; curiosity model of, 43, 45–62, 106–107; disparate nature of, 1; features of, 48, 61, 213; genres of, 5–6; ideal of, 61; as its own genre, 46; Japanese, 31–32; memory and, 10–12, 14; motivations for, 4; overview of, 31–33, 146; postcolonial, 38; reconciliation of accounts in, 52–55; relevance of, 7–15; scholarship on, 3–6, 215–216; See's *On Gold Mountain* as, 65, 107; travel narratives compared to, 38–40; Yung's *My Life in China and America* as, 176. See also return visits
Nationalists (China), 2, 14, 142, 213
Ng, Faye Myenne, 101, 102
Ngon Hung, 83, 90, 94, 101
Nguyen, Viet Thanh, 4, 10, 11–12, 71, 177, 191
Nicholson, Grace, 87
Nieh Hualing, 70
Nonini, Donald, 47

Ohnuki-Tierney, Emiko, 31, 44, 197–198, 200–201, 203, 229n10
Oishi, Gene, 207
Okihiro, Gary, 7, 84
Okubo, Benji, 95
Ondaatje, Michael, 34; *Anil's Ghost*, 9; *Running in the Family*, 9, 39–40
Ong, Aihwa, 21, 34, 46–47, 52–54, 61, 83, 101; *Flexible Citizenship*, 100
On Gold Mountain (See), 41–42, 63–104, 134, 211–214; Chinese heroine paradigm in, 82–88; as family memoir, 71; flexible citizenship in, 97–103; genres utilized in, 65–67, 73–79; as narrative of return, 65, 107; race/ethnicity in, 88–93; racial attitudes in, 80–82; sources for, 73–74, 81–82
Oxfeld, Ellen, 33
Ozeki, Ruth, 7, 31, 40, 43, 177; *A Tale for the Time Being*, 44, 179, 191–207, 216–217

Pacific Asia Museum, Pasadena, 87
Pacific Shuttle, 53
Page Act, 222n4
Paley, Grace, 125
Palubinskas, Helen, 3, 152
paper daughters, 114, 116
paper sons, 99
parachute kids, 53
Parker, Peter, 154, 156–157
Parkes, Harry, 162
Partridge, Jeffrey, 71
Peterson, Martin, 79
Pfaelzer, Jean, 81
Pham, Andrew X., 34, 38; *Catfish and Mandala*, 39

Polo, Marco, 147
postcolonial melancholia: absence of, 215–216; of American-educated Chinese elites, 42; China and, 29–30; Japan and, 37, 178–179; theory of, 28, 205–207, 214–215
postcolonial return visits, 37–38
postcolonial studies, 8
postimperial melancholia, 28, 207, 223n4
postimperial return visits, 37
postmemory: Asian American, 108; Chai and Chai's *The Girl from Purple Mountain* and, 124–125; Chong's *The Concubine's Children* and, 119–120; defined, 5, 107–108, 213; Minatoya's *Strangeness of Beauty* and, 178, 183–184; Ozeki's *A Tale for the Time Being* and, 191–205; readers and, 196–197; selectivity of, 204–205. *See also* countermemory
Pratt, Mary Louise, 147
prostitution, 79
Proust, Marcel (*In Search of Past Time*), 192
Pruett, John and Luscinda, 78–79
Pruett, Letticie (Ticie), 63, 73–80, 82–103, 221n3 (chap. 3)

Qian, Ning, 151
Qing Dynasty, 30, 37, 43, 112, 149–150, 170–176, 215

race/ethnicity: and marriage, 82–83, 88–89, 92, 94, 143–144; in See's *On Gold Mountain*, 80–82, 88–93. *See also* exclusion policies and laws; racism
racialized gender melancholia, 110, 116–117, 212, 222n2
racial melancholia: agency arising from, 26, 56, 121–122; Chai and Chai's *The Girl from Purple Mountain* and, 125–128; Chong's *The Concubine's Children* and, 42, 105–106, 109–111, 113–122, 134–135; effects of, 24–25; features of, 26; immigration linked to, 193; in Korean narratives of return, 33; narratives of return as response to, 6, 207; Ozeki's *A Tale for the Time Being* and, 43, 193–195, 207; sources of, 24–27, 56–62, 111, 117–118, 193; structural features of, 25–26, 56, 58, 117–118, 193; theory of, 23–25, 26, 56, 105–106, 109–111, 146; transmission of, 117; whites and, 24–25, 111, 193; in Wu's "Coming Home," 55–61; Yung's *My Life in China and America* and, 148
racism, Chinese as victims of, 80–81, 90, 92–93, 111, 144
Rak, Julie, 67
reading practices: American, 9–10, 17; ethics associated with, 196–197; reform of, 17; window model of, 5–6, 23
redress movements, 178, 216
remittances, 101, 112
repatriate melancholia, 193, 207
retrospective monologues, 75, 78–79
return visits: actual, 33–34; imagined, 33; permanent (repatriated), 33–34, 36–38; provisional, 33–36; resources for, 50; success/failure as background of, 36; symbolic, 33–34; types of, 33–38; virtual, 33. *See also* narratives of return
Rhoads, Edward, 174–175, 225n9, 227n21
Ricci, Matteo, 158
Rizal, José (*Noli Me Tangere*), 38
Roberts, Issachar, 154, 155, 164
Roberts, Neil, 28
Roosevelt, Theodore, 153
Rowlandson, Mary, 76–77

Said, Edward W., 8
Sakamoto, Kerri, 207
Salaff, Janet W., 53
Sanger, Margaret, 20
Schlund-Vials, Cathy J., 10
screen memories, 138–139, 213
See, Bennie, 75, 82, 86, 91
See, Bertha Weheimer, 92
See, Carolyn Laws, 73, 88
See, Eddy, 75, 78, 82–83, 87, 88, 91–92, 94, 100
See, Fong, 41, 63–68, 73–101, 107; business of, 73, 75–76, 79, 82, 85–87, 89–91, 93–96, 100; facts concerning life of, 77; first marriage of, 77, 100; fourth wife of (Si Ping), 92, 97, 100; and immigration law, 90; immigration records of, 99–100; investments of, in home country, 101–102; returns of, to China, 82–83, 85–86, 94, 97–98; second marriage of (with Ticie), 63, 77, 80, 82–83, 85–90, 94–95, 100; third marriage of (with Ngon Hong), 87, 90, 94, 100, 101

See, Leona, 92
See, Lisa, 22, 31, 35, 65–66. *See also On Gold Mountain*
See, Ming (Milton), 75, 82, 87, 91–92
See, Ray, 75, 82, 86, 89, 91–92, 95, 97
See, Richard, 73, 88
See, Sissee, 75–78, 83, 86, 91–92, 97
See, Stella Copeland, 76, 78, 88, 92
Self-Strengthening Movement, 19, 173
Sheridan, Richard, 168
Shteyngart, Gary, 125
Siam (Thailand), 160
Sianturi, Dinah Roma, 8
Sidharta, Myra, 48
Silverman, Kaja, 23
Si Ping, 92, 97
slave narratives, 67, 147–148, 165–176
Smith, Sidonie, 67, 147
So, Christine, 65, 83–84, 93, 124, 134, 187
Sohn, Stephen Hong, 15, 16; *Transnational Asian American Literature*, 20–21
Sone, Monica (*Nisei Daughter*), 34, 184
South Korea, 12–13
Spence, Jonathan, 157, 158, 174, 225n9; *The Death of Woman Wang*, 134
Srikanth, Rajini, 9–10, 11; *The World Next Door*, 17
Stegner, Wallace, 75
stereotypes: of Asians, 70–71, 101; of Chinese, 81, 152; model-minority, 57–58, 115, 152
Stevens, Edwin, 155
Sugimoto, Etsu, 40; *A Daughter of the Samurai*, 18–19, 44, 178, 184–187, 206, 229n6
suicide, 192–193, 196–200, 203–205, 207, 220n9
Sui Sin Far (pseudonym of Edith Eaton), 15, 67, 88, 150
Suleri, Sara, 38
Sumida, Stephen H., 16, 55
Sun Yatsen (Sun Yat-sen), 137, 152, 176, 227n22
symbolic universes, 46–51, 62

Taiping Rebellion, 155–156, 164–165, 172–173
Taiwan, 12–14

Tan, Amy (*The Joy Luck Club*), 76, 123, 131
Taniguchi, Yuko, 207
Thailand (Siam), 160
Tham, Maria, 48–51
Thompson, Carl, 8
Tiananmen demonstrations, 29, 59
tokkōtai (kamikaze pilots), 32, 192–193, 195–201, 229n10
Tomita, Mary K., 182, 207
transnational commutes, 34–35
transnational subjects, 34–35
transpacific crossings, 64
transpacific families, 34–35, 66, 98
trauerarbeit (working through historical losses), 127, 179, 191, 195, 203, 205, 228n3
travel narratives: cosmopolitan character of, 9; imperialist character of, 8–9; missionary, 159–165; narratives of return compared to, 38–40; popularity of, 7–8; postcolonial studies approach to, 8; Yung's *My Life in China and America* in relation to, 147, 159–165
The Travels of Marco Polo, 147
Treaty of Nanjing, 156, 159
Treaty of Wangxia (Wang-hsia), 156–157
Trudeau, Justin, 112
Tsao Mei-en, 123, 134. *See also* Chai, Ruth
Tsiang, H. T., 70
Tu Wei-ming, 41, 46–48, 50, 62, 102; *The Living Tree*, 47
Twichell, Joseph, 151, 154, 174, 226n13
Ty, Eleanor, 16, 31, 66; *Unfastened*, 21–23

utilitarian familialism, 52–54, 61, 100

Valentino, Gina, 15, 16; *Transnational Asian American Literature*, 20–21

Wan, Peter Pei-de, 151, 153, 172, 227n22
Wang, Chih-ming, 38, 70, 150
Washington, Booker T., 153
Watson, Julia, 67, 147
White, Richard, 85, 86
white supremacy, 18, 43, 70, 150–152
Whitman, Walt (*Leaves of Grass*), 209–210
Williams, Raymond, 25
Wilson, Florence Mills, 229n6
Winnie (Hing), 108–111, 115, 117–121, 135

women and femininity: Chinese heroine paradigm, 82–88; Confucian values concerning, 114, 116–118, 127, 134–135; in "Gone with the Wind" genre, 83–84, 124, 126–127, 215; Japanese ideals of, 185–187; in male slave narratives, 167; modernity associated with, 83–88, 124, 126, 140; naming practices for, 133–134; role of daughters, 53; Yung's *My Life in China and America* and, 167–168. *See also* racialized gender melancholia

Wong, Anna May, 74, 77
Wong, Brad, 51
Wong, Jade Snow, 67, 101
Wong, K. Scott, 151
Wong, Sau-ling Cynthia, 15–16, 21, 22, 34–35, 70–71, 83, 124
Wong, Shawn, 3, 15
Wong, Tyrus, 74, 77
Work, Nancy, 45, 48
World War II: histories and remembering of, 179–182, 228n3; Japan and, 178–182, 186–205, 216–217, 227n3
writers, minority and ethnic: expectations and preconceptions applied to, 70–72, 75–76; life writing among, 68–69
Wu, Lily, 51, 211; "Coming Home," 55–61
Wu Ningkun, 209–210

Yale College, 148–151, 154, 160, 169, 175
Yanagisako, Sylvia, 18
Ye Mingchen (Yeh Ming Hsin), 172–173
Yoshida, Jim, 207
Yung, Bartlett Golden, 148, 154
Yung, Judy, 100
Yung, Morrison Brown, 148, 154
Yung Wing, 7, 70; Chinese service of, 149–151, 154, 157, 166–167, 170, 172, 175, 226n17; and Christianity, 149, 153–159, 168, 174; contradictions in life of, 149, 171–172, 174–175; and decolonization, 30, 43, 158, 215–216; elite status of, 18, 19, 31, 43; first marriage of, 151, 167; and identity/subjectivity, 22, 146–149, 162–171, 175–176, 214; life of, 149–150, 153–154; and missionaries, 149, 153–159; and Qing Dynasty, 149–150; revolutionary activities of, 227n22; second marriage of (with Kellogg), 150, 167, 174; U.S. citizenship of, 149–151, 171; and U.S. education, 19, 145, 147–148, 150–151, 154, 156, 158, 162, 173–175. *See also My Life in China and America*

Zhou Enlai, 140–141
Zong massacre, 163, 226n13

PATRICIA P. CHU is an Associate Professor of English at George Washington University and the author of *Assimilating Asians: Gendered Strategies of Authorship in Asian America*.

ALSO IN THE SERIES *ASIAN AMERICAN HISTORY AND CULTURE:*

Jonathan Y. Okamura, *Ethnicity and Inequality in Hawai'i*
Sucheng Chan and Madeline Y. Hsu, eds., *Chinese Americans and the Politics of Race and Culture*
K. Scott Wong, *Americans First: Chinese Americans and the Second World War*
Lisa Yun, *The Coolie Speaks: Chinese Indentured Laborers and African Slaves in Cuba*
Estella Habal, *San Francisco's International Hotel: Mobilizing the Filipino American Community in the Anti-eviction Movement*
Thomas P. Kim, *The Racial Logic of Politics: Asian Americans and Party Competition*
Sucheng Chan, ed., *The Vietnamese American 1.5 Generation: Stories of War, Revolution, Flight, and New Beginnings*
Antonio T. Tiongson Jr., Edgardo V. Gutierrez, and Ricardo V. Gutierrez, eds., *Positively No Filipinos Allowed: Building Communities and Discourse*
Sucheng Chan, ed., *Chinese American Transnationalism: The Flow of People, Resources, and Ideas between China and America during the Exclusion Era*
Rajini Srikanth, *The World Next Door: South Asian American Literature and the Idea of America*
Keith Lawrence and Floyd Cheung, eds., *Recovered Legacies: Authority and Identity in Early Asian American Literature*
Linda Trinh Võ, *Mobilizing an Asian American Community*
Franklin S. Odo, *No Sword to Bury: Japanese Americans in Hawai'i during World War II*
Josephine Lee, Imogene L. Lim, and Yuko Matsukawa, eds., *Re/collecting Early Asian America: Essays in Cultural History*
Linda Trinh Võ and Rick Bonus, eds., *Contemporary Asian American Communities: Intersections and Divergences*
Sunaina Marr Maira, *Desis in the House: Indian American Youth Culture in New York City*
Teresa Williams-León and Cynthia Nakashima, eds., *The Sum of Our Parts: Mixed-Heritage Asian Americans*
Tung Pok Chin with Winifred C. Chin, *Paper Son: One Man's Story*
Amy Ling, ed., *Yellow Light: The Flowering of Asian American Arts*
Rick Bonus, *Locating Filipino Americans: Ethnicity and the Cultural Politics of Space*
Darrell Y. Hamamoto and Sandra Liu, eds., *Countervisions: Asian American Film Criticism*
Martin F. Manalansan IV, ed., *Cultural Compass: Ethnographic Explorations of Asian America*
Ko-lin Chin, *Smuggled Chinese: Clandestine Immigration to the United States*
Evelyn Hu-DeHart, ed., *Across the Pacific: Asian Americans and Globalization*
Soo-Young Chin, *Doing What Had to Be Done: The Life Narrative of Dora Yum Kim*
Robert G. Lee, *Orientals: Asian Americans in Popular Culture*
David L. Eng and Alice Y. Hom, eds., *Q & A: Queer in Asian America*
K. Scott Wong and Sucheng Chan, eds., *Claiming America: Constructing Chinese American Identities during the Exclusion Era*

Lavina Dhingra Shankar and Rajini Srikanth, eds., *A Part, Yet Apart: South Asians in Asian America*
Jere Takahashi, *Nisei/Sansei: Shifting Japanese American Identities and Politics*
Velina Hasu Houston, ed., *But Still, Like Air, I'll Rise: New Asian American Plays*
Josephine Lee, *Performing Asian America: Race and Ethnicity on the Contemporary Stage*
Deepika Bahri and Mary Vasudeva, eds., *Between the Lines: South Asians and Postcoloniality*
E. San Juan Jr., *The Philippine Temptation: Dialectics of Philippines–U.S. Literary Relations*
Carlos Bulosan and E. San Juan Jr., eds., *The Cry and the Dedication*
Carlos Bulosan and E. San Juan Jr., eds., *On Becoming Filipino: Selected Writings of Carlos Bulosan*
Vicente L. Rafael, ed., *Discrepant Histories: Translocal Essays on Filipino Cultures*
Yen Le Espiritu, *Filipino American Lives*
Paul Ong, Edna Bonacich, and Lucie Cheng, eds., *The New Asian Immigration in Los Angeles and Global Restructuring*
Chris Friday, *Organizing Asian American Labor: The Pacific Coast Canned-Salmon Industry, 1870–1942*
Sucheng Chan, ed., *Hmong Means Free: Life in Laos and America*
Timothy P. Fong, *The First Suburban Chinatown: The Remaking of Monterey Park, California*
William Wei, *The Asian American Movement*
Yen Le Espiritu, *Asian American Panethnicity*
Velina Hasu Houston, ed., *The Politics of Life*
Renqiu Yu, *To Save China, To Save Ourselves: The Chinese Hand Laundry Alliance of New York*
Shirley Geok-lin Lim and Amy Ling, eds., *Reading the Literatures of Asian America*
Karen Isaksen Leonard, *Making Ethnic Choices: California's Punjabi Mexican Americans*
Gary Y. Okihiro, *Cane Fires: The Anti-Japanese Movement in Hawaii, 1865–1945*
Sucheng Chan, *Entry Denied: Exclusion and the Chinese Community in America, 1882–1943*

www.ingramcontent.com/pod-product-compliance
Lightning Source LLC
Chambersburg PA
CBHW041733300426
44116CB00019B/2970